Just Enough AutoCAD 2006

Just Enough AutoCAD® 2006

George Omura

San Francisco London

Publisher: Dan Brodnitz

Acquisitions Editor: Willem Knibbe

Developmental Editor: Mariann Barsolo

Production Editor: Lori Newman

Technical Editor: Scott Onstott

Copy Editor: Pat Coleman

Compositor: Kate Kaminski, Happenstance Type-O-Rama

Graphic Illustrator: Jeff Wilson, Happenstance Type-O-Rama

Proofreaders: Jim Brook, Candace English, Ian Golder, Jennifer Larsen, Nancy Riddiough

Indexer: Nancy Guenther

Book Designer: Judy Fung

Cover Designer: John Nedwidek, Emdesign

Cover Illustrator: John Nedwidek, Emdesign

Library of Congress Card Number: 2004117503

ISBN: 0-7821-4397-0

SYBEX and the SYBEX logo are either registered trademarks or trademarks of SYBEX Inc. in the United States and/or other countries.

Screen reproductions produced with Collage Complete.
Collage Complete is a trademark of Inner Media Inc.

Autodesk, AutoCAD, Design Web Format, and DWF are either registered trademarks or trademarks of Autodesk, Inc., in the U.S.A. and/or certain other countries. Mental ray is a registered trademark of mental images GmbH & Co. KG, licensed for use by Autodesk, Inc. Certain content, including trial software, provided courtesy Autodesk, Inc., © 2005. All rights reserved.

TRADEMARKS: SYBEX has attempted throughout this book to distinguish proprietary trademarks from descriptive terms by following the capitalization style used by the manufacturer.

The author and publisher have made their best efforts to prepare this book, and the content is based upon final release software whenever possible. Portions of the manuscript may be based upon pre-release versions supplied by software manufacturer(s). The author and the publisher make no representation or warranties of any kind with regard to the completeness or accuracy of the contents herein and accept no liability of any kind including but not limited to performance, merchantability, fitness for any particular purpose, or any losses or damages of any kind caused or alleged to be caused directly or indirectly from this book.

Manufactured in the United States of America

10 9 8 7 6 5 4 3 2

To my mother, who always seems amazed that I write for a living.

Acknowledgments

Over the past few years, a growing number of people have been asking me if I knew of a book for the casual AutoCAD user. I hadn't thought that I would be the one to actually write it until Willem Knibbe, acquisitions editor at Sybex, asked me if I had any book ideas. One thing led to another and the results are this book: *Just Enough AutoCAD*.

I'd like to thank Willem for giving me the opportunity to work with Sybex on this project. I'd also like to thank Mariann Barsolo for her great suggestions and her effort to keep me from getting carried away with too many details. Thanks to Lori Newman for coordinating the project and for gently nudging me every now and then to keep up with the schedule. Scott Onstott offered his expertise in making sure I wasn't making up stuff. A big thanks to my copy editor, Pat Coleman, for her dedicated work on each chapter, and to the proofreaders, Jim Brook, Candace English, Ian Golder, Jennifer Larsen, and Nancy Riddiough, for their careful attention to detail.

At Autodesk, Jim Quanci once again gave his full support for our work. Thanks to Shaan Hurley for graciously opening the doors to the AutoCAD beta program. And thanks to Denis Cadu who is always more that willing to help us in our times of need.

Thank you all for making this book possible.

Contents at a Glance

Introduction . . . . *xv*

Chapter 1 • Getting Familiar with AutoCAD 1

Chapter 2 • Understanding the Drafting Tools 35

Chapter 3 • Drawing 2D Objects 71

Chapter 4 • Editing AutoCAD Objects 107

Chapter 5 • Editing with the Modify Toolbar 123

Chapter 6 • Creating 3D Drawings 147

Chapter 7 • Getting Organized with Layers 193

Chapter 8 • Blocks, Groups, Xrefs, and DesignCenter 227

Chapter 9 • Creating Text 255

Chapter 10 • Using Dimensions 285

Chapter 11 • Gathering Information 317

Chapter 12 • Laying Out and Printing Your Drawing 333

Index *367*

Contents

Introduction . . . . *xv*

Chapter 1 • Getting Familiar with AutoCAD 1
Understanding the AutoCAD Window 1
    Getting to Know the Window Components 2
    The Menu Bar 7
    Using the Toolbars 11
    Closing and Opening Toolbars 15
    Other Toolbars 16
    Checking Out the Draw and Modify Toolbars 18
Starting a Drawing 20
Panning and Zooming to Adjust Your View 24
Understanding the Layout Tabs 26
Understanding How Command Options Work 28
Getting Help 30
    Using the Search Tab 31
    Using Context-Sensitive Help 32
    Additional Sources of Help 33
    Staying Informed with the Communication Center 33
Just Enough Summary 34

Chapter 2 • Understanding the Drafting Tools. **35**
Understanding the AutoCAD Coordinate System 35
    Experimenting with Coordinates Using Lines 37
    Specifying Exact Distances 39
Setting Up a Drawing 45
    Selecting the Drawing Units 45
    Other Drawing Unit Options 47
    Determining the Drawing Area 47
Using a Digital T Square and Triangle 50
    Using a Quick T Square Function with Ortho 50
    Using an Adjustable Triangle with Polar Tracking 50
    Modifying Polar Tracking's Behavior 51
Getting a Visual Reference with the Grid Mode 52
Snapping to the Grid or Other Regular Intervals 53
Changing the Grid and Snap Settings 54
    Adjusting the X and Y Spacing 55
    Setting Up for Isometric 2D Drawing 55
    Rotating the Grid, Snap, and Cursor 56
    Aligning the Grid to an Object 57
Selecting Exact Locations on Objects 59
    Setting Up Osnap Locations 59

Automatically Snapping to Locations 60
Selecting Object Snaps on the Fly 61
Understanding the Osnap Options 62
Fine-Tuning the AutoSnap Feature 63
Aligning Objects Using Object Snap Tracking and Tracking Points 64
Using the Temporary Tracking Point Feature 67
Just Enough Summary 69

Chapter 3 • Drawing 2D Objects **71**
Drawing Straight Lines 72
Drawing Circles and Arcs 73
Using the Circle Options 73
Using the Arc Options 74
Drawing Curves 76
Drawing an Ellipse 76
Drawing an Elliptical Arc 77
Drawing Smooth Curves 78
Drawing Curves with Polylines 80
Drawing Parallel Lines 81
Drawing Revision Clouds 83
Drawing a Freehand Revision Cloud 84
Drawing a Revision Cloud Based on the Shape of an Object. 84
Working with Hatch Patterns and Solid Fills 85
Placing a Hatch Pattern: The Basics 86
Using Predefined Patterns 87
Adding Solid Fills 88
Positioning Hatch Patterns Accurately 89
Editing the Hatch Area 91
Modifying a Hatch Pattern 92
Understanding the Boundary Hatch Options 94
Drawing Regular Polygons 100
Using Objects to Lay Out Your Drawing 101
Marking Points in a Drawing 101
Marking Off Equal Divisions 102
Dividing Objects into Specified Lengths 102
Using Construction Lines 103
Just Enough Summary 106

Chapter 4 • Editing AutoCAD Objects **107**
Selecting Objects 107
Using the Standard AutoCAD Selection Method 107
Practice Using Selection Options 108
Selecting Objects with Windows 109
Editing the Windows Way 111
Stretching Lines Using Grips 111
Copy, Mirror, Rotate, Scale, and Stretch with Grips 113
Other Grips Features 114

Changing Objects with Grips and Dynamic Input 115
Controlling Objects Using the Properties Palette 118
Just Enough Summary 121

Chapter 5 • Editing with the Modify Toolbar 123
Selecting Objects 123
Erasing Objects 125
Joining Objects 125
    Joining End to End with Intermediate Arcs 125
    Joining with a Chamfer 127
    Extending or Trimming Lines to Other Objects 129
Moving and Copying 132
    Moving with Accuracy 132
    Copying Objects with the Copy Command 133
    Making Circular Copies 134
    Copying Rows and Columns 135
Scaling, Stretching, and Rotating 137
    Scaling to a Specific Scale Factor 137
    Scaling an Object to Fit Another 137
    Stretching Objects 138
    Rotating Objects 139
    Aligning the Rotation Cursor with an Object 139
Breaking an Object into Two 141
Editing Xrefs and Blocks 142
Editing Polylines 144
Just Enough Summary 146

Chapter 6 • Creating 3D Drawings 147
Understanding the Modeling Methods 147
Surface Modeling Tools 148
    Getting a 3D View 149
    Converting 2D into 3D by Adding Thickness 150
    Adding a 3D Surface 151
    Using Object Snaps in 3D Space 152
    Rotating Objects in 3D 153
    Working with User Coordinate Systems 154
    3D Modeling with Polylines 157
    Creating Curved Shapes with Meshes 159
Using 3D Solids 163
    Extruding a Polyline 163
    Using a Predefined UCS 167
    Subtracting 3D Shapes 169
    Using Other Solid-Editing Tools 171
    Filleting a Corner 172
    Getting a Shaded View to See More Clearly 173
    Extruding along a Path 174

Revolving a Polyline 175
Other 3D Solid Examples 177
3D Solid-Editing Options 177
Manipulating Objects in 3D Space 179
Understanding Your 3D Viewing Options 181
Using the Camera Command to Set Up Your Viewpoint 182
Using 3Dorbit to View in Perspective and Adjust Your View 184
Changing Your Focal Length in Perspective 189
Saving and Restoring Your 3D Views 189
Saving a View 190
Restoring a View 191
Just Enough Summary 191

Chapter 7 • Getting Organized with Layers **193**
Creating and Assigning Layers 193
Understanding the Layer Properties Manager Dialog Box 196
Assigning Layers to Objects 198
Setting the Current Layer 200
Controlling Layer Visibility 201
Controlling Layer Visibility Using the On/Off Option 201
Controlling Layer Visibility with Freeze and Thaw 202
Controlling Layer Visibility in Individual Viewports of a Layout Tab 203
Locking Layers from Printing and Editing 205
Finding the Layers You Want 206
Taming an Unwieldy List of Layers 206
Filtering Layers by Their Properties 207
Creating Layer Groups by Selection 209
Applying Filters to the Properties Toolbar Layer List and Other Options 211
Saving and Recalling Layer Settings 211
Express Tools Layer Options for Managing Layers 213
Saving Layer States through Express Tools 213
Exploring Layers with Layer Walk 214
Changing the Layer Assignment of Objects 215
Controlling Layer Settings through Objects 215
Organizing Visual Content through Properties 216
Assigning Linetypes to Layers 216
Controlling Linetype Scale 219
Setting Line Weights 221
Setting Colors, Linetypes, Linetype Scales, and Line Weights
for Individual Objects 224
Just Enough Summary 226

Chapter 8 • Blocks, Groups, Xrefs, and DesignCenter **227**
Using Blocks to Organize Objects 227
Creating a Block 228
Understanding the Block Definition Dialog Box 229
Inserting a Block 230

Scaling and Rotating Blocks 231
Importing an Existing Drawing as a Block 232
Saving Blocks as AutoCAD Drawing Files 234
Organizing Objects Using Groups 235
Toggling Groups On and Off 235
Working with the Object Grouping Dialog Box 236
Working with the LT Group Manager 237
Finding Files on Your Hard Disk 238
Getting Multiple Uses from Drawings Using External References 240
Attaching a Drawing as an External Reference 241
Updating an Xref While You Draw 242
Differences between External References and Blocks 242
Keeping Track of Drawing Components with DesignCenter 243
Getting Familiar with DesignCenter 244
Opening and Inserting Files with DesignCenter 247
Finding and Extracting the Contents of a Drawing 247
Exchanging Data between Open Files 249
Loading Specific Files into DesignCenter 249
Downloading Symbols from DesignCenter Online 250
Keeping Tools on Hand with Tool Palettes 250
Deleting Tools and Palettes 252
Customizing a Tool 252
Just Enough Summary 253

Chapter 9 • Creating Text 255
Adding and Formatting Text 255
Adjusting the Text Height and Font 256
Using Color, Stacked Fractions, Alignment, Lists, and Special Symbols 257
Adjusting the Text Boundary 259
Setting Indents and Tabs 259
Adjusting Line Spacing 260
Adding a Background Mask to Text 261
Making Changes to Multiple Text Objects 261
Using AutoCAD's Spelling Checker 262
Using AutoCAD's Find And Replace Text Feature 264
Importing Text Files from Other Programs 265
Understanding Text and Scale 265
Using Styles to Organize Your Fonts 266
Creating and Setting a Style 266
Using a Text Style 267
Setting the Current Default Style 268
Adding Single Words with the Single-Line Text Object 269
Adding Tables to Your Drawing 270
Creating a Table 270
Adding Cell Text 271
Combining Cells 271

Adjusting Table Cell Text Orientation 272
Adjusting Table Cell Text Justification 273
Adding or Deleting Rows and Columns of Cells 274
Adding Formulas to Cells 274
Exporting Tables 278
Importing Tables 279
Editing Table Line Weights 279
Changing Cell Background Colors 281
Adding Graphics to Table Cells 281
Creating Table Styles 282
Just Enough Summary 284

Chapter 10 • Using Dimensions **285**
Understanding the Parts of an AutoCAD Dimension 285
Dimensioning in the Model or Layout Tab 286
Drawing Linear Dimensions 287
Placing Horizontal and Vertical Dimensions 287
Continuing a Dimension 288
Drawing Dimensions from a Common Base Extension Line 289
Adding a String of Dimensions with a Single Operation 290
Dimensioning Nonorthogonal Objects 291
Adding Nonorthogonal Linear Dimensions 291
Dimensioning Arcs and Circles 292
Dimensioning Angles and Arc Lengths 294
Adding a Note with an Arrow Using the Leader Tool 295
Using Ordinate Dimensions 296
Adding Tolerance Notation 298
Editing Dimensions 299
Appending Data to Dimension Text 299
Making Changes to Multiple Dimensions 300
Detaching Dimension Text from the Dimension Line 301
Rotating a Dimension Text 302
Skewing Dimension Lines 303
Setting Up the Dimension's Appearance 303
Creating a Dimension Style 303
Setting the Current Dimension Style 314
Editing a Dimension Style 316
Just Enough Summary 316

Chapter 11 • Gathering Information **317**
Measuring Areas 317
Measuring the Area of a Polygonal Shape 318
Measuring the Area of Complex or Curved Shapes 318
Finding the Coordinate of a Point 321
Measuring Distances 322
Measuring Angles 322

Getting the General Status of the Drawing 323
Finding the Time Spent on a Drawing 324
Adding Nondrawing Data to Store with Your Drawing 325
Finding Text in a Drawing 326
Locating and Selecting Named Components 327
  Searching Using Quick Select 328
  Viewing a List of Named Components 328
Finding Missing Support Files 329
  Locating Xrefs 329
  Locating Fonts, Linetypes, and Hatch Patterns 331
Just Enough Summary 332

Chapter 12 • Laying Out and Printing Your Drawing. 333
Setting Up a Drawing for Printing 334
  Exploring the Layout Tab 334
  Using the Layout Tab to Scale Down Your Drawing 338
  Creating Additional Viewports 339
  Controlling How Viewports Display and Print 342
  Setting Layers for Individual Viewports 343
  Adding Layouts 345
Printing Your Drawing 346
  Selecting and Storing Printer Settings 346
  Printer Configuration Options 347
  Selecting a Paper Size and Number of Copies 348
  Determining What View Will Print 349
  Adjusting the Location of Your Printed Image 349
  Setting the Print Scale 349
  Options for Printing 3D Views 350
  Plot Options 351
  Drawing Orientation 352
Storing Your Printer Settings 353
Controlling Color, Lines, and Fills through Plot Styles 355
  Using AutoCAD's Predefined Plot Styles 356
  Choosing between Color and Named Plot Style Tables 357
  Creating a Plot Style Table 358
  Editing and Using Plot Style Tables 358
  Understanding the Options in the Plot Style Table Editor 359
Assigning Named Plot Styles Directly to Layers and Objects 362
  Assigning Plot Styles to Objects 362
  Assigning Named Plot Style Tables to Layers 364
Converting a Drawing from Color Plot Styles to Named Plot Styles 365
Just Enough Summary 366

Index *367*

Introduction

If you're involved in any way with a design and manufacturing industry, you've probably had to work with AutoCAD drawings. AutoCAD has become the standard program for producing technical drawings of all types. It has the depth and range of features that lets the expert user create nearly any type of technical drawing.

But not everyone needs to be an expert at AutoCAD. Many AutoCAD users really need to know only a few of its vast array of tools. Still others only use AutoCAD from time to time to review existing drawings and make minor changes. If you're someone who doesn't need or want to be an AutoCAD power user, but would like to be able use AutoCAD proficiently, this book is for you. You may have taken an AutoCAD course and have forgotten most of what you've learned, or you might be a project manager who only has to work with AutoCAD drawings occasionally. Or perhaps you have had a job that has taken you away from AutoCAD, and you want to get back into using the latest version. You want a resource that gets to the point and lets you find what you need fast without wading through volumes of information. If this sounds like you, you've come to the right place. *Just Enough AutoCAD 2006* is designed with you in mind.

How to Use This Book

Just Enough AutoCAD 2006 covers the basic drawing and editing tools that most users will need to produce quality AutoCAD drawings. You won't find every last detail of every feature. Instead, this book presents AutoCAD's essential features through a combination of tutorials and reference material to give you a concise, easy-to-use companion for your work with AutoCAD. It's designed so that you can quickly learn the tools you need when you need them.

Most chapters start with tutorials covering basic concepts on a particular topic so you can understand how things work in a general way. Later parts of the chapter provide reference material to help you with specific tasks. For example, in Chapter 9, a tutorial at the beginning gives you the basic steps for creating and formatting text. After that, the chapter goes into more depth to show you other features such as importing text, sizing and scaling text, and creating tables. Once you've learned the basics from the beginning tutorial, you can pick and choose from those other topics later in the chapter as the need arises.

The book assumes you have a working knowledge of the Microsoft Windows operating system. You should also know how to locate files on your computer and how menus and toolbars work in a general way. Experience with other graphics programs also helps but is not essential.

What You'll Find

To help you get the most from AutoCAD, the chapters in *Just Enough AutoCAD 2006* are organized into general topics such as Drawing 2D Objects or Laying Out and Printing Your Drawing. Within each chapter, specific tasks such as drawing circles or choosing a printer paper size are discussed in detail.

The first three chapters serve as an introduction to the AutoCAD way of doing things. If you're totally new to AutoCAD, you'll want to pay special attention to these chapters. In **Chapter 1: Getting Familiar with AutoCAD**, you'll be introduced to AutoCAD and how it is laid out. You'll learn where to find things and what the various parts of the AutoCAD screen are for. **Chapter 2: Understanding the Drafting Tools** gets into more detail regarding the way AutoCAD works. You'll learn how to set up a drawing and how to use AutoCAD's basic drafting tools such as the grid and the coordinate system. **Chapter 3: Drawing 2D Objects** discusses the most common AutoCAD drawing and editing tools. Here you'll find out how to draw lines, arcs, and circles, as well as how to add hatch patterns and how to lay out a drawing.

The next two chapters are concerned with editing in AutoCAD. **Chapter 4: Editing AutoCAD Objects** describes the general methods for editing drawings in AutoCAD. This is another good chapter to review if you are new to AutoCAD. **Chapter 5: Editing with the Modify Toolbar** shows you how to use specific tools to make changes to your drawing. Here you learn how to join, move, scale, and stretch objects, as well as many other operations.

Chapter 6: Creating 3D Drawings gives you an introduction to 3D modeling in AutoCAD. You'll learn about the basic concepts for creating and viewing 3D models in AutoCAD.

Chapter 7: Getting Organized with Layers shows you how you can use a feature called layers to organize your drawing. You'll learn how to create and use layers and how to manage large lists of layers. You'll also learn how to employ AutoCAD object properties such as color and line weights to help visually organize your drawings. **Chapter 8: Blocks, Groups, Xrefs, and DesignCenter** shows you how to work more efficiently by grouping objects into assemblies. Here you'll also learn how to use existing files as backgrounds for new projects.

Textual notation plays a major role in technical drawing, and AutoCAD provides some excellent tools to help you with your notation tasks. **Chapter 9: Creating Text** shows you how to create and edit text. You'll learn how to scale text properly for your particular drawing and how you can use AutoCAD's table feature that works just like a spreadsheet. **Chapter 10: Using Dimensions** shows you the dimensioning tools needed to add and display crucial dimensions of your drawing.

One of the greatest features of AutoCAD drawings is the amount of information they hold. **Chapter 11: Gathering Information** shows you how to extract the types of information available from an AutoCAD drawing. You'll learn how to find basic types of information such as distances and areas, plus you'll learn how to search for text and other named components.

Eventually, you'll need to print your drawings, but the nature of technical drawings means that AutoCAD's printing and plotting feature is a bit more complex than your word processor. **Chapter 12: Laying Out and Printing Your Drawing** guides you through the process of getting the output you want on the medium you need. Chapter 12 also shows you how to use AutoCAD's Layout feature to lay out and organize the components of your drawing on a printed sheet.

Besides printing, more users are relying on computer file formats to transmit AutoCAD drawings to their recipients. You can check our website for the bonus chapter, **Preparing Drawings for Transfer or Export**, which discusses the many options you have for sending electronic versions of your drawings to other users across town or across the world.

How to Contact the Author

The idea for this book came from the growing number of casual users I've observed over the years. Instead of wanting to become experts, they want to know how to perform certain tasks with the least amount of fuss. I've tried to incorporate the essential information needed for most users, but if you have ideas about how the book can be improved or if you feel I've left out an essential feature while covering nonessentials, you can send e-mail to me at the address below. If you feel you need more information than this book provides, you might want to consider Sybex's *Mastering AutoCAD 2006 and AutoCAD LT 2006*.

You can also contact Sybex regarding general questions about this and other AutoCAD publications at `www.sybex.com`. Thanks for choosing *Just Enough AutoCAD 2006*.

George Omura
`gomura@yahoo.com`

Chapter 1

Getting Familiar with AutoCAD

If you are totally new to AutoCAD, you'll want to read this chapter. It provides an overview of AutoCAD's layout and shows you what to expect when you start to use it. Even if you've had a class or have used an older version of AutoCAD, you will find this chapter useful.

You'll start by taking a tour of the AutoCAD Window to get familiar with the menus, toolbars, and other components. Then you'll get a chance to try your hand at drawing, and, in doing so, you'll be introduced to the way AutoCAD's commands work. You'll also learn how to use the Zoom and Pan tools to help you get around in a drawing. And you'll take a look at the ways you can view your drawing using the layout tabs. Finally, you'll be introduced to the Help system for those times when you forget to have this book on hand.

This chapter includes the following topics:

◆ Understanding the AutoCAD Window

◆ Starting a Drawing

◆ Panning and Zooming to Adjust Your View

◆ Understanding the Layout Tabs

◆ Understanding How Command Options Work

◆ Getting Help

Understanding the AutoCAD Window

AutoCAD works like most other Windows-based graphics programs, but it also has a few quirks. This section gives you an overview of AutoCAD's layout. Although many elements will be familiar, a few will be new to you.

First let's take a look at the AutoCAD window as it appears when you first open it. After installing AutoCAD, take the following steps:

1. Choose Start ➤ All Programs ➤ Autodesk ➤ AutoCAD 2006 ➤ AutoCAD 2006. You can also double-click the AutoCAD 2006 icon on your Windows Desktop. LT users will click AutoCAD LT 2006 in place of AutoCAD 2006.

The opening greeting, called a *splash screen,* tells you which version of AutoCAD you are using, to whom the program is registered, and the AutoCAD dealer's name and phone number, should you need help. After the splash screen closes, you see the AutoCAD Window with a blank default document named Drawing1.dwg as shown in Figure 1.1.

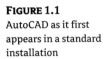

FIGURE 1.1
AutoCAD as it first
appears in a standard
installation

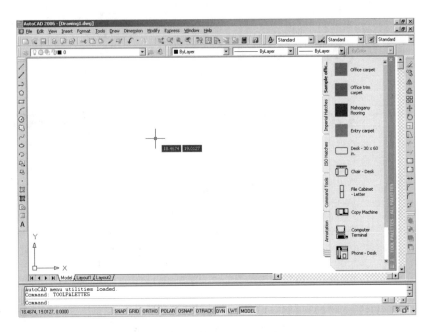

2. In some installations, you may see a Startup dialog box. If this happens to you, click Cancel, and AutoCAD will display the blank default document.

Let's take a detailed look at the AutoCAD window. You'll find that, for the most part, it is a typical Windows-style graphics program window with a few twists.

Getting to Know the Window Components

The AutoCAD window is made up of several parts that are common to most Windows graphics programs:

- Menu bar
- Docked and floating toolbars
- Drawing area
- Command window
- Status bar
- Tool palettes
- Properties palette

The Tool palettes and Properties palette may not appear on the screen, but you can easily retrieve them by clicking buttons on the toolbar at the top of the AutoCAD window. If you don't see them, don't worry. At this point, they aren't essential for new users. Your AutoCAD window should look like Figure 1.1, which shows the default configuration for a new AutoCAD installation. Since AutoCAD is so easily customizable, you may not see exactly the same layout, but the basic components should be there.

As with typical Windows programs, AutoCAD has a menu bar along the top that contains most of the common functions you'll need to work with (see Figure 1.2). Below that are toolbars for quick access to settings and the more common drawing and editing tools. You also have toolbars to the right and left of the window. The Draw toolbar at the left contains tools you use to place new objects in your drawing, and the Modify toolbar at the right contains tools you use to edit objects. These toolbars provide the same functions as the Draw and Modify menu bar options.

FIGURE 1.2

The components of the top of the AutoCAD window

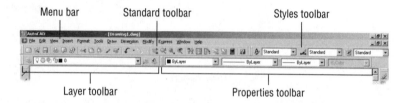

In the middle is the drawing area where you will do your actual drawing. One difference between Figure 1.1 and what you see on your screen is that the background in the default AutoCAD drawing area is black. This helps with the visibility of lines on the computer screen. But in this book, you will see the drawing area background shown in white because in print, drawings with a white background are easier to see.

At the bottom of the screen is the status bar, which provides information regarding many of the settings you'll use in AutoCAD. Just above the status bar is the Command window, which is somewhat unique to AutoCAD. You'll learn more about the Command window a bit later in this chapter.

Just as you can do in other Windows programs, you can move toolbars and reshape them to your liking. The default location of the toolbars is in their *docked* position, which just means that they are merged with the outer edge of the window to save space. You can drag them out into the drawing area and reshape them if you like, or you can reposition them anywhere in the screen. When toolbars are moved away from the edge of the window and appear "free floating," they are said to be *floating toolbars*, as opposed to docked.

Another unique item in AutoCAD's window is the set of Tool palettes shown in Figure 1.3. These palettes let you keep your favorite tools and drawing components in one convenient place for quick access.

Now let's look at some important parts of the AutoCAD window. The drawing area, the status bar, and the Command window work together to give you feedback while you create and edit your drawing. As you move your cursor over the drawing area, you'll see the cursor appear as a crosshair. Along with the crosshair, you may see a pair of numbers.

FIGURE 1.3
The Tool palettes

The crosshair lets you point to portions of the drawing area, and the numeric display, known as the *Dynamic input display*, tells you your XY coordinate within the drawing area. You'll learn more about coordinates in AutoCAD in Chapter 2. As you work with AutoCAD commands, the Dynamic input display changes to text prompts to aid you in determining what to do next.

If you don't see the Dynamic input display next to the crosshair cursor, go to the bottom of the AutoCAD window to the status bar and click the button labeled DYN. This is the Dynamic input setting, which is new in AutoCAD 2006.

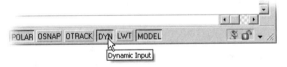

Along with the Dynamic input display, the Command window and status bar just below the drawing area provide feedback as you work with AutoCAD commands (see Figure 1.4). You can also see the XY coordinate in the far left of the status bar in the lower-left corner of the AutoCAD window.

FIGURE 1.4
The status bar and the Command window work with the drawing area to give you feedback as you draw.

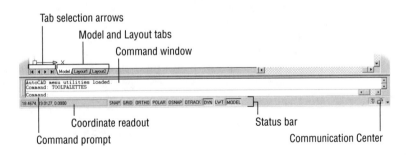

CONTROLLING THE STATUS BAR DISPLAY

To the far right of the status bar, you'll see a downward-pointing arrow, which opens a menu that controls the display of the status bar. You use this menu to turn the items in the status bar on or off. A checkmark by an item indicates that it is currently on. If for some reason you do not see all the buttons mentioned in the previous discussion, check this menu to make sure that all the status bar options are turned on. Note that LT does not have an Otrack option in the status bar.

Finally, you'll notice a set of tabs that appear between the drawing area and the Command window. These tabs provide two types of drawing views. By default, you see the Model tab. This is where you do most of your drawing and editing. The Layout 1 and Layout 2 tabs provide a way to set up your drawing for printing. You'll learn more about layout tabs later in this chapter and in Chapter 11.

TIP In a new installation of AutoCAD, you will see a message balloon in the bottom right corner of AutoCAD. This message balloon alerts you to the latest news and information regarding AutoCAD through a feature called the Communication Center.

GETTING FAMILIAR WITH THE DRAWING AREA

As you might imagine, the drawing area in the middle of the AutoCAD window is the space where you'll be spending a lot of time. It pays to get a feel for how it behaves early on. As your introduction to the drawing area, try the following exercise.

1. Move the cursor around in the drawing area. As you move, notice how the Dynamic input display changes to tell you the cursor's location. It shows the coordinates in an X, Y format. The coordinate readout in the status bar also shows X and Y coordinates, but it adds the Z coordinate.

2. Place the cursor in the middle of the drawing area and click the left mouse button. You have just selected a point. Move the cursor, and a rectangle follows. This is a *selection window*; if there are objects in the drawing area, this window allows you to select them for editing. Also notice that you see the word *Command* in the Dynamic input display. This tells you to check the Command window for more information.

3. Move the cursor a bit in any direction; then click the left mouse button again. Notice that the selection window disappears. Had there been objects within the selection window, they would be selected. This is similar to the way the mouse cursor behaves on the Windows Desktop, only in Windows, you have to click and drag the mouse button to create a selection window.

4. Try selecting several more points in the drawing area. Notice that as you click the mouse, you alternately start and end a selection window.

As you click inside the drawing area, you may notice that, depending on whether you click to the right or the left of the last point, the selection window displays a different color. If you click from left to right, the selection window appears blue. From right to left, it's green (red if you have a white background). These colors indicate a different mode of selection, which you'll learn about a bit later.

If you click the right mouse button, the shortcut menu appears. Just as with most other Windows applications, a right mouse click frequently opens a menu that contains options that are *context sensitive*. This means that the contents of the shortcut menu depend on where you right-click as well as the command that is active at the time of your right-click. If there are no applicable options at the time of the right-click, AutoCAD treats the right-click as ↵. You'll learn more about these options as you progress through the book. For now, if you happen to open this menu by accident, press the Esc key to close it.

TIP The ↵ symbol is used in this book to denote the Enter key. Whenever you see it, press the Enter key, also known as the Return key.

THE UCS ICON

The UCS icon is the L-shaped icon you see at the lower-left corner of the drawing area. It helps you see your orientation at a glance by pointing to the positive X and Y directions. UCS stands for *User Coordinate System*. That name is a hint that you can create and use other coordinates besides the default one that exists in new drawings. The default X direction is from left to right, and the Y direction is bottom to top, but AutoCAD lets you alter your view orientation as well as include additional coordinate systems that can be oriented in different directions. The UCS icon is especially helpful when you start to use these other coordinate systems and display modes, but right now, just be aware that it is there to help you get your bearings.

You might notice a small square at the base of the UCS icon. This square tells you that you are in the World Coordinate System, which is the base coordinate on which other coordinate systems can be built. You'll learn more about the UCS in Chapter 5.

THE COMMAND WINDOW

The horizontal window at the bottom of the AutoCAD window is called the *Command window*. Besides the drawing area, this is where you can get feedback from AutoCAD. It is also where you can type commands and command options. The Command window shows three lines of text. As you work in AutoCAD, the command activity appears in the bottom line of the Command window and scrolls upward.

When AutoCAD is waiting for input, you see the word *Command:* at the bottom of the Command window. This is called the Command *prompt*. As you click a point in the drawing area, you see the message `Specify Opposite Corner`. Simultaneously, a selection window appears in the drawing area. Click another point without selecting anything, and the selection window disappears and the Command prompt returns.

You'll want to pay close attention to the Command window as you start using AutoCAD because it tells you what AutoCAD expects you to do. It also lists information when you query AutoCAD for certain types of information, which you'll learn about in later chapters.

In addition to getting feedback from the Command window, you will also see the Command prompts at the cursor whenever you have Dynamic input display turned on.

The Command window is a little like a chat window when you're online. You "chat" with AutoCAD by responding to messages that appear in the Command window. When AutoCAD asks for specific data, the Command window allows you to type data through the keyboard. It is also an area that provides information about your drawing when you request it.

"CHATTING" WITH AUTOCAD

AutoCAD communicates its needs to you through messages in the Command window. These messages often tell you what to do next or offer options, usually shown in square brackets. Commands often display a series of messages, which you answer to complete the command. If you ever get lost while using a command or forget what you are supposed to do, look at the Command window for clues. As an additional aid, you can right-click to display a context-sensitive shortcut menu. If you are in the middle of a command, this menu provides a list of options specifically related to that command. For example, if you right-click before selecting the first point for the Rectangle command, a menu appears, offering the same options that are listed in the Command prompt, plus some additional options.

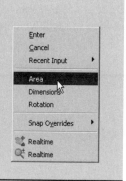

The Menu Bar

Although the Command window is a little unusual for a Windows program, the AutoCAD menu bar provides a familiar means to finding commands. You'll see many of the standard Windows commands such as Cut, Paste, and Copy, File Save, Save As, and AutoCAD's version of the Print command called Plot.

You'll also find lots of other commands and options that are pure AutoCAD, but the basic operation of the menu bar is the same as that of other Windows program. The menu bar lets you issue commands and open dialog boxes to change settings. Some of the menu bar options expand to show additional menu choices in what is called a *cascading* menu.

One helpful feature of the menu bar that you don't often find in other programs are the icons shown to the left of many menu options. These icons help you connect the option names with their equivalent toolbar options. For example, if you open the Modify menu, you'll see that the options there have the same icons that appear in the Modify toolbar along the left side of the AutoCAD window.

Another menu bar feature is the command description in the status bar. As you open a menu from the menu bar and point to options, you'll see a brief description of the option in the status bar. Try the following exercise to get a feel for how the menu bar works.

1. Click View in the menu bar. The list of items that appears includes the commands and settings that let you control the way AutoCAD displays your drawings.

2. Move the highlight cursor slowly down the list of menu items. As you highlight each item, notice that a description of the item appears in the status bar at the bottom of the AutoCAD window. These descriptions help you choose the menu option you need. At the end of the description, you'll see a single word in capital letters. This is the keyboard command equivalent to the highlighted option in the menu or toolbar. You can actually type these keyboard commands to start the tool or menu item that you are pointing to. You don't have to memorize these command names, but knowing them will help you later if you want to customize AutoCAD.

3. Some of the menu items won't show anything in the status bar, but will have triangular pointers to their right. This means the menu option has additional choices. For instance, highlight the Zoom item, and you'll see another set of options appear to the right of the menu. This second set of options is called a *cascading menu*. Whenever you see a menu item with the triangular pointer, you know that it opens a cascading menu with a more detailed set of options.

OPENING DIALOG BOXES

You might have noticed that other drop-down menu options are followed by an ellipsis (...). This indicates that the option displays a dialog box, as the following exercise demonstrates:

1. Move the highlight cursor to the Tools option in the menu bar.

2. Click the Options item at the bottom of the menu to open the Options dialog box.

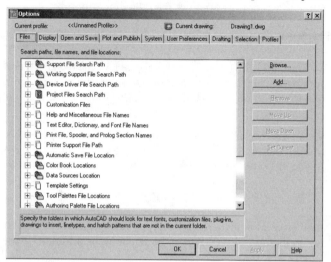

The Options dialog box is like the Preferences dialog box in other programs. Here you can find most of the general AutoCAD settings that affect its behavior. Numerous settings are divided into tabs across the top of the dialog box. The Options dialog box is one of many dialog boxes available through the menu bar.

STARTING COMMANDS

The third type of item you'll find on menu bar menus is a command that directly executes an AutoCAD operation. Let's try an exercise to explore a typical command.

1. First, turn off the Dynamic input display by clicking the DYN button in the status bar. It should look like it is in the off position. You'll start your exploration of commands with this feature turned off as it can be somewhat confusing to the first-time user. You'll get a chance to try out the Dynamic input feature in later chapters, starting with Chapter 2.

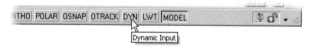

2. If the Tool palettes are open, click the X in the upper-right corner to close them. This will give you a clear view of the whole drawing area.

3. Click the Draw option from the menu bar, and then click the Rectangle command. Notice that the Command window now shows the following prompt:

```
Specify first corner point or [Chamfer/Elevation/Fillet/Thickness/Width]:
```

AutoCAD is asking you to select the first corner for the rectangle, and in brackets, it is offering a few options that you can take advantage of at this point in the command. Don't worry about those options right now. You'll have an opportunity to learn about command options in Chapter 2.

4. Click a point roughly in the lower-left corner of the drawing area, as shown in Figure 1.5. Now as you move your mouse, you'll see a rectangle follow the cursor with one corner fixed at the position you just selected. You'll also see the following prompt in the Command window:

```
Specify other corner point or [Dimensions]:
```

5. Click another point anywhere in the upper-right region of the drawing area. A rectangle appears (see Figure 1.6). You'll learn more about the different cursor shapes and what they mean later in this chapter.

Next try deleting the rectangle you just drew.

1. Place the cursor on top of the rectangle, but don't do anything yet. Notice that as you pass the cursor over the rectangle, it is highlighted. In a crowded drawing, this highlighting can help you determine exactly what will be selected should you click the mouse on an object.

FIGURE 1.5
Selecting the first point of a rectangle

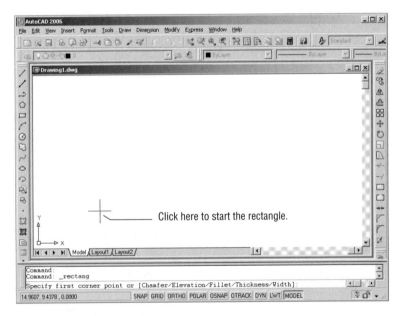

2. With the cursor on the rectangle and the rectangle highlighted, click the left mouse button. The rectangle is selected.

3. Press the Delete key. The rectangle is removed from the drawing.

In step 1, AutoCAD shows you exactly what the cursor is pointing to by highlighting objects that will be selected with the next mouse click.

In drawing and erasing the rectangle, you were exposed to the most common processes you need to know about to work in AutoCAD: you selected a command from the menu bar, and then you selected points in the drawing area while following the messages in the Command window. Commands from the toolbars work in the same way, as you'll see next.

Using the Toolbars

The menu bar provides most of the commands you'll need in a format that most Windows users will find easy to understand, and as a new user, you will probably be most comfortable using the menu bar. As you become more familiar with AutoCAD, you can start to use the toolbars. The toolbars offer the same commands as the menu bar but in a more compact format that is quicker to access. Not all toolbars are displayed on the screen in the default AutoCAD setup, but you'll find the most commonly used toolbars ready for you to use.

The tools in the toolbars perform three types of actions, just like the drop-down menu commands: they display further options, open dialog boxes, and issue commands that require keyboard or cursor input.

FIGURE 1.6

Once you've selected your first point of the rectangle, you see a rectangle follow the motion of your mouse.

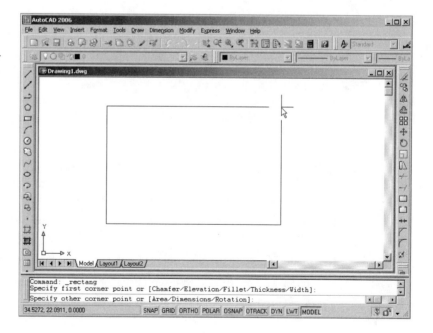

THE TOOLBAR TOOL TIPS

The toolbars are collections of buttons or tools that show icons that represent commands. *Tool tips* are short descriptions that help you understand what the icons represent. To see how tool tips work first hand, try the following exercise.

1. Move the arrow cursor onto one of the toolbar tools and leave it there for a moment. Notice that a brief description of the tool appears nearby—this is the tool tip. In the status bar, a more detailed description of the tool's purpose appears (see Figure 1.7).

2. Move the cursor across the toolbar. As you do, notice that the tool tips and status bar descriptions change to describe each tool. The keyboard command equivalent of the tool is also shown in the status bar at the end of the description.

WORKING WITH FLYOUTS

Earlier, you saw how cascading menus in the menu bar provide a set of additional options that expand from an option in an open menu. A toolbar *flyout* works in a similar way, but instead of menu options, you get an additional set of tools that "fly out" of the toolbar. And just like cascading menus, a toolbar flyout shows a small triangular arrow in the lower-right corner of the tool icon. Try the following to see firsthand how flyouts work.

1. Move the cursor to the Zoom Window tool in the Standard toolbar. Click and hold the left mouse button to display the flyout. Don't release the mouse button.

2. Still holding down the left mouse button, move the cursor over the flyout; notice that the tool tips appear here as well. Also, notice the description in the status bar.

3. Move the cursor to the Zoom Window tool at the top of the flyout and release the mouse button.

4. You don't need to use this tool yet, so press the Esc key to cancel this tool.

As you can see from this exercise, you get a lot of feedback from AutoCAD!

FIGURE 1.7

Tool tips show you the function of each tool, and a description of the tool is also displayed in the status bar.

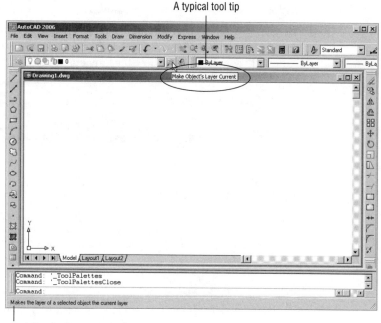

A typical tool tip

Tool description in the status bar

MOVING THE TOOLBARS

Another toolbar feature is its ability to be positioned anywhere on the screen. If you don't like the location of a toolbar, you can move it to another location. Try the following exercise to move the Standard toolbar away from its docked position.

1. Move the arrow cursor so that it points to the vertical bars, called *grab bars*, to the far left of the Standard toolbar, as shown here:

2. Click and hold down the left mouse button. Notice that a gray box in the shape of the toolbar appears by the cursor.

3. Still holding down the mouse button, move the mouse downward. The gray box follows the cursor.

4. When the gray box is over the drawing area, release the mouse button, and the Standard toolbar—now a floating toolbar—moves to its new location.

5. To move the toolbar back into its docked position, place the arrow cursor on the toolbar's title bar and slowly click and drag so that the cursor is in position in the upper-left corner of the AutoCAD window. Notice how the gray outline of the toolbar changes as it approaches its docked position.

6. When the outline of the Standard toolbar is near its docked position, release the mouse button. The toolbar moves back into its previous position in the AutoCAD window.

TIP You can also move a toolbar from a docked position to a floating position by double-clicking the toolbar's grab bar. Double-click the title bar of a floating toolbar to move the toolbar to its docked position.

LOCKING THE TOOLBARS AND PALETTES

The mobility of the toolbars and palettes is a great feature, allowing you to customize AutoCAD's window, but you might find that you can accidentally move or close toolbars. You can lock toolbars in their docked or floating location using a shortcut menu.

Right-click any toolbar and choose Lock Location toward the bottom of the shortcut menu.

You can choose from any of five options. Floating Toolbars and Docked Toolbars let you lock toolbars in either floating or docked locations. Floating Windows and Docked Windows do the same for palettes such as the Tool palette and Info palette. All offer a convenient setting to lock everything at once. When you click one of these options, a checkmark appears next to the selected option, telling you that that option is turned on.

UNDERSTANDING THE COMMAND, TOOL, AND OPTION RELATIONSHIP

One of AutoCAD's greatest assets is its ability to adjust to your way of doing things. If you prefer using toolbars, you can gain access to nearly all AutoCAD functions through toolbars. If you prefer using options from the menu bar, again, you can perform most of what you need through them. Hardcore users know how to use the command line and know nearly all the commands by heart.

The AutoCAD commands are really at the heart of its operations. Menu bar options and toolbar tools are really just different ways to invoke AutoCAD commands. When you click a toolbar tool or a menu option, you are really initiating a command through AutoCAD's menu system, sometimes with predetermined options already selected. In fact, if you watch the command line as you click a menu option or toolbar tool, you'll see that the messages in the Command window are the same regardless of where the command is invoked.

For this reason, I'll often intermix the terms tool, option, and command, because at a practical level, they are really all the same. Just be aware that menu options and toolbar tools invoke commands.

Closing and Opening Toolbars

Many experienced AutoCAD users prefer to start commands through the keyboard rather than through the toolbars. That way, they can remove the toolbars from the screen to maximize the area available for drawing.

If at some point, you find you prefer to remove the toolbars entirely, you can do so easily. Or you can remove and recall toolbars as needed. The next steps show you how.

1. Click and drag the Draw toolbar from its position at the left of the AutoCAD window to a point near the center of the drawing area. Remember to click and drag the grab bars at the top of the toolbar.

2. Click the Close button in the upper-left corner of the Draw floating toolbar. This is the small square button with the X in it. The toolbar disappears.

3. To recover the Draw toolbar, right-click the border or grab bar of any toolbar—but not a toolbar button. A shortcut menu of toolbars appears.

4. Locate and select Draw in the shortcut menu. The Draw toolbar reappears.

5. Click and drag the Draw toolbar back to its docked position in the far-left side of the AutoCAD window.

TIP If you do not want the toolbar to dock but instead want it to appear "floating" near the border of the AutoCAD Window, you can press the Ctrl key before you click and drag the toolbar into position. This prevents toolbars from automatically falling into a docked position.

AutoCAD remembers your toolbar arrangement between sessions. When you exit and then reopen AutoCAD later, the AutoCAD window appears just as you left it.

Other Toolbars

I mentioned earlier that not all the AutoCAD toolbars are open and visible. If they were, there wouldn't be any room for a drawing area. In the last exercise, you saw the list of all the available toolbars. Table 1.1 provides a brief description of each toolbar.

TABLE 1.1:   The Full List of AutoCAD Toolbars

COMMAND	DESCRIPTION
3D Orbit	Tools to control 3D views (not available in LT).
CAD Standards	Tools that let you check the layer, dimension, and text styles against standards that you have created (not available in LT).
Dimension	Commands that help you dimension your drawings. Many of these commands are duplicated in the Dimension drop-down menu. See Chapter 10.
Draw	Commands for creating common objects, including lines, arcs, circles, curves, ellipses, and text. This toolbar appears in the AutoCAD window by default. Many of these commands are duplicated in the Draw drop-down menu.
Draw Order	Commands that let you arrange the order of overlapping objects. If an object covers another object that you need visible, you can use Draw Order to "move" an object behind another or to the back of a set of objects (not available in LT).
Inquiry	Commands for finding distances, point coordinates, object properties, mass properties, and areas.
Insert	Commands for importing other drawings, raster images, and OLE objects.
Layer	Drop-down list and tools for controlling layer properties located just below the Standard toolbar.
Layouts	Tools that let you set up drawing layouts for viewing, printing, and plotting.
Modify	Commands for editing existing objects. You can move, copy, rotate, erase, trim, extend, and so on. Many of these commands are duplicated in the Modify drop-down menu.
Modify II	Commands for editing special complex objects such as polylines, multilines, 3D solids, and hatches.
Properties	Commands for a set of drop-down lists and tools for manipulating the properties of objects. This toolbar is normally docked to the right of the Layer toolbar, just below the Standard toolbar.

TABLE 1.1:   The Full List of AutoCAD Toolbars *(CONTINUED)*

COMMAND	DESCRIPTION
Object Snap	Tools to help you select specific points on objects, such as endpoints and midpoints. See Chapter 3.
Refedit	Tools that allow you to make changes to symbols or background drawings that are imported as external reference drawings. (not available in LT).
Reference	Commands that control cross-referencing of drawings. See Chapter 8.
Render	Commands to operate AutoCAD's rendering feature. (not available in LT).
Shade	Offers tools to control the way 3D models are displayed. See Chapter 6 for more on Shade (not available in LT).
Solids	Commands for creating 3D solids. See Chapter 6 (not available in LT).
Solids Editing	Command for editing 3D solids. See Chapter 6 (not available in LT).
Standard	The most frequently used commands for view control, file management, and editing. This toolbar is normally docked below the menu bar.
Styles	Tools that control style options such as text styles and dimension styles.
Surfaces	Commands for creating 3D surfaces. See Chapter 6 (not available in LT).
Text	Tools for creating and editing text. See Chapter 9.
UCS	Tools for setting up a plane on which to work. This is most useful for 3D modeling, but it can be helpful in 2D drafting, as well. See Chapter 6.
UCS II	Tools for selecting from a set of predefined user coordinate systems.
View	Tools to control the way you view 3D models. See Chapter 6 for more on 3D views.
Viewports	Tools that let you create and edit multiple views of your drawing. See Chapter 6 for more about viewports.
Web	Tools for accessing the World Wide Web.
Workspaces	Tools for managing workspaces.
Zoom	Commands that allow you to navigate your drawing.

Checking Out the Draw and Modify Toolbars

In the next section, you'll start to work in the drawing area by drawing some lines. Before you do that, take a moment to examine the Draw and Modify toolbars. You will be instructed to use them frequently throughout this book, so it will be helpful for you to get a feel for their arrangement and what they contain.

1. In the AutoCAD window, move the arrow cursor to the top icon in the Draw toolbar, which is the vertical toolbar at the far left of the AutoCAD window, and rest it there so that the tool tip appears.

2. Slowly move the arrow cursor downward over the other tools in the Draw toolbar, and read each tool tip.

In most cases, you'll be able to guess what each tool does by looking at its icon. The icon with an arc, for instance, indicates that the tool draws arcs; the one with the ellipse shows that the tool draws ellipses; and so on. For further clarification, the tool tip gives you the name of the tool. In addition, the status bar at the bottom of the AutoCAD window gives you information about a tool. For example, if you point to the Multiline Text tool at the bottom of the Draw toolbar, the status bar reads `Creates a multiple-line text object`. It also shows you the actual AutoCAD command name: `MTEXT`. This command is what you type in the Command window to invoke the Multiline Text tool.

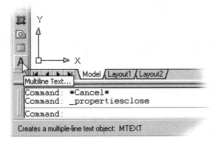

Table 1.2 will aid you in navigating the two main toolbars, Draw and Modify. You'll get experience with many of AutoCAD's tools as you work through this book.

TABLE 1.2: The Options on the Draw and Modify Toolbars

DRAW		MODIFY	
Icon	Tool	Icon	Tool
![Line]	Line	![Erase]	Erase
![Construction Line]	Construction Line (Xline)	![Copy Object]	Copy Object

TABLE 1.2: The Options on the Draw and Modify Toolbars *(CONTINUED)*

DRAW		MODIFY	
Icon	Tool	Icon	Tool
	Polyline (Pline)		Mirror
	Polygon		Offset
	Rectangle		Array
	Arc		Move
	Circle		Rotate
	Revision Cloud		Scale
	Spline		Stretch
	Ellipse		Trim
	Ellispse Arc (new since 2000)		Extend
	Insert Block		Break at Point
	Make Block		Break
	Multiple Point		Join

TABLE 1.2: The Options on the Draw and Modify Toolbars *(CONTINUED)*

DRAW		MODIFY	
Icon	**Tool**	**Icon**	**Tool**
	Hatch		Chamfer
	Gradient		Fillet
	Region		Explode
	Tables		
	Multiline Text		

Starting a Drawing

Let's create a new file.

1. Choose File ➤ Close to close the current file. In the Save Changes dialog box, click No. Notice that the toolbars disappear and that the AutoCAD drawing window appears blank when no drawings are open.

2. Choose File ➤ New to open the Select Template dialog box.

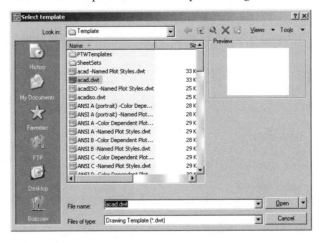

3. Locate and select the `acad.dwt` file, and then click Open to open a blank drawing window.

4. To give your new file a unique name, choose File ➢ Save As to open the Save Drawing As dialog box.

5. Type **My First Drawing**. As you type, the name appears in the File Name text box. Notice that the file will be saved in the `My Documents` folder by default.

6. Click Save. You now have a file called `My First Drawing.dwg`, located in the `My Documents` folder. Of course, your drawing doesn't contain anything yet. You'll take care of that next.

The `acad.dwt` template file you selected in step 3 is really just an AutoCAD drawing file that has been set up with standard settings. AutoCAD uses those settings to create a brand new file. As you saw in the Select Template dialog box, you can choose from several such templates.

This new file you just created shows a drawing area roughly 60 units wide by 30 units high. The units can be inches, meters, or millimeters. You determine what the units are equivalent to through the Drawing Units dialog box, which you will learn about in Chapter 2.

The drawing area you're presented with initially is your workspace, though you're not limited to the 60 by 30 unit area in any way. No visual clues indicate the size of the area. To check the area size for yourself, move the crosshair cursor to the upper-right corner of the screen, and observe the value in the coordinate readout in the lower-left corner of the AutoCAD window. This is the standard AutoCAD default drawing area for new drawings using the `acad.dwt` drawing template.

Point here.

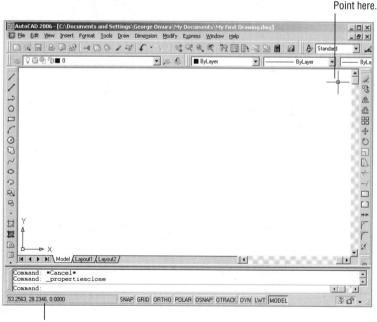

Read the coordinate here.

WARNING The coordinate readout won't show exactly 60 units by 30 units because the proportions of your drawing area are not likely to be exactly 6 x 3. Factors such as the size and resolution of your display and the shape of the AutoCAD window affect the dimensions of the drawing area. Also note that the default drawing that appears when you first open AutoCAD has an area that is roughly 16 units by 9 units.

Next, try drawing a couple of objects just to get comfortable with drawing in AutoCAD. You'll draw a rectangle again, plus some additional objects.

1. Click the Rectangle tool in the Draw toolbar. You can also choose Draw ➢ Rectangle from the menu bar.

2. Click a point in the lower-left of the drawing area as shown in Figure 1.8. Don't worry about the exact location. You're just practicing right now. After clicking, notice that one corner of the rectangle follows the cursor.

3. Click a point in the upper-right of the drawing area as shown in Figure 1.8. Again, it's not important if you don't pick the exact location. The rectangle is now drawn in place.

FIGURE 1.8
Drawing a circle

Click here for the center of the circle.

Click here to "fix" the circle's radius.

Click here to start the rectangle.   Then click here to complete the rectangle.

WHEN YOU NEED TO UNDO

Recently AUGI, the AutoCAD User Group International, conducted a survey to identify the most commonly used features in AutoCAD. They found the Undo and Escape keys were at the top of their list. Everyone makes mistakes, and it would be impossible to get any work done if it weren't for these two features. Undo and the Escape key are just two of a set of features you can use to reverse something you have done. If you find you've done something unintentionally, here is a listing of options you can use to get out of trouble.

Backspace (♦)   If you make a typing error, press the Backspace key to back up to your error, and then retype your command or response.

Escape (Esc)   When you need to quickly exit a command or a dialog box without making changes, just press the Esc key in the upper-left corner of your keyboard.

U⏎   If you accidentally change something in the drawing and want to reverse that change, click the Undo tool in the Standard toolbar (the left-pointing curved arrow). You can also type **U⏎** at the command prompt. Each time you do this, AutoCAD undoes one operation at a time, in reverse order. The last command performed is undone first, then the next-to-last command, and so on. The prompt displays the name of the command being undone, and the drawing reverts to its state prior to that command. If you need to, you can undo everything back to the beginning of an editing session.

Undo⏎   If you decide that you want to back up a few steps of an operation you just performed, you can use the Undo tool (the right-pointing curved arrow) in the Standard toolbar. Or type **Undo⏎**. Each click of the Undo tool steps you back one operation. In AutoCAD 2006, you can also select the exact command to undo by using the Undo drop-down list. You can open the Undo drop-down list by clicking the downward-pointing arrow found to the right of the Undo tool.

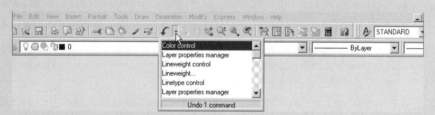

Redo⏎   If you accidentally Undo one too many commands, you can redo the last undone command by clicking the Redo tool (the right-pointing curved arrow) in the Standard toolbar. Or type **Redo⏎**. In AutoCAD 2006, Redo allows you to redo several operations that you might have undone with the Undo command. You can also select the exact command to redo by using the Redo drop-down list. To open the Redo drop-down list, click the downward-pointing arrow found to the right of the Redo tool.

Now add a circle to the drawing.

1. Click the Circle tool in the Draw toolbar.

2. Click the location shown in Figure 1.8 to place the center of the circle. Now as you move the cursor, a circle appears whose radius follows the location of the cursor.

3. Click another point as shown in Figure 1.8 to "fix" the circle's radius in place. You can also enter a radius value for a circle with an exact radius.

You now have a circle and a rectangle. As you can see, you create objects by placing key points of their geometry within the drawing area. For the rectangle, it was two corners; for the circle, it was the center and a location on the radius.

Once you've placed an object in the drawing, you can edit them using a variety of tools. In later chapters, you'll learn more about those editing tools. In the following section you'll learn how to get around in your drawing.

Panning and Zooming to Adjust Your View

One of the greatest features of AutoCAD is its ability to draw accurately through a wide range of scales. For example, you can draw a football field, zoom into a blade of grass, and draw its cell structure. With such a broad range of views to work with, you need to be familiar with AutoCAD's view features. The Zoom and Pan commands are the most frequently used of the view features, so you'll want to become familiar with them right away.

Try the following exercise to see how Zoom works.

1. Choose View ➤ Zoom ➤ Window or select Zoom Window from the Standard toolbar.

2. Click the first point indicated in Figure 1.9. You don't have to be too accurate.

3. Click the second point indicated in Figure 1.9. The area you selected expands to fill the drawing area. Notice that the transition to the zoomed view is smooth. This helps you keep track of exactly where in the drawing the zoom occurs.

4. Choose View ➤ Pan ➤ Realtime or click the Pan Realtime tool in the Standard toolbar. Notice that the cursor changes to a hand icon.

5. Click and drag in the drawing area. Notice how the view moves as you drag the cursor.

6. Press Escape to exit the Pan command. You can also right-click and choose Exit from the shortcut menu.

7. Finally, to get your original view of the overall drawing, choose View ➤ Zoom ➤ Previous or click the Zoom Previous tool in the Standard toolbar. The view smoothly transitions to the previous view, allowing you to see clearly where the previous view occurs in relation to the current one.

If you have a mouse with a scroll wheel, you can use it to zoom in and out of your drawing view. You can also use it to pan across your drawing. To zoom, scroll the wheel. To pan, click and drag the wheel.

FIGURE 1.9

Selecting a Zoom window

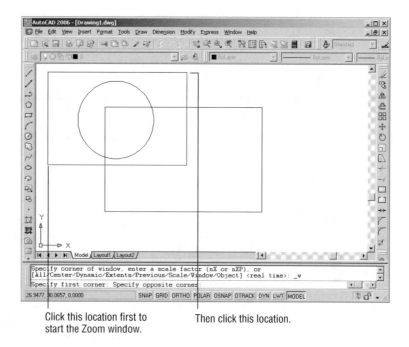

Click this location first to start the Zoom window.

Then click this location.

WARNING If you have a mouse that uses special drivers, you might not be able to use the wheel to control pans and zooms.

There are several other Zoom- and Pan-related commands, but those you've just tried are the ones you'll use 90 percent of the time. You can try the other Zoom and Pan options, which are displayed when you choose View ➤ Zoom. They are also options in the Zoom Command window options list:

```
[All/Center/Dynamic/Extents/Previous/Scale/Window/Object] <real time>:
```

Here is a list of the options and how they are used.

Realtime is the default Zoom option. It displays a magnifying glass cursor. With this option, you can click and drag up or down to change your magnification in real time. You can right-click to access the other Zoom options, plus Exit and Cancel.

Previous displays the previous view like an Undo for the Zoom command.

Dynamic changes the display to an overall view. A rectangle also appears, which lets you select an area to zoom into. To change the size of the rectangle, left-click the mouse. This allows you to adjust the size of the rectangle and thus change the size of the zoom area. Click again to fix the rectangle size. Right-click and select Enter to zoom in to the selected area.

Scale lets you zoom in or out by a specific value. It allows you to enter a specific view scale.

Center allows you to center a location on the screen.

Object lets you select a view area based on the area occupied by an object. For example, if you want to zoom in so that a particular object fills the display area, use this option.

In is the same as using the Scale option and entering 2x to magnify your view two times.

Out is the same as using the Scale option and entering 0.5x to view twice the current view area.

All displays the area of your drawing defined by the drawing limits plus any part of your drawing that falls outside the limits.

Extents displays a view that encompasses all the objects in you drawing. This option ignores the limits of your drawing.

You've just about completed your first look at AutoCAD. There are just a couple of other features you'll want to know about. In the next section, you'll be introduced to a display feature in AutoCAD that helps you set up your drawing for printing.

ACCURATE PANNING

Realtime pan is a great tool for quickly getting around in a drawing, but sometimes you need to pan in an exact distance and direction. A version of the Pan command lets you do just that.

If you choose View ➤ Pan ➤ Point, you see the prompt:

```
Specify base point or displacement:
```

This is the prompt you see for the Move or Copy commands, though in this case you're not affecting the objects in your drawing. When you select a point at this prompt, you see a rubber-banding line in conjunction with the next prompt:

```
Specify second point:
```

The rubber-banding line indicates the direction and distance of your pan. As with any other command that displays a rubber-banding line, you can select points to indicate distance and direction, or you can enter coordinates. This allows you to specify exact distances and directions to pan your view.

Understanding the Layout Tabs

Aside from the Command prompt, you've probably noticed that AutoCAD behaves like most other Windows programs. One element in AutoCAD's window is a little different from other Windows graphics programs.

At the bottom of the AutoCAD window, you'll see a set of tabs labeled Model, Layout 1, and Layout 2. If you have followed the exercises in this chapter or if you've just opened a brand new drawing, the Model tab is the one that is currently selected. This tells you that you that the drawing area you are currently viewing is the *model space* of AutoCAD. Model space is the display you'll use to do most of your drawing. It's like your main workspace.

The layout tabs are like page previews with the added advantage of allowing you to draw within them. The layout tabs also give you control over the printed scale of your drawing.

Another way to look at the layout tabs is to think of them as a drawing paste-up area. In the layout tab, you can set up multiple views of the drawing you create in model space. You can also add a title to your drawing and include borders or other graphic design features.

Try the following exercise to see firsthand how the layout tabs work.

1. Click the Layout 1 tab at the bottom of the drawing area. The drawing area changes to show your drawing, plus some additional display elements as shown in Figure 1.10. The Layout tab shows you how your drawing will look when it is printed.

2. Move the cursor over the rectangle that immediately surrounds your rectangle and circle drawing, as shown in Figure 1.10.

3. Click the highlighted rectangle, and then press the Delete key. Your drawing disappears.

4. Click the Model tab to return to model space. You see that the objects you drew are still there.

5. Click the Undo tool in the Standard toolbar twice to return to the Layout 1 tab and undo your deletion of the outer rectangle. The view of the rectangle and circle return.

6. Click the Model tab to return to the original drawing area.

In step 3, your entire drawing disappeared when you deleted the outer rectangle. This is because that rectangle is really a *viewport* into the drawing you created in the Model tab. When you are in a layout tab, a viewport acts like a window into your drawing. By default, AutoCAD creates a single viewport to show your drawing, but you can have multiple viewports of various sizes, each displaying different parts of your drawing. When you deleted that viewport, you essentially closed your view into your drawing in the Model tab, so your rectangle and circle disappeared from view. They didn't really go anywhere. It's just that your view of them was deleted.

FIGURE 1.10
Your drawing as it appears in a layout tab.

Click this outline and press the Delete key.

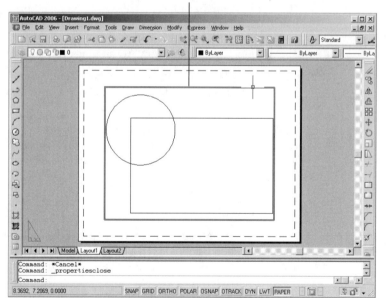

You might have also noticed that a layout tab displays a white area over a gray background. This white area represents the area of the paper onto which your drawing will be printed.

The white area also shows a dashed line close to its edge. This dashed line represents the printable area of your paper. Both the paper area and dashed line are determined by the current default printer connected to your computer.

If you have a printer that accepts paper of different sizes, you can select a different sheet size, and the new sheet size will be reflected in the white area shown in the layout tab. You'll learn how to control sheet sizes in the chapter on printing.

As you might guess, you use the layout tabs to lay out your drawing for printing. You can print from the Model tab if you like, but you have much more control over your printer output from a layout tab.

Understanding How Command Options Work

Nearly every AutoCAD command offers a set of options that are shown in the Command window prompt. These options let you alter the behavior of a command to suit your current drawing. To help demonstrate how command options work, and to get a feel for the drawing process in general, you'll draw an arc and then place it exactly in the inside corner of the rectangle.

1. Click the Arc tool in the Draw toolbar. The prompt Specify start point of arc or [Center]: appears, and the cursor changes to Point Selection mode.

   If you examine this Specify start point of arc or [Center]: prompt, you'll see the start point contains two options. The default option is stated in the main part of the prompt: Specify start point. If other options are available, they appear within brackets, as in the [Center] option that appears in the Arc Command prompt. This [Center] option tells you that you can also start your arc by selecting a center point instead of a start point. If multiple options are available, they appear within the brackets and are separated by forward slashes (/). The default is the option AutoCAD assumes you intend to use unless you tell it otherwise.

2. Type **C↵** to select the Center option. The prompt Specify center point of arc: appears. Notice that you only had to type the **C** and not the entire word **Center**.

   When you see a set of options in the Command window, note their capitalization. If you choose to respond to prompts using the keyboard, these capitalized letters are all you need to enter to select that option. In some cases, the first two letters are capitalized to differentiate two options that begin with the same letter, such as LAyer and LType.

3. Now select a point for the center of the arc as shown in Figure 1.11. The prompt Specify start point of arc: appears. You also see a rubber-banding line from the center point you just selected to your cursor.

   If you point directly to the right, you see that the rubber-banding line snaps to an exact horizontal orientation, and you see a tool tip appear at the cursor. This is a feature called *Polar Tracking vector*, and it help you to draw in exact horizontal and vertical directions much like a T square and a triangle. The tool tip shows your cursor's location relative to the center point you just selected. It displays this information in what is known as a polar coordinate. You can learn more about polar coordinates in Chapter 2.

FIGURE 1.11

Using the Arc command

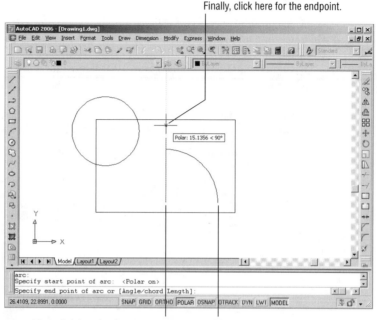

Finally, click here for the endpoint.

First, click here for the arc center.   Then click here for the start point.

4. With the rubber-banding line pointing to the right, click the left mouse button to select a point, as shown in Figure 1.11. The prompt `Specify end point of arc or [Angle/chord Length]:` appears.

5. Move the mouse, and a temporary arc appears, originating from the start point of the arc that you just selected and rotating about the center of the arc.

   As the prompt indicates, you now have three options. You can enter an angle, a chord length, or the endpoint of the arc. The prompt default, to specify the endpoint of the arc, lets you select the arc's endpoint. Again, the cursor is in Point Selection mode, telling you it is waiting for point input. To select this default option, you need only select a point on the screen indicating where you want the endpoint.

6. Move the cursor so that it points vertically from the center of the arc. You'll see the Polar Tracking vector snap to a vertical position as shown in Figure 1.11.

7. Click any location with the Polar Tracking vector in the vertical position. The arc is now fixed in place.

As you can see, AutoCAD has a distinct structure in its prompt messages. You first issue a command, which in turn presents options in the form of a prompt. Depending on the option you select, you get another set of options or you are prompted to take some action, such as selecting a point, selecting objects, or entering a value. The prompts offer a great deal of help "prompting" you to take an action.

Getting Help

AutoCAD provides a good set of help options that can answer most of the questions you might have while working on a drawing. If you're stuck with an AutoCAD problem, give the AutoCAD help options a try.

To get more familiar with the AutoCAD Help window, try the following:

1. Choose Help ➢ Help from the menu or press F1 to open the AutoCAD 2006 Help window.

2. Click the Contents tab, which contains a table of contents. The other four tabs—Index, Search, Favorites, and Ask Me—provide assistance in finding specific topics.

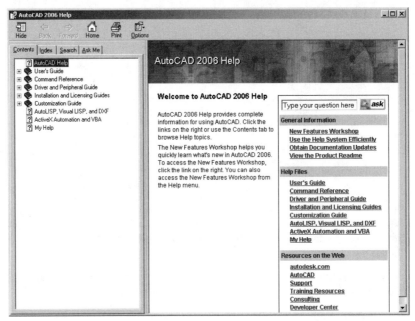

3. Scan down the screen until you see the topic Command References, and double-click it. Both panels of the Help window change to show more topics.

4. In the panel on the right, click the item labeled C just to the right of the Command listing. The panel expands to display a list of command names that start with the letter C.

5. Look down the list and click the word *Copy*. A description of the Copy command appears in the panel to the right.

You also have the Concepts, Procedures, and Reference tabs along the top of the panel on the right. These options provide more detailed information on the use of the selected item. If you want to back up through the steps you have just taken, click the Back button on the toolbar.

Using the Search Tab

If you're a beginning AutoCAD user looking for help, the Help window's table of contents may not be as useful as it could be. To use it, you have to know a little about what you're looking for. Sometimes it's quicker to use the Search feature of the Help window.

1. Click the Search tab in the left panel. If this is the first time you've selected the Search tab, you might see a message telling you that AutoCAD is setting up an index for searches.

2. Type **Change** in the text box at the top of the Search tab, and then click List Topics or press ↵. The list box displays all the items in the Help system that contain the word *Change*.

In this example, the list that is returned is quite large. You can use Boolean AND, OR, NEAR, and NOT in conjunction with other keywords to help filter your searches. Once you've found the topic you're looking for, select it from the Select Topic list and then click the Display button to display the topic information.

Another useful tool in the Help dialog box is the Ask Me tab. This tab lets you ask "natural language" questions. Try the following steps to see how it works.

1. Click the Ask Me tab.

2. In the top text box, enter **How do I zoom into my view**. The list below the text box changes to show several items that relate to adjusting views in AutoCAD.

3. Click Magnify A View (Zoom). The right panel changes to display a description of how the Zoom command works.

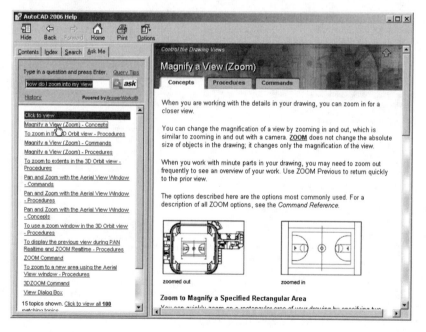

As you use the Help window, you will notice a three-letter abbreviation to the right of some of the items in the Ask Me tab. These tell you the document source for the listed option. For example, the Magnify A View (Zoom) item is listed in the AutoCAD User Guide, or AUG. Other items show ACR for AutoCAD Command Reference. You can also limit the query to specific document sources by selecting a source from the List Of Components To Search list box.

If you scroll down to the bottom of the Ask Me list, you'll find a Search The Web For: option. This does just what it says. If you don't find a satisfactory answer in the AutoCAD help system, you can select this option to open a search web page in the panel on the right. (Make sure you are connected to the Internet if you use this option.)

The Index tab lets you locate specific topics in the AutoCAD help system by entering a word in a list box. The Favorites tab lets you store locations in the help system that you refer to frequently.

Using Context-Sensitive Help

AutoCAD also provides *context-sensitive help* to give you information related to the command you are currently using. To see how this works, try the following:

1. Close or minimize the Help window and return to the AutoCAD window.

2. Click the Move tool in the Modify toolbar to start the Move command.

3. Press F1, or choose Help from the menu bar to open the Help window. A description of the Move command appears in the panel on the right.

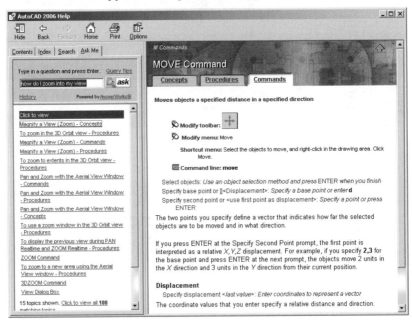

4. Click the Close button or press the Esc key.

5. Press the Esc key to exit the Move command.

If you gain some confidence with AutoCAD's Help window, you can go far in helping yourself to learn basic AutoCAD commands. But if you really get stuck, this book should help to get you past your barriers.

Additional Sources of Help

The Help Topics tool is the main online source for reference material, but you can also find answers to your questions through the other options in the Help menu. Here is a brief description of the other Help menu options:

Info Palette   A popup window that offers immediate help with the command that you are using. It's helpful for first-time users. When you issue a command with the Info palette open, you will see an option or list of options in the palette. These options offer a brief tutorial or other information regarding the current command.

Developer Help   Information specifically for developers. This includes anyone interested in customizing AutoCAD.

New Features Workshop   Descriptions and tutorials focused on the new features found in AutoCAD 2006. You can update this unique support tool through the Autodesk website.

Online Resources   Offers additional options that start your default web browser and open pages in the Autodesk PointA website. You can find the most up-to-date information regarding AutoCAD support and training by using these options.

About   Information about the version of AutoCAD you are using.

Staying Informed with the Communication Center

Nearly every major Windows program is somehow linked to the Internet to offer the latest news and updates for software. AutoCAD provides the Communication Center, which appears as a satellite dish icon in the lower-right corner of the AutoCAD window. You might see a balloon message pointing to this icon telling you of some new feature or news regarding AutoCAD.

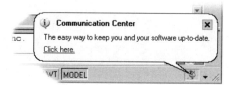

Click the Communication Center icon to open the Communication Center Welcome dialog box.

As the Communication Center Welcome dialog box explains, the Communication Center provides a way to stay informed about the latest software updates and support issues for AutoCAD. Click the Settings button to open the Configuration Settings dialog box.

The Communication Center works best if you use an "always on" Internet connection such as a DSL connection or high-speed cable connection. If you don't have such a connection, you can set the Check For New Contents option to On Demand. You can then check for updates when you connect to the Internet.

Just Enough Summary

AutoCAD is a rare example of a program that has successfully made the transition from a text-based DOS program to a fully Windows compliant one. As with most of today's drawing programs, you can use toolbars and menu options to access AutoCAD's features. The trick to using AutoCAD is in learning how to use it to input exact distances and directions. Once you've mastered the input methods AutoCAD offers, you're well on your way to producing accurate drawings. If you find you have questions along the way, hopefully this book will provide the right amount of help, but don't forget the AutoCAD Help system. It is full of great information and can be a real lifesaver.

That does it for your introduction to AutoCAD. You might want to practice what you've learned thus far. When you're ready to get down to some serious drawing, check out the next chapter. There you'll be introduced to the drawing tools you'll need to produce accurate drawings.

Chapter 2

Understanding the Drafting Tools

A lot of programs let you draw lines, circles, and arcs, but AutoCAD lets you draw with a level of precision that goes way beyond most other drawing programs. To take advantage of that precision, however, you need to know how to use the Drafting tools.

This chapter covers the set of tools that allow you to place objects exactly where you want them. You'll start by learning about the AutoCAD coordinate system, which will be basic to your understanding of precision in AutoCAD. Then you'll learn how to set up a drawing and how AutoCAD uses units of measure. The last half of this chapter covers the tools that let you select points in your drawing accurately. You'll learn how to select exact endpoints or midpoints of lines, for example, and how to align one object with another.

This chapter includes the following topics:

- ◆ Understanding the AutoCAD Coordinate System
- ◆ Setting Up a Drawing
- ◆ Using a Digital T Square and Triangle
- ◆ Getting a Visual Reference with the Grid Mode
- ◆ Snapping to the Grid or Other Regular Intervals
- ◆ Selecting Exact Locations on Objects
- ◆ Aligning Objects Using Object Snap Tracking and Tracking Points

Understanding the AutoCAD Coordinate System

Before you get too far in your use of AutoCAD, you'll want to know a little about the coordinate system in AutoCAD. Coordinates are important because they allow you to specify exact locations in your drawing. You'll use coordinates frequently to set the size and location of objects, to move and copy objects, and to align objects relative to each other.

AutoCAD uses a standard X Y Cartesian coordinate notation with a horizontal X axis and a vertical Y axis as shown in Figure 2.1.

FIGURE 2.1

AutoCAD's coordinate
system

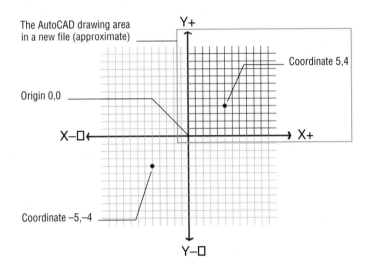

In a new drawing, AutoCAD shows the positive X and Y range of coordinates with the 0,0 coordinate, or origin, placed in the lower-left corner of the drawing area. The origin is an important coordinate location because it can be used as a reference for multiple drawings. For example, you can use the origin in a set of house plans to coordinate locations among a site plan drawing, a landscape drawing, and a floor plan.

Many AutoCAD commands ask you to choose a location by entering a point. For example, if you start the Line command, you see the prompt:

```
Specify first point:
```

You can specify exact coordinates by entering the X and Y coordinates separated by a comma. The X coordinate is given first and then the Y. For example, a location that is 5 units in the X direction and 4 in the Y is entered as 5,4 (see Figure 2.1). If you want to include the Z coordinate for a 3D location, you include it at the end of the list with a comma as in 5,4,2 where 2 is the Z coordinate. When you enter coordinates in this way, you are said to be using *absolute* coordinates, since these are exact locations in the overall coordinate system.

But for the most part, you won't be entering absolute coordinates to specify locations in a drawing. Usually you'll want to specify locations that are relative to a point you select in the drawing area. You can specify a distance and direction from a selected point using *relative* coordinates.

You specify relative coordinates in the same way you specify absolute coordinates, with one major exception: you must precede the coordinate with the @ sign. The @ sign means "the last point selected." For example, suppose you want to draw a horizontal line 3 units long in a random location in the drawing. You can start the Line command and then at the prompt

```
Specify first point:
```

you can select a point anywhere on the screen by clicking in the drawing area. The next prompt asks for the next point of the line:

```
Specify next point or [Undo]:
```

At this point, you enter @3,0. This tells AutoCAD to draw a line that is 3 units in the X coordinate and 0 units in the Y coordinate from the last point selected.

Another way to specify distance and direction is to use *polar* coordinates. With polar coordinates, you specify a distance and an angle. For example, if you want to specify a point that is 4 units from another point and at a 45°angle, you enter @ 4<45. Here the @ sign tells AutoCAD that you want to select a point relative to the last point selected, the 4 is the distance, and the <45 is the angle, as shown in Figure 2.2.

FIGURE 2.2

Drawing a line at a 45° angle

A line is drawn that is 4 units in length at a 45° angle.

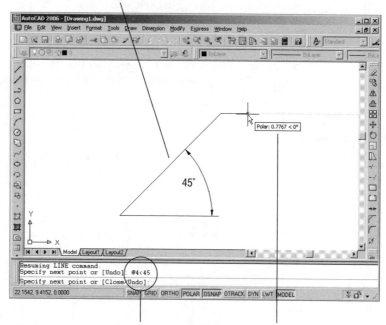

For the next point, type @4<45.   AutoCAD then waits for your next point of input.

You won't have to use coordinates for everything you draw. You can accurately select locations on objects using *object snaps*, or *osnaps* for short. Osnaps are a way of selecting exact locations on existing objects in a drawing, such as the endpoint or midpoint of a line or the intersection of a line and a circle. See "Setting Up Osnap Locations" later in this chapter for more on osnaps.

Experimenting with Coordinates Using Lines

The preceding explanation of AutoCAD's coordinate system, though brief, can serve as a reference or a reminder as you work with AutoCAD. If you need some additional practice, try the following to see firsthand how to use the coordinate methods. You'll use the Line command as a practice tool. These exercise will also help you become more familiar with the way AutoCAD works in general, so if you are totally new to AutoCAD, it is a good idea to do the exercises in this section.

To begin a line, follow these steps:

1. Start by making sure the Dynamic Input option is off by clicking the DYN button in the status bar. It should appear in the "up" position. You'll get a chance to use this feature later.

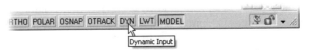

2. Click the Line tool on the Draw toolbar, or type **L↵** to start the Line command. AutoCAD responds in two ways. First, in the Command window, you see the message

```
Specify first point:
```

asking you to select a point to begin your line. The cursor has also changed its appearance; it no longer has a square in the crosshairs. This is a clue telling you to select a point to start a line (see Figure 2.3).

FIGURE 2.3
A rubber-banding line

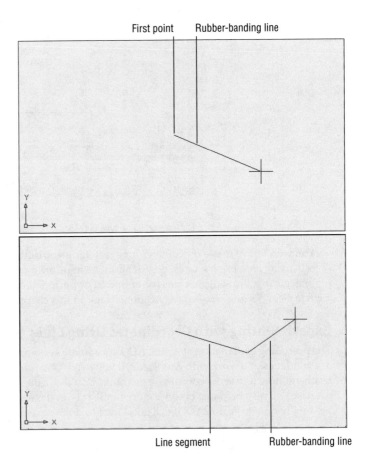

3. Using the left mouse button, select a point on the screen a little to the left of center. As you select the point, AutoCAD changes the prompt to

```
Specify next point or [Undo]:
```

Now as you move the mouse, notice a line with one end fixed on the point you just selected and the other end following the cursor (see the first image in Figure 2.3). This action is called *rubber-banding*.

If you move the cursor to a location directly to the left or right of the point you clicked, you'll see a dotted horizontal line, along with a message at the cursor. This action also occurs when you point directly up or down. In fact, your cursor will seem to jump to a horizontal or a vertical position.

TIP   This feature is called Polar Tracking. It helps restrict your line to an exact horizontal or vertical direction as a T square and triangle would. You can turn Polar Tracking on or off by clicking the Polar button in the status bar. If you don't see it, chances are it's turned off.

Now continue with the Line command:

4. Move the cursor to a point below and to the right of the center of the drawing area, and click the left mouse button again. The first rubber-banding line is now fixed between the two points you selected, and a second rubber-banding line appears. (See the second image in Figure 2.3).

5. If the line you drew isn't the exact length you want, you can back up during the Line command and change it. To do this, click Undo (left) in the Standard toolbar, or type **U↵**.

TIP   The Undo tool in the Standard toolbar contains an Undo drop-down list from which you can select the exact command you want to undo. See the "Chapter 1 for more information.

Now the line you drew previously will rubber-band as if you hadn't selected the second point to fix its length. You've just drawn, and then undrawn, a line of an arbitrary length. The Line command is still active. Two items tell you that you are in the middle of a command. If you don't see the word Command in the bottom line of the Command window, a command is still active. Also, the cursor will be the plain crosshair without the box at its intersection.

TIP   From now on, I will refer to the crosshair cursor without the small box as the *Point Selection mode* of the cursor. If you look ahead to Figure 2.10, you'll see all the modes of the drawing cursor.

Specifying Exact Distances

Next, you will draw a simple rectangle 10 units wide by 2 units high. By drawing a rectangle to a specific dimension, you'll get a chance to specify exact distances. You can use either relative polar coordinates or Cartesian coordinates to draw in AutoCAD. You'll start by using relative polar coordinates, which is the most common method for distance input.

SPECIFYING POLAR COORDINATES

To enter the exact distance of 10 units to the right of the last point you selected using polar coordinates, do the following:

1. Type **@10<0**. As you type, the letters appear at the Command prompt.

2. Press ↵. A line appears, starting from the first point you selected and ending 10 units to the right of it (see Figure 2.4). You have just entered a relative polar coordinate.

FIGURE 2.4
Notice that the rubber-banding line now starts from the last point selected. This tells you that you can continue to add more line segments.

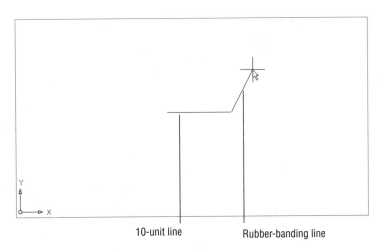

10-unit line   Rubber-banding line

Remember, you specify polar coordinates by starting with the "at" sign (@) followed by the distance, a less-than symbol (<), and finally the angle.

TIP If you are accustomed to a different method for describing directions, you can set AutoCAD to use a vertical direction or downward direction as 0°. See Chapter 3 for details.

Angles are given based on the system shown in Figure 2.5, in which 0° is a horizontal direction from left to right, 90° is straight up, 180° is horizontal from right to left, and so on. You can specify degrees, minutes, and seconds of arc if you want to be that exact. I'll discuss angle formats in more detail in Chapter 3.

SPECIFYING RELATIVE CARTESIAN COORDINATES

For the second line segment, let's try the Cartesian method for specifying exact distances. Follow these steps:

1. Enter **@0,2**↵. A line appears above the endpoint of the last line.

    As in the polar coordinate method, the @ tells AutoCAD that the distance you specify is from the last point selected. But, in this example, you give the distance in *x* and *y* values. The *x* distance, 0, is given first, followed by a comma, and then the *y* distance, 2. This is how to specify distances in relative Cartesian coordinates.

2. Enter **@-10,0**↵.The result is a drawing that looks like Figure 2.6.

FIGURE 2.5
AutoCAD's default system for specifying angles

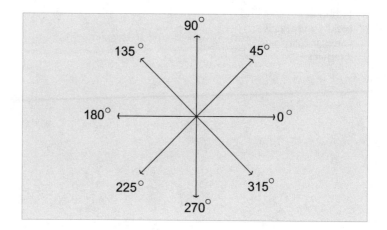

FIGURE 2.6
These three sides of the rectangle were drawn using the Line tool. Points are specified using either relative Cartesian or polar coordinates.

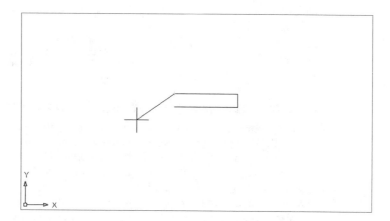

The distance you entered in step 2 was also in *x,y* values, but here you used a negative value to specify the *x* distance. Positive values in the Cartesian coordinate system are from left to right and from bottom to top (see Figure 2.7). (You may remember this from your high school geometry class!) If you want to draw a line from right to left, you must designate a negative value. It is also helpful to know where the origin of the drawing lies. In a new drawing, the origin, or coordinate 0,0, is in the lower-left corner of the drawing.

TIP To finish drawing a series of lines without closing them, you can press Esc, ↵, or the spacebar.

3. Type **C**↵. This C stands for the Close option of the Line command. It closes a sequence of line segments. A line connecting the first and last points of a sequence of lines is drawn (see Figure 2.8), and the Line command terminates. The rubber-banding line also disappears, telling you that AutoCAD has finished drawing line segments. You can also use the rubber-banding line to indicate direction while simultaneously entering the distance through the keyboard.

You can also use these methods when you need to specify distances when moving or copying objects or any time you need to specify a distance and direction.

FIGURE 2.7
Positive and negative
Cartesian coordinate
directions

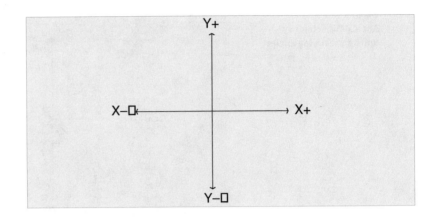

FIGURE 2.8
The finished rectangle

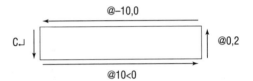

USING THE DIRECT DISTANCE METHOD FOR QUICK RELATIVE COORDINATES

A third way to enter distances is to simply point in a direction with a rubber-banding line and then enter the distance through the keyboard. For example, to draw a line 5 units long from left to right, click the Line tool on the Draw toolbar, click a start point, and then move the cursor so that the rubber-banding line points to the right at some arbitrary distance. While holding the cursor in the direction you want, type **5⏎**. The rubber-banding line becomes a fixed line 5 units long.

Using this method, called the *Direct Distance method*, along with Polar Tracking, can be a fast way to draw objects of specific lengths. Use the standard Cartesian or polar coordinate methods when you need to enter exact distances at angles other than those that are exactly horizontal or vertical.

USING THE DYNAMIC INPUT OPTION

Many users find it bothersome to have to look at the Command window while drawing and entering data. AutoCAD 2006 provides the *Dynamic Input* option that offers a kind of "heads up" display for the Command window. Dynamic Input displays the Command window prompts at the cursor so you don't have to look down to see them. It also offers yet another method for entering distances and directions. Try the following exercise to see how Dynamic Input works.

1. Click the DYN button in the status bar to turn on Dyanamic Input. The button should look like it is in the down or on position. Also turn off the Polar option. This will let you see more clearly how Dynamic Input works.

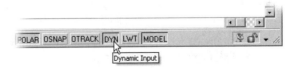

2. Click the Line tool in the Draw toolbar. Now as you move the cursor, you see the `Specify first point` prompt at the cursor. You also see the coordinate readout.

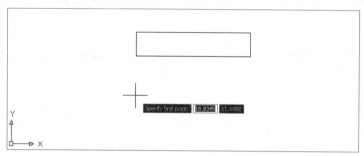

3. Click a point below the left corner of the rectangle you just drew. Now as you move the cursor, you see the actual dimension of the rubber-banding line as well as its angle near the cursor. You also see the `Specify next point or` prompt at the cursor.

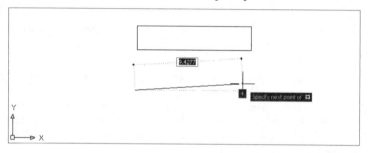

4. Notice that the length dimension is highlighted. This tells you that you can enter a value for that dimension. Type **10**, and then press the Tab key. As you type 10, it appears in the horizontal dimension. Once you press the Tab key, the line remains fixed at a length of 10 units while the angle continues to follow the cursor.

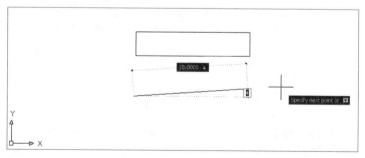

5. Notice that the angle value is now highlighted. Type **0↵** to fix the angle at zero degrees. The line is now fixed in place, and the next line segment is ready to be entered.

For the next line segment, try entering the angle first.

1. Press the Tab key. Notice that the angle value is now highlighted without affecting the length dimension.

2. Type **90**, and press the Tab key. The angle is fixed at 90°, but the length is still variable. After you press the Tab key, the length dimension is highlighted.

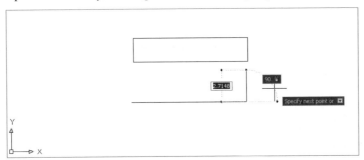

3. Type **2**↵ for the length. Now you have a vertical line segment 2 units long.

   Now try entering a Cartesian coordinate.

4. Type **-10,0**↵. A line segment is drawn from right to left. Notice that you didn't have to include the "at" sign (@). With Dynamic Input turned on, AutoCAD automatically assumes you want to specify the object's dimension rather than a coordinate in the overall coordinate system. This only applies to points you enter after the initial point you select to start the object. If you prefer, for consistency, you can still use the @ sign while entering relative coordinates with the Dynamic Input display.

5. Type **C**↵ to close the set of lines.

6. Turn off the Dynamic Input option by clicking the DYN button in the status bar.

As you worked through the exercise, you might have noticed a little downward-pointing arrow in the Command line at the cursor. This tells you that you can press the Down arrow key to access command options. The options are the same as those inside the square brackets in the Command window.

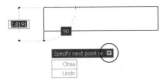

The Dynamic Input option offers yet another method for drawing and editing objects. As you can see from this example, you can enter a value for an object's dimension, and then use the Tab key to move to the next value displayed by the cursor. If you prefer, you can tab to a different value from the current highlighted value without entering anything, or you can just enter distances in the usual way, using Cartesian or polar coordinates.

Other commands such as Rectangle or Circle offer different dimension values that are more appropriate to the object being drawn, but the process is still the same: enter a value for the highlighted dimension by the cursor and then tab to the next dimension. If you want to enter Cartesian or polar coordinates, you don't have to include the @ sign, though you can if you want to for consistency. You can also use the Direct Distance method mentioned earlier, with the added benefit of using the angle readout of the Dynamic Input display. Use the Dynamic Input display's angle readout to point the rubber-banding line at the desired angle, then enter the length you want followed by ↵. The line will be drawn at the length you specify and at the indicated angle.

Now that you have some general practice, you're ready to set up an actual drawing.

TIP   For the rest of the book, unless I'm specifically discussing the Direct Input option, I will assume that it is turned off. Although it is a great tool, it can create some confusion for new users and can create some visual clutter in some of the exercises and examples. You might also be receiving help from others who are not familiar with the Dynamic Input option, which would create further confusion for you as a new user. As you become more accustomed to using AutoCAD, you might want to turn it on and experiment with it on your own. I'll also explain other features of the Direct Input option in later chapters.

Setting Up a Drawing

When you first open AutoCAD, you are presented with a default drawing called Drawing1. You can start drawing right away in Drawing1 without having to set up a drawing area or determining the drawing units you want to use. And even if you do set up a drawing for a particular area and type of drawing unit, you can always change them at any time. So as you learn how to set up a drawing, keep in mind that you can alter, expand, and modify the setup at any time.

Selecting the Drawing Units

Though not absolutely essential, it is helpful to set up the drawing units in AutoCAD before you start your drawing. And eventually, you'll want to set up the drawing units, so you might as well make a habit of setting them up right off the bat.

You'll most likely use either Imperial or metric measurement systems though you are not limited to those two systems. You can regard the base AutoCAD unit as anything you want as long as you are consistent in your use of that unit.

The most commonly used system in the United States is the Imperial system of inches and feet. Since the Imperial system has some special requirements, AutoCAD provides additional options when you're using it.

To select a drawing unit, you use Drawing Units dialog box.

TIP   If you want to just start drawing right away without setting up the drawing units, you can assume that the basic unit is the inch. Metric users can decide to use millimeters, centimeters, decameters, or meters, but whichever you choose to be the basic unit, make sure you stick with it throughout the drawing. You can tell AutoCAD what you want that unit to represent later using the Drawing Units dialog box.

1. Choose Format ➤ Units to open the Drawing Units dialog box (see Figure 2.9).

2. In the Length group, click the Type drop-down list, and then select the option that best represents the unit of length you will be using in your drawing. (See Table 2.1 for a description of these options.) If you are creating an architectural drawing using Imperial units, select the Architectural option. This will let you specify distances in feet and inches.

FIGURE 2.9

The Drawing Units
dialog box

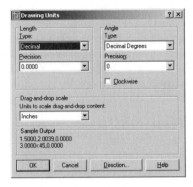

TIP As you highlight an option in the Type drop-down list, you'll see a sample of the type in the Sample Output box at the bottom of the dialog box.

3. In the Angle group, click the Type drop-down list, and then select the option that best represents the type of angle you plan to use. (See Table 2.2 for a description of these options.) The Decimal Degrees option is the most commonly used angle option for most drawings, but if you are drawing a site plan, you can select the Surveyor's Units to use a "metes and bounds" style of distance measurement.

4. Click OK.

Once you've set up the drawing units, you can use that unit as you specify distances in AutoCAD. For example, if you select Architectural, you can specify distances in feet and inches. The Engineering option lets you specify distance in feet and decimal feet. If you are using a metric system, stick with the default decimal type option.

TABLE 2.1: The Length Options

TYPE	DESCRIPTION
Architectural	Feet, inches, and fractional inches, as in 12´-6 ½″.
Engineering	Feet and decimal feet as in 12.5´ or 12´-6.5″.
Decimal	Whole and decimal units that can be anything (metric distances, decimal inches, decimal feet, or decimal miles, for example).
Fractional	Whole and fractional units that can be anything (fractional metric distances, fractional inches, feet, or miles, for example).
Scientific	Scientific notation for distances. Units can be anything (meters, angstroms, miles, astronomic units, parsecs, or light years, for example).

TABLE 2.2:   The Angle Options

TYPE	DESCRIPTION
Decimal Degrees	Whole and decimal degrees of angle.
Deg/Min/Sec	Degrees, minutes, and seconds of angle.
Grads	Angles specified in grads. For example, 45° of angle is specified as 50g.
Radians	Angles specified in radians. For example, 45° is specified as 1r.
Surveyor's Units	Angles are specified in degrees from north or south to east or west, as in N45dE.

Other Drawing Unit Options

You might want to know about a few other options in the Drawing Units dialog box. These are not as important as the type of length and angle you want to use, but they might play an important role in your work at some point.

Precision   The Precision option lets you control how AutoCAD reports length and angle values. This option does not actually affect the precision of the objects in the drawing. For example, if you select Decimal Degrees as the length type and 0.0 for the precision, AutoCAD displays a distance of 1.2 for a distance of 1.167. If you choose 0.000 for the precision option, you will see the full distance of 1.167 whenever AutoCAD displays a distance.

Direction   By default, AutoCAD assumes that 0° is a horizontal direction from left to right. Ninety degrees is directly vertical, and 180° is a horizontal direction from right to left. Angle values increase from 0° in a counterclockwise fashion. Figure 2.5 shows the cardinal directions and their degree values in a default AutoCAD setup.

If your drawing requires a different direction for 0°, you can use the Direction option to choose an angle. When you click the Direction button, the Direction dialog box opens. Click one of four radio buttons to select the 0° direction from the four cardinal directions. If your desired 0° direction does not conform to the cardinal directions, you can specify an angle numerically or graphically by selecting the Other option.

Clockwise   By default, angle values increase counterclockwise, but you can change this to clockwise by turning on the Clockwise option in the Angle group of the Drawing Units dialog box.

Drag-And-Drop Scale   AutoCAD can automatically scale a drawn object using the Design-Center feature. If you draw an object in inches, but you later need to import that object into a drawing created using millimeters, AutoCAD can automatically scale your object so it is the correct size in the metric drawing. To take advantage of this feature, you must specify the type of unit you are using for the current drawing in the Drag-And-Drop Scale drop-down list. For example, if the current drawing uses feet and inches, select inches from the list.

Determining the Drawing Area

One important concept you need to know is that AutoCAD's drawing area is virtually limitless. Although your view of a new drawing might show you an area that is only 60 units by 30 units, you are not confined to that area. If you like, you can include the entire western hemisphere of the world in your drawing area, even if you are only drawing a plan of your backyard.

With such a limitless area to work with, you need to set boundaries. To set up your drawing area, think of a reasonable area for the drawing you are about to start. You don't have to be too precise as you can always change it.

DRAWING A REFERENCE RECTANGLE

The first step is to determine what the drawing unit represents and then think of the area you want in real-world terms. You can go about this in a number of ways. This first example uses a rectangle to help you see the drawing area more easily.

Suppose you are starting a drawing of a house plan. You know that the lot size is 100' by 50'. First set up your drawing units to be Architectural and then do the following:

1. Choose Rectangle from the drawing. In the Command window, you'll see the prompt

   ```
   Specify first corner point or [Chamfer/Elevation/Fillet/Thickness/Width]:
   ```

2. Enter **0,0**. This tells AutoCAD you want the first corner of the rectangle at the origin of the drawing, which is the lower-left corner of a new drawing. If you remember your high school geometry, 0,0 is the coordinate for the origin of an XY graph. You'll see the next prompt

   ```
   Specify other corner point or [Dimensions]:
   ```

3. Enter **100',50'** to draw a 100' by 50' rectangle. The value you entered, 100',50' is a coordinate that is 100' in the X direction and 50' in the Y direction.

4. The rectangle is larger than the display of a new drawing, so to view the entire rectangle, choose View ➤ Zoom ➤ Extents.

You've now set up your view to include the entire area enclosed by the rectangle. This is a quick way to set up your drawing area, and it gives you the visual reference of the 100' by 50' rectangle.

USING LIMITS TO SET UP THE DRAWING AREA

In the previous section, you saw how to use a rectangle to set up a drawing area. Another tool for setting up the area is the Limits command. Unlike drawing a rectangle, the Limits command just defines an area. No visual clues show you what that area looks like, but you can choose View ➤ Zoom ➤ All to display the area set by Limits.

Here's how to set up the limits of a drawing:

1. Choose Tools ➤ Drawing Limits. You'll see the prompt

   ```
   Reset Model space limits:
   Specify lower left corner or [ON/OFF] <0.0000,0.0000>:
   ```

2. Press ↵ to accept the default location for the lower-left corner, which is the origin of the drawing. You then see the prompt

   ```
   Specify upper right corner <16.0000,9.0000>:
   ```

3. Enter a coordinate value representing what you want to use for your drawing. It should be the actual area at full scale. To use the example of the site plan from the previous section, enter **100′,50′**. Once you've entered a value, it will appear as though nothing has happened.

4. Choose View ➢ Zoom ➢ All. Again, nothing apparently has happened. However, now as you move your cursor to the upper-right corner of the drawing area, you'll see that the coordinate readout in the lower left of the AutoCAD window shows a coordinate of about 100′ by 50′.

INTERPRETING THE CURSOR MODES AND UNDERSTANDING PROMPTS

The key to working with AutoCAD successfully is understanding the way it interacts with you. You need to become familiar with some of the ways AutoCAD prompts you for input. Understanding the format of the messages in the Command window and recognizing other events on the screen will help you learn the program more easily.

The Command window aids you with messages, and the cursor also gives you clues about what to do.

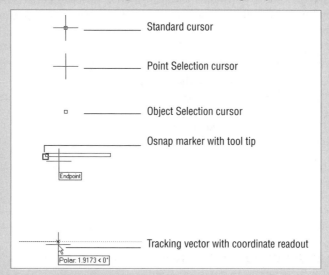

Standard cursor

Point Selection cursor

Object Selection cursor

Osnap marker with tool tip

Endpoint

Tracking vector with coordinate readout

Polar: 1.9173 < 0°

The Standard cursor tells you that AutoCAD is waiting for instructions. You can also edit objects using grips when you see this cursor. Grips are squares that appear at endpoints and midpoints of objects when they are selected. (You may know them as *workpoints* from other graphics programs.)

The Point Selection cursor appears whenever AutoCAD expects point input. It can also appear in conjunction with a rubber-banding line. You can either click a point or enter a coordinate through the keyboard. The Object Selection cursor tells you that you must select objects—either by clicking them or by using any of the object selection options available. The *Osnap (object snap)* marker appears along with the Point Selection cursor when you invoke an osnap. The tracking vector appears when you use the Polar Tracking or Object Snap Tracking feature. Polar Tracking aids you in drawing orthogonal lines, and Object Snap Tracking helps you align points in space relative to the geometry of existing objects. Object Snap Tracking works in conjunction with an osnap.

The drawback to the Limits command is that it does not give you any visual feedback. So why use it? It provides the following features that can be quite useful:

◆ You can choose View ➤ Zoom ➤ All to quickly display the area set by the Limits command.

◆ You can use the ON/OFF option of the Limits command to force your drawing to stay within the boundary set by the Limits command.

◆ The Grid feature, which displays a grid of dots, displays only within the boundary set by the Limits command. (This is important if you plan to use the Grid feature.)

TIP If you find that you use the same drawing setup over and over, you can create template files that are already set up to your own, customized way of working. Templates are discussed in Chapter 5.

Using a Digital T Square and Triangle

Before CAD became so prevalent in drafting rooms, most people used T squares and triangles to draw horizontal and vertical lines. AutoCAD provides two features that perform the same function as these hand-drafting tools: Ortho mode and Polar Tracking.

Using a Quick T Square Function with Ortho

The Ortho mode is the simpler of the two. It forces the cursor to point in either a vertical or a horizontal direction. You can use the Ortho mode in two ways. If you just need to temporarily restrain a rubber-banding line to a vertical or horizontal orientation, hold down the Shift key while selecting points. This is a common method found in many drawing programs. You can also click the Ortho button in the AutoCAD status bar to lock the Ortho mode on.

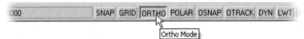

Once you've turned Ortho mode on in the status bar, your cursor will be continually restrained to a vertical or horizontal orientation as you draw objects or move, rotate, or copy objects.

Using an Adjustable Triangle with Polar Tracking

Another T square–like tool is Polar Tracking, which also helps restrain the cursor to horizontal or vertical motion. Polar Tracking is much more flexible than Ortho because it doesn't force you to point in strictly horizontal or vertical directions. Instead, it causes the cursor to "snap" to a horizontal or vertical orientation as your cursor approaches such an orientation.

Try the following exercise to see how Polar Tracking works:

1. Click the Line tool in the Draw toolbar.

2. Click the Polar button in the AutoCAD status bar to turn it on.

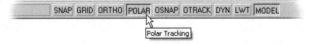

3. Click a point on the screen to start the line.

4. Point the cursor so that the rubber-banding line is at a 45° angle, and then slowly rotate the rubber-banding line to a horizontal orientation. Notice that as the rubber-banding line comes close to being horizontal, it "snaps" to a horizontal orientation. You also see a tool tip that displays the length and direction of the line.

5. Try pointing the rubber-banding line vertically. It "snaps" into a vertical orientation.

6. Press the Esc key to exit the Line command without drawing anything.

Modifying Polar Tracking's Behavior

Polar Tracking is not limited to vertical and horizontal orientations. You can set it to allow for other angles as well, much like an adjustable triangle in hand drafting. You can change the behavior of Polar Tracking through the Drafting Settings dialog box. To open the Drafting Settings dialog box, do one of the following:

◆ Right-click the Polar button in the status bar to open the shortcut menu, and then choose Settings.

◆ Choose Tools ➢ Drafting Settings, then select the Polar Tracking tab.

◆ Enter **DS**↵ at the Command prompt, and then select the Polar Tracking tab (see Figure 2.10).

With the Drafting Settings dialog box open at the Polar Tracking tab, you can set Polar Tracking to "snap" to any angle you need. First, select the Track Using All Polar Angle Settings option from the Object Snap Tracking Settings group. Then select an angle from the Incremental Angle drop-down list, which is in the Polar Angle Settings group. If you don't see the angle you want in the drop-down list, you can turn on the Additional Angle option. Click New, and then enter an angle in the list box. Table 2.3 shows the Polar Tracking options and their functions.

FIGURE 2.10
The Polar Tracking tab

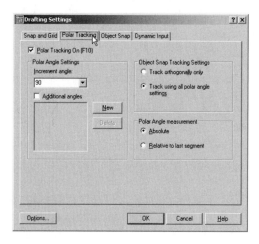

TABLE 2.3: Options in the Polar Tracking Tab of the Drafting Settings Dialog Box

SETTING	PURPOSE
Polar Angle Settings	You can set additional angles to which Polar Tracking will snap with these settings. Use a predefined angle from the Increment Angle drop-down list, or enter a custom angle by turning on the Additional Angles option and clicking New.
Object Snap Tracking Settings	Use the settings you choose in the Polar Angle Settings group by selecting the Track Using All Polar Angle Settings option.
Polar Angle Measurement	Set polar angles relative to the base coordinate system in AutoCAD or to the last angle used.

Getting a Visual Reference with the Grid Mode

If you're a CAD user, chances are you've used grid paper to help sketch out an idea for one design or another. Grids can help you get an idea of proportion or approximate distances when you don't have a scale.

The AutoCAD Grid mode displays an array of nonprinting dots within the drawing area. These dots can give you a reference for distance or location. You can set the spacing of the dots and easily turn them on or off using one of the following methods:

◆ Click the Grid button in the status bar.

◆ Press F7 or Ctrl+G.

You can also enter **Grid↵ on↵**. An array of dots appears in the drawing area as shown in Figure 2.11. You can turn off the grid by repeating the operation you used to turn the grid on, or you can enter **Grid↵ off↵** at the Command prompt.

FIGURE 2.11
An AutoCAD grid

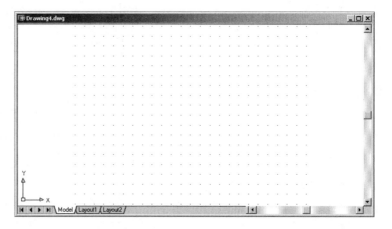

If you do not see a grid when you know you've turned it on, there are two possible explanations:

◆ The current display area is outside the limits of the drawing. (See "Using Limits to Set Up the Drawing Area" earlier in this chapter.) The grid is displayed only within the drawing limits.

◆ The grid spacing is too small to display properly in the current view. In this situation, you will see the message Grid too dense to display in the Command window.

You might also see a grid that appears only in a small area, as shown in Figure 2.12. This happens when the limits of the drawing are smaller than the area currently being displayed.

FIGURE 2.12

The grid as it appears when the limits of the drawing are smaller than the current display

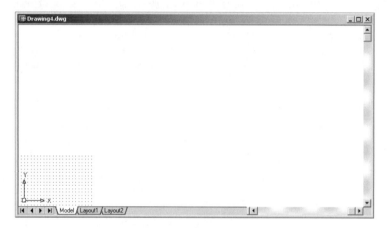

As described in "Using Limits to Set Up the Drawing Area," you can choose View ➤ Zoom ➤ All to adjust the display so that the limit of the drawing roughly equals the display area. If parts of the drawing are outside the limits of the drawing, choosing View ➤ Zoom ➤ All displays the limits of the drawing and any parts of the drawing that fall outside the limits.

You can make a wide range of settings for the way grids display. See "Changing the Grid and Snap Settings" later in this chapter for more information.

Snapping to the Grid or Other Regular Intervals

Depending on the type of drawing you are doing, it can be helpful to have the cursor "snap" to the grid. The Snap mode in AutoCAD forces the cursor to "snap" to regular intervals. For example, if you are drawing an object whose dimensions fall exactly within 1-unit increments, you can turn on the Snap mode and set it to 1 unit. When you then start to draw, the cursor jumps to 1-unit increments.

NOTE   Units can be inches, metric measurements, or any unit of measure you choose.

To control the Snap mode, do one of the following.

◆ Click the Snap button in the status bar.

◆ Press F9 or Ctrl+B.

You can also turn on the Snap mode by entering **Snap↵ on↵** at the Command prompt.

To turn off the Snap mode, repeat the operation you used to turn it on. You can also enter **Snap↵ off↵** at the Command prompt.

By default, the grid and snap spacing are the same; so if you turn on the grid and snap at the same time, the cursor appears to snap to the grid points. It is possible to set the grid and snap spacing to different values. For example, you might want the grid to show at a 12-inch interval while the snap spacing is set to 1 inch.

If the Snap mode does not seem to have an effect, the snap spacing might be set to a value too small to be noticeable in relation to your current view. For example, if your view encompasses an area the size of a football field and your snap spacing is set to 1/2 inch, you won't notice the effects of the Snap mode.

In a new drawing, the snap interval is set to 0.5 units. (This is 0.5 inches if you are using the Architectural or Engineering unit type in the Drawing Units dialog box.) The snap spacing can be anything you want, plus you can rotate the snap interval orientation, have a different X and Y snap spacing, or set the snap intervals to align with a specific location such as the corner of a box or the center of a circle. You'll learn how to make these adjustments in the next section.

Changing the Grid and Snap Settings

The Grid and Snap modes have a wide range of settings. You can modify their spacing and rotation and even set up a grid for 2D isometric drawing. To edit these settings, you use the Drafting Settings dialog box, which you can open by doing one of the following:

♦ Right-click the Grid Or Snap button in the status bar and choose Settings from the shortcut menu.

♦ Choose Tools ➢ Drafting Settings to open the Drafting Settings dialog box, and then select the Snap And Grid tab.

♦ Enter **DS↵** at the Command prompt to open the Drafting Settings dialog box, and then select the Snap And Grid tab (see Figure 2.13).

From here, you can adjust both the grid and snap settings. The following sections describe the settings in this dialog box.

FIGURE 2.13

The Snap And Grid tab

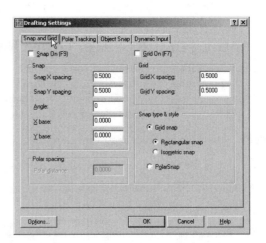

Adjusting the X and Y Spacing

You can set the X or Y grid spacing for either the grid or snap interval using the Snap X Spacing and Snap Y Spacing text boxes in the Grid and Snap groups. The *y* spacing value automatically adjusts to match the *x* spacing value for both Snap and Grid settings. For example, if you enter 4 for the Grid X Spacing value, the Grid Y Spacing value automatically changes to 4. To set the X and Y spacing to different values, first set the *x* spacing value and then set the *y* spacing value.

TIP   The grid spacing automatically follows the snap spacing if you set both Grid X and Y Spacing to zero.

Setting Up for Isometric 2D Drawing

Using isometric drawings is a common drafting method for drawing a 3D view of an object. Lines are drawn at 30° increments to simulate a 3D look. If you want to use the grid or snap to help you draw an isometric drawing, select the Isometric Snap option (Figure 2.14) in the Snap Type & Style group of the Drafting Settings dialog box.

FIGURE 2.14
The Isometric
Snap option

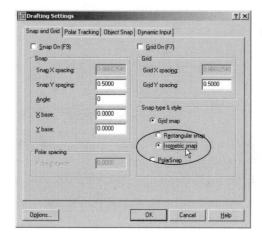

With the Isometric Snap option turned on, the grid changes to an isometric pattern, and the cursor changes to conform to the grid. To further aid in drawing an isometric view, you can toggle the cursor orientation between the left, right, or top Isoplane mode by pressing F5 or Ctrl+E. Figure 2.15 shows the cursor orientation for each isoplane mode.

FIGURE 2.15
The isoplane cursors

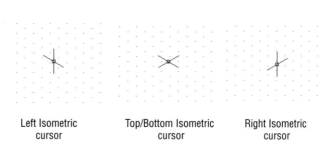

Left Isometric   Top/Bottom Isometric   Right Isometric
cursor   cursor   cursor

Since this is still a 2D drawing, the cursor's Isoplane mode is only an aid to help you visualize your 3D surface and does not affect the objects you draw.

Rotating the Grid, Snap, and Cursor

At times, it's helpful to temporarily rotate your grid to draw objects at an angle. For example, you might need to draw an assembly of rectangular-shaped objects at a 30° angle to the screen orientation, as shown in Figure 2.16. AutoCAD lets you rotate not only the grid, but the cursor and snap points as well, facilitating the construction of such a drawing.

FIGURE 2.16

A rotated grid and lines

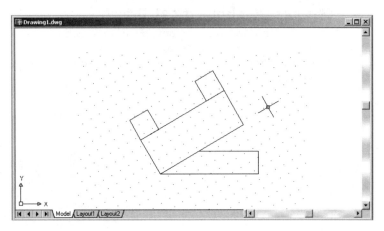

You can rotate the grid in two ways: you can use the Snapang command, or you can enter an angle in the Drafting Settings dialog box. Here's how Snapang works:

1. At the Command prompt, enter **Snapang**↵.

2. At the `Enter new value for SNAPANG <0>:` prompt, enter the angle that you want for the snap or grid.

The grid displays at the angle you indicated in step 2.

You can also indicate an angle visually in step 2 by clicking two points. For example, to align the grid to a line you've drawn at an angle, use the endpoint object snaps, and select the two endpoints of the line, as shown in Figure 2.17.

If you know the numeric value of the angle you want, you can also enter it in the Angle text box in the Snap And Grid tab of the Drafting Settings dialog box (see Figure 2.18).

Rotating the snap and grid won't affect how rectangles and the Polar Snap tool work. They still operate according to the default angle type, which is usually horizontal and vertical. If you need to do an extensive amount of drawing at an angle, you can create a *user coordinate system*, or UCS for short. See Chapter 6 for more on the UCS.

FIGURE 2.17
Using osnaps in conjunction with Snapang to align the grid to an object

Use the Endpoint osnap, and select this endpoint

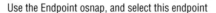

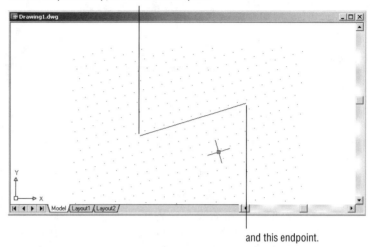

and this endpoint.

FIGURE 2.18
You can enter the specific angle in the Angle text box.

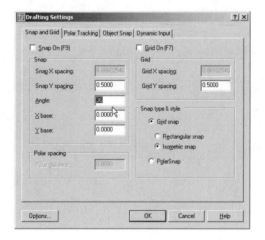

Aligning the Grid to an Object

In addition to rotating the grid, you can also align the grid's origin, or "base," to an object. This is useful when you want to use the grid to propagate from a specific location in a drawing such as the corner of a room or the center of a hole (see Figure 2.19).

FIGURE 2.19

The grid at the left is not aligned, but the grid on the right was aligned with the center of the circle using Snapbase.

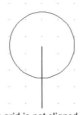

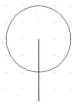

The grid is not aligned with the center of the circle.

The grid is aligned with the center of the circle.

To align the grid or snap to an object, do the following:

1. At the Command prompt, enter **Snapbase**↵.

2. At the Enter new value for SNAPBASE <0.0000,0.0000>: prompt, select a location that you want to use as the base or origin of the grid or snap, or enter a coordinate for the base.

As the command's name indicates, Snapbase sets the base for the snap. It also sets the base for the grid, even if the grid is set to a different X and Y interval from the Snap setting.

If you know the coordinate of the Snapbase you want, you can also enter it instead of selecting a point in step 2. Or you can enter the coordinate in the X Base and Y Base settings in the Snap And Grid tab of the Drafting Settings dialog box (see Figure 2.20).

FIGURE 2.20

The X Base and Y Base settings

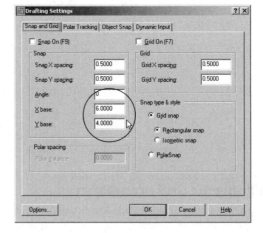

Selecting Exact Locations on Objects

One of the main reasons for using AutoCAD is to create accurate representations of your designs. And one of the most important tools you'll use to draw accurately is the *object snap*, or *osnap*. Object snaps allow you to select specific locations in your drawing as you draw or edit objects. For example, you can draw a new line from the exact endpoint of another using object snaps. Or you can quickly start or end a line from the exact center of an arc or circle.

These examples may sound trivial, but they reflect some of the most common activities you'll do in AutoCAD. Therefore, understanding osnaps is vital to using AutoCAD successfully.

Setting Up Osnap Locations

You can set up AutoCAD to automatically snap to endpoints, midpoints, and a variety of other locations on objects in your drawing. This first exercise shows how this works:

1. Open a new AutoCAD drawing.

2. Choose Tools ➤ Drafting Settings to open the Drafting Settings dialog box, and then select the Object Snap tab.

3. Click the Clear All button at the right of the dialog box to turn off any options that might be selected.

4. Click the Endpoint, Midpoint, and Intersection check boxes so that they contain a checkmark (see Figure 2.21).

FIGURE 2.21
Checking Endpoint, Midpoint, and Intersection

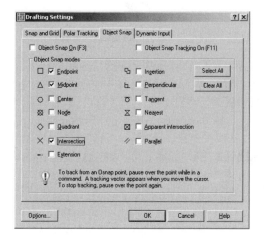

Automatically Snapping to Locations

After setting up osnaps as in the previous example, you are ready to use them. You can turn on the Osnap mode so that AutoCAD automatically selects the nearest osnap on an object as you approach the osnap location. This is called a *Running Osnap*. Now let's see how a Running Osnap works.

1. First turn on the Osnap mode by clicking the Osnap button in the status bar.

2. Click the Rectangle tool in the Draw toolbar, and then draw a rectangle in the drawing area about the size and location shown in Figure 2.22. You'll use this rectangle to test the osnap settings.

FIGURE 2.22
Draw this rectangle to practice using osnaps.

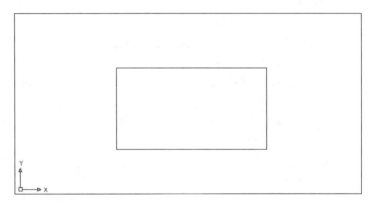

3. Start the Line command, place the cursor at the lower-left corner of the rectangle, but don't click yet. Notice that the cursor snaps to the corner and that a square appears. Also, a tool tip appears after a moment showing you the name of the osnap that is active; Endpoint.

4. Click the mouse while the Endpoint osnap is displayed. The line is now fixed to the corner of the rectangle.

5. Move the cursor to the middle of the right side of the rectangle, as shown in Figure 2.23. The Midpoint osnap appears. This time you see a triangle that gives you immediate feedback as to which osnap is active. Leave the cursor there for a moment, and you see the Midpoint tool tip.

6. Click the mouse while the Midpoint osnap is displayed. The line is now fixed between the lower-left corner and the midpoint of the right side.

7. Move the cursor to the upper-left corner, click when you see the Endpoint osnap marker, and then press ↵ to exit the Line command.

As you can see, osnaps let you quickly select a location on an object without too much intervention on your part.

TIP When you see an Osnap marker on an object, press Tab to move to the next osnap point on the object. If you have several Running Osnap modes on (Endpoint, Midpoint, and Intersection, for example), pressing Tab cycles through those osnap points on the object. This feature can be especially useful in a crowded area of a drawing.

FIGURE 2.23
Using the Midpoint
osnap

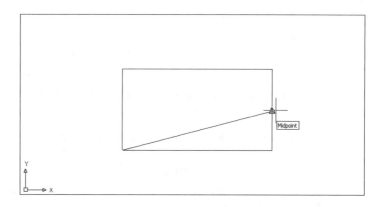

Selecting Object Snaps on the Fly

As helpful as object snaps are, they can get in the way. In a crowded drawing, osnaps can cause you to accidentally select a point you don't want. In these situations, you can turn off the Osnap mode. When you then need to select an osnap, you can do so from a Shift right-click menu. This lets you be more selective in the osnap you choose. The following exercise shows how this method works.

1. If you don't already have a rectangle in the drawing, start a new drawing and place a rectangle roughly in the middle of the drawing area.

2. Make sure the Osnap button in the status bar is in the "up" or off position. If it isn't, click the Osnap button or press F3.

3. Click the Line tool, hold down the Shift key, and right-click. A menu appears at the cursor, displaying a list of osnap options (see Figure 2.24).

4. Select Midpoint, and then place the cursor near the midpoint of line at the bottom of the rectangle. The Midpoint osnap marker appears.

FIGURE 2.24
Osnap options

5. Shift+right-click again, and select Endpoint from the shortcut menu.

6. Move the cursor to the upper-right endpoint of the rectangle. This time the Endpoint osnap marker appears.

7. Left-click the corner while the Endpoint osnap marker is still visible.

8. Press ⏎ to exit the Line command.

TIP If you accidentally select too many objects, you can remove them from your selection by holding down the Shift key and clicking the objects.

Understanding the Osnap Options

In the previous exercise, you made several of the osnap settings automatic so that they were available without having to select them from the Osnap pop-up menu. Another way to display the osnap options is to type their keyboard equivalents while selecting points or to right-click while selecting points to open the Osnap shortcut menu.

Here is a summary of all the osnap options, including their keyboard shortcuts. You've already used many of these options in this chapter and in the previous chapter. Pay special attention to those options you haven't yet used in the exercises but might find useful to your style of work. The full name of each option is followed by its keyboard shortcut in brackets. To use these options, you can enter either the full name or the abbreviation at any point prompt. You can also select these options from the pop-up menu that is displayed when you Shift+right-click.

TIP Sometimes you'll want one or more of these options available as the default selection. Remember that you can set Running Osnaps to be on at all times. Choose Tools ➢ Drafting Settings to open the Drafting Settings dialog box, and then click the Object Snap tab. You can also right-click the Osnap button in the status bar and choose Settings from the shortcut menu.

Apparent Intersection [apint]   Selects the apparent intersection of two objects. This is useful when you want to select the intersection of two objects that do not actually intersect. You will be prompted to select the two objects.

Center [cen]   Selects the center of an arc or a circle. You must click the arc or circle itself, not its apparent center.

Endpoint [endp]   Selects all the endpoints of lines, polylines, arcs, curves, and 3D face vertices.

Extension [ext]   Selects a point that is aligned with an imagined extension of a line. For example, you can select a point in space that is aligned with an existing line but is not actually on that line. To use that point, type **ext**⏎ during point selection or select Extension from the Osnap pop-up menu; then move the cursor to the line whose extension you want to use, and hold it there until you see a small, cross-shaped marker on the line. The cursor also displays a tool tip with the word *extension*, letting you know that the Extension osnap is active.

From [fro]   Selects a point relative to a selected point. For example, you can select a point that is 2 units to the left and 4 units above a circle's center. This option is usually used in conjunction with another osnap option, such as From Endpoint or From Midpoint.

Insert [ins]   Selects the insertion point of text, blocks, Xrefs, and overlays.

Intersection [int]   Selects the intersection of objects.

Midpoint [m]   Selects the midpoint of a line or an arc. In the case of a polyline, it selects the midpoint of the polyline segment.

Mid Between 2 Points [m2p]   Selects a point midway between two points.

Nearest [nea]   Selects a point on an object nearest the pick point.

Node [nod]   Selects a point object.

None [non]   Temporarily turns off Running Osnaps.

Osnap Settings   Opens the Object Snap tab of the Drafting Settings dialog box to allow you to make Osnap setting changes.

Parallel [par]   Lets you draw a line segment that is parallel to another existing line segment. To use this option, type **par**↵ during point selection or select Parallel from the Osnap pop-up menu; then move the cursor to the line you want parallel to and hold it there until you see a small, cross-shaped marker on the line. The cursor also displays a tool tip with the word *parallel*, letting you know that the Parallel osnap is active.

Perpendicular [per]   Selects a position on an object that is perpendicular to the last point selected. Normally, this option is not valid for the first point selected in a string of points.

Point Filters   Opens an additional set of options that let you select just the X, Y, or Z coordinate of a point or a combination of any pair of these coordinates, such as X and Z or Y and Z. This feature is most useful when creating 3D models.

Allows you to use the Object Snap Tracking feature "on the fly." See "Using the Temporary Tracking Point Feature" later in this chapter.

Quadrant [qua]   Selects the nearest cardinal (north, south, east, or west) point on an arc or a circle.

Tangent [tan]   Selects a point on an arc or a circle that represents the tangent from the last point selected. Like the Perpendicular option, Tangent is not valid for the first point in a string of points.

Temporary Track Point [tt]   Allows you to use the Object Snap Tracking feature "on the fly." See "Using the Temporary Tracking Point Feature" later in this chapter.

Fine-Tuning the AutoSnap Feature

When you click the Options button in the Object Snap tab of the Drafting Settings dialog box, you'll see the Drafting Settings tab of the Options dialog box. This tab provides options pertaining to the AutoSnap feature (see Table 2.4). AutoSnap looks at the location of your cursor during osnap selections and locates the osnap point nearest your cursor. AutoSnap then displays a graphic called a marker showing you the osnap point it has found. If it is the one you want, simply left-click to select it.

You can also get to this tab by choosing Tools ➤ Options and then selecting the Drafting Settings tab.

TABLE 2.4:   The AutoSnap Settings in the Drafting Settings Tab of the Options Dialog Box

OPTION	USE
Marker	Turns the graphic marker on or off
Magnet	Causes the Osnap cursor to "snap to" inferred osnap points

TABLE 2.4: The AutoSnap Settings in the Drafting Settings Tab of the Options Dialog Box (CONTINUED)

OPTION	USE
Display AutoSnap Tooltip	Turns the Osnap tool tip on or off
Display AutoSnap Aperture Box	Turns the old-style osnap cursor box on or off
AutoSnap Marker Size	Controls the size of the graphic marker
AutoSnap Marker Color	Controls the color of the graphic marker

Aligning Objects Using Object Snap Tracking and Tracking Points

Osnaps are great for selecting exact locations directly on existing objects, but what if you want to find a point that is aligned with an object but not necessarily on the object? *Object Snap Tracking,* or *Osnap Tracking,* is like an extension of Object Snaps that allows you to *align* a point to the geometry of an object instead of just selecting a point on an object. This alignment point is referred to as a *tracking point* since the cursor "tracks" from the selected osnap point.

With Osnap Tracking you can select a point that is exactly at the center of a rectangle. In the following exercise, you'll place a circle inside a rectangle to see how Osnap Tracking works firsthand.

WARNING The Object Snap Tracking feature is not available in AutoCAD LT 2006. If you are using LT, you can use the Temporary Tracking feature described later in this chapter.

First, make sure Running Osnaps are turned on and that they are set to the Midpoint option. Then make sure Osnap Tracking is turned on.

1. Right-click the Otrack button in the status bar and choose Settings from the shortcut menu to open the Drafting Settings dialog box (see Figure 2.25) at the Object Snap tab.

FIGURE 2.25
The Drafting Settings dialog

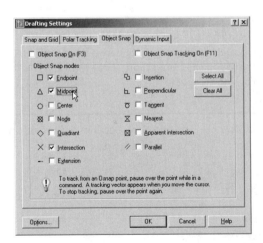

2. Make sure that the Midpoint option in the Object Snap Modes group is checked.

3. Also make sure that Object Snap On and Object Snap Tracking On are both checked. Click OK.

Now you're ready to draw.

1. Draw a rectangle large enough to fill most of the drawing area with some margin around the outside, as shown in Figure 2.26.

2. Click the Circle tool in the Draw toolbar or enter **C↵**.

3. At the `Specify center point for circle or [3P/2P/Ttr (tan tan radius)]:` prompt, type **C** or right-click and choose Center from the shortcut menu.

4. Move your cursor to the top, horizontal edge of the rectangle, until you see the midpoint tool tip.

FIGURE 2.26
Draw this rectangle to practice using Object Snap Tracking.

5. Move the cursor directly over the Midpoint Osnap marker. Without clicking the mouse, hold the cursor there for a second until you see a small cross appear. Look carefully because the cross is quite small. This is the Osnap Tracking marker.

TIP You can alternately insert and remove the Osnap Tracking marker by passing the cursor over it.

Tracking marker

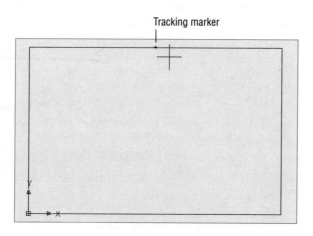

Now as you move the cursor downward, a dotted line appears, emanating from the midpoint of the horizontal line. The cursor also shows a small X following the dotted line as you move it.

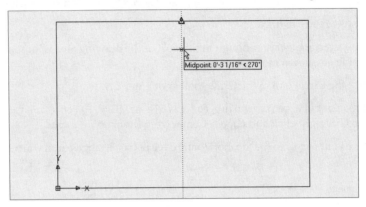

6. Move the cursor to the midpoint of the left vertical side of the rectangle. Don't click, but hold it there for a second until you see the small cross. Now as you move the cursor away, a horizontal dotted line appears with an X following the cursor.

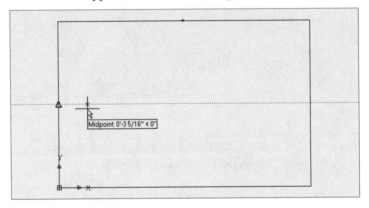

7. Move the cursor to the center of the rectangle. The two dotted lines appear simultaneously, and a small X appears at their intersection.

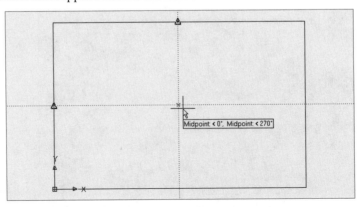

8. With the two dotted lines crossing and the X at their intersection, left-click to select the exact center of the rectangle.

9. At the Specify radius of circle or [Diameter]: prompt, click a point anywhere to finish the circle. The radius doesn't really matter here. The circle appears in the exact center of the rectangle, as shown in Figure 2.27.

FIGURE 2.27
The completed circle centered on the rectangle

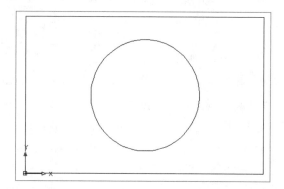

Although you only used the Midpoint Osnap setting in this exercise, you are not limited to only one osnap setting. You can use as many as you need to in order to select the appropriate geometry. You can also use as many alignment points as you need, although in this exercise, you only used two. If you like, erase the ellipse and repeat this exercise until you get the hang of using the Osnap Tracking feature.

TIP As with all the other buttons in the status bar, you can turn Osnap Tracking on or off by clicking the Otrack button. You can also press F11.

Using the Temporary Tracking Point Feature

The Osnap Tracking feature described in the previous section automatically selects tracking points for you when you momentarily hold the cursor on a location. Osnaps must be turned on for this feature to work. But what if you want to use Osnap Tracking "on the fly" when Osnaps are turned off?

The Temporary Tracking Point feature lets you specify tracking points even if osnaps are turned off or if your current osnap settings do not include an osnap that you want to use as a tracking point. For example, what if you want to use the Endpoint osnap for a tracking point but you only have Midpoint turned on for your Running Osnaps?

The following exercise demonstrates how you can use Temporary Tracking Points to use any osnap option you need "on the fly."

1. If you haven't done so already, draw a rectangle large enough to fill most of the drawing area with some margin around the outside, as shown in Figure 2.22.

2. If you did the exercise in the previous section, erase the circle you drew in the center of the rectangle by clicking it and pressing Del.

3. Turn off Osnap mode by clicking the Osnap button in the status bar. It should be in the "up" position.

Now you're ready to try the Temporary Tracking Point feature.

1. Click the Circle tool in the Draw toolbar or enter **C**↵.

2. At the `Specify center point for circle or [3P/2P/Ttr (tan tan radius)]:` prompt, type **C** or right-click and choose Center from the shortcut menu.

3. Shift+right-click, and choose Temporary Tracking Point.

4. Shift+right-click again, and choose Midpoint.

5. Move your cursor to the top, horizontal edge of the rectangle, until you see the midpoint tool tip and click that point.

6. Shift+right-click, and choose Temporary Tracking Point again.

7. Shift+right-click, and choose Midpoint.

8. Move the cursor to the midpoint of the left vertical side of the rectangle, and click that point.

9. Move the cursor to the center of the rectangle. The two dotted lines or tracking vectors appear simultaneously, and a small X appears at their intersection.

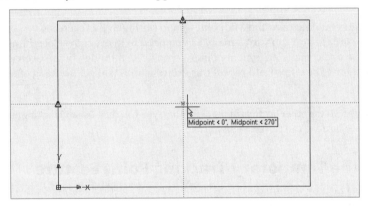

10. With the two dotted lines crossing and the X at their intersection, left-click to select the exact center of the rectangle.

11. At the `Specify radius of circle or [Diameter]:` prompt, click a point anywhere to finish the circle. The radius doesn't really matter here.

When a drawing gets crowded, Running Osnaps might get in the way of your work. The Temporary Tracking Point feature lets you access the Osnap Tracking vector without having to turn on Running Osnaps.

The Temporary Tracking Point feature and the other tools that use tracking vectors take a little practice to use, but once you understand how they work, they are an indispensable aid in your drawing.

USING OSNAP TRACKING AND POLAR TRACKING TOGETHER

In addition to selecting as many tracking points as you need, you can also use angles other than the basic orthogonal angles of 0, 90, 180, and 270 degrees. For example, you can locate a point that is aligned vertically to the top edge of the rectangle and at a 45° angle from a corner.

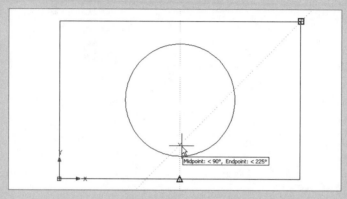

To do so, use the settings in the Polar Tracking tab of the Drafting Settings dialog box. (See the "Modifying Polar Tracking's Behavior" section earlier in this chapter.) If you set the increment angle to 45° and turn on the Track Using All Polar Angle Settings option, you will be able to use 45° in addition to the orthogonal directions.

Just Enough Summary

The drawing area and drawing units are often the most mystifying aspects of AutoCAD, if only because they have few limits. Once you understand how drawings are set up for area and units, you can start to draw with more confidence.

Next, you'll want to brush up on your high school geometry so you can understand the way AutoCAD determines the location of objects.

Since AutoCAD is all about drawing accurately, you'll want to become intimately familiar with the tools that help you maintain accuracy, such as osnaps and osnap tracking. This chapter covers all the osnap methods, but if you focus on just knowing how to get to them through the shortcut menus, you'll have all you need to make good use of osnaps.

Chapter 3

Drawing 2D Objects

This is one of the basic topics covered in this book, and many users will jump in and start to draw without a great need to consult this chapter. Still, some tools and tool characteristics might not be obvious or might trip you up as you begin to draw. If you find you need a little extra help when you draw something, you can review this chapter.

When you draw in AutoCAD, you are creating AutoCAD objects: lines, circles, arcs, ellipses, and hatch patterns. And each and every object has a set of properties. There are geometric properties such as the endpoints of a line or the center and radius of a circle. There are also properties not directly related to the geometry of an object, such as its color or its layer assignment. (See Chapter 7 to find out what layers do.)

When you draw objects, you are really specifying their geometric properties. The other properties are assigned by whatever defaults are currently in place, such as the current color and layer assignments. You can set these defaults in the Properties toolbar. You can always change the properties of an object (see Chapter 4), so don't feel that you need to be too careful when you're drawing.

- ◆ Drawing Straight Lines

- ◆ Drawing Circles and Arcs

- ◆ Drawing Curves

- ◆ Drawing Parallel Lines

- ◆ Drawing Revision Clouds

- ◆ Working with Hatch Patterns and Solid Fills

- ◆ Drawing Regular Polygons

- ◆ Using Objects to Lay Out Your Drawing

Drawing Straight Lines

The basic object in AutoCAD is the *line*. If you worked through the exercises in earlier chapters, you've already used lines. Drawing lines consists of four basic actions:

1. Click the Line tool or enter **L↵** at the Command prompt.

2. Click a start point or enter a coordinate.

3. Continue to select points, either by clicking them or entering coordinates, to place a series of contiguous line segments.

4. Press ↵ to exit the Line command, or enter **C↵** to join the last line endpoint with the first.

When you draw a series of contiguous line segments using the Line command, each line segment behaves like an individual object. You can move the segments separately or change their individual properties.

You typically don't just draw a line and leave it alone. Lines tend to get edited a lot. Some of the most commonly used editing commands for lines are Trim, Extend, Fillet, and Offset. Trim and Extend either trim lines to intersecting lines or extend lines to other objects. Fillet joins two lines exactly end to end or adds an arc between them. And Offset makes a parallel copy of a line at a specific distance.

As useful as lines are, you might find that you need your contiguous line segments to behave as a single object instead of as a series of individual lines. Another type of object called a *polyline* is just such an object. Using the Polyline command, you can draw a series of line segments, and they will behave as a single object. In fact, the rectangle is really a polyline that is closed. So are regular polygons created by the Polygon command, described later.

To draw straight lines with the Polyline command, click the Polyline tool in the Draw toolbar or choose Draw ➤ Polyline. Then start selecting points, just as you would with the Line command. Press ↵ when you finish drawing your lines.

When you click a polyline, instead of just selecting a line segment, you select the entire polyline. You can "break down" a polyline into its constituent parts by using the Explode command (see Chapter 4 for more on Explode).

Polylines can help you construct some types of objects very quickly. Figure 3.1 shows some examples of polylines that have been created from standard AutoCAD commands or edited to form complex shapes.

FIGURE 3.1
Although different commands were used to create them, these objects are all polylines and can be edited as such.

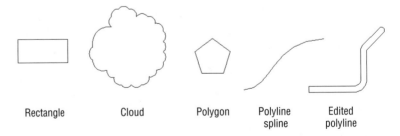

Rectangle   Cloud   Polygon   Polyline spline   Edited polyline

Drawing Circles and Arcs

Next to lines, *circles* and *arcs* are the easiest objects to draw. But like everything else in AutoCAD, they offer a wide range of options to allow you to draw them in nearly any situation.

Using the Circle Options

Click the Circle tool in the Draw toolbar, click the location for the center, and then click a point to indicate a radius or enter a radius value. You can use osnaps to select points on objects to determine the center and radius. You can also specify the diameter instead of the radius by typing **D**↵ after selecting a center point.

USING THE 2P OPTION TO INDICATE DIAMETER

If you want to draw a circle based on two points, you can do so by using the 2P option. Here's how it works:

1. Click the Circle tool in the Draw toolbar, or enter **C**↵ at the Command prompt.

2. Enter **2P**↵. You can also right-click and select 2P from the shortcut menu.

3. At the `Specify first end point of circle's diameter:` prompt, click the first point.

4. At the `Specify second end point of circle's diameter:` click the second point. A circle appears using the two selected points to determine the circle's diameter.

You can also choose Draw ➤ Circle ➤ 2 Points, which automatically issues the 2P option in step 2. Use osnaps to select points on objects in steps 3 and 4.

USING THE 3P OPTION TO SPECIFY 3 POINTS ON THE CIRCLE

If you know you want a circle to pass through three points, but you don't know the center point or radius, you can use the 3P option. This lets you select 3 points to indicate the location of the circle.

1. Click the Circle tool in the Draw toolbar.

2. Enter **3P**↵ or right-click and select 3P from the shortcut menu.

3. Select three points through which you want the circle to pass.

You can also choose Draw ➤ Circle ➤ 3 Points, which automatically issues the 3P option in step 2. Use osnaps to select points on objects in step 3. One use of the 3P option in conjunction with osnaps is to draw a circle tangent to three other circles or arcs. Choose Draw ➤ Circle ➤ 3 Points, and then use the Tan osnap to select a circle. Repeat using the Tan osnap to select two more circles (see Figure 3.2). The new circle is drawn tangent to the selected circles. This is how the Draw ➤ Circle ➤ Tan Tan Tan option works.

FIGURE 3.2

Drawing a circle tangent to three other circles

Use the 3P option in the Circle command, and then use the Tangent osnap to select these locations.

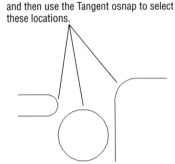

The circle is drawn tangent to the arcs and the circle.

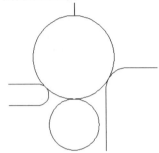

USING THE TAN TAN RADIUS TO SELECT TANGENT OBJECTS AND A RADIUS

You can also draw a circle tangent to two objects. You must also specify a radius:

1. Click the Circle tool in the Draw toolbar.

2. Enter **ttr⏎** or right-click and select Ttr (tan tan radius) from the shortcut menu.

3. Select two objects to which the circle is to be tangent, and then enter a radius value (see Figure 3.3).

    Optionally, you can choose Draw ➢ Circle ➢ Tan, Tan, Radius

AutoCAD does its best to draw a circle to your specifications, but if it's impossible, don't expect miracles.

Using the Arc Options

The default method for drawing an arc is the following:

1. Click the Arc tool in the draw toolbar or enter **A⏎**.

2. Select the start point.

FIGURE 3.3

Drawing a circle tangent to two objects

Use the 2P option of the Circle command, and then use the Tangent osnap and select these arcs.

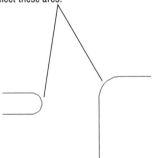

Specify a radius that allows a circle to be drawn that is tangent to the two arcs.

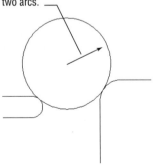

3. Select a second point through which the arc is to pass.

4. Select the endpoint.

If this default method for drawing arcs does not fill your needs, you can use several other AutoCAD methods. Choose Draw ➢ Arc to display a list of 11 other ways to draw an arc. The first option, 3 Points, is the default just described. Figure 3.4 shows you how the other options work.

The Continue option, shown last, lets you continue an arc from the last line or arc drawn. You might notice that there isn't a Continue option in the Arc Command prompt. To continue an arc, choose Draw ➢ Arc ➢ Continue, or start the Arc command, and then press ↵ instead of selecting a point or entering an option. The arc begins from the last line or arc that was drawn.

FIGURE 3.4

The methods for drawing an arc. The numbers indicate the order of point selection.

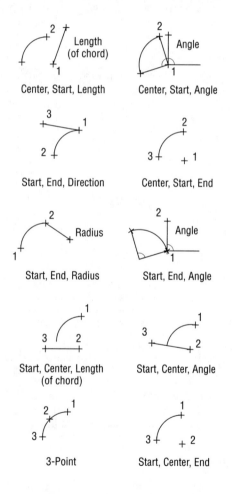

Center, Start, Length

Center, Start, Angle

Start, End, Direction

Center, Start, End

Start, End, Radius

Start, End, Angle

Start, Center, Length (of chord)

Start, Center, Angle

3-Point

Start, Center, End

TIP You can draw an arc by first drawing a circle and then crossing the circle with two lines or other objects. Use the Trim command to trim the arc back to the crossing objects. This method is useful for constructing an arc that is connected to another object. See Chapter 4 for more on the Trim command.

Drawing Curves

Not everything you draw will be made of straight lines and perfect circles. For those more complex curves, AutoCAD offers some additional objects. *Ellipses* and *elliptical arcs* are two objects that are self-explanatory. *Splines* are specially designed to draw smooth curves that are mathematically accurate. *Polylines* are the all-purpose lines that let you draw anything from a closed irregular polygon to contour lines on a topographical map. If you think you'll need to draw any of these types of objects, check out this section.

Drawing an Ellipse

When drawing an ellipse, remember that it has a major and a minor axis as shown in Figure 3.5. You'll see prompts that ask you to select an axis. It doesn't matter which axis you select first; it can be either the major or the minor axis.

FIGURE 3.5
Drawing an ellipse

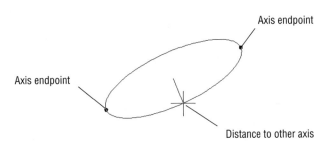

The default method for drawing an ellipse is to select two points defining one axis and then select a third point defining the other axis. Here are the steps:

1. Click the Ellipse tool in the Draw toolbar or enter **el↵**. You can also choose Draw ➤ Ellipse ➤ Axis, End.

2. At the `Specify axis endpoint of ellipse or [Arc/Center]:` prompt, click the first point defining one end of an axis of the ellipse as shown in Figure 3.5.

3. At the `Specify other endpoint of axis:` prompt, click another point for the axis as shown in Figure 3.5. You see an ellipse that is "fixed" at the two points you've selected. As you move the cursor, the ellipse changes shape to follow the cursor.

4. At the `Specify distance to other axis or [Rotation]:` prompt, click another point to complete the ellipse.

You might notice the Rotation option in the prompt in step 4. Selecting this option lets you simulate the way a circle looks on the side of an isometric or other 3D view. If you enter **R↵** in step 4 instead of clicking a point, you can enter a value indicating the angle from which you are viewing the circle.

TIP   You might use osnaps to determine the location of the points on the ellipse.

If you need to place the center of an ellipse at a specific location, you can use the Center option of the Ellipse command.

1. Click the Ellipse tool in the Draw toolbar or enter **el⏎**.

2. Enter **C⏎** or right-click and choose Center from the shortcut menu, and then select a point for the center of the ellipse (see Figure 3.6). A rubber-banding line emanates from the point you select.

FIGURE 3.6
Drawing an ellipse
from a center point

Then select an axis endpoint.

Select the center.

Finally, select the other axis.

3. At the Specify endpoint of axis: prompt, select a point to define one axis of the ellipse.

4. At the Specify distance to other axis or [Rotation]: prompt, select a point to define the other axis of the ellipse.

Drawing an Elliptical Arc

You draw elliptical arcs using the Ellipse command. In the menu bar options and Draw toolbar, you'll find an Elliptical Arc tool. Drawing an elliptical arc is the same as drawing an ellipse with the addition of prompts that ask you for a beginning and end angle defining the arc. Here's how it works:

1. Click the Ellipse Arc tool in the Draw toolbar, or choose Draw ➤ Ellipse ➤ Arc.

2. At the Specify axis endpoint of ellipse or [Arc/Center]: prompt, click the first point defining one end of an axis of the ellipse as shown in Figure 3.7.

FIGURE 3.7
Drawing an elliptical arc

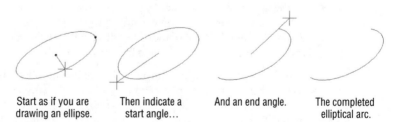

Start as if you are
drawing an ellipse.

Then indicate a
start angle…

And an end angle.

The completed
elliptical arc.

3. At the `Specify other endpoint of axis:` prompt, click another point for the axis. Once this is done, you see an ellipse that is "fixed" at the two points you've selected. As you move the cursor, the ellipse changes shape to follow the cursor.

4. At the `Specify distance to other axis or [Rotation]:` prompt, click another point to indicate the overall ellipse shape that defines the arc.

5. At the `Specify start angle or [Parameter]:` prompt, notice that a rubber-banding line emanates from the center of the ellipse. This helps you visualize the beginning of the arc, or click a point to determine its beginning.

6. At the `Specify end angle or [Parameter/Included angle]:` prompt, notice that an elliptical arc now appears from the location you selected in the previous step. As you move the cursor, the arc expands or contracts depending on the cursor location. Click a point to fix the arc in position.

Drawing Smooth Curves

Whether you're a naval architect drawing a ship's hull or a civil engineer drawing map contours, you'll eventually need some way to draw smooth curves. AutoCAD provides two commands that do just that. Splines let you draw curves that conform to NURBS. Polylines are a general purpose line type that can simulate a smooth curve.

If you need accurate curves, use the Spline command to generate NURBS curves (see Figure 3.8). To draw a spline, do the following:

1. Click the Spline tool in the Draw toolbar, or choose Draw ➢ Spline.

2. At the `Specify first point or [Object]:` prompt, select a point to start the spline.

3. At the `Specify next point or [Close/Fit tolerance] <start tangent>:` prompt, continue to select points. As you select points a curve appears that passes through each point.

4. When you complete your curve, press ↵.

5. At the `Specify start tangent:` prompt, you see a rubber-banding line eminate from the spline's starting point. This lets you adjust the tangent angle of the beginning of the spline. Press ↵ to accept the default angle or indicate a direction with the rubber-banding line and click. You can always change it later if you need to.

6. At the `Specify end tangent:` prompt, you see a rubber-banding line eminating from the spline's endpoint. Here, you can adjust the tangent angle of the end of the spline. Press ↵ to accept the default angle, or indicate a direction with the rubber-banding line and click. You can always change the tangent angle later if you need to.

By default, the spline is drawn through the points you select. You can change the Fit Tolerance option as you draw so that the points you select indicate a direction for the curve rather than a point along the curve. In step 3 of the previous exercise, you see two options in the Command prompt—Close and Fit Tolerance. If you enter **F↵**, you can enter a value to indicate the amount of "pull" the selected points have on the curve. A value of 0 "pulls" the curve through the point, and a value greater than zero draws the curve toward the point but not through it, as shown in Figure 3.9.

FIGURE 3.8
Drawing a spline curve

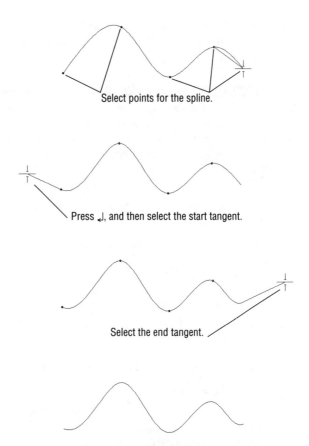

Select points for the spline.

Press ↵, and then select the start tangent.

Select the end tangent.

The finished spline.

FIGURE 3.9
The effect of the Fit
Tolerance option on
a spline

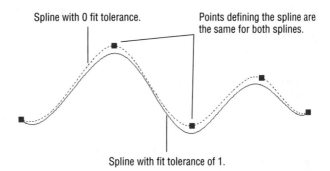

Spline with 0 fit tolerance.

Points defining the spline are the same for both splines.

Spline with fit tolerance of 1.

TIP The Fit Tolerance value affects all the points along the spline, not just the currently selected point. You can modify the fit tolerance of individual points using the Splinedit command described in Chapter 5.

Drawing Curves with Polylines

If you don't need the most accurate spline curves, you might want to draw your curves using the Polyline command. Polylines are the most versatile object type in AutoCAD because they can be shaped and duplicated quickly. You can quickly find the area enclosed by a polyline, and you can "explode" a polyline to smaller components when the need arises, which is something you cannot do to a spline.

To use a polyine to draw a curve, do the following:

1. Click the Polyline tool in the Draw toolbar, choose Draw ➢ Polyline, or enter **pl**⏎ at the Command prompt.

2. At the Specify start point: prompt, select a point.

3. At the Specify next point or [Arc/Halfwidth/Length/Undo/Width]: prompt, continue to select points. A line appears between each point you select.

4. Press ⏎ when you finish selecting points or right-click and choose Enter.

Your polyline doesn't look like much of a curve, but you can alter the way it's drawn using the Pedit command.

1. Choose Modify ➢ Object ➢ Polyline or enter **pe**⏎.

2. At the PEDIT Select polyline or [Multiple]: prompt, select the polyline you just drew.

3. At the Enter an option [Close/Join/Width/Edit vertex/Fit/Spline/Decurve/Ltype gen/Undo]: prompt, enter **S**⏎ to select the Spline option. The straight lines of the polyline change to form a curve, as shown in Figure 3.10.

Notice that the spline version of the polyline does not pass through the points selected to generate the polyline. Instead, the curve is "pulled" toward the points without passing through them. This is similar to the behavior of a spline drawn with the tolerance option set to 1.

FIGURE 3.10
The effect of the Pedit command's Spline option on a straight line polyline

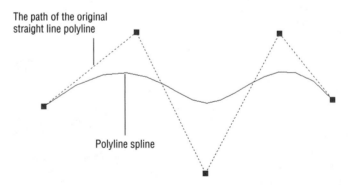

The path of the original straight line polyline

Polyline spline

Another way to turn a straight line polyline into a curve is to use the Fit option in the Pedit command. Instead of using the Spline option in step 3 of the previous exercise, enter **F**↵ to use the Fit option, which changes the straight line polyline into a set of arcs, as shown in Figure 3.11.

FIGURE 3.11

The Fit option applied to a straight line polyline

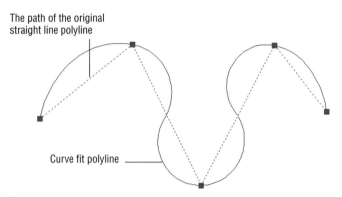

The path of the original straight line polyline

Curve fit polyline

Since arcs are used, the curve is not as smooth, but the polyline passes through each point that defined the corners of the original straight line polyline.

If you've created a spline curve using the Polyline command, but you decide you'd rather have a true spline, you can convert it using the Spline command. This lets you apply some of the spline-editing options to a curve generated using polylines.

To convert a polyline spline curve into a true spline curve, use the Object option in the Spline command.

1. Click the Spline tool in the Draw toolbar, or choose Draw ➤ Spline.

2. At the `Specify first point or [Object]:` prompt, type **O**↵, or right-click and choose Object.

3. At the `Select objects` prompt, select the spline fitted polyline curves you want to convert.

4. Press ↵ to finish your selection. You can also right-click and choose Enter. The polylines are converted to splines.

These steps will only work on "spline fitted" polylines. You will get an error message if you try to do this on other types of polylines.

Drawing Parallel Lines

Another common CAD function is to draw parallel lines. You frequently want parallel lines when drawing the walls of a floor plan or drawing a cross-section of a flat metal assembly, for example. In AutoCAD, you can do this in two ways. You can use the Multiline command, which draws parallel lines and arcs, and you can use the Offset command to copy objects to a set distance. The overall effect of the Offset command is to draw a line parallel to an existing one.

The Offset command makes parallel copies of objects and is the most flexible way to draw parallel lines. It works with lines, arcs, circles, splines, and polylines, so you can produce just about any parallel line you might need (see Figure 3.12). Since it works with splines and polylines, you can easily draw complex parallel curves.

FIGURE 3.12

Examples of parallel
lines created using Offset

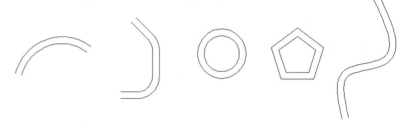

No matter what type object you're trying to make parallel copies of, the operation is the same. Here are the steps to use the Offset command:

1. Click the Offset tool in the Modify toolbar, choose Modify ➢ Offset, or enter **O**↵ at the Command prompt.

2. At the `Specify offset distance or [Through] <0.0000>:` prompt, indicate a distance by either entering a distance through the keyboard or selecting two points in the drawing area. You can use osnaps to indicate distances based on existing objects in the drawing.

3. At the `Select object to offset or <exit>:` prompt, select the object you want to copy.

4. At the `Specify point on side to offset:` prompt, select the side of the object where you want the copy to appear. AutoCAD creates a parallel copy at the distance you specified in step 2.

5. Repeat steps 3 and 4 for more parallel copies or press ↵ to exit the Offset command.

You might notice the Through option in step 2. If you enter **T**↵ at the prompt in step 2 to invoke the Through option, AutoCAD prompts you to Specify through point: at step 4. You can then select a point through which the parallel copy is to pass. This option is useful when you know where the parallel line is to pass but you do not know the distance.

WHAT ARE MULTILINES?

Multilines are double lines that you can use to represent anything that needs parallel lines, such as walls or borders. You can also customize multilines to display solid fills, center lines, and additional line types. You can save your custom multilines as Multiline styles, which are in turn saved in special files for easy access from other drawings.

Multilines are not flexible and are difficult to work with, so you might not encounter them often. If you do encounter multilines and find you need to edit them, you can explode and edit them using the standard AutoCAD editing tools. When a multiline is exploded using the Explode command, it is reduced to its component lines. Line-type assignments and layers are maintained for each component. If you are working as part of a team, you will want to consult with your team members before you explode multilines in an AutoCAD drawing. (See Chapter 4 for more on the Explode command.)

Drawing Revision Clouds

Revision clouds are common in all types of technical documents. They draw attention to areas of a drawing that have been modified or updated since the last official version of a drawing, as shown in Figure 3.13.

FIGURE 3.13

An example of a revision cloud in an architectural drawing

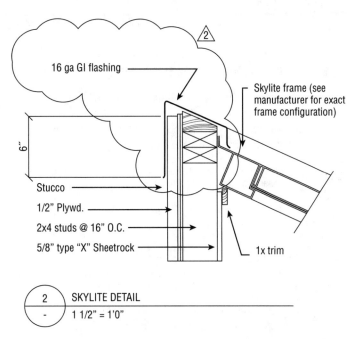

16 ga GI flashing

Skylite frame (see manufacturer for exact frame configuration)

6"

Stucco

1/2" Plywd.

2x4 studs @ 16" O.C.

5/8" type "X" Sheetrock

1x trim

2 / - SKYLITE DETAIL

1 1/2" = 1'0"

AutoCAD lets you use two types of revision clouds: *normal* and *calligraphy style,* as shown in Figure 3.14:

FIGURE 3.14

The normal (left) and calligraphy cloud

Drawing a Freehand Revision Cloud

The following describes the default "freehand" method for drawing revision clouds:

1. Click the Revcloud tool in the Draw toolbar or choose Draw ➤ Revision Cloud. You can also enter **revcloud↵** at the Command prompt. In the Command window, you'll see the message

```
Minimum arc length: 2.5722   Maximum arc length: 2.5722   Style: Calligraphy
```

2. At the `Specify start point or [Arc length/Object/Style] <Object>:` prompt, click a point in the drawing area to start the revision cloud. You'll see the message

```
Guide crosshairs along cloud path...
```

3. Start to move the cursor to encircle the revision area in your drawing. As you move the mouse, the revision cloud appears.

4. As you come full circle to the starting point of the revision cloud, the cloud automatically closes, and you see the message

```
Revision cloud finished.
```

Drawing a Revision Cloud Based on the Shape of an Object

If you want to place your revision cloud more carefully, you can draw a closed polyline or a circle around the area you want to cloud and then use the Object option of the Revcloud command.

1. Click the Revcloud tool in the Draw toolbar or choose Draw ➤ Revision Cloud. You can also enter **revcloud↵** at the Command prompt.

2. At the `Specify start point or [Arc length/Object/Style] <Object>:` prompt, press ↵ to select the default Object option or right-click and select Object.

3. Click the object that defines the path of the cloud, such as a closed polyline, spline, or circle. A revision cloud replaces the object you select. You also see the prompt

```
Reverse direction [Yes/No] <No>:
```

4. You can reverse the direction of the revision cloud by entering **Y↵**, or you can press ↵ to accept the cloud as it is. You can also right-click and select Yes or No from the shortcut menu.

As you draw the revision cloud, you might find that the individual arcs that make up the cloud are too small or too big. You can adjust the size of the revision cloud arc by using the Arc length option.

1. Start the Revcloud command, and then at the `Specify start point or [Arc length/ Object/Style] <Object>:` prompt, enter **A↵** or right-click and choose Arc Length.

2. At the `Specify minimum length of arc <2.5722>:` prompt, enter a size for the arc.

3. At the `Specify maximum length of arc <1.0000>`: prompt, you can press ↵ to accept the default maximum arc length, which is equal to the minimum, or you can enter a larger value to vary the arc size.

4. Draw the revision cloud, or press Esc to exit the Revcloud command.

You might find that the revision cloud does not stand out enough in your drawing. You can change the way the arcs are drawing by changing the revision cloud style.

1. Start the Revcloud command, and then at the `Specify start point or [Arc length/ Object/Style] <Object>`: prompt, enter **S**↵ or right-click and choose Style.

2. At the `Select arc style [Normal/Calligraphy] <Normal>`: prompt, enter **C**↵. You see the message

```
Arc style = Calligraphy
```

3. Draw the revision cloud or press the Esc to exit the Revcloud command.

You can change back to the normal style by taking the same steps, but instead of entering **C**↵ in step 2, enter **N**↵.

TIP   Revclouds are really polylines, so you can edit them just as you edit any polyline. If you use the normal revcloud style, you can use the Pedit command to adjust the thickness of the revcloud arcs. See Chapter 5 for more on editing polylines.

Working with Hatch Patterns and Solid Fills

Just about every drawing program has a paint bucket tool that lets you fill a closed area with a color or a pattern. AutoCAD has a tool that performs a similar function, though it is considerably more complex than a simple paint bucket tool.

The Boundary Hatch command lets you add patterns, solid fills, and gradient colors to any closed polygon (see Figure 3.15). The closed polygon can be made up of any combination of objects. The only requirement is that the area to be hatched must not have large gaps.

FIGURE 3.15

Examples of hatch patterns within random shapes formed by a spline, a circle, an arc, and a rectangle

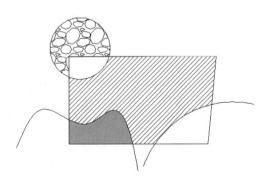

Placing a Hatch Pattern: The Basics

A paint bucket tool usually just requires you to select a pattern and then click inside an area to be filled. AutoCAD requires you to work through a dialog box to select patterns and areas to fill. This first section describes the basic methods for adding hatches and fills.

You can select a hatch pattern from a set of predefined patterns, or if you need just a simple hatch pattern, you can use a user defined pattern, which is really just the standard crosshatch lines. This first example describes how to use a user-defined hatch pattern.

WARNING   If you are using LT, you will not see the Gradient tab in the Boundary Hatch dialog box shown in step 1 of the next exercise.

1. To open the Hatch And Gradient dialog box, click the Hatch tool on the Draw toolbar or type H↵. Hatch is also located in the Draw drop-down menu.

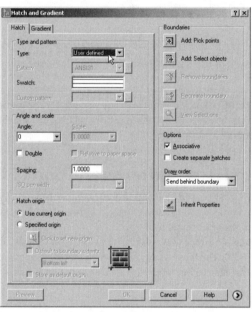

2. In the Type drop-down list box in the Type And Pattern section, select User Defined. The User Defined option lets you define a simple crosshatch pattern by specifying the line spacing of the hatch and whether it is a single- or double-hatch pattern. The Angle and Spacing input boxes become available so that you can enter values.

3. Enter the spacing between the crosshatching in the Spacing input box.

4. Enter the angle for the crosshatching in the Angle input box.

5. Turn on the Double option (just above the Spacing input box) if you want a cross-hatch hatch pattern. Also notice that the Swatch sample box in the Type and Pattern group displays a sample of your hatch pattern.

6. In the Boundaries section, click the Add Pick Points button. The dialog box momentarily closes, allowing you to select a point inside the area you want hatched.

7. Click a point anywhere inside the area you want hatched. Notice that a highlighted outline appears in the area. This is the boundary AutoCAD has selected to enclose the hatch pattern. You can select additional closed areas at this step.

TIP If you have text in the hatch boundary, AutoCAD avoids hatching over it, unless the Ignore option is selected in the Boundary Style options of the Advanced Hatch settings.

8. Press ↵ to return to the Hatch And Gradient dialog box.

9. Click the Preview button in the lower-left corner of the dialog box. The hatch pattern appears in the area you indicated in step 6. You also see the prompt:

```
Pick or press Esc to return to dialog or <Right-click to accept hatch>:
```

10. Press Esc or the spacebar to return to the dialog box to make further changes or right-click to apply the hatch pattern. You can also press ↵ to apply the hatch pattern.

In this example, you selected only one area to fill. You can select multiple areas as indicated in step 6. If after you have previewed the hatch pattern in step 8 you decide you need to select more areas, you can do so by clicking the Add Pick Points button again and selecting more areas.

In step 6, AutoCAD finds the actual boundary for you. Many options give you control over how a hatch boundary is selected. For details, see the section "Understanding the Boundary Hatch Options" later in this chapter.

TIP Say you want to add a hatch pattern that you have previously inserted in another part of the drawing. You might think you have to guess at its scale and rotation angle. But with the Inherit Properties option in the Boundary Hatch And Fill dialog box, you can select a previously inserted hatch pattern as a prototype for the current hatch pattern. However, this feature does not work with exploded hatch patterns.

Using Predefined Patterns

The user-defined hatch pattern is just one type of hatch you can apply to a drawing. AutoCAD also provides sets of predefined patterns. Figure 3.16 shows you all the patterns available. You can also create your own custom patterns, though that process is beyond the scope of this book.

To use any of these patterns, select the Predefined option from the Type drop-down list in the Boundary Hatch And Fill dialog box.

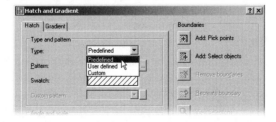

FIGURE 3.16

The predefined hatch patterns available in AutoCAD

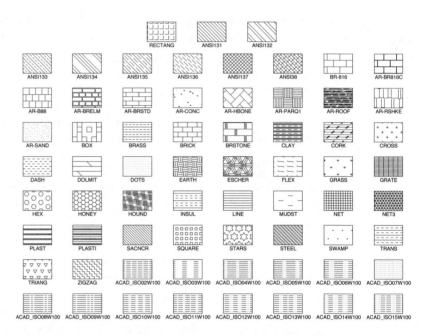

You can then select a predefined hatch pattern by clicking the Browse button to the right of the Pattern drop-down list to open the Hatch Pattern Palette dialog box.

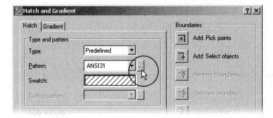

From here you can select a pattern from one of four tabs: ANSI, ISO, Other Predefined, and Custom. The ANSI and ISO patterns are standard patterns used with the ANSI and ISO standards. The Other Predefined patterns are architectural and other patterns you may find useful. The Custom patterns are ones that users have created on their own and placed in a special file.

Within the Other Predefined tab, patterns with the AR prefix are architectural patterns that are drawn to full scale. In general, you will want to leave their scale settings at 1. You can adjust the scale after you place the hatch pattern using the Properties palette, as described later in this chapter.

Adding Solid Fills

To add solid fills, you use the same process as adding a predefined hatch pattern, but you use a specific predefined pattern called a solid. You can see the solid pattern at the top left of the Other Predefined tab of the Hatch Pattern Palette dialog box.

When you use this pattern, a solid color, initially black, fills the area you select for hatching. You can change the color by altering the color property of the solid hatch pattern. See Chapter 4 for more on editing the properties of objects.

TIP   You can drag and drop solid fills and hatch patterns from the tool palettes you saw in Chapter 1.

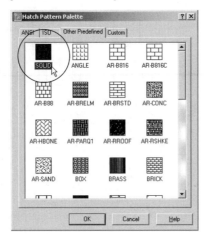

Positioning Hatch Patterns Accurately

In the previous example, you placed the hatch pattern without regard for the location of the lines that make up the pattern. In most cases, however, you will want accurate control over where the lines of the pattern are placed. For example, you might want to place a floor tile pattern in a specific location in a floor plan. Or you might want to find the most efficient location for ceiling tiles in a ceiling plan. In the top image in Figure 3.17, a floor tile pattern is placed without regard for the snap origin. The hatch pattern around the perimeter is not evenly spaced. With some careful planning, the hatch pattern's origin is moved to the location shown in the lower image in Figure 3.17. This results in a more evenly spaced tile pattern around the perimeter of the room.

TIP   You can also click the Swatch button to browse through a graphical representation of the predefined hatch patterns.

Hatch patterns use the same origin as the snap origin. (See Chapter 2 for more information about the snap origin). By default, this origin is the same as the drawing origin, 0,0. You can change the snap origin (and thus the hatch pattern origin) by using the Snapbase command. The hatch pattern then uses the new snap base as its origin.

The Hatch And Gradient dialog box also contains a set of options that let you select an origin for the pattern you are currently placing in the drawing. You can use the Hatch Origin option group in the lower-left corner to determine a point in the drawing to be the hatch origin.

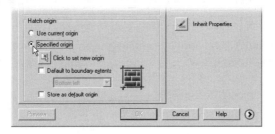

FIGURE 3.17

Placing a floor tile pattern where you want it using the snap base

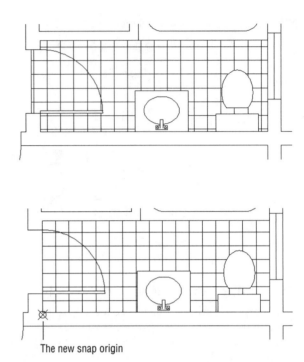

The new snap origin

To set a hatch origin, select the Specified Origin option. You can then determine the origin in two ways. You can click the Click To Set New Origin button. The dialog box temporarily closes to let you select an origin in the drawing. The Hatch And Gradient dialog box then returns so that you can apply more options to your hatch pattern.

The other way to set the hatch origin is to use the Default To Boundary Extents option. This option lets you set the origin based on the extents of the hatch boundary rather than on a point you select. The hatch boundary extents is an imaginary rectangle that represents the outermost boundary of the pattern. If you are hatching a rectangular area, the hatch boundary extents is the same as your selected boundary, but if the area is an irregular shape, an imaginary rectangular area defines the outermost boundary of the pattern, as shown in Figure 3.18. In that figure, the pattern outside the irregular shape shows you the relationship between the visible pattern and the boundary extents. In reality, only the dark pattern within the irregular shape is drawn.

When you select this option, you can select options from the drop-down list: Bottom Right, Bottom Left, Top Right, Top Left, and Center. You can select one of these five options to position the hatch origin in relation to the boundary extents. A graphic appears to the right of the list to show the location of the hatch origin. A red cross appears on the graphic telling you where the origin will be when you add the pattern.

The Store As Default Origin option maintains the origin you select as the default hatch origin for later hatch pattern insertions.

FIGURE 3.18
Boundary extents are
shown in gray. The hatch
pattern only appears
within the irregular
shape.

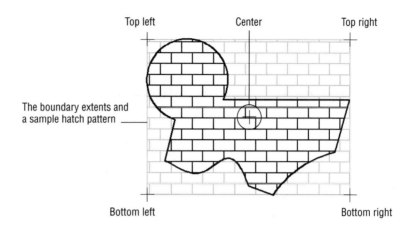

Editing the Hatch Area

The Hatch command has an option, Associative, that automatically adjusts the shape of a pattern to any changes in the boundary of the hatch pattern. (The Associative option is in the Options section in the Hatch tab in the Hatch And Gradient dialog box.)

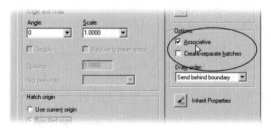

When the Associative option is turned on, the hatch pattern "flows" into any changes you make to the boundary of the pattern. In the right image in Figure 3.19, the diagonal hatch pattern in the center of the rectangle changes when the arc is moved. (The original pattern is shown in the left image.)

The Associative option can save time when you need to modify your drawing, but you need to be aware of its limitations. A hatch pattern can lose its associativity when you do any of the following:

- Erase or explode a hatch boundary

- Erase or explode a block that forms part of the boundary

- Move a hatch pattern away from its boundary

These situations frequently arise when you edit an unfamiliar drawing. Often, boundary objects are placed on a layer that is off or frozen, so the boundary objects are not visible. Or the hatch pattern may be on a layer that is turned off, and you proceed to edit the file, not knowing that a hatch pattern exists. When you encounter such a file, take a moment to check for hatch boundaries so you can deal with them properly.

FIGURE 3.19
The Associative hatch option causes hatch patterns to automatically adjust to changes in the pattern's boundary.

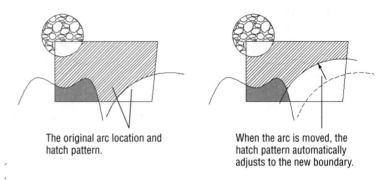

The original arc location and hatch pattern.

When the arc is moved, the hatch pattern automatically adjusts to the new boundary.

Modifying a Hatch Pattern

Like everything else in a project, a hatch pattern might eventually need to be changed in some way. Hatch patterns are like blocks in that they act like single objects. You can explode a hatch pattern to edit its individual lines. The Properties tool in the Object Properties toolbar contains most of the settings you'll need to make changes to your hatch patterns.

1. Double-click the hatch pattern you want to edit. The Hatch Edit dialog box is the same as the Hatch And Gradient dialog box.

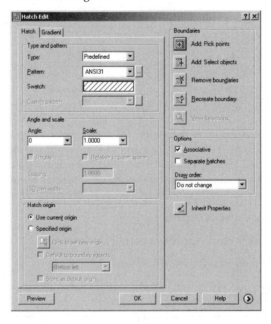

TIP When you double-click a hatch pattern, you don't display the typical Properties palette. Double-clicking complex objects such as text, blocks, attributes, and hatch patterns opens a dialog box in which you can edit the object in a more direct way. You can still access the Properties palette for any object by selecting the object, right-clicking, and choosing Properties from the shortcut menu.

2. Click the Browse button to the right of the Pattern drop-down list to open the Hatch Pattern Palette dialog box.

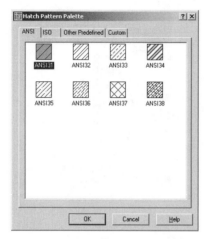

3. Locate and double-click the pattern you want to use.

4. Click OK to accept the change to the hatch pattern. The selected pattern appears in place of the original pattern.

In this example, a predefined pattern was used. You can also replace a pattern with a user-defined pattern if you prefer. Select User Defined from the Type drop-down list, and then specify spacing and angle values.

The other items in the Hatch Edit dialog box duplicate some of the options in the Hatch And Gradient dialog box. They let you modify the individual properties of the selected hatch pattern. The section "Understanding the Boundary Hatch Options" describes these other properties in detail.

TIP If you create and edit hatch patterns frequently, you will find the Modify II toolbar useful. It contains an Edit Hatch tool that gives you ready access to the Hatch Edit dialog box. To open the Modify II toolbar, right-click any toolbar, and then click the Modify II check box in the Toolbars dialog box that opens.

If you prefer, you can still use the older method to edit a hatch pattern. To open the Properties palette, right-click a pattern, and choose Properties from the shortcut menu. The Properties palette displays a Pattern category, which offers a Pattern Name option.

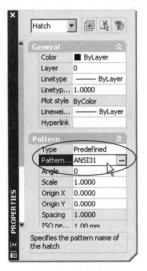

When you click this option, a Browse button appears. Click it to open the Hatch Pattern Palette dialog box. You can then select a new pattern from the dialog box. The Type option in the Properties palette lets you change the type of hatch pattern from Predefined to User Defined.

Understanding the Boundary Hatch Options

The Hatch And Gradient dialog box contains many other options that you didn't explore in the previous exercises. For example, instead of selecting the area to be hatched by clicking a point, you can select the actual objects that bound the area you want to hatch using the Add: Select Objects button. Clicking the Swatch sample box in the Type And Pattern group opens the Hatch Pattern Palette dialog box, which lets you select a predefined hatch pattern from a graphic window.

Other options in the right column of the Hatch And Gradient dialog box include the following:

Remove Boundaries   Lets you remove objects that you do not want to include as part of the boundary. An example of this might be furniture outlines in a floor pattern or some objects that you might have accidentally selected as part of a boundary set.

Recreate Boundary   Allows you to recreate a boundary after you've added a polyline or region to an existing hatch pattern boundary.

View Selections   Temporarily closes the dialog box and then highlights the objects that have been selected as the hatch boundary by AutoCAD.

Create Separate Hatches   Hatches several separate areas at once in AutoCAD, but by default, even though the hatches are in separate areas, they behave as one object. You can force separate hatch areas to behave as separate hatch objects by turning on this option.

Draw Order Lets you control whether your hatch pattern is drawn over existing objects or whether they are to be placed "underneath" existing objects. Hatch patterns can cover or draw over existing graphics. This is especially true of solid fill or gradient hatch patterns.

Inherit Properties Lets you select a hatch pattern from an existing one in the drawing. This is helpful when you want to apply a hatch pattern that is already used, but you do not know its name or its scale, rotation, or other properties.

At the bottom of the column of options in the Options button group is the Associative option. This option lets you determine whether the hatch pattern being inserted is associative or nonassociative. As discussed earlier, an associative hatch pattern automatically changes to fill its boundary whenever that boundary is stretched or edited.

CONTROLLING THE BEHAVIOR OF HATCH PATTERNS AND FILLS

AutoCAD's Boundary Hatch command has a fair amount of intelligence. It can detect the shape of an area and fill the area accordingly. Boundary Hatch can also detect objects within a closed area, such as an "island" and hatch around it as shown in Figure 3.20.

If you prefer, you can control how AutoCAD treats these island conditions and other situations by expanding the Hatch And Gradient dialog box. To do this, click the More Options button in the lower-right corner of the dialog box.

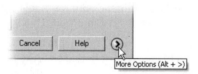

The dialog box expands to the right showing several more options.

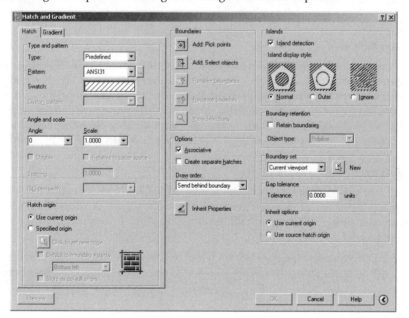

FIGURE 3.20
A hatch pattern can fill a complex shape and detect "islands" within the shape.

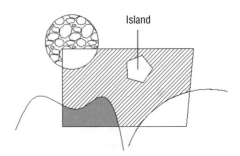

In addition to controlling the Island Detection feature of hatch patterns, the additional Hatch and Gradient options lets you fine-tune other aspects of hatch pattern creation.

Islands

The options in the Islands section control how nested boundaries affect the hatch pattern. The graphics show the effect of the selected option. The Islands options include the following:

Island Detection Detects an island within a boundary and causes the hatch pattern to ignore it.

Normal Causes the hatch pattern to alternate between nested boundaries. The outer boundary is hatched; if a closed object is within the boundary, it is not hatched. If another closed object *is* inside the first closed object, *that* object is hatched. This is the default setting.

Outer Applies the hatch pattern to an area defined by the outermost boundary and by any boundaries nested within the outermost boundary. Any boundaries nested within the nested boundaries are ignored.

Ignore Supplies the hatch pattern to the entire area within the outermost boundary, ignoring any nested boundaries.

Boundary Retention

The Boundary Hatch command can also create an outline of the hatch area using one of two objects: 2D regions, which are like 2D planes, or polyline outlines. Boundary Hatch actually creates such a polyline boundary temporarily, to establish the hatch area. These boundaries are automatically removed after the hatch pattern is inserted. If you want to retain the boundaries in the drawing, make sure the Retain Boundaries check box is checked. Retaining the boundary can be useful if you know you will be hatching the area more than once or if you are hatching a fairly complex area.

Boundary Set

If the current view contains a lot of graphic data, AutoCAD can have difficulty or be slow in finding a boundary. If you run into this problem, or if you want to single out a specific object for a point selection boundary, you can further limit the area that AutoCAD uses to locate hatch boundaries by using the Boundary Set options.

New Lets you select the objects from which you want AutoCAD to determine the hatch boundary, instead of searching the entire view. The screen clears and lets you select objects. This option discards previous boundary sets. It is useful for hatching areas in a drawing that contain many objects that you do not want to include in the hatch boundary.

Current Viewport   Tells you that AutoCAD will use the current view to determine the hatch boundary. Once you select a set of objects using the New button, you also see Existing Set as an option in this drop-down list. You can then use this drop-down list to choose the entire view or the objects you select for the hatch boundary.

The Boundary Set options are designed to give you more control over the way a point selection boundary is created. These options have no effect when you use the Select Objects button to select specific objects for the hatch boundary.

Gap Tolerance

This option lets you hatch an area that is not completely enclosed. The Tolerance value sets the maximum gap size in an area that you want to hatch. You can use a value from 0 to 5000.

CHOOSING COLORS AND PATTERNS FOR GRADIENT FILL SHADING

You might have noticed that one of the hatch patterns offered is a solid. The solid hatch pattern lets you apply a solid color to a bounded area instead of a pattern. AutoCAD also offers a set of gradient patterns that let you apply a color gradient to an area.

You can apply a gradient to an area in the same way that you apply a hatch pattern, but instead of using the Hatch tab of the Hatch And Gradient dialog box, you use the Gradient tab to select a gradient pattern.

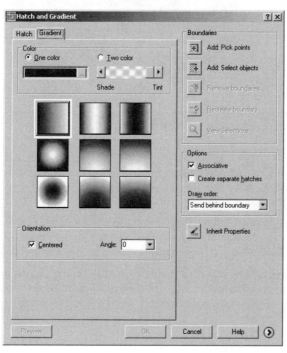

Instead of hatch patterns, the Gradient tab presents a variety of gradient patterns. It also lets you control the color of the gradient. For example, if you want to set shades of blue, you can click the One Color button and then double-click the blue color swatch.

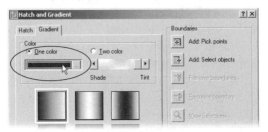

When you double-click the color swatch, the Select Color dialog box opens, displaying a palette of true color options.

TIPS FOR USING THE BOUNDARY HATCH

Here are a few tips on using the Boundary Hatch feature:

◆ Watch out for boundary areas that are part of a large block. AutoCAD examines the entire block when defining boundaries. This can take time if the block is quite large. Use the Boundary Set option to "focus in" on the set of objects you want AutoCAD to use for your hatch boundary.

◆ If the area to be hatched will be large yet will require fine detail, first outline the hatch area using a polyline. Then use the Select Objects option in the Hatch And Gradient dialog box to select the polyline boundary manually, instead of depending on Boundary Hatch to find the boundary for you.

◆ Consider turning off layers that might interfere with AutoCAD's ability to find a boundary. Boundary Hatch works on nested blocks as long as the nested block entities are parallel to the current UCS and are uniformly scaled in the X and Y axes.

You can then select the color you want for the gradient. The Shade/Tint slider just to the right of the color swatch in the Gradient tab lets you control the shade of the single color gradient.

If you want the gradient to transition between two colors, select the Two Color radio button. When you select Two Color, the slider to the right of the Two Color option changes to a color swatch. You can double-click the swatch or click the browse button to the right of the swatch to open the Select Color dialog box.

Just below the One Color and Two Color options are the gradient pattern options. You can choose from nine patterns, plus you can select an angle for the pattern from the Angle drop-down list box. The Centered option places the center of the gradient at the center of the area selected for the pattern.

To place a gradient pattern, select a set of objects or a point within a bounded area, just as you would for a hatch pattern. You can then click the Preview button to preview your hatch pattern, or you can click OK to apply the gradient to the drawing.

HOW TO QUICKLY MATCH A HATCH PATTERN AND OTHER PROPERTIES

Another tool to help you edit hatch patterns is Match Properties, which is similar to Format Painter in the Microsoft Office suite. This tool lets you change an existing hatch pattern to match another existing hatch pattern. Here's how to use it.

1. Click the Match Properties tool in the Standard toolbar.

2. Click the source hatch pattern you want to copy.

3. Click the target hatch pattern you want to change.

The target pattern changes to match the source pattern. The Match Properties tool transfers other properties as well, such as layer, color, and line-type settings. You can select the properties that are transferred by opening the Property Settings dialog box.

To open this dialog box, type **S**↵ after selecting the object in step 2, or right-click and choose Settings from the shortcut menu. You can then select the properties you want to transfer from the options shown. All the properties are selected by default. Note that text and dimension style settings can also be transferred. You'll learn more about text and dimension styles in Chapters 9 and 10.

Drawing Regular Polygons

If you need to draw a regular polygon, such as a hexagon or pentagon, you can use the Polygon tool in the Draw toolbar. This tool creates a polyline in the shape of a regular polygon.

The default method for drawing regular polygons is as follows:

1. Click the Polygon tool in the Draw toolbar, choose Draw ➤ Polygon, or enter **pol↵** at the Command prompt.

2. At the `Enter number of sides <4>:` prompt, enter the number of sides you want for your polygon.

3. At the `Specify center of polygon or [Edge]:` prompt, select the center point for the polygon.

4. At the `Enter an option [Inscribed in circle/Circumscribed about circle] <I>:` prompt, press ↵ to specify the distance from the center to a vertex of the polygon. You can also enter **C↵** if you want to specify the distance from the center to a point tangent to one side of the polygon (see Figure 3.21).

FIGURE 3.21

The polygon on the left uses the Inscribed option in step 4, and the polygon on the right uses the Circumscribed option. The radius is the same for both images.

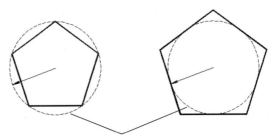

The circle and radius are shown for reference only.

5. At the `Specify radius of circle:` prompt, enter a radius value. This value, in conjunction with the option you select in step 4, determines the size of the polygon. Once you enter a radius, the polygon appears in the drawing.

You also have the option to specify the size of the polygon based on the length of one side of the polygon. To do this, enter **E↵** at the prompt in step 3. You will see the prompt

    Specify first endpoint of edge:

Select a point. You then see the prompt

    Specify second endpoint of edge:

You also see the polygon follow the cursor with one vertex on the point you selected at the first endpoint prompt.

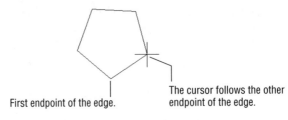

First endpoint of the edge.

The cursor follows the other endpoint of the edge.

Select a point to place the polygon in the drawing. Remember that you can specify a relative coordinate to specify an exact length for the side of the polygon.

Using Objects to Lay Out Your Drawing

Often when you are sketching with pencil and paper, you draw some lines to help lay out your sketch. You can do the same in AutoCAD using any object. But AutoCAD also provides a few tools specifically designed to help you lay out your drawing.

You can use Divide and Measure to mark off an object at regular intervals. If you are familiar with manual drafting tools, you can think of Measure as analogous to a divider. Measure marks off exact distances along an object. The Divide command is similar to Measure, but instead of marking off a known distance you specify, it marks divisions of an object to exact, equal segments. For example, if you want to mark off a line of unknown length into 12 equal divisions, you use the Divide command.

You can use point objects to mark exact points in a drawing. In fact, the Divide and Measure commands use points as markers. Point objects can be helpful in surveying to mark off datum locations or waypoints, for example.

Ray and Xline are two commands that create lines with special characteristics. Ray creates a line that starts at a selected point and extends into an infinite distance much like the rays of light from the sun. Xline creates a line that has an infinite length in both directions. Unlike rays, xlines do not have a beginning point. You specify a point through which the Xline passes and a direction.

Marking Points in a Drawing

Point objects are AutoCAD objects that are commonly used to mark an exact point in a drawing. Point objects are used as markers by commands that mark off equal divisions on objects. You can also create point objects by using the Point command. To place a point in a drawing, choose Draw ➢ Point ➢ Single Point or Draw ➢ Point ➢ Multiple Points.

Point objects can be difficult to see. Fortunately, you can alter their appearance to make them more visible. To see point objects more clearly, follow these steps:

1. Choose Format ➢ Point Style to open the Point Style dialog box.

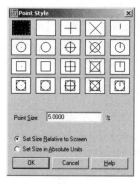

2. Click the X point style in the upper-right of the dialog box, click the Set Size Relative To Screen button, and then click OK.

3. If you have already used the Divide or Measure command or have placed points in your drawing, choose View ➢ Regen or enter **Re↵**. The point objects in the drawing change into Xs as shown in Figure 3.22.

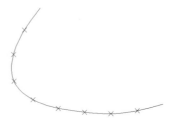

You can change the point style any time, and all the points in a drawing will change to the new style.

TIP   If you are using point objects as visual markers only, and do not want them to print, you can put them on a layer you create specifically for points objects and then set that layer as a nonprinting layer. See Chapter 7 for more on layers.

Marking Off Equal Divisions

You can use the Divide command to divide an object into a specific number of equal segments. The Divide command places a set of point objects on a line, an arc, a circle, a spline or a polyline, marking off exact divisions. This exercise shows how it works.

1. Choose Draw ➢ Point ➢ Divide, or type **Div**↵.

2. At the `Select object to divide:` prompt, select the object you want to mark off.

3. The `Enter number of segments or [Block]:` prompt that appears next is asking for the number of divisions you want on the selected object. Enter the number of divisions you want.

The Command prompt now returns, and it may appear that nothing has happened. AutoCAD has placed several point objects on the selected object. These point objects indicate the locations of the divisions you requested. They do not actually cut the object. They just mark the object. You can use the Node osnap to select a point exactly at the point objects' location.

Dividing Objects into Specified Lengths

The Measure command acts just like Divide; however, instead of dividing an object into equal-length segments, the Measure command marks intervals of a specified distance along an object. For example, suppose you need to mark off segments exactly 4 units long along a curve (see Figure 3.23). The following steps describe how the Measure command is used to accomplish this task.

1. Choose Draw ➢ Point ➢ Measure or type **Me**↵.

2. At the `Select object to measure:` prompt, click the object closest to the end from which you want the measured divisions to start.

3. At the `Specify length of segment or [Block]:` prompt, enter the length you want. The point objects appear at the specified distance.

FIGURE 3.23
Marking off 4-unit
segments on a curve

Typical 4-unit segment marked by point objects

Using Construction Lines

Many graphics programs include an alignment guide, which is usually a nonprinting line that can be dragged into the work area. AutoCAD offers a similar function in the construction line, otherwise known as the Xline command.

Unlike the alignment guide of other programs, AutoCAD's construction line prints. You can also edit construction lines so that they become a standard line in the AutoCAD drawing, place them with accuracy, and rotate them to any angle you like.

MARKING OFF INTERVALS USING DRAWING ASSEMBLIES INSTEAD OF POINT OBJECTS

Marking off regular distances isn't the only use for the Divide and Measure commands. You can also place drawing assemblies, such as symbols or parts, at regular intervals along an object.

For example, you can use the Block option of Divide or Measure to place a row of sinks equally spaced along a wall or place a row of parking spaces along a curb.

To replace the point objects with assemblies, you use the Block option in the Divide or Measure command. Blocks are an assembly of objects that form an image that can be readily copied, like a rubber stamp (see Chapter 8 for more on blocks). The blocks take the place of the point objects as markers.

Here's how to use blocks as markers:

1. Be sure the block you want to use is part of the current drawing file.

2. Start either the Divide or Measure command.

3. At the `Specify length of segment or [Block]:` prompt, enter **B**↵.

4. At the `Enter name of block to insert:` prompt, enter the name of a block.

5. At the `Align Block with Object? [Yes/No]:` prompt, press ↵ if you want the blocks to follow the alignment of the selected object. (Entering **N**↵ inserts each block to at a 0° angle.)

6. At the `Enter the number of Segments:` prompt, enter the number of segments. The blocks appear at regular intervals on the selected object.

The block's insertion point is placed on the divided or measured object in the location where the point object would normally be placed.

DRAWING MULTIPLE CONSTRUCTION LINES THROUGH A POINT

1. Click the Construction Line tool in the Draw toolbar, choose Draw ➤ Construction Line, or enter **Xline⏎** at the Command prompt.

2. At the `Specify a point or [Hor/Ver/Ang/Bisect/Offset]:` prompt, select a point through which the construction line is to pass. If you don't have an exact location, you can always move the construction line later.

3. At the `Specify through point:` prompt, you'll see a temporary construction line that passes through the point you selected in step 2 and follows the cursor. Select another point to indicate the angle for the construction line.

4. You can continue to select points to draw several construction lines through the first point you selected in step 2.

5. Press ⏎ to exit the Construction Line tool.

Once you nave a construction line in the drawing, you can move, copy, and edit the line as you would other lines.

DRAWING MULTIPLE HORIZONTAL, VERTICAL, OR ANGLED CONSTRUCTION LINES

Using the default method shown in the previous steps, you can draw multiple construction lines passing through the same point. But what if you want to draw multiple lines that are all vertical or horizontal or even at an angle? The Construction Line tool offers several options that allow you to add multiple horizontal or vertical lines as well as lines at a specified angle. Here's how these options work:

1. Click the Construction Line tool in the Draw toolbar, choose Draw ➤ Construction Line, or enter **Xline⏎** at the Command prompt.

2. At the `Specify a point or [Hor/Ver/Ang/Bisect/Offset]:` prompt, enter **H⏎** for multiple horizontal lines or **V⏎** for multiple vertical lines.

3. Select points in the drawing to place your construction lines.

4. Press ⏎ to exit the Construction Line tool.

For multiple construction lines at the same angle, do the following:

1. Click the Construction Line tool in the Draw toolbar, choose Draw ➤ Construction Line, or enter **Xline⏎** at the Command prompt.

2. At the `Specify a point or [Hor/Ver/Ang/Bisect/Offset]:` prompt, enter **A⏎**, and then enter the angle for the lines you want to place in the drawing.

3. Select points in the drawing to place your construction lines.

4. Press ⏎ to exit the Construction Line tool.

Optionally, in step 2, you can enter **R⏎** and then select an existing line whose angle you want to match.

DRAWING A BISECTING CONSTRUCTION LINE

If you need to draw a line that bisects two other lines, you can do so with the Bisect option of the Construction Line tool. Here's how the Bisect option works:

1. Click the Construction Line tool in the Draw toolbar, choose Draw ➢ Construction Line, or enter **Xline↵** at the Command prompt.

2. At the `Specify a point or [Hor/Ver/Ang/Bisect/Offset]:` prompt, enter **B↵**.

3. At the `Specify angle vertex point:` prompt, use the Intersect osnap and select the intersection of the two lines you want to bisect (see Figure 3.24)

FIGURE 3.24

Bisecting a pair of lines with a construction line

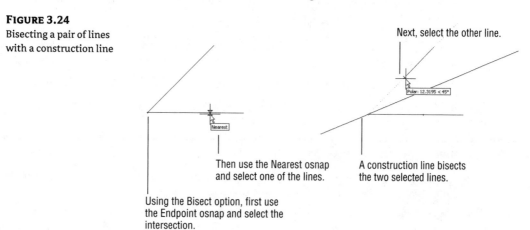

Next, select the other line.

Polar: 12.3195 < 45°

Nearest

Then use the Nearest osnap and select one of the lines.

A construction line bisects the two selected lines.

Using the Bisect option, first use the Endpoint osnap and select the intersection.

4. At the `Specify angle start point:` prompt, use the nearest osnap and select one of the pair of lines you want to bisect.

5. At the `Specify angle end point:` prompt, use the Nearest osnap and select the other line. A construction line appears that bisects the pair you selected.

6. You can continue to place bisecting construction lines or press ↵ to exit the command.

CREATING A CONSTRUCTION LINE PARALLEL TO AN EXISTING LINE

The last construction line option lets you create a construction line that is parallel to an existing line. This option works just like the Offset command described earlier in this chapter, but instead of creating a copy of an object, the Offset option creates a straight construction line.

1. Click the Construction Line tool in the draw toolbar, choose Draw ➢ Construction Line, or enter **Xline↵** at the Command prompt.

2. At the `Specify a point or [Hor/Ver/Ang/Bisect/Offset]:` prompt, enter **O↵**.

3. At the `Specify offset distance or [Through] <0.0000>:` prompt, indicate a distance by either entering a distance through the keyboard or selecting two points in the drawing area. You can use osnaps to indicate distances based on existing objects in the drawing.

4. At the `Select object to offset or <exit>:` prompt, select the object you want to copy.

5. At the `Specify point on side to offset:` prompt, select the side of the object where you want the copy to appear. AutoCAD creates a parallel copy at the distance you specified in step 2.

6. Repeat steps 3 and 4 for more parallel construction lines or press ↵ to exit the Offset command.

PLACING A RAY CONSTRUCTION LINE

The construction line is unusual in that it has no endpoint. It extends into a virtual infinity in two directions. If you want a construction line that has a starting point, you can use a ray. A ray can be useful when editing circular objects because they can be easily rotated about an origin point. Here's how to place a ray in a drawing.

1. Choose Draw ➤ Ray from the toolbar or enter **ray**↵ at the Command prompt.

2. At the `Specify start point:` prompt, select a point for the beginning of the ray.

3. At the `Specify through point:` prompt, select another point to indicate the direction of the ray.

4. Continue to place more rays by selecting points or press ↵ to exit the command.

OTHER DRAWING METHODS

You create most 2D drawings in AutoCAD using the commands presented in this chapter, but you can use two other methods: the region and freehand sketching.

The region object acts more like a paper cutout shape. Regions are always closed outlines of shapes, and you can even convert a closed polyline into a region. You can add and subtract regions to build 2D shapes using what are called *Boolean operations*. (See Chapter 5 for more on Boolean operations.) Since Regions are not commonly used, you won't find a detailed discussion of them in this book.

The Sketch command lets you draw freehand, though this method of drawing really doesn't make sense unless you are using a drawing tablet. Even then, the Sketch command is rarely used.

If you'd like to find out more about regions and the Sketch command, check the AutoCAD help system. You'll also find information on these features in *Mastering AutoCAD 2006 and AutoCAD LT 2006*, published by Sybex.

Just Enough Summary

If you like to experiment, you've probably tried to create a few objects on your own before even reading this chapter. And if you've read the first two chapters of this book and have understood the basic way in which AutoCAD operates, drawing objects should be easy to understand.

Things do get tricky, however, when you start to use hatch patterns and gradient shading. If you find you need to draw hatch patterns and gradient fills, you'll want to study the sections that cover those topics more carefully. Also, curved lines can be difficult to master without some practice, so try using spline fit polyines and splines before you try to use them in a "serious" drawing.

The Layout tools also take a little practice, and you might find that you don't use them that frequently. But when you need them, they are indispensable, so it's a good idea to at least be aware of them, and remember where they are in this book for a quick reference.

Chapter 4

Editing AutoCAD Objects

By *editing*, I mean performing the operations to change existing objects in your drawing. If you want to know how to move, copy, or rotate an object, this chapter is the place to look. Of course, AutoCAD is capable of doing much more.

If you're not in a hurry, you might want to skim this chapter to get an idea of what you can do in AutoCAD in terms of editing objects. Or if you are looking for some instruction right now, check the list of chapter topics to see if the information you need is here.

If you're completely new to AutoCAD, you might want to read the first half of this chapter as a primer, especially since editing in AutoCAD is an integral part of creating new drawings.

The beginning of this chapter covers some basic information that is crucial to just about all the AutoCAD editing commands. Selecting objects, for example, is something you'll be doing a lot, so it is explained in detail. Grip editing, a method of editing that is fairly common in most graphics programs, is also explained. You'll learn how Dynamic Input, a new feature in AutoCAD 2006, provides a way to edit the properties of individual objects. Finally, you'll be introduced to the Properties palette, an important tool for editing in AutoCAD.

- ◆ Selecting Objects
- ◆ Editing the Windows Way
- ◆ Changing Objects with Grips and Dynamic Input
- ◆ Controling Objects Using the Properties Palette

Selecting Objects

Like most of today's graphics programs, AutoCAD lets you select objects in a drawing in a variety of ways. Unfortunately, these methods aren't always consistent throughout AutoCAD's set of commands. In this section, you'll learn about the most common methods for selecting objects.

Using the Standard AutoCAD Selection Method

Many AutoCAD commands prompt you to `Select objects:`. Along with this prompt, the cursor changes from a crosshair to a small square.

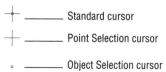

Standard cursor

Point Selection cursor

Object Selection cursor

Whenever you see the `Select objects:` prompt and the square cursor, called a pickbox, you have a couple of options while making your selection. You can click objects individually or select groups of objects using a rectangular selection area. AutoCAD also provides options to select areas using an irregular polygon boundary.

AutoCAD's behavior when you are selecting an object is a little different from that of other graphics programs. If you see the `Select objects:` prompt, you are actually in a selection mode, and every action you take is inferred by AutoCAD to be a selection operation. You can continue to add or subtract selections, but AutoCAD won't know you're finished selecting objects until you press ↵.

As already mentioned, you can click objects to select them. Each time you click an object, it is added to the *selection set*, which is the set of objects to be edited by the current command. You can also select objects using a window, commonly called a marquee in other programs. To remove a selection, Shift+click the object. This is opposite to most other graphics programs that require a Shift+click to add objects to your selection.

Practice Using Selection Options

Let's take a look at the most common selection options in AutoCAD and see what to do when you make the wrong selection.

Before you continue, you'll turn off Running Osnaps and Osnap Tracking. Although extremely useful, these feature can be confusing to new users. .

1. Look at the Osnap and Otrack buttons in the status bar at the bottom of the AutoCAD window. If they are turned on, they look like they are pressed. Click them to turn them off.

2. You'll want to draw something to practice on. Click the Line tool in the Draw toolbar, and then draw the four sides of a rectangle roughly like the one shown in Figure 4.1. Remember that you can draw the first three sides and then enter **C**↵ to "close" the rectangle.

3. Click the Arc tool in the Draw toolbar, and select three points to draw an arc roughly where one is shown in Figure 4.1. The Arc does not have to be exact, but it should be placed above the rectangle.

FIGURE 4.1
A rectangle drawn using the Line tool and an arc

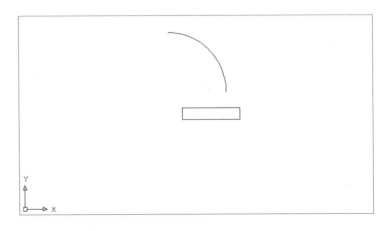

Now let's go ahead and see how to select an object in AutoCAD. In this first exercise, you'll practice using a single click to select objects one at a time.

1. Place the cursor over any object, but do not click the mouse just yet. As the cursor hovers over an object, notice that the object highlights. This does two things: it shows you the object AutoCAD will select if you click the mouse, and it shows you the extent and shape of the object you are about to select.

2. Click each of the two horizontal lines of the rectangle. As you select an object, it is highlighted, as shown in Figure 4.2.

   Once you've made a selection, you can "un-select" objects that have been selected accidentally.

3. Hold down the Shift key and click one of the highlighted lines. It reverts to a solid line, showing you that it is no longer selected for editing.

4. Shift+click the remaining selected line. Now you're back to having nothing selected.

Clicking objects is perhaps the most intuitive and easiest way to select objects. The additional highlighting helps you determine if you are about to select the right object.

Single clicks work fine when you need to be precise about selecting individual objects, but you'll also need a way to select multiple objects efficiently. Next we'll look at Autoselect and the selection window, which lets you quickly select groups of objects.

Selecting Objects with Windows

When you use Autoselect, AutoCAD automatically starts a selection window when you click in a blank area of the drawing during the selection process. A selection window lets you enclose a set of objects to select them. The following exercise demonstrates how it works.

1. Select a point above and to the left of the rectangle shown in the top image of Figure 4.3. Be sure not to select the rectangle itself. Now a window appears that you can drag across the screen as you move the cursor. If you move the cursor to the left of the last point selected, the window appears dotted (see the first image in Figure 4.3) and has a yellow (or green if you are using a white background) tint. If you move the cursor to the right of that point, it appears solid with a blue tint (see the second image in Figure 4.3).

FIGURE 4.2
Selecting the lines of the rectangle and seeing them highlighted

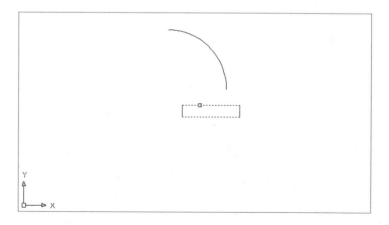

FIGURE 4.3

The dotted window (left image) indicates a crossing selection; the solid window (right image) indicates a standard selection window.

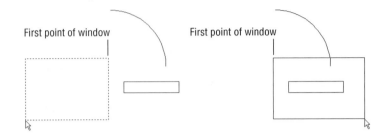

2. Select a point below and to the right of the door so that the rectangle is completely enclosed by the window, as shown in the right image in Figure 4.3. The rectangle is highlighted. Notice that the arc is not selected, even though you may have partially included it in the window.

3. Press Esc to clear the entire selection at once.

The two windows you have just seen—the solid, blue tinted one and the dotted, yellow (or green) one—represent a standard window and a crossing window. If you use a standard window, anything that is completely contained within the window is selected. If you use a crossing window, anything that crosses through the window is selected. These two types of windows start automatically when you click any blank portion of the drawing area with a Standard cursor or Point Selection cursor, hence the name Autoselect.

Next, you will select objects with an automatic crossing window.

1. Select a point below and to the right of the rectangle as shown in Figure 4.4. As you move the cursor left, the crossing (dotted) window appears, and the window area is tinted yellow or green if you are using a white background.

2. Place the window so that it encloses the rectangle and part of the arc (see Figure 4.4), and then click the mouse to confirm your selection area. Both the rectangle and arc are highlighted.

FIGURE 4.4

The rectangle enclosed by a crossing window

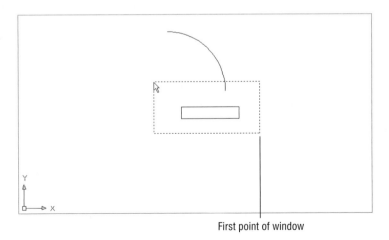

The combination of the autoselect window and single clicks are all you need to select objects in AutoCAD. Often you can select a group of objects with either the standard or crossing window and then use a Shift+click to remove anything from the selection set that you don't want to include in the selection. If you are working in a crowded drawing, you can use the scroll wheel of your mouse to zoom in and out while you are selecting objects. It also helps to turn off the snap mode while making your selections.

Editing the Windows Way

You might have noticed that when you click an object, AutoCAD displays the object's *grips*, which are special square points on the object. These grips most commonly appear on the endpoints of objects, though they can also appear at the midpoint of lines and arcs and at other geometric features of objects. You can use grips to make direct changes to the shape of objects or to quickly move, copy, rotate, or scale the object. The exercise in the following section gives you a feel for how grip editing works.

WARNING   In the unlikely event that you do not see grips when you click objects, your version of AutoCAD may have the Grips feature turned off. To turn it on, right-click a blank area of the drawing, and choose Options from the shortcut menu. In the Options dialog box, select the Selection tab. Turn on the Enable Grips option in the Grips section.

Stretching Lines Using Grips

In this exercise, you'll stretch one corner of the rectangle by grabbing the grip points of two lines. In these beginning exercises, you'll work with the Dynamic Input option turned off. Later, you'll see how to use Dynamic Input to make detailed changes to objects.

1. Press Esc to make sure you're not in the middle of a command, and then make sure the DYN button in the status bar is in the off or "up" position.

2. Click a point below and to the left of the rectangle to start a selection window.

3. Click above and to the left of the rectangle, and then place a crossing window around the rectangle to select it. Notice that the lines of the rectangle are selected and that the grips appear.

4. Place the cursor on the lower-left corner grip of the rectangle, *but don't click the mouse yet.* Notice that the cursor jumps to the grip point and that the grip changes color.

5. Move the cursor to another grip point. Notice again how the cursor jumps to it. When placed on a grip, the cursor moves to the exact center of the grip point. This means, for example, that if the cursor is placed on an endpoint grip, it is on the exact endpoint of the object.

6. Move the cursor to the upper-left corner grip of the rectangle and click it. The grip becomes a different color and is now a *hot grip*. The prompt displays the following message:

   ```
   **STRETCH**
   Specify stretch point or [Base point/Copy/Undo/eXit]:
   ```

   This prompt tells you that stretch mode is active. Notice the options in the prompt. As you move the cursor, the corner follows, and the lines of the rectangle stretch (see Figure 4.5).

FIGURE 4.5

Stretching lines using hot grips. The left image shows the rectangle's corner being stretched upward. The right image shows the new location of the corner at the top of the arc.

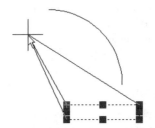
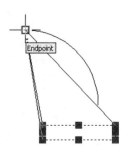

When you select a grip by clicking it, it turns a solid color (typically red) and is a hot grip. If you want to select more than one grip, you can first click one grip and then Shift+click additional grips to include them in your grip selection. Shift+click again on a hot grip to remove it from the selection.

7. Move the cursor upward toward the top end of the arc and click that point. The rectangle deforms, with the corner placed at your selection point (see Figure 4.5).

When you click the corner grip point, AutoCAD selects the overlapping grips of two lines. When you stretch the corner away from its original location, the endpoints of both lines follow.

Here you saw that an option called STRETCH is issued simply by clicking a grip point. A handful of other hot grip options are also available.

1. Notice that the objects are still selected and the grips are still available. Click the grip point that you moved before to make it a hot grip again.

2. Right-click to open a shortcut menu that contains a list of grip edit options.

Now try copying the selected objects.

3. Choose Move from the shortcut menu, and then click a point directly to the left of the hot grip as shown in Figure 4.6. The entire set of objects moves.

4. Click the grip you selected before, right-click, and choose Move again.

FIGURE 4.6
Click the location shown
to copy the grip.

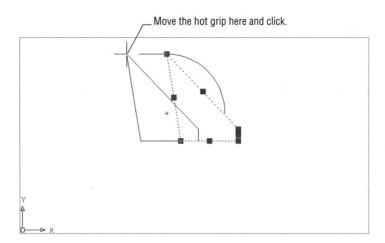

Move the hot grip here and click.

5. Right-click again and choose Copy. You can also enter **c** ↵.

6. Select a point below the hot grip. A copy appears.

7. Press ↵ or enter **X**↵ to exit the grip edit. You can also right-click again and choose Exit from the shortcut menu.

In this last set of exercises, you saw how you can select a grip and then select grip edit options from the shortcut menu. You also saw how you can stretch grips, move objects, and make a copy.

You can also specify distances and directions using relative Cartesian or polar coordinates. For example, instead of just moving the hot grip and clicking a new location, you can enter a polar coordinate in steps 5 and 6 of the previous exercise. (See Chapter 2 for more on Cartesian and polar coordinates.) The grip will then move or be copied to the exact distance you specify. A third option is to turn on the Dynamic Input feature and use it to specify an exact distance and direction. You'll learn more about the Dynamic Input feature later in this chapter.

Copy, Mirror, Rotate, Scale, and Stretch with Grips

The shortcut menu presents options other than Move. When you select a grip and right-click, you can choose from Mirror, Rotate, Scale, or Stretch. Stretch is the default option, and you've seen how that works with the Move options in the previous exercise. The other options are self-explanatory. You can use the Copy option to make mirrored, rotated, scaled, or stretched copies. Just remember to select the main option first and then choose Copy since the Copy option affects the current editing mode.

TIP You can also "cycle" through the Move, Rotate, Scale, and Stretch options by pressing the spacebar while a hot grip is selected.

Another option, Base Point, lets you change the location of the cursor in relation to the current hot grip. By default, the cursor and the hot grip are in the same location and move together. You can right-click, select Base Point, and then select another point to change the location of the cursor in relation to the hot grip.

The base point is moved away from the grip.

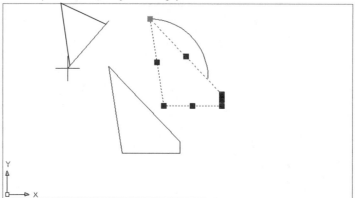

Since you can move the base point, you aren't limited to the actual grip location. This is handy if you want to use other objects as a reference for your grip edits. For example, you can use the Base Point option to rotate your selection about a point other than a grip point.

TIP   You can use the osnaps while grip editing by using a Shift+right-click to open the Osnap menu.

Other Grips Features

Grips let you perform the most common editing tasks you'll encounter as you work with AutoCAD. Along with what you've been shown so far, you'll want to be aware of the following grip features:

- ◆ You can click endpoint grips to reposition those endpoints.

- ◆ Clicking midpoint grips of lines lets you move the entire line. If multiple objects are selected, all the objects also move.

- ◆ If two objects meet end to end and you click their overlapping grips, both grips are selected simultaneously.

- ◆ You can select multiple grips by holding down the Shift key and clicking the desired grips.

- ◆ When a hot grip is selected, the Stretch, Move, Rotate, Scale, and Mirror options are available from the shortcut menu.

- ◆ You can cycle through the Stretch, Move, Rotate, Scale, and Mirror options by pressing ↵ or the spacebar while a hot grip is selected. Watch the Command window to see which option is currently active.

- ◆ All the hot grip options let you copy the selected objects by either using the Copy option or holding down the Shift key while selecting points.

- ◆ All the hot grip options let you select a base point other than the originally selected hot grip. Choose Base from the shortcut menu.

Changing Objects with Grips and Dynamic Input

So far, you've looked at grip editing with the Dynamic Input feature turned off. This gives you a direct view of the basic grip-editing features that let you perform the more common editing tasks. But once you turn on Dynamic Input, you can begin to edit the actual geometry of the selected objects in a more accurate way. You can alter the length and angle of lines to exact measurements or adjust the radius or length of an arc.

In this first exercise, you start with a simple editing task of changing the length of a line. This will show you the basic operation of grip editing with Dynamic Input.

1. Erase all the objects in your drawing, and then draw a line similar to the one in Figure 4.7.

FIGURE 4.7
A diagonal line to test grips and Dynamic Input

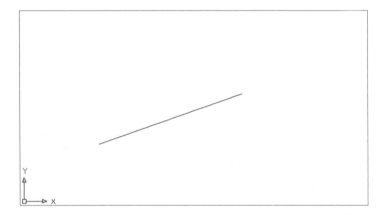

2. Click the DYN button in the status bar to turn on the Dynamic Input display. The button should be in the on, or "down," position.

3. Click the line you just drew.

4. Place the cursor over the grip at the right end of the line, but don't click yet. You see the length dimension and angle of the line displayed. Make a mental note of the length and angle.

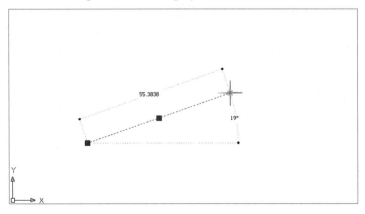

5. Place the cursor over the grip at the left end of the line. Now you see the length and angle from a different orientation.

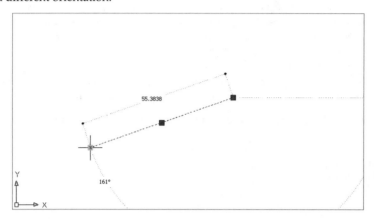

As you can see from this example, you can get immediate information regarding an object just by placing the cursor over its grip points. Next you'll edit the line's length.

1. Click the grip at the right end of the line. You now see a highlighted text box near the cursor. If you don't move the cursor, the text box displays the value of 0.000. This value represents the change in the length of the line.

2. Move the cursor around. As the line follows the cursor, the highlighted dimension shows you the change in the length of the line. You'll also see the overall dimension change.

3. Now enter **10**↵. The value in the highlighted text box changes to 10 as you type, and then when you press ↵, the length of the line increases by exactly 10 units. The angle does not change.

In this example, you used the Dimension Input box to increase the length of the line 4 units. You can also enter negative values to reduce the length of the line. But suppose you want to change the line based on the overall length. Here's how that's done.

1. Click the grip on the right end of the line again. Once again you see the dimension Input text box highlighted.

2. Press the Tab key and move the cursor a bit. Now the overall dimension is highlighted.

3. Enter **22**↵. The line becomes exactly 22 units long.

Finally, you can change the angle of a line without affecting the length.

1. Click the grip on the right end of the line again.

2. Press the Tab key twice until you see the Angle text box highlighted. You may have to move the cursor around to see it.

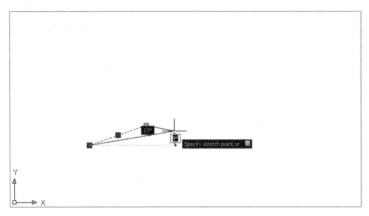

3. Enter **45↵** for a 45° angle. The line is reoriented to a 45° angle.

Finally, you can use Dynamic Input as a kind of "heads up" display while editing. For example, as you enter Cartesian or polar coordinates to move an object, you'll see your input appear at the cursor, so you don't have to look at the Command window to make sure you're entering the right values. Try the following exercise to see how this works firsthand.

1. Select the line you've been working on in the previous exercise.

2. Click the right end grip.

3. Right-click and choose Move. Notice that the cursor changes to show the Specify move point or prompt. You also see the displacement value highlighted followed by an at sign (@) and the angle.

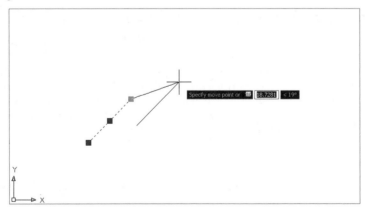

4. Type **10**, then press the Tab key. Now as you move the cursor, it remains at a fixed distance of 10 units from the endpoint no matter where the cursor is placed, but as you move the cursor, the line "circles" the original grip point allowing you to specify an angle. Also notice that the angle value is highlighted, showing that you can enter an angle value.

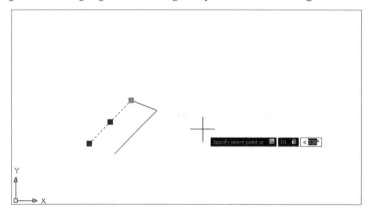

5. Enter **0**↵. The line is now fixed at a distance of 10 units directly to the right of its original location.

In this example, you used a polar coordinate to indicate a distance and an angle for the direction of the move. You can also enter a Cartesian coordinate of 10,0 in step 4 to achieve the same result.

In these examples, you edited only a single line, but the general method is the same for editing all objects: select the object, click a grip, tab to the property value you want to change, and enter a new value. For circles and arcs, you will see radius and arc lengths. If you select a grip that includes multiple line endpoints, you can press the Tab key repeatedly until you get to the property value of the particular line you want to edit.

Controlling Objects Using the Properties Palette

Besides editing objects directly on the screen, you can also edit them by changing their properties in the Properties palette. The properties of an object include many of the object's geometric values such as the radius of a circle or the coordinates of the endpoints of a line. Properties also include colors, line types, and layer assignments. Many users find the Properties palette so useful that they keep it open all the time. You can gather information at a glance by clicking an object and viewing its properties in the Properties palette. For example, you can find the area of a closed polygon or region by selecting the object and looking at the area listing in the Properties palette.

You can open the Properties palette (see Figure 4.8) in two ways: by clicking the Properties tool in the Standard toolbar or right-clicking an object and choosing Properties.

NOTE   The Properties palette title bar can appear on the left or right depending on which side of the AutoCAD window it is placed.

The information displayed in the Properties palette depends on the object you've selected. Two categories, General and Geometry, are displayed for nearly every type of object. The General properties are described in Table 4.1.

FIGURE 4.8

AutoCAD's Properties palette

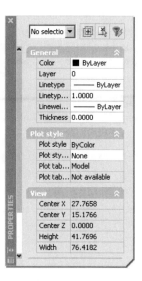

TABLE 4.1:   The General Properties Displayed in the Properties Palette

PROPERTY	MEANING
Color	The object's color assignment. The default Bylayer means that the object inherits the color of the layer to which the object is assigned.
Layer	The object's layer assignment. All objects have a layer assignment. (See Chapter 7 for more on layers.)
Linetype	The object's line type assignment. By default, objects use the Bylayer linetype, which is set according to the object's layer assignment. Typically, this is a continuous linetype. AutoCAD offers a variety of linetypes through the Linetype tools. (See Chapter 7 for more on linetypes.)
Linetype Scale	Controls the appearance of noncontinuous linetypes. This setting lets you set the frequency of line intervals. For example, if you have a dashed line, the Linetype Scale can set how often the dashes appear within a certain length of the drawing. A global linetype scale is also available that sets scale for all linetypes.
Plot Style	Determines how lines are drawn in the final output of your drawing. You can set up a style to control the color, shading, and corner condition of lines to fine-tune the appearance of your drawing. (See Chapter 12 for more on plot styles.)
Lineweight	Sets the plotted line weight of an object .
Hyperlink	Sets up or locates a hyperlink from an object to another drawing or file.

The information in the Geometry section (see Figure 4.9) of the Properties palette depends on the object. Lines show their endpoint coordinates as well as their length and angle. Circles show their center coordinates and radius as well as circumference and area. Closed polylines show segment widths, areas, and vertex coordinates.

FIGURE 4.9

The Geometry section (bottom) of the Properties palette

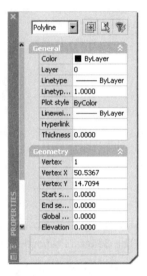

You can edit almost all the options listed in the Properties palette. To edit an item, click its name in the left column. The value to the right of the item either turns into a drop-down list from which you can choose an option or a text box that you can edit. Some text boxes also include a Browse button (a series of periods), as you can see in Figure 4.10.

If an option is not available for editing, it is shown in gray, though some items, such as the Area listing for circles, cannot be edited but can be selected for cutting and pasting elsewhere.

If you aren't certain of the function of an option, you can click it to select it and view the description at the bottom of the palette. If you don't see a description there, click the Properties button at the bottom of the Properties palette title bar and select Description from the menu that appears.

You can control the display of the Properties palette through a set of options at the bottom of the title bar. If you click the Auto-hide button at the bottom of the title bar, the palette is minimized to its title bar.

FIGURE 4.10
Some boxes in the
Properties palette
include a Browse button.

When the palette is "hidden," you can quickly display its contents by placing the cursor on the title bar. This option lets you maximize your drawing area without completely closing the Properties palette.

Just Enough Summary

When you're in a hurry, and you are working with an unfamiliar program, you may be tempted to try methods that you've used in other programs. You can do that in AutoCAD, and if you're lucky, you might get the results you want. But you might also be a bit confused about some of the behaviors AutoCAD presents.

This chapter has given you a bit more information on what to expect when you start to click objects in an AutoCAD drawing. Once you've mastered the features presented here, you'll be on your way to gaining control over those mysterious objects in AutoCAD.

Chapter 5

Editing with the Modify Toolbar

The previous chapter contained information about how to perform the basic editing tasks by clicking objects. In addition to those editing features, you can use editing tools and commands that are unique to CAD drawing.

This chapter provides information on the editing tools in the Modify toolbar. These tools do everything from joining line endpoints, to extending objects to meet other objects, to breaking objects in two. In this chapter, you'll also learn how to edit blocks and external references (xrefs), which are collections of objects that act like a single object. And since polylines are fairly complex, they have their own editing tools, which you'll learn about toward the end of this chapter.

The topics in this chapter are organized by the following tasks.

- ◆ Selecting Objects
- ◆ Erasing Objects
- ◆ Joining Objects
- ◆ Moving and Copying
- ◆ Scaling, Stretching, and Rotating
- ◆ Breaking an Object into Two
- ◆ Editing Xrefs and Blocks
- ◆ Editing Polylines

Selecting Objects

If you read the previous chapter, you know that you can select objects by clicking them or by clicking a blank area to start a selection window. Once objects are selected in this way, you can use grips to make changes to your selection.

But you can also select objects in another way. Most of the tools in the Modify toolbar or menu present the `Select objects:` prompt. When you see this prompt, you can use the methods shown in Chapter 4 plus some additional options that give you more flexibility in selecting objects.

When you see the `Select objects:` prompt, you can use any of the options in the following list to refine your selection. For example, if you press ↵ at the `Select objects:` prompt, the entire contents of a drawing is selected. Or if you enter **p**↵, the previous set of objects you edited is reselected. After you make a selection, the `Select objects:` prompt returns, allowing you to continue to select objects. To indicate that you've finished selecting objects, press ↵.

NOTE   When single clicks or selection windows aren't powerful enough, you can use these section options. Some of tools in the Modify toolbar require only that you select a single object, so these options do not apply to them.

All [all↵]   Selects all the objects in a drawing except those in frozen or locked layers. (See Chapter 7 for information on layers.)

Crossing [c↵]   Similar to the Select Window option but selects anything that crosses through the window you define.

Crossing Polygon [cp↵]   Lets you select an area by enclosing it with an irregularly shaped polygon boundary. Acts exactly like Window Polygon (see the "Window Polygon" entry later in this list) but, like the Select Crossing option, selects anything that crosses through a polygon boundary.

Fence [f↵]   Selects objects that are crossed over by a temporary line called a fence. This operation is like crossing out the objects you want to select with a line. When you invoke this option, you can then select points, as if you are drawing a series of line segments. When you finish drawing the fence, press ↵, select other objects, or press ↵ again to finish your selection.

Last [l↵]   Selects the last object you entered.

Multiple [m↵]   Lets you select several objects first, before AutoCAD highlights them. In a large file, selecting objects individually can cause AutoCAD to pause after each selection, while it locates and highlights each object. The Multiple option can speed things up by letting you first select all the objects quickly and then highlight them all by pressing ↵. This option has no menu equivalent.

Previous [p↵]   Selects the last object or set of objects that were edited or changed.

Window [w↵]   Forces a standard selection window. Once you enter **w**↵, you select two points to define a selection window. This option is useful when your drawing area is too crowded to use the Autoselect feature to place a window around a set of objects. It prevents you from accidentally selecting an object with a single click when you are placing your window.

Window Polygon [wp↵]   Lets you select objects by enclosing them in an irregularly shaped polygon boundary. When you use this option, you see the prompt `First polygon point:`. You then select points to define the polygon boundary. As you select points, the prompt `Undo/<Endpoint of line>:` appears. Select as many points as you need to define the boundary. You can undo boundary line segments as you go by clicking the Undo tool on the Standard toolbar or by pressing the U key. With the boundary defined, press ↵. The bounded objects are highlighted, and the `Select object:` prompt returns, allowing you to use more selection options.

Erasing Objects

In AutoCAD, you can erase objects in different ways. You can select an object or a set of objects, and press Del. This works for nearly every type of AutoCAD object with the exception of OLE objects. Or you can use the Erase tool in the Modify toolbar or choose Modify ➤ Erase. Erase works with all AutoCAD objects; so if for some reason you encounter an object you cannot erase by pressing Del, try the Erase tool. To use Erase, click the Erase tool, select the objects you want to erase, and then press ↵ Del.

Some objects will persist either in the current file or as external files, even after being erased. You can reinsert blocks if they are erased from a drawing. Xrefs also remain as external files and are not deleted when erased from a drawing. Image files behave in a way similar to xrefs and are not deleted from your hard drive when you delete them from your AutoCAD drawing.

To delete bitmap images that have been inserted using the Image or Imageattach command, use the Del key, but you must select the image frame and not the image itself.

Finally, if you happen to erase an object by accident, you can usually retrieve it by clicking the Undo tool in the Standard toolbar. AutoCAD lets you Undo several steps. (See Chapter 2 for more on Undo.) To restore the last set of deleted objects, use the Oops command. Oops is useful if you want to restore objects you deleted several steps back and do not want to undo your work to the point of deletion.

Joining Objects

The whole idea of using AutoCAD is to draw precisely. Not surprisingly, you end up joining objects in exacting ways. One of the most common tasks is joining the endpoints of objects so that they meet exactly end to end.

AutoCAD provides several tools that join the endpoints of objects, particularly arcs, lines, and polylines. In this instance, *joining* means shortening or extending a line, an arc, or a polyline to meet another object, without disturbing the object's orientation.

Joining End to End with Intermediate Arcs

The Fillet command is one of the more frequently used commands because it is great at doing one thing: it joins lines end to end no matter where the endpoints of those lines are. Optionally, Fillet adds an intermediate arc between the joined lines to form a "bullnose," or rounded corner, as shown in Figure 5.1. Fillet also joins two parallel lines with an arc. The following steps describe Fillet's default behavior:

1. From the Modify toolbar, choose Fillet.

2. At the following prompt:

   ```
   Current settings: Mode = TRIM, Radius = 0.0000
   Select first object or [Polyline/Radius/Trim/mUltiple]:
   ```

   click one line.

3. At the `Select second object:` prompt, select the other line. The lines will join end to end without disturbing their orientation.

FIGURE 5.1
Fillet will join the two
lines at left end to end
(center) or join them
with an intermediate arc
(right).

Fillet join lines, arcs, and polylines. If you join a polyline with a line or an arc, the line or arc becomes part of the polyline.

ROUNDING CORNERS

Fillet also lets you round corners by adding an intermediate arc. You might notice several options in step 2, including a Radius option. If you enter **R↵** in step 2, you will see the prompt

```
Specify fillet radius <0.0000>:
```

You can enter a radius value and then proceed to select two objects. Instead of joining the objects end to end, an arc is added between the objects.

NOTE The Fillet command continues to add arcs until you change the Radius option back to zero.

TIP If you use Fillet to join two parallel lines, an arc is automatically used to join the two lines.

You can also round the corners of a polyline, as shown in Figure 5.2, by using the Radius option in conjunction with the Polyline option.

FIGURE 5.2
The polyline on the right
is the result of using the
Fillet command on the
polyline on the left.

Start the Fillet command, enter **R↵** and a radius, enter **P↵**, and select the polyline. The vertices of the polyline change into arcs of the specified radius.

ROUNDING WITHOUT TRIMMING

If you want to add an arc that is tangent to two objects, but you don't want the objects trimmed to join the arc, you can change the Trim setting of the Fillet command. Figure 5.3 shows the effect of Fillet's No Trim option. (Note that the Chamfer command has a similar option that works the same way. See the section "Joining with a Chamfer" later in this chapter.)

To change the way Fillet trims objects, start the Trim command, and then enter **T↵** You'll see the prompt

```
Enter Trim mode option [Trim/No trim] <Trim>:
```

Enter **N↵**.

FIGURE 5.3
Fillet with the No Trim
setting turned on

NOTE The No Trim option becomes the default method that Fillet uses to join lines until you set the option back to Trim.

CONTROLLING FILLET'S BEHAVIOR

Some additional options are available with the Fillet command that control how Fillet behaves. The following list describes them.

Polyline applies the Fillet to all the corners of a polyline composed of straight line segments. (See Figure 5.2 earlier in this chapter.)

Radius lets you set the radius of the fillet.

Trim lets you specify whether lines are trimmed when they are filleted. By default, lines are trimmed. You can specify No Trim to leave the lines as they are. Once Trim/No Trim is set, it becomes the default until it is changed.

Multiple lets you select multiple sets of lines to fillet.

Joining with a Chamfer

Another common editing operation is joining two lines with another intermediate line to form a chamfer, as shown in Figure 5.4. The Chamfer command works much like the Fillet command, with some different options.

FIGURE 5.4
Chamfer is used to join
the two lines at left to
form the chamfered
corner shown at right.

To join lines with a chamfer, do the following:

1. In the Modify toolbar, click the Chamfer tool, choose Modify ➢ Chamfer, or enter **cha↵** at the Command prompt. You will see the message

   `(TRIM mode) Current chamfer Dist1 = 0.0000, Dist2 = 0.0000`

   This tells you the current settings for the Chamfer distances.

2. At the `Select first line or [Polyline/Distance/Angle/Trim/Method/mUltiple]:` prompt, enter **d↵** to specify a Chamfer distance.

3. At the Specify first chamfer distance <1.0000>: prompt, enter a distance value. The value you enter determines the distance from the intersection of the two lines being chamfered to the beginning of the chamfer, as shown in Figure 5.5.

FIGURE 5.5

The Chamfer distance shown by arrows. The first Chamfer distance is determined by the line that is selected first (at the Select first line: prompt).

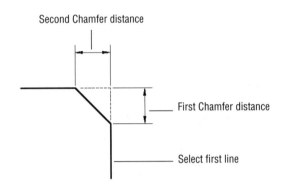

Second Chamfer distance

First Chamfer distance

Select first line

4. At the Specify second chamfer distance <2.0000>: prompt, enter a value for the other Chamfer distance. Press ⏎ if you want the first and second Chamfer distance to be equal.

5. At the Select first line or [Polyline/Distance/Angle/Trim/Method/mUltiple]: prompt, select one line.

6. At the Select second line: prompt, select the other line. The two lines are joined with a Chamfer, as shown in Figure 5.6.

Once you've set the distances in steps 3 and 4, AutoCAD remembers them for the current drawing. The next time you use Chamfer, you won't have to set the distances. You can immediately select two lines as soon as you invoke the Chamfer command, skipping steps 2, 3, and 4.

Chamfer works on lines and polylines with straight line segments only. You cannot Chamfer an arc to a line, for example.

You might notice other options in the previous steps. The following list describes what they do. Remember that to use an option, enter its capitalized letter at the prompt. For example, to use the Trim option in step 5 of the previous example, enter **t**⏎. For the mUltiple option, enter **U**⏎.

Polyline Applies the Chamfer to all the corners of a polyline composed of straight line segments (see Figure 5.6).

FIGURE 5.6

The polyline on the right is the result of using the Chamfer command on the polyline on the left.

Distance   Lets you specify the distance of the Chamfer from the intersection of two lines. The distance can be equal for each line, or lines can have different values. (Also see Method later in this list.)

Angle   Lets you specify an angle for the Chamfer. You are first asked for a distance value and then for the angle (see Figure 5.7). (Also see Method later in this list.)

FIGURE 5.7

Chamfer's Angle option lets you specify the Chamfer based on a distance and an angle. The angle is relative to the first line selected at the `Select first line:` prompt.

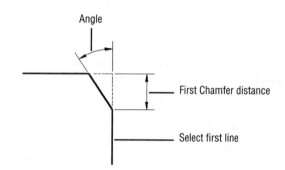

Angle

First Chamfer distance

Select first line

Trim   Lets you specify whether lines are trimmed when they are Chamfered. By default, lines are trimmed. You can specify No Trim to leave the lines as they are (see Figure 5.8). Once Trim/No Trim is set, it becomes the default until it is changed. This option affects both Chamfer and Fillet.

FIGURE 5.8

A Chamfer with the default Trim option is shown on the left, and the No Trim option is shown with the fillet on the right.

Method   Lets you choose whether Chamfer uses the Distance or the Angle settings by default. (See the Distance and Angle entries in this list.)

mUltiple   Lets you select multiple sets of lines to Chamfer.

Extending or Trimming Lines to Other Objects

One fairly common operation in AutoCAD is to extend a line to meet another object or to trim a line or other object back to meet another object. For example, you can quickly trim two rectangles with a circle to form a wrench shape, as shown in Figure 5.9. Or you can extend a pair of lines to meet another line to form a wall extension, as shown in Figure 5.10.

FIGURE 5.9

Use the Trim command and select the locations indicated by the dots at left to quickly draw a new shape at right.

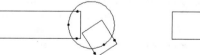

FIGURE 5.10
Extending the vertical
lines shown at left to
form an extension to
a wall at right

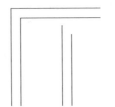 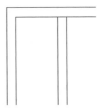

Trim and Extend work on most AutoCAD objects with the exception of hatch patterns, text, splines, and regions. You can explode hatches and regions to their constituent parts to be trimmed or extended. You can use Trim or Extend on blocks and xrefs by first using the Refedit command. (See Chapter 8 for more on blocks and xrefs.)

TRIMMING OBJECTS

You can use the Trim command to both trim and extend objects. The following steps show how you might use Trim to truncate a circle, as shown in Figure 5.11.

FIGURE 5.11
Trimming a circle
and line at left to form a
truncated circle at right

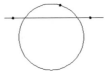

1. In the Modify toolbar, click the Trim tool, choose Modify ➤ Trim, or enter **tr**↵ at the Command prompt. You see the message

   ```
   Current settings: Projection=UCS, Edge=Extend
   ```

2. At the Select cutting edges ...: prompt, select the object or set of objects you want to trim to, and then press ↵. In this example, select the circle and line shown in Figure 5.11.

3. At the Select object to trim or shift-select to extend or [Project/Edge/Undo]: prompt, select the portion of the object you want to trim. In the circle example, select the locations indicated by the dots in the left image in Figure 5.11.

4. When you are finished, press ↵.

EXTENDING OBJECTS

To extend an object, start the Trim command as in the first two steps of the previous example, but instead of clicking the ends you want to trim, Shift+click to select the objects you want to extend, as shown in Figure 5.12.

To extend a series of lines to another object, as shown in Figure 5.13, use the Fence Selection option.

FIGURE 5.12
Shift+click to select the
lines shown on the left
to get the results on
the right.

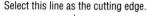
Select this line as the cutting edge.

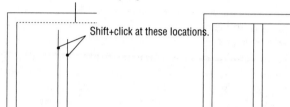
Shift+click at these locations.

FIGURE 5.13
Extending a set of lines to
a curve using the Fence
Selection option. Hold
down the Shift key while
placing the fence.

Line to extend to

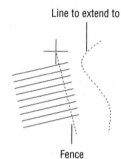

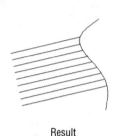

Fence   Result

Another option is to use the Extend tool in the Modify menu or the Modify toolbar. Extend works just like Trim, but by default, it assumes you want to extend an object to another object rather than trim objects.

TRIM AND EXTEND OPTIONS

You can control the way the Trim and Extend commands work through their options. Three options are available in both commands: Project, Edge, and Undo. The following list describes their function:

Project If you are working in 3D, the effects of the Trim or Extend command depend on your viewpoint. Project lets you control whether Trim or Extend are determined by the UCS or the current view. (See Chapter 6 for more on the UCS.)

Edge You might want to extend or trim to an object that does not actually cross the object's path, as shown in Figure 5.14. You can use the Edge option to allow the Trim command to work whether or not objects actually cross.

Undo This option lets you undo a trim operation. It undoes a single trim or extends a selection.

FIGURE 5.14
Even though the lines do
not cross as shown in the
left image, you can turn
on the Edge option to
trim to the edge defined
by the dotted line in the
middle image.

Moving and Copying

Chapter 4 described how to use grips to move and copy objects. So why have specific commands for moving and copying when you can use grips? Part of the reason is that grip editing is a feature that was added later in AutoCAD's history, and the Move and Copy commands are the original methods for performing those functions. If you are building macros, you can use the Move and Copy commands but not the grip-editing options. Finally, the Move and Copy commands descried in this chapter, along with Rotate, Stretch, and Scale, can all take advantage of the selection options described earlier in this chapter. Grip editing cannot. If you have to move or copy a set of objects that cannot be selected easily with single clicks or selection windows, use the Move or Copy commands in the Modify toolbar or menu.

Moving with Accuracy

The Move command is deceptively simple. It's easy enough to move objects in a general way. It gets a little more complicated when you want to move objects with any accuracy. Here are the basic steps for using the Move command:

1. In the Modify toolbar, click the Move tool, choose Modify ➤ Move, or enter **m**↵ at the Command prompt.

2. At the `Select objects:` prompt, select the objects you want to move.

3. At the `Specify base point or displacement:` prompt, select a base point. If you want to enter a relative coordinate, you can select any point on the screen, or you can enter @↵. The @ means "the last point selected."

4. At the `Specify second point of displacement or <use first point as displacement>:` prompt, you'll see the selected objects move with the cursor. You can select the second point with the cursor or enter an absolute or relative coordinate. (See Chapter 2 for more on coordinates in AutoCAD.)

TIPS FOR NEW USERS

The trickiest part of the Move command is understanding the base point and the second point in steps 3 and 4 in the previous exercise. The base point can be anywhere on the drawing. It does not have to be on the object or objects you are trying to move. Once you select a base point, its position stays fixed in relation to the selected objects. This is most obvious when you select a random point for a base point. As you move the cursor, the selected objects move in unison with the cursor, even if the cursor is nowhere near the objects.

Another function that can trip up a new user is the selection process. It is a good idea to become intimately familiar with the many ways you can select objects in AutoCAD. Study the section "Selecting Objects" in the first part of this chapter.

ALIGNING OBJECTS WITH OSNAPS

Finally, you can use osnaps to accurately place the objects you are moving. For example, if you want to move an object so that its corner meets the corner of a second object, do the following. Use the endpoint osnap (as in step 3 in the previous exercise) to select the corner of the selected object. Then in step 4, use the endpoint osnap again to select the corner of the second object (see the middle image in Figure 5.15). This is just one example of using osnaps with the Move command. You can use osnaps to join any part of one object to any part of another. For example, you can move the midpoint of a line to the center of a circle using osnaps in steps 3 and 4.

FIGURE 5.15

Use the endpoint osnap to select the corner of the object you want to move (left image), and then use it again to select the corner you want to move the object to (center image).

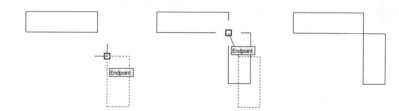

Copying Objects with the Copy Command

The Copy command is virtually identical to the Move command with the obvious difference that Copy makes copies instead of moving objects. Another difference is that you can place multiple copies in the drawing by repeatedly clicking locations or entering coordinates.

To practice with the Copy command, follow the steps shown in the previous section. The main difference is that after step 4, AutoCAD continues to prompt you to Specify a second point:. You can then continue to make copies by clicking in your drawing, or you can press ↵ to exit the Copy command.

TIP   To make parallel copies of objects, use the Offset command, as described in Chapter 3.

PROVIDING BASE POINTS

When you use the Move or Copy command, AutoCAD prompts you for a base point, which can be a difficult concept to grasp. You must tell AutoCAD specifically from where and to where the move occurs. The *base point* is the exact location from which you determine the distance and direction of the move. Once the base point is determined, you can tell AutoCAD where to move the object in relation to that point.

The base point can come in handy when you want to move or copy an object using a geometric feature of the object. For example, if you want to move the upper-right corner of a rectangle so that it connects exactly to the endpoint of a line, select the exact corner of the rectangle as the base point for the move. The following steps describe how to do this.

1. Start the Move command, select the rectangle, and press ↵.

2. At the Base point or displacement: prompt, Shift+right-click and select the endpoint osnap from the shortcut menu.

3. Click the corner of the rectangle you want to connect to the line.

4. At the Specify second point of displacement: prompt, Shift+right-click again and select Endpoint.

5. Click the endpoint of the line. The corner of the rectangle moves to meet the endpoint of the line.

Making Circular Copies

To make copies in a circular pattern, you use the Array dialog box. You can create patterns such as the tick marks on a clock or the teeth in a gear. You can also set up your circular copies to remain in a fixed orientation, like the numbers on a clock.

Here are the basic steps for using the Array dialog box.

1. In the Modify toolbar, click Array or type **AR** to open the Array dialog box (see Figure 5.16).

2. Click the Select Objects button. The dialog box temporarily closes, allowing you to select objects.

3. Select the objects you want to copy, and then press ↵. The Array dialog box reopens.

4. Click the Polar Array radio button at the top of the dialog box to tell AutoCAD you want a circular array. The Array dialog box displays the polar array options, as shown in Figure 5.17.

5. Click the Pick Center Point button (Figure 5.17). The Array dialog box temporarily closes to allow you to select a center point about which the copies will be made.

6. Select the point that represents the center of the circular array. If you have an object representing the center of the array, you can use an Osnap to select the object. Once you've indicated a point, the Array dialog box reopens.

FIGURE 5.16

The Array dialog box

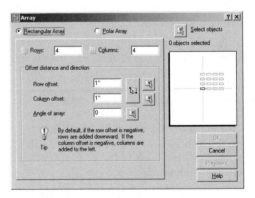

FIGURE 5.17

The Polar Array options

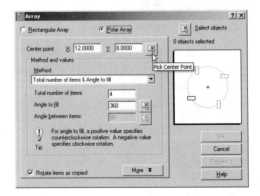

At this point, you've selected an object to array, and you've indicated the center location of the array. If you've selected the wrong object or the wrong center point, you can go back and specify these options again.

Now, to complete the process, tell AutoCAD the number of copies in the array and the extent of the array through the circle.

1. In the Array dialog box, enter the number of copies you want in the Total Number of Items text box. The number you enter should include the original object.

2. In the Angle to Fill text box, enter the angle in degrees that you want your circular copies to fill. For example, if you enter 360, AutoCAD spreads the copies evenly over the full 360° of the circle. If you enter 180, the array fills half a circle. You can also click the Pick Angle to Fill button to the right of the Angle to Fill box to graphically select an angle in the drawing.

3. If you want the object to rotate about the array center, turn on the Rotate Items As Copied check box in the lower-left corner of the dialog box. If you turn this option off, the copies are all oriented in the same direction as the original object.

4. Click the Preview button to display the results of your array settings plus a dialog box that offers Accept, Modify, and Cancel options.

5. Click Accept if you are satisfied with the array. Click Modify if you need to make adjustments.

6. When you are finished setting up the array, click OK in the Array dialog box. The circular array appears in the drawing.

Copying Rows and Columns

You can use the Array dialog box to copy rows and columns. Here are the steps.

1. In the Modify toolbar, click the Array tool type **AR**↵ to open the Array dialog box.

2. Click the Select Objects tool to temporarily close the Array dialog box.

3. Select the objects you want to copy, and then press ↵ to confirm your selection.

4. In the Array dialog box, click the Rectangular Array radio button.

5. Change the Rows text box to the number of rows you want.

6. Change the Columns text box to the number of columns you want.

7. To set the distance between rows, enter a distance in the Row Offset text box.

8. To set the distance between columns, enter a distance in the Column Offset text box (see Figure 5.18).

9. When you are satisfied with the Array settings, click OK.

AutoCAD usually draws a rectangular array from bottom to top and from left to right. You can reverse the direction of the array by entering negative values for the distance between columns and rows in steps 7 and 8.

TIP At times, you might want a rectangular array at an angle. To accomplish this, enter the angle in the Angle of Array input box. You can also select the angle graphically by clicking the Pick Angle of Array button just to the right of the Angle of Array input box.

FIGURE 5.18

Copying rows and
columns

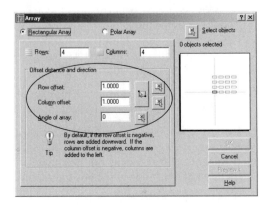

If you prefer, you can graphically indicate an *array cell,* using the options in the Offset Distance and Direction section of the Array dialog box (see the bottom image in Figure 5.19). An array cell is a rectangle defining the distance between rows and columns (see the top image in Figure 5.19). You might want to use this option when objects are available to use as references from which to determine column and row distances. For example, you might have drawn a crosshatch pattern, as on a calendar, within which you want to array an object. You use the intersections of the hatch lines as references to define the array cell, which is one square in the hatch pattern.

You can also indicate row or column distances individually using the Pick Row Offset or Pick Column Offset buttons to the right of the Pick Both Offsets button.

FIGURE 5.19

An array cell and the
Array dialog box options
that let you graphically
indicate array cells

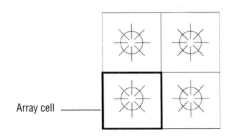

Array cell

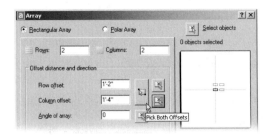

Scaling, Stretching, and Rotating

You can scale, stretch, and rotate as well as move and copy objects with grips. But as described for the Move and Copy commands, you can also use specific commands for each of these operations. Like the Move and Copy commands, the Scale, Stretch, and Rotate commands give you more flexibility in your selection of objects.

Scaling to a Specific Scale Factor

To use the Scale command to change the size of an object or a set of objects, do the following:

1. From the Modify toolbar, choose Scale, or choose Modify ➤ Scale, or enter **sc**↵ at the Command prompt.

2. At the `Select objects:` prompt, select the objects you want to scale and press ↵.

3. At the `Specify base point:` prompt, select a point about which to scale. If you select a corner of a rectangle, for example, the corner remains in place while the rest of the rectangle expands or contracts around the corner.

4. At the `Specify scale factor or [Reference]:` prompt, enter a scale value. The selected objects change to the specified scale.

Scaling an Object to Fit Another

A useful feature of the Scale command is the Reference option, which lets you scale an object to match the size of another. The following example shows how to use the Reference option to change the size of a door in a floor plan to fit an enlarged opening.

1. From the Modify toolbar, choose Scale, or choose Modify ➤ Scale, or enter **sc**↵ at the Command prompt.

2. At the `Select objects:` prompt, select the door.

3. At the `Specify base point:` prompt, use the endpoint osnap to select the corner of the door, as shown in the left image in Figure 5.20.

4. At the `Specify scale factor or [Reference]:` prompt, enter **r**↵.

FIGURE 5.20
Scaling a door to fit
an opening

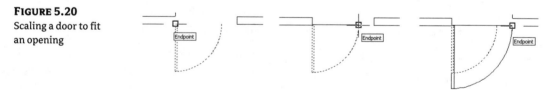

5. At the `Specify reference length <1>:` prompt, use the endpoint osnap, and select the same corner of the door you selected in step 3. You can also enter @↵ since the last point you selected was the point you selected in step 3.

6. At the `Specify second point:` prompt, select the endpoint of the arc that represents the door swing, as shown in the middle image in Figure 5.20.

7. At the `Specify new length:` prompt, notice that the door swing endpoint follows the cursor while the corner of the door stays fixed in its corner location. Use the endpoint osnap again, and select the other corner of the door opening as shown in the right image in Figure 5.20.

In this example, a door is scaled to fit an opening. This door already had one corner at the same location as one side of the opening. To scale an object to fit another, you need to first align the location you will use as a base point to one end of the object or area to which you want to scale.

Stretching Objects

To move the endpoint of a line or a vertex of a polyline, you can use the Stretch command. Stretch lets you select a single vertex or several vertices and move them to reshape a drawing.

The basic method for using Stretch is as follows:

1. In the Modify toolbar, click the Stretch tool, choose Modify ➤ Stretch, or enter **s**↵ at the Command prompt.

2. At the `Select objects:` prompt, enter **c**↵. This invokes the crossing selection window.

3. Enclose the vertices you want to stretch with the crossing selection window, as shown in the left image in Figure 5.21, and then press ↵. You cannot use a standard window for this operation.

FIGURE 5.21

Use a crossing window to select the vertexes you want to stretch (left image), and then select a base point. The vertices will move with the cursor (right image).

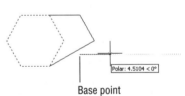

Base point

4. At the `Specify base point or displacement:` prompt, select a base point.

5. At the `Specify second point of displacement or <use first point as displacement>:` prompt, you'll see the vertices move as you move the cursor. Select a new location for the vertices, or enter a coordinate.

Although the Stretch command is useful, the grip-editing version of Stretch is just as capable and a bit easier to understand.

TIP See the section "Moving and Copying" earlier in this chapter for tips on selecting base points and objects.

Rotating Objects

From Chapter 4, you also learned that you can rotate objects using grips, but in addition you can use the Rotate command to do so. To rotate an object with the Rotate command, do the following:

1. In the Modify toolbar, click the Rotate tool, choose Modify ➤ Rotate, or enter **ro**↵ at the Command prompt. You'll see the message

   ```
   Current positive angle in UCS:  ANGDIR=counterclockwise  ANGBASE=0
   ```

2. At the `Select objects:` prompt, select the object or objects you want to rotate, and then press ↵.

3. At the `Specify base point:` prompt, select a point about which the objects are to be rotated. The objects rotate about the selected point as you move your cursor.

4. At the `Specify rotation angle or [Reference]:` prompt, enter a rotation angle value or use the cursor to select a rotation angle.

The message you see in step 1 lets you know the current settings for the angle direction and base angle. This helps you decide whether to enter a positive or a negative value for rotation angles.

Aligning the Rotation Cursor with an Object

In step 3 of the previous example, the selected objects and the cursor rotate about the selected base point. Frequently, the angle indicated by the cursor and the angle of the objects you are rotating do not coincide. This can be a problem, particularly if you want to graphically rotate the selected objects. You can align the cursor with the objects you are rotating using the Reference option. This can be helpful if you are trying to rotate one edge of an object to a specific angle or to another object. The following steps describe how you can use the Reference option to align a randomly placed rectangle with the cursor to rotate the rectangle to a specific angle.

1. Start the Rotate command and select the objects you want to rotate.

2. At the `Specify base point:` prompt, select a point about which the objects are to be rotated. In the example in Figure 5.22, the base point is represented by the cross with the circle. Once you select a base point, the objects rotate about the selected point as you move your cursor.

3. At the `Specify rotation angle or [Reference]:` prompt, enter **r**↵.

FIGURE 5.22
Using the Reference option to align the selected objects to the cursor

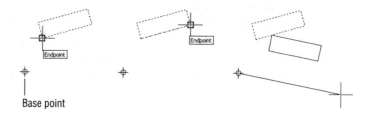

Base point

4. At the `Specify the reference angle <0>:` prompt, use the endpoint osnap to select the endpoint of the line you want aligned with the cursor, as shown in the left image of Figure 5.22.

5. At the `Specify second point:` prompt, select the other end of the line you want to align with the cursor, as shown in the middle image of Figure 5.22

6. At the `Specify the new angle:` prompt, notice that the object is now aligned with the cursor as it rotates about the base point. You can enter an angle value or select a point to finish the command.

You can also use the Reference option to select a specific point on an object as the location being rotated. For example, suppose you want to rotate a set of circles inside a hexagon to align with the corner of the hexagon, as shown in Figure 5.23.

FIGURE 5.23

The goal is to rotate the circles inside the hexagon (left view) to align with the corners of the hexagon (right view).

 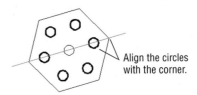

Align the circles with the corner.

To do this, you can use the Reference option as follows:

1. Start the Rotate command and select the objects you want to rotate.

2. At the `Specify base point:` prompt, use the center osnap to select the center of the hexagon as represented by the central circle (see the left image in Figure 5.24). Once you do this, the objects rotate about the selected point as you move your cursor.

FIGURE 5.24

Rotating the circles to align with the corners of the hexagon

  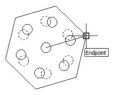

3. At the `Specify rotation angle or [Reference]:` prompt, enter **r↵**.

4. At the `Specify the reference angle <0>:` prompt, use the center osnap to select the center of the hexagon again. You can also enter @↵ since the last point you selected was the center.

5. At the `Specify second point:` prompt, use the center osnap to select the center of one of the circles you are rotating, as shown in the center image of Figure 5.24. Now as you move the cursor, the circle whose center you selected is aligned with the cursor angle.

6. At the `Specify the new angle:` prompt, use the endpoint osnap to select one of the corners of the hexagon as shown in the right image in Figure 5.24. The circles align with the corners.

TIP To rotate an object about a point that is some distance from your current view, draw a temporary circle whose center is at the location of the rotation center and whose radius intersects with the object you want to rotate. You can then zoom into the object you want to rotate and use the center osnap to locate the center of the circle as the rotation base point. Delete the circle when you are done, or keep it for future edits. Consider creating a nonprinting layer on which you can keep construction objects such as the circle.

Breaking an Object into Two

If you need to place a gap in a line or an arc, or if you just need to cut a line in half, you'll want to use the Break command. Break is simple to use, but it does have a few quirks. First, it does not work on all types of objects. You can place gaps in lines, polylines (including rectangles, polygons, and clouds), splines, arcs, and circles using Break. Break also lets you cut an object without actually placing a gap in the object. This option will not work on circles, however.

To use Break to place a gap in an object, do the following.

1. In the Modify toolbar, click the Break tool, choose Modify ➤ Break, or enter **br⏎** at the Command prompt.

2. At the `Select object:` prompt, select the object you want to break at the location where you want the gap to begin.

3. At the `Specify second break point or [First point]:` prompt, select the second point on the object for the opposite side of the gap. The gap appears on the object.

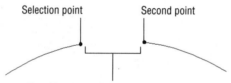

The object breaks between the two points.

Sometimes you want the beginning of the gap at an intersection of two objects, in which case you can't click the object to select the beginning of the gap location. Break lets you select an object independent of the beginning and end points of the gap by using the First Point option. Here's how it works:

1. In the Modify toolbar, click the Break tool, choose Modify ➤ Break, or enter **br ⏎** at the Command prompt.

2. At the `Select object:` prompt, select the object you want to break.

3. At the `Specify second break point or [First point]:` prompt, enter **f⏎**, and then select the beginning location for the gap.

4. At the `Specify second break point:` prompt, select the second point on the object for the opposite side of the gap. The gap appears on the object.

To break an object at a single point without creating a gap, enter @↵ in step 4. This tells AutoCAD that the first and second points of the gap are the same. You can also use the Break at Point tool in the Modify toolbar to accomplish this.

Editing Xrefs and Blocks

Blocks are AutoCAD objects that are assemblies of other objects. For example, you can draw a chair and then convert the chair into a block named "chair." This block behaves as if it were a single object. All blocks have names to easily identify them during other editing functions. Blocks are useful in creating symbols such as doors and windows in an architectural drawing, chairs and office equipment in a plan layout, or anything that will be repeated frequently in a drawing.

Xrefs are entire drawing files that are imported into other drawing files. When a file has been imported as an xref, it behaves like a single object just like a block (see Chapter 8). Xrefs can be nested, and they can also contain blocks.

Even though blocks and xrefs behave as single objects, you can still edit the individual components from which they are made using the Refedit command. However for casual or new users, it's much easier to simply open the source xref file and make changes there.

You can also use Refedit to edit blocks, but new in AutoCAD 2006 is the Block Definition Editor, which greatly simplifies block editing.

In Chapter 3, you learned that you can often edit an object just by double-clicking the object. This opens either the Properties palette or a specific dialog box that lets you edit the object. Double-clicking a block opens the Edit Block Definition dialog box (see Figure 5.25).

FIGURE 5.25
The Edit Block Definition dialog box

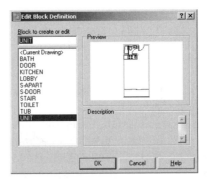

This dialog box lists all the blocks in the drawing. The block you double-click is automatically selected from the list. To the right is a preview window displaying a thumbnail version of the currently selected block.

After you select a block name from the list and click OK, you might see a dialog box asking if you want to see how dynamic blocks are created. Click No as this is an advanced topic.

TIP   If you feel adventurous, you can take a look at the Dynamic Block demonstration and try the advanced features on your own.

Once past the Dynamic Block message, the entire drawing area changes to show just your selected block on a yellow background. This is the Block Editor window (see Figure 5.26). You'll also see the Block Authoring palette, which offers some advanced block features.

FIGURE 5.26

The Block Editor window with the Block Authoring palette shown to the left.

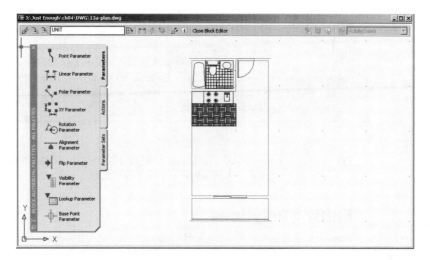

You won't find a discussion of this Block Authoring palette here as this is for more advanced users. However, you will find that once in the Block Editor, you can edit the block using all the usual editing tools described in this and the previous chapter.

Once you've finished editing your block, you can use the Save Block Definition option in the Block Editor toolbar to save any changes you made to the drawing. You can then use the Close Block Editor option to close the Block Editor and return to the standard AutoCAD window.

Save Block Definition.

Closes the Block Editor and asks if you want to save changes.

If you decide not to save your changes, click the Close Block Editor option and select No when you are asked to save your changes.

While you're editing a block and you encounter a nested block that you want to edit, double-click the nested block. You'll be asked if you want to save the changes to the current block. Click Yes or No, and then the Edit Block Definition dialog box reopens, this time with the nested block name highlighted. Click OK, and the nested block appears in the Block Editor window. You can then proceed to edit the nested block.

Another way to open another block while in the Block Editor window is to click the Edit or Create Block Definition option in the Block Editor toolbar.

Edit or Create Block Definition

You're asked if you want to save the current block, and then the Edit Block Definition dialog box you saw at the beginning of this section opens. From there, you can select the block name you want to edit from the list on the left.

REDUCING BLOCKS AND POLYLINES TO SIMPLE LINES AND ARCS WITH EXPLODE

The Explode command can reduce some of the more complex AutoCAD objects to basic objects. Polylines, for example, can be reduced to lines or arcs. Blocks can be "unblocked" into their constituent objects. Hatch patterns can be reduced to lines. Explode is easy to use. In the Modify toolbar, click the Explode tool, or choose Modify ➢ Explode, or enter **x↵** at the Command prompt. At the Select object: prompt, click the object or objects you want to explode and press ↵.

TIP If you are working on a team and others are editing the same files as you are, make sure that you notify your team members when you modify blocks in a drawing.

Editing Polylines

Polylines are a great drawing tool because you can use them to perform a number of functions. If you outline an area with a polyline, you can quickly get the area of the outline by checking the properties of the polyline. You can easily convert closed polylines to 3D objects. You can form curves or quickly round the corners of polylines using the Fillet command.

As with other objects, you can edit a polyline using AutoCAD's grip-editing feature. You can click a polyline to expose its grips and then move the individual grips to reshape the polyline. But an object as versatile as the polyline requires a special tool for editing. The Pedit command lets you fine-tune a polyline's shape. You can add line segments to polylines with Pedit, as well as straighten a polyline or add a new vertex. You can even adjust the overall width of a polyline or taper a polyline to form an arrow.

To use the Pedit command, do the following:

1. Choose Modify ➢ Object ➢ Polyline or enter **Pe↵** at the Command prompt.

2. At the Select polyline or [Multiple]: prompt, select the polyline you want to edit. If you want to edit multiple polylines, enter **m↵**, and then select them. You'll see the prompt

   ```
   Enter an option [Close/Join/Width/Edit vertex/Fit/Spline/Decurve/Ltype gen/
   Undo]:
   ```

3. Enter the capitalized letter of the option you want to use, and then follow the prompts to complete the edit.

TIP If you have Dynamic Input turned on, the prompt options appear as a list by the cursor. You can then select the option you want.

Once you've performed the edit, you are returned to the Pedit prompt. To exit Pedit, press ↵ at the prompt without selecting an option. Table 5.1 describes the functions of the Pedit options.

TIP Pedit also lets you convert a line or arc into a polyline. Start the Pedit command, and then at the Select polyline prompt, select the line or arc. You are asked if you want to convert the object into a polyline. Press ↵ to accept the default Yes option.

TABLE 5.1:   The Pedit Options

OPTION	FUNCTION
Close/Open	If the polyline is closed, the Open option appears and allows you to change the polyline from closed to open. If the polyline is open, Close lets you close it.
Join	Lets you join polylines, arcs, and lines to form a single polyline. Objects must be connected end to end. If you have problems joining objects, try adjusting the Hpgaptol system variable to a higher number.
Width	Lets you adjust the width of a polyline. You can also use the Properties palette to do this.
Edit vertex	Opens another set of options that let you edit the vertices of a polyline. You can remove vertices, insert new vertices, and change the width of the polyline at specific vertices to name a few options. See Table 5.3.
Fit	Changes the polyline to a series of arcs that pass through the vertices. See Chapter 3.
Spline	Changes the polyline into a spline curve. See Chapter 3.
Decurve	Converts a fit or spline polyline into one of straight line segments.
Ltype gen	Adjusts the way linetypes are displayed. With Ltype gen turned on, linetypes ignore vertices when generating line patterns.
Undo	Undoes the last Pedit change of the current Pedit session.

If you select the Edit option of the Pedit command, you are presented with the following prompt:

`[Next/Previous/Break/Insert/Move/Regen/Straighten/Tangent/Width/eXit] <N>:`

These options let you manipulate the vertices of a polyline. You'll also see an X marker at the beginning of the polyline. The X shows you the vertex that is currently available for editing. It indicates which vertex will be affected by the edit options. Table 5.2 explains what these options do.

TABLE 5.2:   The Edit Options of the Pedit Command

OPTION	FUNCTION
Next	Moves the X marker to the next vertex for editing.
Previous	Moves the X marker to the previous vertex for editing.
Break	Lets you break the polyline from the current vertex marked by the X to the next. You will see the prompt `[Next/Previous/Go/eXit] <N>:`, which lets you move the X marker to the next or previous vertex. The Go option performs the break after you've moved the X marker.

TABLE 5.2: The Edit Options of the Pedit Command *(CONTINUED)*

OPTION	FUNCTION
Insert	Lets you insert a vertex. The inserted vertex is added in the direction of the next vertex.
Move	Lets you move a vertex.
Regen	Regenerates the polyline after you've made a change using one of the edit options.
Straighten	Lets you straighten a polyline between two vertices. You will see the prompt `[Next/` `Previous/Go/eXit]` `<N>:`, which lets you move the X marker to the next or previous vertex. The Go option straightens the polyline by removing intermediate vertices after you've moved the X marker.
Tangent	Lets you change the tangent direction of a vertex.
Width	Lets you change the width of the polyline at the current vertex.
EXit	Exits the Edit option of the Pedit command. You are returned to the Pedit prompt.

Just Enough Summary

You'll use the editing features discussed in this chapter frequently during typical editing sessions, though you may find you use some more than others. For example, you'll often use Fillet to join two lines to make a corner, and you'll probably use Scale only once in a while to resize objects. Block and xref editing are also features that you might not use all that often, but when you need them, they can be a lifesaver.

Chapter 6

Creating 3D Drawings

One of the most underrated features in AutoCAD is 3D modeling, especially for users in the building industry. AutoCAD provides enough 3D features to fill an entire book. This chapter gives you a taste of what can be done, and I hope you'll be able to take some of this information and create your own basic 3D models.

You'll find a mix of tutorials and command descriptions in this chapter. Tutorials walk you through features that you'll use more frequently. Other features that are not as important for new users are described with figures and a less formal discussion of their use.

- ◆ Understanding the Modeling Methods
- ◆ Surface Modeling Tools
- ◆ Using 3D Solids
- ◆ Manipulating Objects in 3D Space
- ◆ Understanding Your 3D Viewing Options
- ◆ Saving and Restoring Your 3D Views

Understanding the Modeling Methods

You can work with two type of modeling in AutoCAD: solid and surface. In solid modeling, you treat objects as if they were solid material. For example, you can create a box and then remove shapes from the box as if you were carving it, as shown in Figure 6.1.

FIGURE 6.1
Solid modeling lets you remove or add shapes.

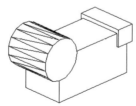
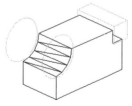

In surface modeling, you create hollow shapes from surfaces. For example, you can quickly turn a line into a vertical surface, as shown in Figure 6.2.

FIGURE 6.2

You can create surface models by changing the thickness property of standard 2D objects.

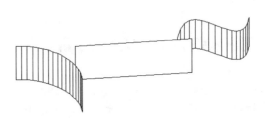

In the first section, you'll try your hand at creating a surface model. You'll get a chance to do some 3D modeling, and at the same time, you'll be introduced to some of the more common modeling tools. The following section shows you how to create a similar object using solid modeling tools. You'll get a chance to see how surface modeling differs from solid modeling, and you'll learn how each modeling method is best used.

The rest of the chapter provides reference material on the individual tools for 3D modeling and editing that you are introduced to in the first two sections. You won't find a comprehensive explanation of all the 3D modeling tools, but you'll get enough information to get started. If you're doing a simple study model, you might find all you need in this chapter.

Surface Modeling Tools

In this section, you'll create some simple 3D forms. First, you'll turn a 2D rectangle into a box by giving the rectangle a thickness value. Nearly all types of objects can be given a thickness that extends the object into the third dimension. Next, you'll see how to use polylines to create more complex shapes. Polylines are an extremely useful object type in 3D modeling with AutoCAD, so getting an early appreciation of their usefulness will give you a head start in creating 3D models. You'll also find out how to get around in 3D space.

The following exercises will let you get your feet wet and expose you to a couple of the more common functions of creating a 3D object: adding thickness to an object in the Z axis, and viewing it from a 3D orientation. As a basis for your exploration of 3D surface modeling, you'll need a simple rectangle.

1. Start AutoCAD now.

2. In the Draw toolbar, click the Rectangle icon.

3. At the Specify first corner prompt, enter **17,8** ↵. For the other corner, enter **@20,15** ↵ (see Figure 6.3).

    You've created a simple 2D rectangle. You could have selected any two points using your mouse, but you selected specific points for the purposes of this demonstration.

FIGURE 6.3
Draw a rectangle
as shown.

Getting a 3D View

Next, you'll turn the rectangle into a 3D wireframe box, but before you do that, let's alter your view of the drawing area so you can see the drawing in a 3D format. Choose View ➤ 3D Views ➤ SW Isometric. Your view changes to show your rectangle in an isometric format, as shown in Figure 6.4.

FIGURE 6.4
The SW Isometric view in
relation to the XY plane
and the Z coordinate

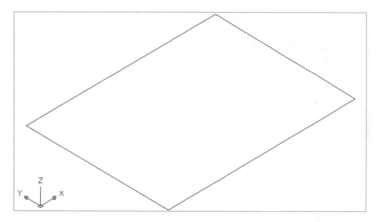

You can use the UCS icon to orient yourself to your drawing. Notice that your point of view is above and to the left of your rectangle, in an isometric format. Remember that you clicked SW Isometric View from the View tool palette, so your position is southwest of your drawing (see Figure 6.4). Think of the cardinal directions north, south, east and west on your drawing as they would appear on a typical map, with north pointing up. You can also view your 3D model in one of six orthographic views: top, left, right, front, back, and bottom.

You might have noticed other 3D view options in the menu bar when you selected SW Isometric. Through other options elsewhere in the menu system, you can fine-tune your view by selecting your viewpoint angle. Or you can view your drawing in a perspective mode that lets you control camera and target position and field of view. You can learn more about other 3D viewing options in the section "Understanding Your 3D Viewing Options" later in this chapter. Now let's move on to the next step, adding 3D depth to your rectangle.

Converting 2D into 3D by Adding Thickness

To add a third dimension to your rectangle, you change its thickness property. When you change an object's thickness, you give the object a value in the Z axis. Normally, in 2D drawings, you don't encounter this Z axis, but it's always available. In a typical 2D drawing, you never see or use the Z axis, since it is pointing directly toward you. But once you change your viewpoint, as in the previous exercise, you can easily see the Z axis, as shown in the UCS icon in the lower left in Figure 6.4.

Now let's see firsthand how changing an object's thickness property can turn it into a 3D object.

1. Choose View ➢ Zoom ➢ Out. This will give you some room to view the changes you will make to the rectangle.

2. Click the Properties button in the Properties toolbar at the top of the AutoCAD window to open the Properties palette.

3. Click the rectangle to display the rectangle's properties in the Properties palette.

4. Click the Thickness box, and then type **4** ↵. The rectangle now appears to be a 3D box, as shown in Figure 6.5.

FIGURE 6.5
The rectangle after increasing its thickness property

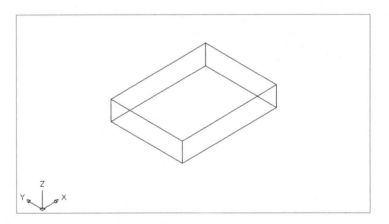

5. Close the Properties palette by clicking the X in its title bar.

6. Press Esc so that the rectangle is no longer selected.

In step 4, you told AutoCAD to change the thickness of your rectangle to 4 units. As you saw in the exercise, the thickness of an object gives the object a third dimension.

Adding a 3D Surface

Right now, you see the box as a wireframe view. You can use the Hide tool to hide lines that are behind surfaces in the foreground to give you a more realistic view of your cube. Choose View ➢ Hide. You can now see your rectangle's orientation more clearly, as shown in Figure 6.6.

FIGURE 6.6
The rectangle with hidden lines removed

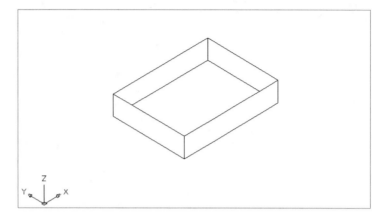

Notice that your box appears to have an open top. The top and bottom sides of the rectangle were not defined by an object, so they remain open. To close the top of the box, you need to use another object called a 3D Face. Here's how to add a 3D Face to your cube to close the top.

1. Choose Draw ➢ Surfaces ➢ 3D Face or enter **3dface** ↵ at the Command prompt.

2. Using the Endpoint override, select the top four corners of the cube in a clockwise sequence (see Figure 6.7).

3. Press ↵ to tell AutoCAD you are finished selecting points.

4. Choose View ➢ Hide. Notice that this time, AutoCAD displays the cube as an enclosed box (see Figure 6.8).

FIGURE 6.7
Select the points in the sequence indicated to draw the 3D face at the top of the box.

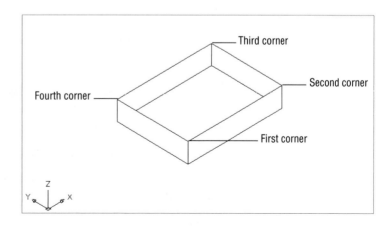

FIGURE 6.8
The box with a top
added and hidden
lines removed

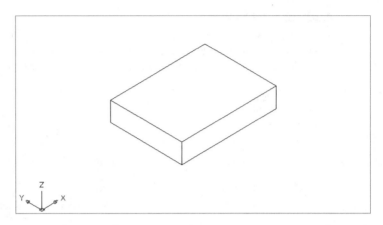

When you added the 3D face to the top of the box in step 3, your wireframe view of the box didn't look any different from before. You've encountered one of the more persistent problems in 3D modeling. Often objects overlap, like the 3D face and the top of the rectangular box, and it will not be obvious from the wireframe view whether all the faces are there until you use the Hide tool. For this reason, you'll want to use the Hide tool frequently to check your work as you go.

Using Object Snaps in 3D Space

If you need to place objects in precise locations in 3D, such as endpoints or midpoints of other objects, you can do so using object snaps, just as you would in 2D.

1. Choose View ➤ Regen to clear the effects of the Hide command.

2. Click the 3D face, and select the endpoint grip closest to you, near the middle of the screen.

3. Right-click, choose Move from the shortcut menu, and then Shift+right-click to open the Osnap menu.

4. Choose Midpoint, and then select the middle of the front corner of the box, as shown in Figure 6.9.

5. Choose View ➤ Hide to see how your box looks now.

FIGURE 6.9
Moving the 3D face to the
middle of the box

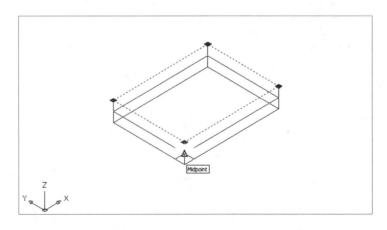

As you can see from this example, osnaps work in 3D in just the same way that they work on 2D drawings. Osnaps are especially useful in 3D because they help locate objects more easily in the sometimes-confusing world of 3D space.

Rotating Objects in 3D

Everything you've done so far has been limited to a rectangular orientation. Suppose you want to create forms that are at odd angles to the X, Y, and Z axes. One way to do this is to create objects of the shape and size you want, and then move and rotate them into position. You've already seen how you can move an object. Next, try the 3D Rotate tool.

1. Choose Modify ➢ 3D Operation ➢ Rotate 3D.

2. At the `Select object:` prompt, click the box and the 3D face that forms the top, and then press ↵ to finish your selection.

3. At the `Specify first point on axis or define axis by [Object/Last/View/Xaxis/` `Yaxis/Zaxis/2points]:` prompt, use the endpoint osnap overrides, and select the two bottom corners of the box, as shown in Figure 6.10. Be sure to select the points in the sequence shown in the figure.

FIGURE 6.10

Selecting the two points for the 3D rotation and the final results

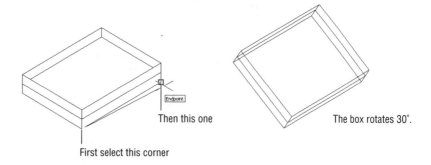

Then this one

First select this corner

The box rotates 30°.

4. At the `Specify rotation angle or [Reference]:` prompt, enter **30**. The box rotates about the axis defined by the two points you selected.

Your box is now standing on edge. With the 3D Rotate tool and the Move and Copy tools, you can position objects in just about any position in 3D space you want. As you can see in the prompt in step 3, you can use the X, Y, or Z axis to determine the rotation axis, or you can use an object (Object/Last) or a view.

TIP The standard Rotate command (Rotate in the Modify toolbar) rotates objects about the Z axis, so another way to rotate objects in 3D is to orient the UCS (described next) in such a way that the Z axis is oriented perpendicular to the plane of rotation. You can then use Rotate as you would for 2D objects. (See Chapter 4 for more on Rotate.)

Now suppose you want to now add an object to one of the sides of the rotated box. The next section will show you another essential tool you can use to do just that.

Working with User Coordinate Systems

In Chapter 2, you learned about the AutoCAD coordinate system. For most drawings, you can use that standard coordinate system, otherwise known as the World Coordinate System, and you'll be fine. But to work in 3D, you need to be able to move the coordinate system into 3D space. This is where the *user coordinate system* (UCS) comes in.

You can place a UCS in any location and in any orientation in space. Once you create a UCS, you can draw as you would in 2D, but your work is aligned with your new UCS. So if you create a UCS that is tilted in relation to the AutoCAD world coordinate system, your objects will also be tilted.

The idea of a UCS might be a bit difficult to grasp, so try the following exercises to see firsthand how the UCS works.

TIP   You aren't limited to creating a UCS in 3D modeling. You can also use UCSs in 2D drawing to create local 2D coordinates.

CREATING A UCS

In this exercise, we'll create and use a new coordinate system to add an arc to the side of the now-tilted box.

1. Choose Tools ➢ New UCS ➢ 3point.

2. At the `Origin point <0,0,0>:` prompt, use the endpoint osnap override, and select the corner of the box closest to you, as shown in the left image in Figure 6.11.

FIGURE 6.11
Selecting points to define a new UCS

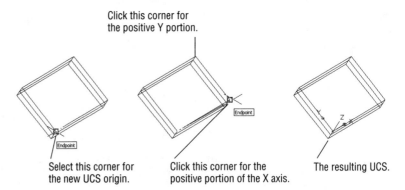

Click this corner for the positive Y portion.

Select this corner for the new UCS origin.

Click this corner for the positive portion of the X axis.

The resulting UCS.

3. At the `Point on positive portion of the X-axis:` prompt, select the corner at the other end along the X axis, as shown in the middle image in Figure 6.11. As you do so, notice the rubber-banding line. This visually shows you the X axis of your newly defined UCS.

4. At the `Point on positive-Y portion of the UCS XY plane:` prompt, select the corner along the Y axis from the origin point, as shown in the middle image in Figure 6.11. Again notice the rubber-banding line indicating the Y axis of your new UCS.

NOTE   At the positive-Y portion of the UCS XY plane prompt, you don't have to select a location exactly on the Y axis of your new UCS. The point you select to define the X axis will define the UCS's X axis orientation. The point you select in step 5, the positive Y location, can be anywhere as long as it defines the general direction of the Y axis.

Notice how the UCS icon moves and changes to match the front face of the box. (See the right image in Figure 6.11.)

Your new UCS is like a drawing board placed on the top edge of the rectangle. Anything you draw now is placed on the XY plane of your new UCS, unless you specifically use osnaps to place objects at different places in your drawing.

USING YOUR UCS

You've just created a UCS that is parallel to the front plane of the tilted box. Its origin is the corner of the box you selected in step 3. Now let's add an arc to the surface of this box.

1. In the Draw toolbar, click the Arc tool.

2. To draw the arc, select the three points indicated in the left image in Figure 6.12.

FIGURE 6.12

Placing the arc on the box surface and adding thickness

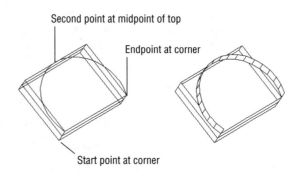

Second point at midpoint of top

Endpoint at corner

Start point at corner

To make it more interesting, give the arc a thickness value to make it a 3D arc.

1. In the Properties toolbar, click the Properties tool.

2. Click the arc.

3. In the Properties palette, click the Thickness option, and then enter 2 in the Thickness text box. The arc becomes a 3D arc in the current UCS.

4. Choose View ➢ Hide to get a better look at the model so far. (See the right image in Figure 6.12.)

The new UCS becomes the default coordinate system. Its origin and X, Y, and Z axes become the default coordinate system when you construct objects. In this example, you used the 3 Point UCS tool and the surface of the tilted box as a template to create the new UCS. You can create a UCS in several other ways, and we'll explore them later in this book.

SAVING AND RESTORING YOUR UCS

Now suppose you want to return to the WCS to construct some additional objects in that plane. You can easily return to the WCS and then go back to the UCS you created, using the UCS Control dialog box.

1. Choose Tools ➢ Named UCS to open the UCS dialog box.

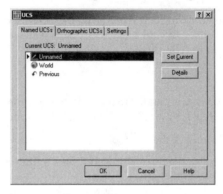

Notice the options listed in the list box. The "name" of available UCSs are listed with the current UCS indicated by a solid triangular arrow to the left. The current UCS is named "Unnamed."

2. Click World in the list box, and then click the Set Current button. Notice that the arrow moves to indicate that World is now the current UCS.

3. Click OK. The UCS icon moves back to its original orientation.

4. Choose Tools ➢ Named UCS or press ↵ to open the UCS dialog box again.

5. Click Previous in the list box, and then click the Set Current button.

6. Click OK. The UCS icon moves back to the new UCS orientation, indicating that you have returned to the new UCS.

Here you've seen how you can switch back and forth between the WCS and your UCS. If you leave things as they are, you can continue to switch between the WCS and your UCS for as long as your drawing is open. If you close the drawing while in the WCS, however, you will loose the UCS you created. To save your UCS, you need to give it a name.

1. Choose Tools ➢ Named UCS or press ↵ again.

2. Click Unnamed UCS (the current one), and then enter **first3D** to rename it. You can also right-click the name and choose Rename from the shortcut menu.

3. Click OK. You have now saved your UCS for future edits.

4. Choose File ➢ Save As, and save your drawing as first3d.

5. Open the UCS dialog box once more and restore the WCS.

Now, whenever you open this drawing, this UCS will be available for quick retrieval.

You can edit and create a UCS in many other ways, and you can have as many UCSs in a drawing as you need. Most of the time, you will create temporary UCSs without naming them. See the section "Working with User Coordinate Systems" later in this chapter to learn more about them.

WARNING　Although you used the face of the 3D box to create a new UCS, the UCS is not associated with the box in any way. If you move or reorient the box, the UCS remains where you created it.

3D Modeling with Polylines

AutoCAD includes a wealth of tools for creating 3D shapes. But none is as versatile as the polyline. Polylines are the starting points for many AutoCAD 3D tools, and they can stand alone as tools for simulating solid objects. Because a polyline is like a compound object, that is, a single object made up of several line segments and arcs, it can help speed up the creation of your 3D models by reducing the number of objects you deal with at once. Let's take a look at a simple application of this versatile object.

DRAWING 3D CURVES

The methods you've used so far are enough to let you create 3D models of floor plans. For example, just by extruding wall lines and using the tools on the View toolbar you can better visualize spaces in an office layout. But our world doesn't always fit in a neat box. Next, we'll look at how you can introduce other shapes into your model. The following exercise shows you how to add a curved polyline to the 3D model.

1. If you haven't done so already, restore the WCS to current status.

2. In the Draw toolbar, click the Polyline tool, and then select the first point of the polyline at the drawing origin (0,0,0) shown in Figure 6.13. You might have to zoom out a bit to draw it.

3. Continue to draw the line segments as shown in the left image in Figure 6.13. When you are done, press ↵.

4. Choose Modify ➢ Object ➢ Polyline, and then select the polyline you just drew.

5. At the `Enter an option [Close/Join/Width/Edit vertex/Fit/Spline/Decurve/ Ltype gen/Undo]:` prompt, enter **s** ↵ to convert the polyline into a spline curve.

6. In the Standard toolbar, click the Properties tool to open the Properties palette, and then click the polyline spline.

7. In the Properties palette, click the Thickness option, and then enter **4** ↵. The polyline now looks like a curved surface.

FIGURE 6.13
Creating a 3D polyline
with thickness

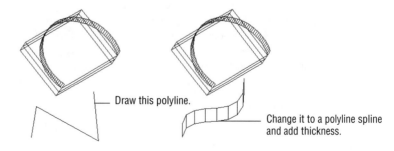

Draw this polyline.

Change it to a polyline spline
and add thickness.

Giving Polylines a "Solid" Appearance

You've seen how easy it is to create a curved surface by adding thickness to a polyline. You can create curved surfaces in many other ways, but using a polyline is a quick way to do so. Now continue by giving the curved surface a solid appearance using the Pedit command:

1. Choose Modify ➢ Object ➢ Polyline, and then click the polyline spline.

2. At the `Enter an option [Close/Join/Width/Edit vertex/Fit/Spline/Decurve/Ltype gen/Undo]:` prompt, enter **W** ↵, and then enter **1** ↵ to give the polyline a width of 1 unit.

3. From the Render toolbar, choose Hide. Notice that the polyline appears as a solid shape (see Figure 6.14). Here you can see how a polyline with width and thickness appears as a solid object when you use the Hide tool.

FIGURE 6.14
The box and polyline with hidden lines removed

All objects, with the exception of 3D polylines, 3D faces, and regions, can be given a thickness in the way shown in these exercises. Only polylines can be given a width, however.

Using the polyline is a quick way to create numerous types of 3D objects. For example, you can use polylines to create window mullions, as shown in Figure 6.15.

FIGURE 6.15
A close-up view of a building with window mullions created with polylines

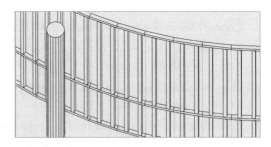

TIP You might notice that the polyline spline appears segmented. You can increase the number of segments, thereby giving the polyline spline a smoother appearance, by using the Splinesegs system variable. At the Command prompt, enter **Splinesegs** ↵, and then enter a higher value than the default of 8. Once you've increased the Splinesegs setting, use the Spline option of the Pedit command again on the polyline.

The Polyline Paradox

You've seen firsthand how to give polylines thickness and width. Later in this book, you'll see how polylines can also be useful in creating 3D solids. But with all its power, the polyline is the one of the most constrained objects when it comes to 3D editing. First, its vertex points must be coplanar. Other objects, such as 3D faces, 3D meshes, lines and 3D polylines are not limited this way. Second, the ability to edit polylines depends on the user coordinate system. Here is a list of what you can and cannot do with polylines with regard to user coordinate systems:

You Can...   Copy, move, rotate, array, 3D array, scale, mirror, align, explode while in *any* UCS.

You Cannot...   Change properties, edit vertices, use the Edit Polyline tool (Pedit) unless you are in a UCS that is parallel to the plane defined by the polyline vertices.

Finally, you cannot snap to an apparent endpoint of a wide, extruded polyline like the curve you created in the earlier exercise. For example, if you use the Endpoint Object Snap option to select the endpoint of the curve, it snaps to its actual endpoint, not to the apparent corner of the wide curve. Figure 6.16 illustrates this limitation.

FIGURE 6.16

Using the Endpoint Object Snap to select a corner of a wide, extruded polyline results in selecting the actual endpoint of the polyline.

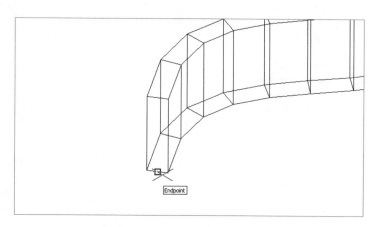

Even with these limitations, polylines are essential to constructing your 3D models. This will become more apparent in later chapters.

Creating Curved Shapes with Meshes

Several 3D surface modeling commands use polylines and other 2D objects to create 3D mesh surfaces. In the limited space of this book, I can't give a full tutorial on their use, but the following examples at least give you an idea how you can use these commands.

Stretching a Surface between Two Objects

You can create a surface that transitions from one shape to another, like stretching a rubber sheet across two shapes (see Figure 6.17). The Rulesurf command draws a 3D surface between two objects. To use it, first draw two objects that define opposite ends of the surface you want to create, and then choose Draw ➤ Surface ➤ Ruled Surface. Click the two objects to display the surface.

FIGURE 6.17

A surface created using
the Rulesurf command

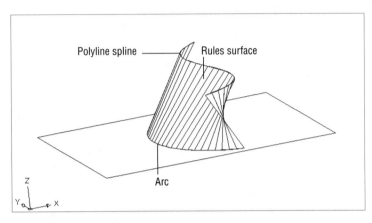

FIGURE 6.17

A surface created using
the Rulesurf command

The point at which you click the objects to select them is important. Make sure you click the objects from the same end; otherwise, the surface twists. Figure 6.18 shows a ruled surface created using the same arc and polyline spline to create the surface in Figure 6.17, but with opposite ends of the arc and polyline selected.

FIGURE 6.18

A ruled surface in which
the objects were selected
at opposite ends

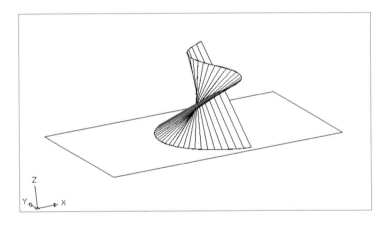

NOTE By default, a rulesurf mesh has 6 facets. To increase the number of facets to give the surface a smoother look as shown in Figures 6.17 and 6.18, you can use the Surftab1 setting. See "Controlling the Number of Facets on a Mesh" later in this section.

USING A LINE TO DETERMINE THE MESH DIRECTION

Earlier, you saw how you can change the thickness property to extend a 2D object into the third dimension. But what if you need to extend a 2D object at an angle instead of straight up? You can use the Tabsurf command to do just that. To use Tabsurf, draw a profile shape and a line indicating the direction of the extension into 3D (see Figure 6.19 for an example). Choose Draw ➢ Surfaces ➢ Tabulated Surface, and then select the profile. Next, select the line. The profile extends in the direction of the line.

FIGURE 6.19

Draw the mesh profile and line representing the length and direction of the mesh.

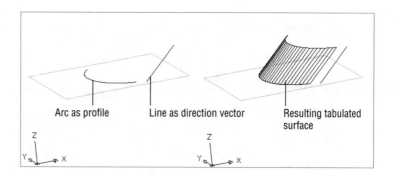

Arc as profile — Line as direction vector — Resulting tabulated surface

NOTE   The mesh in Figure 6.19 uses 12 for the Surftab1 setting. See "Controlling the Number of Facets on a Mesh" in this section for more on this setting.

REVOLVING A SHAPE SUCH AS A LATHE

You can create a circular shape that is a revolved extension of a profile, such as a lathe or a potter's wheel. The Revsurf command lets you create a vase or a wineglass, for example, using two objects: a profile and a line. The profile can be made of a polyline, a spline, a circle, or an arc. It can only be a single object. For example, to draw a vase, follow these steps:

1. Draw the vase profile using a polyline or a spline as shown in the left image in Figure 6.20.

FIGURE 6.20

A revolved surface using a spline profile and a line representing the center axis

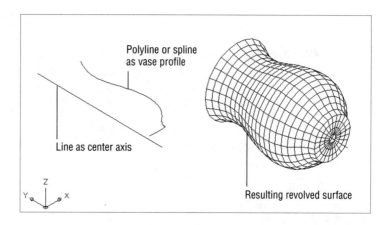

Polyline or spline as vase profile

Line as center axis

Resulting revolved surface

2. Draw a line representing the center axis of the vase, as shown in the left image in Figure 6.20.

3. Choose Draw ➢ Surfaces ➢ Revolved Surface, and then click the profile object.

4. Click the line representing the center axis.

5. At the Specify start angle <0>: prompt, press ↵ to accept the default.

6. Enter the number of degrees you want the profile to be revolved, or press ↵ if you want a full 360°. The profile is revolved according to your responses. (See the right image in Figure 6.20.)

NOTE The vase in Figure 6.20 uses 24 for both the Surftab1 and Surftab2 settings. See the "Controlling the Number of Facets on a Mesh" section for more on these settings.

DEFINING A MESH USING FOUR EDGES

Edgesurf, another 3D surface command, draws a mesh based on four objects that define the four edges of the mesh. This is a great tool for creating free-formed curved surfaces. You'll need to first draw four objects defining the edges of the mesh. They must meet end to end as shown in Figure 6.21. Choose Draw ➤ Surfaces ➤ Edge Surface, and then select the four edges sequentially. A 3D mesh fills the edge objects.

FIGURE 6.21
Edgesurf draws a surface using four 2D objects to define the edge of a mesh.

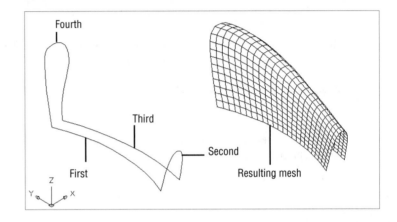

CONTROLLING THE NUMBER OF FACETS ON A MESH

You can control the number of facets on the mesh using the Surftab1 and Surftab2 system variables. These settings behave like commands in that you can enter them at the Command prompt to make changes. For example, the left image in Figure 6.22 shows a surface created using the Edgesurf command with the default Surftab1 and Surftab2 settings of 6. To increase the number of facets for mesh objects, enter **Surftab1** at the Command prompt, and then enter the number of facets you want. If you are creating a revolved or edge surface, enter **Surftab2** and then enter the number of facets you want in the second direction of the mesh.

FIGURE 6.22
Increasing the Surftab1 and Surftab2 values increases the number of facets in a mesh.

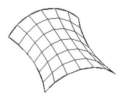 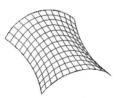

Surftab1 and Surftab2 set to 6   Surftab1 and Surftab2 set to 12

USING CANNED 3D SURFACES

Before you move on to the 3D solids tutorial, you'll want to know about a set of predefined 3D surface objects. These are common shapes such as wedges, spheres, and boxes that you might need in your modeling. To access them, choose Draw ➢ Surfaces ➢ 3D Surfaces to open the 3D Objects dialog box.

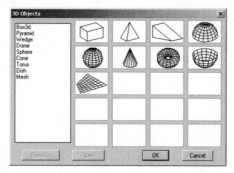

Click the object you want, and then follow the prompts to place the object in the drawing. You are prompted for the dimensions and location of the object, as well as the number of facets.

Using 3D Solids

Solid modeling is great for quickly creating shapes from basic, 2D objects. Solids are considered more intuitive to use, but they are more difficult to edit. You cannot use grip editing, for example, nor can you easily stretch 3D solids.

If you're an architect wanting a massing model, you'll want to take a look at solid modeling because it lends itself to creating rectilinear shapes quickly. The following tutorial shows some basic methods for creating and editing 3D solids. You can learn more about specific tools in later sections of this chapter.

Extruding a Polyline

You can insert a variety of solid shapes into your drawing. For example, you can create a sphere by choosing Draw ➢ Solids ➢ Sphere. You can then select a center point and a radius, just as you would for a circle, but you end up with a solid sphere.

Another way to create solids is to extrude them from closed polylines. This is a more flexible way to create shapes because you can create a polyline of any shape and extrude it to a fairly complex form.

In the following exercise, you'll start with a rectangle, which is actually a simple closed polyline. From that rectangle, you'll use a variety of tools to form a box

1. Open a new file in AutoCAD using the `acad.dwt` template.

2. Click the Rectangle tool, and click at coordinate 12,8. You don't have to be exact about the location just as long is you're close visually to the lower-left corner shown in Figure 6.23.

3. Enter @30,15 to create a rectangle that is 30 by 15 units.

FIGURE 6.23
Drawing the rectangle from which a 3D object will be created

You now have a rectangle like any other you may have drawn. Next you'll change your view to see it in 3D. Even though it is a 2D object, you can view the rectangle as if it were drawn on the floor of a 3D space.

1. Choose View ➢ 3D Views ➢ SWIsometric. Your view changes to an isometric style.

2. Choose View ➢ Zoom ➢ Out to adjust your view to look like Figure 6.24.

OBJECTS YOU CAN EXTRUDE

The 3D solids tutorial shows how to extrude a polyline, but you aren't limited to closed polylines. You might find that you need to use other types of objects in your extrusion. Here is a list of objects that are available for 3D extrusions:

◆ 3D Faces

◆ 2D Solids (choose Draw ➢ Surfaces ➢ 2D Solids)

◆ Circles

◆ Closed splines

◆ Regions

3D faces can be especially useful because they are components of 3D meshes (described earlier in this chapter). You can use the Explode command to reduce a mesh into its component 3D faces. (Each facet of a mesh becomes a 3D face.) You can then extrude the individual 3D face of the exploded mesh.

In addition, you can extrude a surface of an existing 3D solid by choosing Modify ➢ Solid Editing ➢ Extrude Faces.

FIGURE 6.24
Adjust your view to look
like this figure.

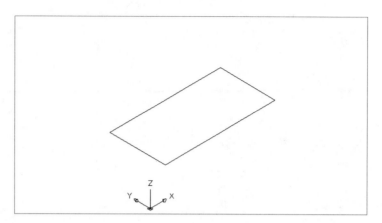

Now you're ready to change this rectangle into a 3D object.

1. Choose Draw ➢ Solids ➢ Extrude.

2. At the `Select objects:` prompt, select the rectangle, and then press ↵.

3. At the `Specify height of extrusion or [Path]:` prompt, enter **10** ↵ to make the height of the extrusion 10 units.

4. At the `Specify angle of taper for extrusion <0>:` prompt, press ↵ to accept the default of 0°. The rectangle expands to become a box, as shown in Figure 6.25.

   You've just created a solid in the form of a box that is 30 × 15 × 10 units. Right now, you see it in what is known as a wireframe view, which means that you see all the corners and sides as though the object were transparent.

FIGURE 6.25
The rectangle extruded
into a box

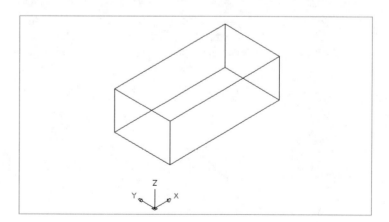

5. To see the true form of the box, choose View ➤ Hide. The box now appears as a solid box.

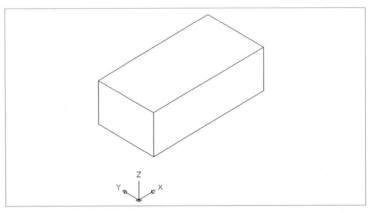

6. Choose View ➤ Regen to get back to the wireframe view.

In this exercise, you extruded a simple rectangle, but you can extrude any shape you can dream up using closed polylines. For example, you can extrude a complex curved shape, as shown in Figure 6.26.

USING POLYLINE SPLINES TO CREATE 3D SOLIDS

You can use polyline splines to create 3D solids, but using them successfully involves a few tricks. Sometimes when you attempt to extrude a closed polyline spline, you get unexpected results, and the extrusion does not reflect the shape of the spline curve. To avoid this problem, use the Offset command to create a copy of the spline, and then use the offset copy as part of your closed polyline spline, not the original spline. You can then extrude the offset copies of the polyline spline and get the results you want, as shown here:

In the left image, the polyline spline is offset in two directions. Next, intermediate lines are added, and the Pedit Join option is used to join all the objects into a single closed polyline, as shown in the middle image. Finally, the Extrude command is used to extrude the closed polyline into the third dimension.

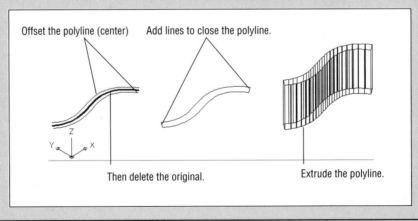

FIGURE 6.26

Sample of an extruded
closed polyline

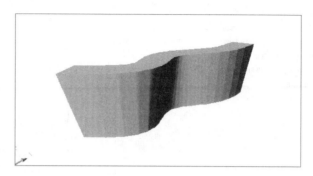

Right now the box is not very interesting. You can add some detail to any of the sides by creating a UCS that is aligned with the side on which you want to work.

Using a Predefined UCS

In the surface modeling exercise at the beginning of this chapter, you learned how to create a UCS by indicating the X and Y axes plus the origin of the UCS. You can also go from the WCS to a pre-defined UCS. For example, if you want to align a UCS to a vertical side of a 3D box, you can do the following:

1. Adjust your view so you can see your 3D object in a way similar to Figure 6.25 earlier in this chapter.

2. Choose Tools ➤ Orthographic UCS ➤ Front to change the UCS so that the Y axis points up. This is an orientation that is aligned with the front of the box. Figure 6.27 shows the orthographic (top) and isometric (bottom) views in relation to a 3D box.

The UCS is in the correct orientation but is floating in space. You'll want to place the UCS directly on the side of the box.

1. Choose Tools ➤ Move UCS.

2. Shift+right-click, and choose Endpoint from the Osnap menu.

3. Using the endpoint osnap, click the lower-left corner of the front face of the box as shown in Figure 6.28. The UCS moves to the corner.

The front UCS is now aligned with one side of the box. Note that while the UCS is aligned with the box, it is not attached to it in any way. If you move the box, the UCS remains where it is.

With the UCS aligned with the side of the box, start to draw directly on the side. The objects you create are aligned with the new UCS, which also happens to be aligned with the side of the box. The net effect is that as you draw objects, they can appear on the side of the box, as shown in Figure 6.29. You can draw anywhere in the drawing away from the box, and objects are still aligned with the UCS and the side of the box.

FIGURE 6.27
The orthographic views are shown at the top, and isometric views are shown in the bottom image.

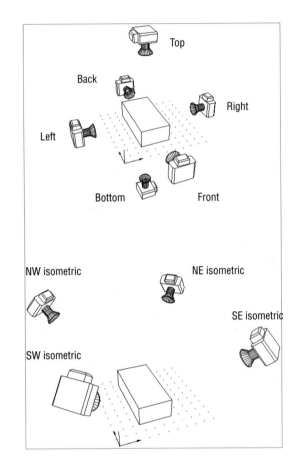

FIGURE 6.28
Use the endpoint osnap, and select the corner shown here.

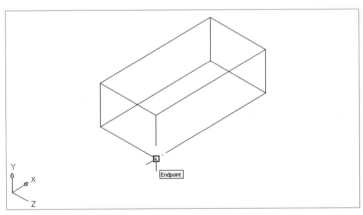

FIGURE 6.29

Drawing on the box's surface

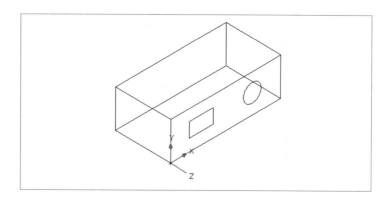

Subtracting 3D Shapes

In the previous examples, you saw how to align a UCS to a surface and then draw on that surface. This all leads up to another feature of 3D solid modeling: you can use 3D solids to sculpt shapes from other solids.

For example, suppose you wanted to cut holes in the side of the rectangle of the previous example. First, you extrude the shapes you want to cut out. You can extrude the rectangle and circle that were drawn on the side of the solid box. You extrude them in a negative direction so that they protrude into the box.

Next, you subtract the extruded circle and rectangle from the box. To do this, choose Modify ➢ Solid Editing ➢ Subtract, select the solid you want to subtract from, and press ↵. Next, select the extruded solids as the solids to subtract, and press ↵. To view the effects of the subtraction, choose View ➢ Hide. The hidden line view shows that the box now has two holes in its side, as you can see in Figure 6.30.

NAMING A UCS

Though not essential, you can give your new UCS a name in case you need to return to it later. Follow these steps:

1. Choose Tools ➢ Named UCS to open the UCS dialog box, which displays three UCSs. The highlighted one is current.

2. Right-click the highlighted UCS (unnamed), and choose Rename. The listing changes so that you can change the name.

3. Enter **Front of box** ↵ to rename the UCS.

4. Click OK.

You can also name the current UCS by following these steps:

1. Enter **UCS** ↵ at the Command prompt, and then enter **s** ↵ to use the Save option.

2. Enter the name for the UCS.

FIGURE 6.30

The circle and rectangle subtracted from the box

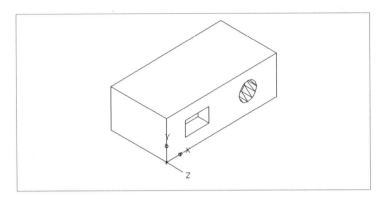

In this example, two smaller shapes are subtracted from the larger one to form holes. You can place solid objects anywhere, and as long as they intersect, you can subtract one from another. You can, for example, carve a cylindrical shape from the corner of the box by first creating a 3D solid cylinder with its center on the corner and then subtracting it as shown in Figure 6.30.

The subtraction of one object from another is called a Boolean operation, named after George Boole, a 19th-century mathematician. Other Boolean operations include union, intersection, and interfere. An overview of these other Boolean operations follows.

COMBINING AND SEPARATING SOLIDS

You saw how you can subtract 3D solids to create new shapes. You can also add solids together. Figure 6.31 shows how a window might be constructed using the Union command to join a set of solids.

In the window example, the outlines of the mullions and frame are created using rectangles. The rectangles are extruded by choosing Draw ➢ Solids ➢ Extrude. The frame and mullions are joined into one object by choosing Modify ➢ Solid Editing ➢ Union.

FIGURE 6.31

Adding solids together

Separate solids created for the frame and mullions.

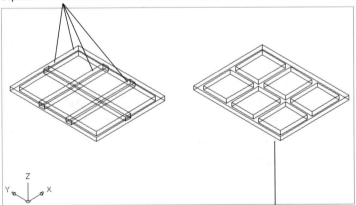

The Union command is applied to the solids to create a single solid.

GETTING THE INTERSECTION OF SOLIDS

Another useful tool for editing solids is the Interfere command. Interfere lets you find the intersection of two solids. This can be helpful if you need to reproduce a section of a solid.

Interfere works by creating a third 3D solid that is the shape of the intersection of two other solids. Figure 6.32 shows how an extruded cornice and a simple box are used to make a copy of a small piece of the cornice.

FIGURE 6.32

Making a copy of a section of a 3D solid using Interfere

Wall with cornice   Box

The Interfere command creates the intersection of the two, which can be moved to other parts of the drawing.

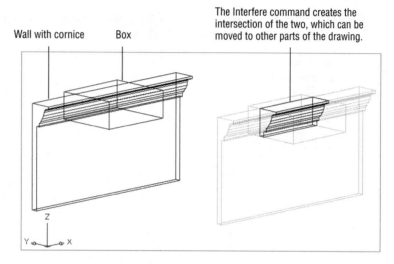

To work with the Interfere command, follow these steps:

1. At the Command prompt, enter **Interfere** ↵.

2. To select the cornice, press ↵.

3. To select the box, press ↵ again.

4. At the `Create interference solids? [Yes/No] <N>:` prompt, enter **Y** ↵.

TIP   If you just want to create the intersection of two solids and discard the original solids, you can use the Intersection command. Choose Modify ➢ Solid Editing ➢ Intersect, and then select the two objects whose intersection you want.

Using Other Solid-Editing Tools

Boolean operations aren't the only methods available for editing 3D solids. You can extend surfaces, change their angle, and much more. To see quite a few other options, choose Modify ➢ Solid Editing. Many of these other options are beyond the scope of this book. If you feel you want to do more in the area of 3D, take a look at *Mastering AutoCAD 2006 and AutoCAD LT 2006*.

Filleting a Corner

One useful editing command for 3D solids is more commonly used in 2D drawings. If you want to round the corner of a 3D solid, you can do so using the Fillet command. But Fillet behaves in a slightly different way when applied to 3D solids. Once you've issued the Fillet command by selecting it from the Modify menu or toolbar, you select the solid edge you want to fillet (see Figure 6.33). The selected edge is highlighted, and you are prompted for a fillet radius. Once you've entered a radius, you can select other contiguous edges to fillet. Press ↵, and the edges are filleted as shown in Figure 6.34.

TIP You can also use the Chamfer command to chamfer the corners of 3D solids. Chamfer works in a way similar to the Fillet command.

FIGURE 6.33
Selecting the edge to fillet

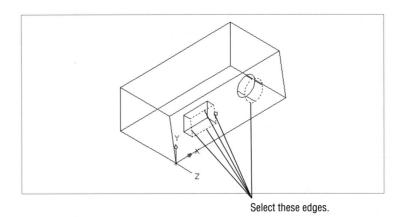

Select these edges.

FIGURE 6.34
The resulting fillet

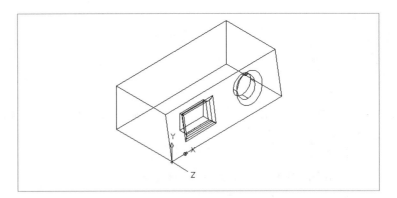

Getting a Shaded View to See More Clearly

Sometimes it helps to get a shaded view of your 3D model as you work to make sure you're on the right track. AutoCAD includes several shaded view options. Try the following to see how your model looks so far.

1. Choose View ➤ Shade ➤ Gouraud Shaded. Your model appears as a dark, shaded object. The Gouraud Shaded option uses the object's color to shade the entire object. You'll want a lighter color to see the object more clearly.

2. Click the corner of the solid to select it.

3. Click the Color drop-down list in the Properties toolbar and select yellow.

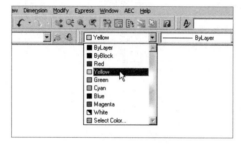

With the lighter color, you can see the shading more clearly, and you can get a better feel for the form of your 3D solid. The Gouraud Shaded view is especially helpful in showing off the rounded corners of the two holes.

Once you are satisfied with the form your model is taking, you can get back to the wireframe view by doing the following:

1. Choose View ➤ Shade ➤ 2D Wireframe.

2. Click the solid object, click the Color drop-down list in the Properties toolbar, and choose Bylayer to return the color of the object to its original.

You might have noticed a few other options in the Shade menu. Figure 6.35 shows those options as they are applied to a sphere.

FIGURE 6.35

The Shade options applied to a sphere

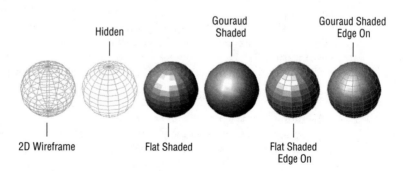

Extruding along a Path

At the beginning of the 3D solid modeling tutorial, you learned how to extrude a polyline into the third dimension. This method let you create some basic 3D shapes, but what if you want to create something a bit more complex?

You might have noticed that, while using the Extrude command (choose Draw ➤ Solids ➤ Extrude), the Path option was available. This option lets you extrude a closed polygon shape along a path. The path can be defined by a polyline or a spline.

Figure 6.36 shows how to create the exterior wall of a building using a polyline outline of the wall's profile and a polyline path of the wall's footprint on the ground.

FIGURE 6.36
The 2D drawings of a
building wall section and
footprint

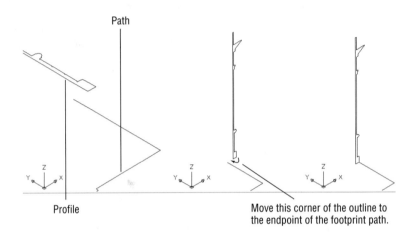

To see how the Path option works, follow these steps:

1. Draw the outline of the shape you want to extrude, and then draw the path you will use to extrude the outline. Figure 6.36 shows an example of an outline and a path in an isometric view.

The outline is a profile or wall section of a building. The path is the building footprint. The footprint has a gap to provide a place to locate the outline, as you will see later.

Once you've drawn the outline and path, you need to orient the outline so that it is perpendicular to the path and is in its proper relationship to the path. You can use the methods described earlier in this chapter to rotate the wall profile into a vertical orientation as shown in the middle part of Figure 6.36. Once the wall profile is vertical, you will have to place the profile on the polyline footprint path.

With everything in place, you can use the Extrude command to create the 3D wall.

1. Choose Draw ➤ Solids ➤ Extrude, select the profile outline, and press ↵.

2. At the `Specify height of extrusion or [Path]:` prompt, enter **p** ↵ to select the Path option, and then select the polyline footprint path. The outline is extruded along the path to form the wall, as shown in the bottom image of Figure 6.37.

FIGURE 6.37
The extrusion along a path

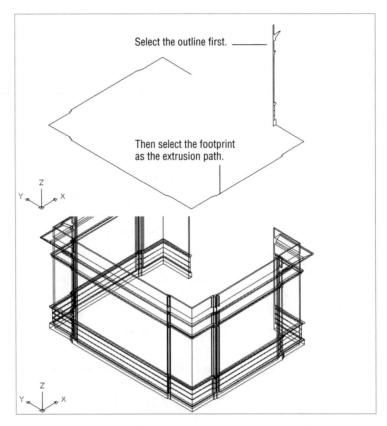

Select the outline first. ———

Then select the footprint as the extrusion path.

Although we used a building in this example, you can use this method to create any number of extruded shapes along a path. The shape can be as simple as a circle extruded along a curve to form a tube or a wall section along a footprint, as in this example.

Revolving a Polyline

You've seen how the Extrude command lets you create solids in two ways: you can extrude in a straight line or along a path. The Revolve command lets you create a 3D solid by rotating a shape. It extrudes a circle, an ellipse, a closed polyline, or a region along a circular path up to 360°. You draw the profile of the shape you want, define an axis of rotation about which the shape will be "rotated," and then use Revolve to turn the shape into a rounded 3D object. It's just like the Rotated Surface option described earlier in this chapter, but instead of creating a surface mesh, you get a solid.

Figures 6.38 and 6.39 show the progression from 2D objects to revolved 3D solids. In Figure 6.38, an ellipse and a line are drawn. The ellipse is the shape that is to be revolved, and the line is the axis of revolution.

FIGURE 6.38

Draw the ellipse and the line.

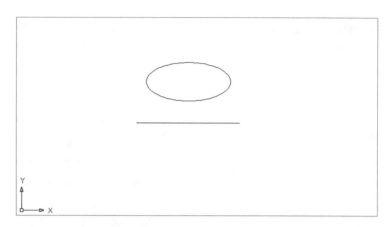

To revolve the ellipse, follow these steps:

1. Choose Draw ➤ Solids ➤ Revolve, select the ellipse, and press ↵.

2. At the Specify start point for axis of revolution or define axis by [Object/X (axis)/Y (axis)]: prompt, enter **o** ↵ to use the Object option, and then select the line representing the axis of revolution.

3. At the Specify angle of revolution <360>: prompt, enter the angle you want for the rotation.

For the revolved shape in Figure 6.39, an angle of 180° is used. A revolved surface won't look like much until you view it using one of the Shade options in the View menu. For example, to display the view in Figure 6.39 I chose View ➤ Shade ➤ Gouraud Shade.

Figure 6.40 shows an ellipse as an example, but you can use any closed shape you want. Just make sure that when you draw your closed shape, the outline does not cross over itself, like a figure eight.

FIGURE 6.39

An ellipse that has been revolved into a solid

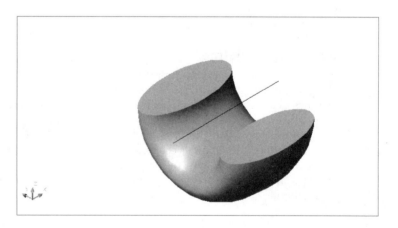

Other 3D Solid Examples

The 3D solid examples so far have shown you how the Extrude and Revolve commands work, but they haven't shown their use in real applications. One practical use of the Extrude command is in modeling building elevations. Figure 6.40 shows how to create a building entry using solids. Figure 6.41 shows a simple window made of 3D solids.

Figure 6.42 shows a part from a mechanical assembly that was created using solids along with the aid of the Fillet command.

3D Solid-Editing Options

In the 3D solid-editing tutorial, you were introduced to a few of the 3D solid-editing options. Several other options can help when you need to modify a 3D solid. Table 6.1 describes several of the options in the Solid Editing menu. As a beginning user, you probably won't need them, but you'll want to know what they do for future reference.

FIGURE 6.40
A building entry made from 3D solids

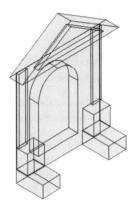

FIGURE 6.41
A window made from 3D Solids

TABLE 6.1: The Solid-Editing Options

OPTION	PURPOSE
Extrude Faces	Lets you extrude the face of a 3D solid. This option behaves in a similar way to the Extrude command, allowing you to apply a taper angle.
Move Faces	Lets you move a face of a 3D solid. When you click a corner, the two faces attached to the corner are highlighted. You can then change the location of the corner, thereby moving the two faces. Useful in moving holes in a solid by selecting the entire hole.
Offset Faces	Lets you offset the face of a 3D Solid. This is similar to the Offset command for 2D objects in that it moves the selected faces in a parallel direction either outward or inward from their current location. Useful in increasing or decreasing the size of holes in solids.
Delete Faces	Deletes an intermediate surface from a solid. For example, you can use Delete Faces to remove a chamfered edge on a box.
Rotate Faces	Rotates a surface on a solid. Useful in rotating holes in a solid.
Taper Faces	Lets you extrude a face in a tapered fashion. Useful in changing a straight hole into a tapered one.
Color Faces	Lets you change the color of a surface.
Copy Faces	Lets you copy a surface. This creates a region that is the same shape as the surface. You can then use the region to create new solids or to use in other 3D applications.
Imprint	Lets you place a 2D shape on a surface. You can then extrude the imprinted shape. The shape can be any closed polyline, spline, or circle.

TABLE 6.1:   The Solid-Editing Options *(CONTINUED)*

OPTION	PURPOSE
Clean	Removes redundant edges, such as imprinted shapes that have not been extruded or other coplanar surfaces that share edges.
Shell	Creates a shell from a solid. You are asked for a shell thickness.
Check	Validates the integrity of a solid.

Manipulating Objects in 3D Space

When you draw in 2D, the Z axis is fairly unimportant. By default, objects you create reside at the 0 (zero) coordinate of the Z axis. In other words, everything you draw is on the plane defined by the X and Y axes. But just as you can move and copy objects anywhere in the XY coordinate plane, you can also move and copy them along the Z axis.

In the surface model tutorial at the beginning of this chapter, the polyline and 3D face box resides on the XY plane of the WCS. The UCS icon in the lower-left corner of the screen indicates the X and Y axes of this WCS. This is typically the base coordinate system for all your 2D work. You might think of it as the surface of a "virtual" drafting table.

But once you start working in 3D, you find you need to work on other surfaces, such as the side elevation of a building or the front panel of an electronic device. As you saw in earlier examples, you can create your own user coordinate system that coexists with the WCS. For example, you can create a user coordinate system that is aligned with one of the vertical sides of the polyline box you created. You can then draw on that vertical surface as you would in the WCS using all the standard AutoCAD drawing tools.

Just as you can specify exact distances in 2D drawings, you can specify locations and distances in 3D space using the @X,Y,Z notation. If you want to move something only within the XY plane, you can leave off the Z coordinate in the specification, and AutoCAD assumes you want to maintain the object's current Z coordinate. To specify relative distances in 3D, you can specify the Z coordinate as needed, as in:

    @2,1,1↵

If you enter this at the To point: prompt in the Move or Copy command, your object not only moves 2 units to the right and 1 unit up, it also moves 1 unit vertically, in the positive direction of the Z axis (see Figure 6.43).

NOTE   If you only want to move an object in the Z axis, enter a zero for both the X and Y axes, as in **@0,0,2**↵. This moves your selected object 2 units in the positive direction of the Z axis.

A negative value for the Z axis moves an object in the negative direction. Figure 6.44 shows the three axes for a typical 2D WCS, with their positive and negative directions.

FIGURE 6.43

The image on the top shows an object moved within the XY plane within the WCS. The image on the bottom shows the same move with an additional Z component.

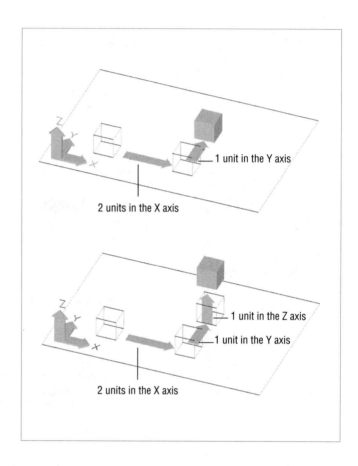

FIGURE 6.44

The X, Y, and Z axes and their positive and negative directions

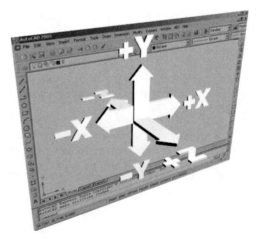

NOTE You might find it easiest to remember the @X,Y,Z format for specifying distances in 3D, but, in typical AutoCAD fashion, you can use two other formats for spatial distances. In the limited space of this book, however, I can't show all the methods for specifying distance in 3D. For future reference, the other methods are the *Cylindrical* format and the *Spherical* format. Both are extensions of the standard AutoCAD polar coordinate format you use in 2D drawing. You can find out more about these formats in *Mastering AutoCAD 2006 and AutoCAD LT 2006*.

Understanding Your 3D Viewing Options

Earlier in this chapter, you were introduced to the 3D options available in the View menu. Those options are fine if you need to take a quick look at your 3D model, but you'll eventually want more control over the way you view your model.

Several AutoCAD tools let you see your model from almost any orientation. You can also save views so that you can quickly return to them later for studies or for printing. In this section, you'll look at the 3Dorbit command and the Camera command. These two commands combined give nearly any view you might want.

Before you delve into these commands, set up a drawing that you can use for practice.

1. Create a new drawing from the acad.dwt template.

2. Draw the rectangle and two circles, as shown in Figure 6.45. The rectangle is 20 × 10 units; the larger circle has a radius of 2.5 units, and the smaller one has a radius of 0.5 units. You don't have to be exact as these objects will be used to demonstrate 3D viewing.

3. In the Standard toolbar, click the Properties tool, and then select the box.

4. In the Properties palette, click the Thickness value, and enter **8** ↵ to give the box a thickness of 8 units.

FIGURE 6.45
The rectangle and two circles

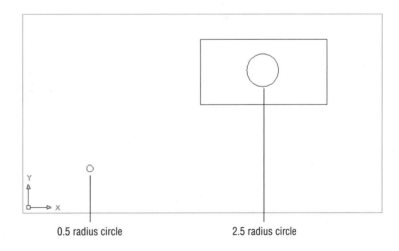

0.5 radius circle   2.5 radius circle

5. Press Esc to clear the selection, and then click the circle.

6. In the Properties palette, click the Thickness value, and enter **4** ↵ to give the box a thickness of 4 units.

7. Click Esc again, click the smaller circle, and change its Thickness value to 5.5.

8. Click the X in the Properties palette title bar to close it.

9. Choose View ➢ 3D Views ➢ SW Isometric to display an isometric view of the three items.

Now you're ready to explore AutoCAD 3D viewing capabilities. The smaller circle will be used as your camera location, and the larger circle will be used as the camera target.

Using the Camera Command to Set Up Your Viewpoint

The Camera command lets you specify an exact location for your viewpoint location and the view target. This gives you much greater control over what you see in your views. For example, if you are trying to select a view from a particular location in an architectural model, you can use objects such as circle or lines to locate the person viewing the building and the point of interest at which the person is looking. You can then use the Camera command to select those objects as the camera and target location. Try the following steps to see how the Camera command works.

1. At the Command prompt, enter **Camera** ↵.

2. At the `Specify new camera position <-30.8222,-42.2347,60.4218>:` prompt, select your camera location. Shift+right-click, select the center osnap, and then select the center of the smaller circle (see Figure 6.46).

FIGURE 6.46
The isometric view of the three objects

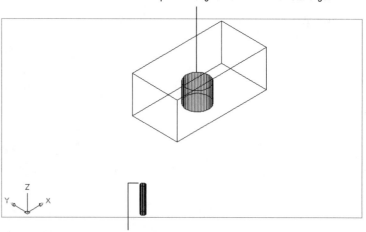

Click the center of the top of the larger circle for the camera target.

Select the top of the small circle for the camera location.

3. At the Specify new camera target <13.6707,2.2583,15.9289>: prompt, select the object you want your camera to be looking at. Shift+right click again, select the center osnap, and then select the center of the larger circle (see Figure 6.47). This has the effect of looking from the top of the smaller circle directly at the top of the larger one. Your view changes to one like that in Figure 6.47.

You can see that the two circles are aligned, showing you that you are looking through the two points you selected. Next, you'll see how to use the Orbit tool to get a perspective view for a little more realism.

FIGURE 6.47
The view after using the camera command

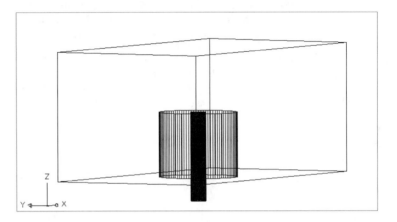

GETTING BACK TO A PLAN OR TOP VIEW

Eventually, you'll want to get to a plan or top view of your 3D model. You can do this by using the Plan command. Choose View ➤ 3D Views ➤ Plan View ➤ World UCS or enter **plan** ↵ ↵ at the Command prompt. If you want a plan view of a particular UCS, you can choose View ➤ 3D Views ➤ Plan View ➤ Named UCS, and then enter the name of the UCS. Or you can use the Current UCS option for the plan view of the current UCS.

You can also use the View dialog box (choose View ➤ Named Views) to select the top view from the list in the Orthographic & Isometric Views tab.

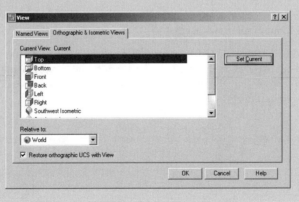

Using 3Dorbit to View in Perspective and Adjust Your View

Your current view is a parallel projection view; that is, all parallel lines appear parallel in your view as in an isometric view. To get a better idea of how your model looks, you'll want to switch to a perspective view.

In the following exercise, you'll use the 3Dorbit command to switch to a perspective view, and then you'll explore some of the other capabilities of 3Dorbit.

1. Choose View ➢ 3D Orbit or enter **3do** ⤶ the Command prompt. You see a circle called an arcball with four smaller circles at the top, bottom, left, and right of the arcball. The UCS also changes into one made up of three colors. The arcball and its smaller circles let you manipulate your view. You might also notice that the cursor has changed shape.

2. Right-click, and then choose Projection ➢ Perspective from the shortcut menu. Your view changes to show the model in perspective, as shown in Figure 6.48.

FIGURE 6.48

The box in perspective

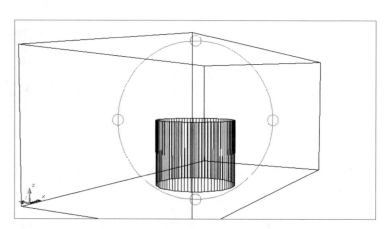

3. Right-click and choose Exit to exit the 3Dorbit command.

ROTATING YOUR VIEW USING THE ARCBALL

You remain in the 3Dorbit command as you can still see the arcball. Next you'll see how you can use the arcball to manipulate your view.

1. Choose View ➢ 3D Orbit or enter **3do** ⤶ the Command prompt, and then move the cursor in and out of the arcball to see what happens to the cursor. Inside the arcball, the cursor looks like two ellipses. Outside, it looks like a circle. These different cursors give you hints about the way the cursor affects your view.

2. With the cursor outside and to the right of the arcball, click and drag the mouse upward and downward. Notice that the view rotates.

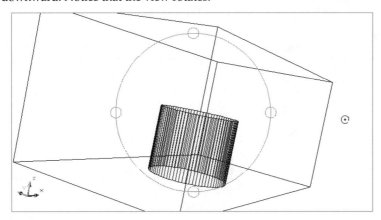

3. Level the view, and then place the cursor on the small circle on the right side of the arcball. Notice how the cursor changes to a horizontally oriented ellipse.

4. Click and drag the small circle on the right side of the arcball. The view rotates horizontally as if you were moving around the box. The small circles at the left and right of the arcball both have the same effect. They rotate your view horizontally about your camera target.

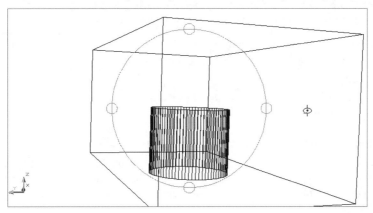

5. Place the cursor on the small circle at the top of the arcball. Now the cursor changes to a vertically oriented ellipse.

6. Click and drag the small circle at the top of the arcball. Now the view rotates vertically as if you were rising up or dropping down in relation to the box. The top and bottom circles on the arcball both behave the same way. They rotate your view vertically.

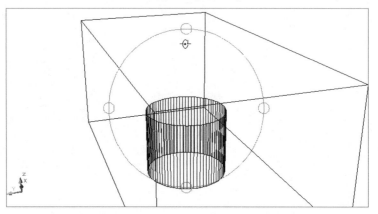

7. Now click and drag in a circular motion inside the arcball. Your views rotate in all directions in a free-form manner.

TIP   Clicking and dragging inside the arcball can start to tilt your view in an undesirable way. You can set 3Dorbit to keep the view straight while clicking and dragging inside the arcball. In the 3Dorbit command, right-click and choose More ➢ Orbit Maintains Z.

8. Right-click, choose Exit to exit the 3Dorbit command, and then use the Undo tool to return to the original perspective view shown in Figure 6.51.

As you can see, you can adjust your view using the arcball in the 3Dorbit command. You can also view your model in perspective. If you want to return to a parallel projection view, start the 3Dorbit command again, right-click, and then choose Projection ➢ Parallel.

ADJUSTING YOUR DISTANCE FROM THE CAMERA TARGET

Along with rotating your view, you will want to be able to adjust your distance from the camera target. In other words, you will want to be able to move into or away from your model to get a close-up view or more of an overall view. To do this, you use the Distance option of the 3Dorbit command.

1. At the Command prompt, choose View ➢ 3D Orbit or enter **3do** ↵.

2. Right-click and choose More ➢ Adjust Distance. Notice that the cursor changes to a double-headed arrow.

3. Click and drag the mouse downward. Your view changes as if you are moving away from the box. You might see the smaller circle come into view.

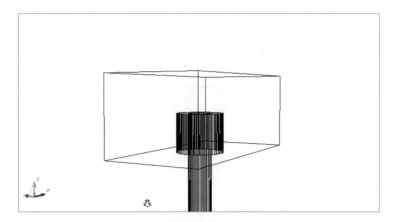

4. Click and drag upward. Your view moves toward the box.

Panning Your View in Perspective Mode

While you are in perspective mode, you cannot use the standard Pan command to pan your view, but you can use the Pan option in the 3Dorbit shortcut menu. Try it in this next exercise.

1. While in the 3Dorbit command, right-click and choose Pan.

2. Click and drag the mouse to the left. Your view will pan as if both the camera and the camera target move in unison.

3. Press ↵ to exit the 3Dorbit command.

If you change back to the parallel projection mode, you can use the standard Pan command to pan your view.

Other 3Dorbit Options

You've just run through the more commonly used 3Dorbit functions. Many other options are available through the 3dorbit shortcut menu. Table 6.2 gives you an overview of them. As a beginner, you may not find these other options useful, or they may not give the results you want, but knowing about them can help you become a more proficient user.

TABLE 6.2:   The 3Dorbit Options

Option	What It Does
Exit	Exits the 3dorbit command.
Pan	Pans your view.

TABLE 6.2:   The 3Dorbit Options *(CONTINUED)*

OPTION	WHAT IT DOES
Zoom	Lets you zoom in. In perspective mode, zoom behaves like a zoom lens, changing your focal length and field of view.
Orbit	Turns on the arcball.
More	Displays additional options. See Table 6.3.
Projection	Lets you select from parallel or perspective projected views.
Shade Modes	Lets you select a shade mode similar to the Shade options in the View menu.
Visual Aids	Lets you turn on a grid or a compass and controls the UCS visibility.
Reset View	Returns to the last view before the most recent 3Dorbit view change.
Preset Views	Displays the same preset parallel projection views found by choosing View ➢ 3D Views.

In addition to the options in the main shortcut menu, you'll find several other options under the More option. Table 6.3 describes those options.

TABLE 6.3:   The Options under the More Option

OPTION	FUNCTION
Adjust Distance	Lets you adjust the distance between the camera and the target in perspective views. Has the same effect as Zoom when in parallel projection mode.
Swivel Camera	In perspective projection mode, has the effect of swiveling the camera so the target location changes.
Continuous Orbit	Displays a kind of animated view by continuously revolving the camera around the camera target, much like the earth rotates about the sun. Select this option, and then click and drag the mouse in the direction of the desired rotation.
Zoom Window	Zooms in to a selected area using a window. In perspective mode, this has the effect of changing your focal length.
Zoom Extents	Zooms out to view all the objects in the drawing.
Orbit Maintains Z	Maintains a vertical Z axis when using the arcball.
Orbit uses AutoTarget	Maintains the camera target location. You can reset the camera target location using the Camera command.

TABLE 6.3:   The Options under the More Option *(CONTINUED)*

OPTION	FUNCTION
Adjust Clipping Planes	Opens a dialog box that lets you adjust clipping planes. See Front Clipping On and Back Clipping On.
Front Clipping On	Turns on the Front Clipping plane. A clipping plane defines a plane parallel to the view plane beyond which objects are hidden. This is useful if you want to view the interior of a room where walls obscure your vision.
Back Clipping On	Turns on the Back Clipping plane. A clipping plane defines a plane parallel to the view plane beyond which objects are hidden. This is useful if you want to hide objects beyond a certain point in your view.

Changing Your Focal Length in Perspective

The 3Dorbit command includes a Zoom option that behaves like a zoom lens when you are in perspective mode. It has the effect of changing the focal length of your view. Unfortunately, the 3Dorbit Zoom option does not give you much control over that focal length and can distort your view if you are not careful. A better way to adjust the focal length is to use the Dview command.

Dview has many options, and before the 3Dorbit command was introduced, Dview was the only way to work in perspective. To use Dview to adjust your perspective view's focal length, follow these steps:

1. Make sure you are in perspective mode.

2. At the Command prompt, enter **dv** ↵.

3. Select an object or set of objects in your model that you will use as a visual reference while you are making your adjustments, and then press ↵.

4. At the `Camera/Target/Distance` prompt, enter **Z** ↵, and then enter a focal length value.

5. Press ↵ to exit Dview.

Saving and Restoring Your 3D Views

Getting the exact view you want in a 3D model can be a painstaking process. Once you've gotten that perfect view, you'll want to preserve it in some way. AutoCAD offers the View command for just that purpose. The View command stores your views so that you can recall them at any time. You can store as many views as you need and quickly switch between them.

TIP   Although I've placed the View command in the 3D chapter, you can use the View command to save 2D views as well. Saving 2D views works the same way as saving 3D views.

Saving a View

To use the View command, take the following steps:

1. Choose View ➤ Named Views or enter **v** ↵ at the Command prompt to open the View dialog box (see Figure 6.49).

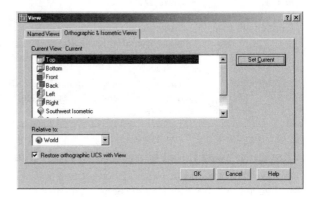

2. If it isn't already selected, click the Named Views tab (see Figure 6.50). You see a list of views available. If there are no saved views, you will see a listing of the current view.

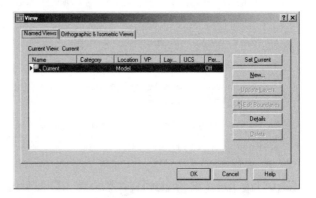

3. With the Current view listing selected, click the New button to open the New View dialog box (see Figure 6.51).

4. In the View Name text box, enter a name for your view.

5. You can optionally enter additional information in the View Category text box to help you identify the view.

6. Make sure the Current Display option is selected in the Boundary section.

FIGURE 6.51

The New View dialog box

7. You can also choose to save the current layer settings and UCS with the view in the Settings section.

8. Click OK. Your view appears in the list box of the View dialog box.

9. Click OK to exit the View dialog box.

Restoring a View

To restore a saved view, do the following:

1. At the Command prompt, choose View ➢ Named Views or enter **v** ↵.

2. In the View dialog box, select the view you want from the list box, and then click Set Current.

3. Click OK to exit the View dialog box.

Your saved view appears in the AutoCAD window.

Just Enough Summary

In this chapter, you've learned about the main tools needed to work in 3D. If you are the adventurous type, you might want to experiment with what you now know. You'll be surprised at how much you can accomplish with your newfound knowledge.

I didn't cover all the tools and options available for 3D modeling. In particular, the vports command can be helpful to get several simultaneous views of a 3D model while you're editing. Still, armed with the information in this chapter, you will be able to do most of the basic 3D modeling tasks you encounter.

Chapter 7

Getting Organized with Layers

The most frequently used tool for getting organized is the layering feature. Layers let you sort parts of your drawing into categories. For example, in a typical architectural floor plan, you can have one layer for the walls, another for doors, and yet another for cabinets. You can create other layers for existing conditions if the plan contains renovation work, or you can include electrical and heating diagrams. You can then turn layers on or off so that your drawing displays only the data you need at any given time. You can set layers to have color and line weights, and objects will inherit those properties. You can even have layers visible on your screen but not have them print. This feature can be useful if you have a lot of layout information you need to keep with your drawing.

In this chapter, you'll learn how to create and manipulate layers and how objects interact with layers.

- ◆ Creating and Assigning Layers
- ◆ Setting the Current Layer
- ◆ Controlling Layer Visibility
- ◆ Locking Layers from Printing and Editing
- ◆ Finding the Layers You Want
- ◆ Taming an Unwieldy List of Layers
- ◆ Saving and Recalling Layer Settings
- ◆ Express Tools for Managing Layers
- ◆ Organizing Visual Content through Properties

Creating and Assigning Layers

You use the Layer Properties Manager dialog box to create and edit layers. When you are just starting a drawing, especially a complex one, you will probably spend a lot of time in this dialog box setting up and managing layers. Though it isn't absolutely necessary, setting a color for a new layer is a good thing to do right off the bat. Colors are a great way to see at a glance the layer an object is assigned to.

The following steps introduce you to the Layer Properties Manager dialog box and show you how to create a new layer.

1. In the Properties toolbar, click the Layer Properties Manager tool shown in Figure 7.1, choose Format ➤ Layer, or type **LA**↵ to open the Layer Properties Manager dialog box.

FIGURE 7.1

The Layer Properties
Manager tool

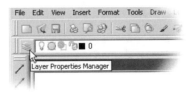

NOTE The Layer Properties Manager dialog box shows you at a glance the status of your layers. Right now, you have only one layer, but as your work expands, so will the number of layers. You will then find this dialog box indispensable.

2. Click the New Layer button at the top of the dialog box (see Figure 7.2). Its icon looks like a sun. A new layer named Layer1 appears in the list box. The name is highlighted so you can immediately start typing a name for it.

FIGURE 7.2

Click the New Layer
button toward the top
of the Layer Properties
Manager dialog box.

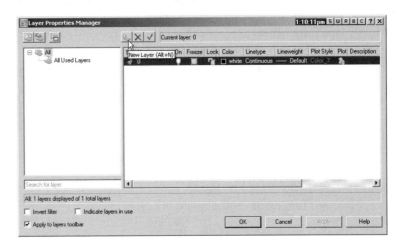

3. As you type, your entry replaces the Layer1 name in the list box. Don't worry if you aren't certain about the name; you can always change it later.

TIP As a project grows, so does its list of layers. It helps to have a system for naming layers so that you'll be able to find them and sort them easily. For example, you might use a prefix for your layer names like FP for floor plan and EP for electrical plan. You can also use industry guidelines, such as the American Institute of Architects' layer naming standards.

4. With your new layer name highlighted, click the Color icon in that layer's listing shown in Figure 7.3. The color icon is in the Color column and currently shows White as its value.

The Select Color dialog box appears as shown in Figure 7.4.

5. In the row of standard colors, click the color you want and then click OK. Notice that the color swatch in the new layer listing is now the color you selected.

6. When the Layer Properties Manager dialog box returns, click OK to close it.

FIGURE 7.3
The Color icon in the
layer listing of the Layer
Properties Manager
dialog box

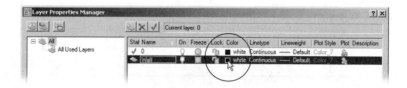

FIGURE 7.4
The Select Color
dialog box

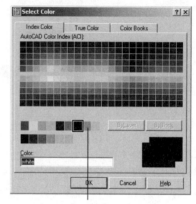

Standard colors

From this point on, any object assigned to your new layer appears in the color you selected in step 5 unless the object is specifically assigned a different color property.

USING TRUE OR PANTONE COLORS

When you choose a color from the Index Color tab of the Select Color dialog box, you'll most often find enough colors to suit your needs. But if you are creating a presentation drawing in which color selection is important, you can choose colors from either the True Color or the Color Books tab of the Select Color dialog box.

The True Color tab offers a full range of colors through a color palette similar to one in Adobe Photoshop and other image-editing programs.

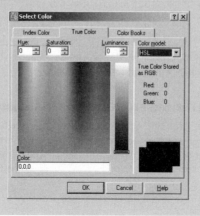

You can use hue, saturation, and luminance, which is the HSL color model, or you can use the RGB (red, green, blue) color model. You can select HSL or RGB from the Color Model drop-down list in the upper-right corner of the dialog box.

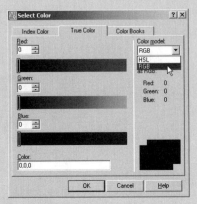

If you installed the PANTONE color option when you installed AutoCAD, you can also select from a PANTONE "color book" using the Color Books tab.

The color book option allows you to match colors to a PANTONE color book for offset printing.

TIP   The Files tab of the Options dialog box (choose Tools ➢ Options) contains the Color Book Location option, which tells AutoCAD where to look for the Color Book settings.

Understanding the Layer Properties Manager Dialog Box

The Layer Properties Manager dialog box shown in Figure 7.5 conforms to the Windows interface standard. The most prominent feature of this dialog box is the layer list box. Notice that the bar at the top of the list of layers includes several buttons for the various layer properties. Just as you can adjust

Windows Explorer, you can adjust the width of each column in the list of layers by clicking and dragging either side of the column head buttons. You can also sort the layer list based on a property simply by clicking the property name at the top of the list. You can Shift+click names to select a block of layer names, or you can Ctrl+click individual names to select multiples that do not appear together. These features become helpful as your list of layers enlarges.

FIGURE 7.5

The Layer Properties Manager dialog box

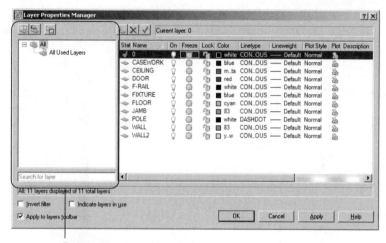

Tools for layer management tasks

Above the layer list, you'll see a box displaying the current layer. Just to the left of the current layer name are three tool buttons as shown in Figure 7.6.

FIGURE 7.6

Three tool buttons of the Layer Properties dialog box that let you create a new layer, delete a layer, or make a selected layer the current one

You've already seen how the New Layer tool works. The tool with the X icon is the Delete Layer tool. Select a layer or a group of layers and click this button to delete layers. Be aware that you cannot delete layer 0, locked layers, or layers that contain objects. The tool with the checkmark icon is the Current Layer tool. It allows you to set the current layer on which you want to work. The green checkmark under the Status column of the layer list indicates the current layer.

TIP   Another way to create or delete layers is to select a layer or set of layers from the list box and then right-click to display a menu that includes the same functions as the tools above the layer list.

You'll also notice another set of three tools farther to the left of the Layer Properties Manager dialog box. These tools offer features to organize your layers in a meaningful way. You'll get a closer look at these tools a little later in this chapter.

Assigning Layers to Objects

When you create an object, that object is automatically assigned to the current layer. In a brand-new drawing, there is only one layer called 0 (zero); so when you start to draw in a new drawing, objects are automatically assigned to the 0 layer. When you start to create new layers, you can reassign objects to them using the Properties palette:

1. Select the objects whose layer assignment you want to change.

2. With the cursor in the drawing area, right-click and choose Properties from the shortcut menu to open the Properties palette as shown in Figure 7.7.

FIGURE 7.7

The Properties palette

3. Click the Layer option. Notice that an arrow appears in the layer name to the right of the Layer option.

4. Click the downward-pointing arrow to the far right of the Layer option to display a list of all the available layers.

5. Select the desired layer name from the list. Press Esc to deselect.

6. Close the Properties palette by clicking the X button in the upper-left corner.

NOTE   If the color property of the selected objects is set to ByLayer, the objects take on the color of their new layer. The same is true for their linetype and line weight. On the other hand, if objects have their color property set to a specific color, linetype, or line weight, their layer assignment will not affect their appearance.

Another way to assign layers to existing objects is to use the Layer list in the Layers toolbar.

FIGURE 7.8
Selecting a layer from
the Layers toolbar

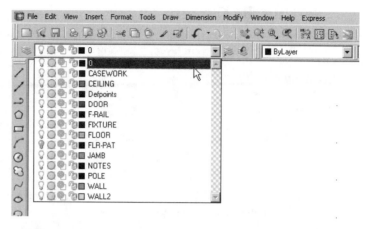

Normally this list displays the current layer, and you can set the current layer by selecting it from this list. But when you click an object with no other command active, the list changes to show you the name of the layer to which the selected object is assigned. Once an object is selected, you can easily change its layer assignment by selecting a new name from the layer list.

If you have multiple objects selected, and they all have different layer assignments, the list appears blank until you select a new layer from the list.

CONTROLLING COLORS AND LINETYPES OF BLOCKED OBJECTS

Layer 0 has special importance to blocks (see Chapter 8 for more on blocks). When objects assigned to Layer 0 are used as parts of a block, and that block is inserted on another layer, those objects take on the characteristics of their new layer. On the other hand, if those objects are on a layer other than Layer 0, they maintain their original layer characteristics even if you insert or change that block to another layer. For example, suppose the tub is drawn on the Door layer, instead of on Layer 0. If you turn the tub into a block and insert it on the Fixture layer, the objects the tub is composed of maintain their assignment to the Door layer, although the Tub block is assigned to the Fixture layer.

It might help to think of the block function as a clear plastic bag that holds together the objects that make up the tub. The objects inside the bag maintain their assignment to the Door layer even while the bag itself is assigned to the Fixture layer. This may be a bit confusing at first, but it should become clearer after using blocks for a while.

AutoCAD also allows you to have more than one color or linetype on a layer. For example, you can use the Color and Linetype buttons in the Change Properties palette (click the Object Properties button on the Standard toolbar) to alter the color or linetype of an object on Layer 0. That object then maintains its assigned color and linetype—no matter what its layer assignment. Likewise, objects specifically assigned a color or linetype are not affected by their inclusion in blocks.

Setting the Current Layer

All objects have a layer assignment, and by default, an object is assigned to the current layer. You can quickly identify the current layer by looking at the layer list in the Layer toolbar shown in Figure 7.9.

FIGURE 7.9

The layer list in the Layers toolbar

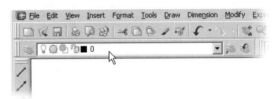

This list also lets you quickly control some of the layer features, including the current layer. Here's how to change the current layer.

1. Click the arrow button to the right of the layer name on the Object Properties toolbar to display a drop-down list, showing you all the layers available in the drawing as shown in Figure 7.10.

2. Click a layer name. The drop-down list closes, and the selected name appears in the toolbar's layer name box. It is now the current layer.

FIGURE 7.10

The opened layer list in the Layers toolbar

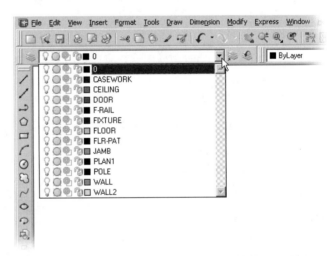

You might have noticed several icons that appear next to the layer names; these control the status of the layer. You'll learn how to work with these icons later in this chapter. Also notice the box directly to the left of each layer name. This shows you the color of the layer.

Controlling Layer Visibility

AutoCAD offers two methods for controlling layer visibility. The On and Off options turn a layer's visibility on or off. The Freeze and Thaw options not only control layer visibility, but when a layer is frozen, ignore the objects in the frozen layer. For large drawings, this can improve the speed of object snaps and other operations that search the drawing database.

Freeze and Thaw also have an effect on blocks that is different from the On and Off functions. A block inserted into a layer that has been turned off remains visible if its component objects are on a layer that is still turned on. But a block inserted into a layer that is frozen becomes invisible even though its component objects are on layers that are visible.

The Freeze and Thaw layer options offer a third option that involves viewports in the layout tabs. You can have multiple viewports in a layout tab (see Chapter 12 for more on viewports in layout tabs), and with the Freeze and Thaw options, you can control the visibility of layers for each viewport. This allows one viewport to display one set of layers, for example, and another viewport to display an entirely different set of layers. Figure 7.11 shows the contents of a layout tab with two viewports, each displaying the same drawing but with different Freeze and Thaw settings.

FIGURE 7.11

Two layout viewports displaying the same drawing with different layers frozen

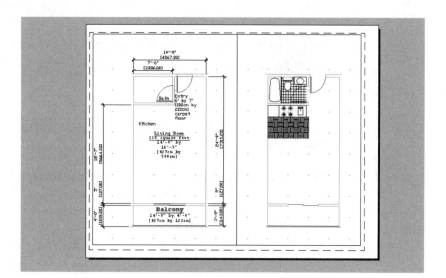

Controlling Layer Visibility Using the On/Off Option

You can use the Layer Manager to turn off layers:

1. Open the Layer Properties Manager dialog box.

2. In the Layer list, click the layer you want to turn off.

3. In the selected layer listing, click the lightbulb icon. The lightbulb icon changes from yellow to gray to indicate that the layer is off, as shown in Figure 7.12.

4. Click the OK button to exit the Layer Properties Manager dialog box. When you return to the drawing, all the objects on the layer you selected in step 2 disappear.

FIGURE 7.12
The lightbulb icon in the
Layer Properties Manag-
er dialog box

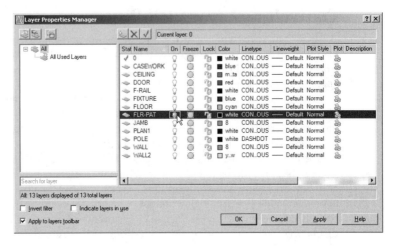

You can also control layer visibility using the Layer drop-down list on the Object Properties
toolbar:

1. On the Object Properties toolbar, click the Layer drop-down list.

2. Find the layer you want to turn off, and notice that its lightbulb icon is yellow. This tells you
   that the layer is on and visible.

3. Click the lightbulb icon to make it gray.

4. Now click the drawing area to close the Layer drop-down list, and the objects on the layer you
   turned off will disappear.

Controlling Layer Visibility with Freeze and Thaw

The Freeze and Thaw options work just like the On and Off options:

1. Open the Layer Properties Manager dialog box.

2. In the Layer list, click the layer you want to freeze.

3. In the selected layer listing, click the sun icon. The sun turns into a snowflake to indicate that
   the layer is frozen.

4. Click the OK button to exit the Layer Properties Manager dialog box. When you return to the
   drawing, all the objects on the layer you selected in step 2 disappear.

You can also control layer visibility using the Layer drop-down list on the Object Properties
toolbar.

1. On the Object Properties toolbar, click the Layer drop-down list.

2. Find the layer you want to freeze and click its sun icon. The options tool tip reads "Freeze or
   Thaw in All Viewports," as shown in Figure 7.13.

FIGURE 7.13

The Freeze Or Thaw In
All Viewports icon in the
Layer drop-down list

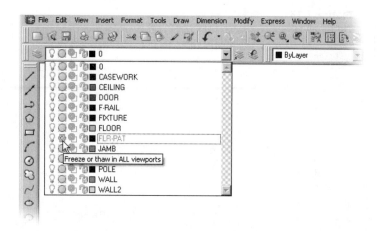

Controlling Layer Visibility in Individual Viewports of a Layout Tab

If you are in a layout tab and you open the Layer Properties Manager dialog box, you'll see two additional columns for each layer: Current VP Freeze and New VP Freeze, as shown in Figure 7.14.

FIGURE 7.14

The Current VP Freeze
and New VP Freeze icons
in the Layer Properties
Manager dialog box

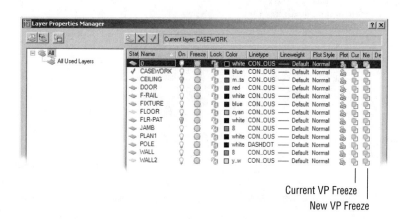

Current VP Freeze

New VP Freeze

The Current VP Freeze option controls the visibility of layers for the currently active viewport. This allows you to control layer visibility in one viewport without affecting the visibility of layers in other viewports in the layout tab. You use it just like the Freeze and Thaw option by clicking the Current VP Freeze sun icon to freeze a layer. You must, however, be in the floating model space of the viewport you want to affect. Here's how to get to the floating model space for a viewport:

1. Select the layout tab you want to use by clicking on a layout tab as shown in Figure 7.15.

2. Click the Paper button in the status bar as shown in Figure 7.16. This button is actually called the Model or Paper space button because its name changes depending on the current layout state.

   The button changes to read Model. You'll also notice that a UCS icon appears in each viewport and that one viewport has a darker border, as shown in Figure 7.17.

FIGURE 7.15
The layout tabs

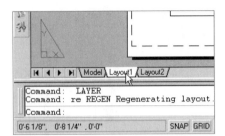

FIGURE 7.16
The Model or Paper
space button

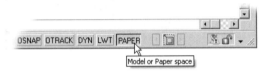

FIGURE 7.17
The UCS icon appears in
each viewport, and the
current viewport has a
darker border.

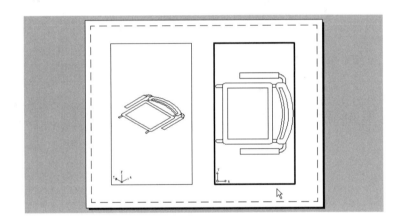

3. Click inside the viewport whose layer visibility you want to set.

4. Use the Current VP Freeze option in the Layer Properties Manager dialog box to set the visibility of layers for the selected viewport.

5. Exit the floating model space mode by clicking the Model button in the status bar (see Figure 7.18).

FIGURE 7.18
The Model button in
the status bar

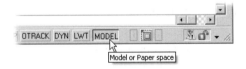

As an alternative, you can also use the Layer drop-down list to select the Current VP Freeze option. Click the Freeze Or Thaw In Current Viewport icon in the drop-down list to control layer visibility in individual viewports. It is the sun icon with a box behind it as shown in Figure 7.19.

FIGURE 7.19

The Freeze Or Thaw In Current Viewport icon in the Layer drop-down list

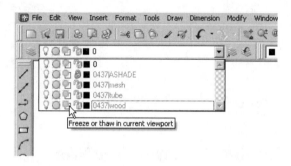

Locking Layers from Printing and Editing

You can lock layers so that you don't accidentally change objects assigned to them. This feature is useful when you are working on a crowded drawing and you don't want to accidentally edit portions of it. You can lock all the layers except those you intend to edit and then proceed to work without fear of making accidental changes. The lock option doesn't prevent others from editing the layer. It's just a tool to temporarily lock a layer from editing.

To use the lock option, click the lock icon in the layer listing in the Layer Properties Manager shown in the top half of Figure 7.20.

The Lock option also appears in the Layer drop-down list of the Object Properties toolbar (see the bottom image in Figure 7.20). The icon changes from an open padlock to a closed one.

Another similar tool is the Plot option. You can click the printer icon (in the Plot column) in the layer listing of the Layer Properties Manager dialog box to prevent a layer from plotting or printing (see Figure 7.21). The Plot option does not appear in the Layer drop-down list, however.

FIGURE 7.20

The Lock icon in the Layer Properties Manager dialog box

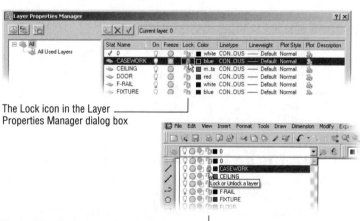

The Lock icon in the Layer Properties Manager dialog box

The Lock icon in the Layer drop-down list

FIGURE 7.21
The printer icon in the
Layer Properties Manag-
er dialog box

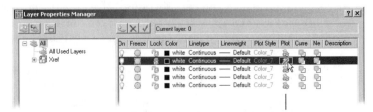

The Plot option shown as a printer icon

The layer is still visible, but it just won't print. This is a great option for layers that you use for layouts.

Finding the Layers You Want

With only a handful of layers, it's fairly easy to find the layer you want to turn off. It becomes much more difficult, however, when the number of layers exceeds 20 or 30. The Layer Properties Manager dialog box lets you control the list of layers in the same way that you can control filenames in Windows Explorer.

Suppose you have several layers whose names begin with C, such as C-lights, C-header, and C-pattern, and you want to find those layers quickly to turn them off. You can click the Name button at the top of the layer list to sort the layer names in alphabetic order. (You can click the Name button again to reverse the order.) To select those layers for processing, click the first layer name that starts with C; then scroll down the list until you find the last layer of the group and Shift+click it. All the layers between those layers are selected. You can then turn all the selected layers off by clicking one of the lightbulb icons of the selected group of layers.

To deselect some of those selected layers, hold down the Ctrl key while clicking the layer names you don't want to include in your selection. Or Ctrl+click other layer names you do want selected.

The Color and Linetype buttons at the top of the list let you sort the layer list by color or linetype assignments. Other buttons sort the list by virtue of the status: On/Off, Freeze/Thaw, Lock/Unlock, and so forth.

TIP You can quickly select all the layers in the list by right-clicking in the Layer Properties Manager dialog box and then choosing Select All. You can also choose Clear All to clear any selections, select all but current selections, and invert selections.

In the previous example, you turned off a set of layers with a single click of a lightbulb icon. You can freeze/thaw, lock/unlock, or change the color of a group of layers in a similar manner by clicking the appropriate layer property. For example, clicking a color swatch of one of the selected layers opens the Select Color dialog box, in which you can set the color for all the selected layers.

Taming an Unwieldy List of Layers

Chances are, you will eventually end up with a fairly long list of layers. Managing such a list can become a nightmare, but AutoCAD provides some tools that help you organize layers so that you can keep track of them more easily. Figure 7.22 shows the tools in the Layer Properties Manager dialog box that let you manage your layer lists and settings.

FIGURE 7.22
The filter and layer
state options in the Layer
Properties Manager
dialog box

In the upper-left corner of the Layer Properties Manager dialog box, you'll see a toolbar containing three tools that are designed to help with your layer management tasks. From left to right they are as follows:

New Property Filter Lets you filter your list of layers to display only layers with certain properties, such as specific colors or names.

New Group Filter Lets you create named groups of layers that can be quickly recalled at any time. It is helpful if you often work with specific sets of layers. For example, you might have a set of layers in an architectural drawing that pertains to the electrical layout. You can create a group filter called Electrical that filters out all layers except those pertaining to the electrical layout.

Layer State Manager Lets you create sets of layer states. For example, if you want to save the layer settings that just have the wall and door layer turned on, use the Layer State Manager tool.

The filters don't affect the layers in any way; they simply specify which layers are displayed in the main layer list.

Filtering Layers by Their Properties

Below the filter tools is the filter list, which is a hierarchical list displaying the sets of layer properties and group filters. Right now, you don't have any filters in place, so you only see the All and All Used Layers. The following steps show you how these tools and the filter list box work. You'll start with a look at the New Properties Filter tool.

1. Open the Layer Properties Manager dialog box.

2. Click the New Property Filter tool in the upper-left corner of the dialog box (see Figure 7.22) to open the Layer Properties Filter dialog box, as shown in Figure 7.23.

   You see two list boxes. The Filter Definition list box at the top is where you enter your filter criteria. The Filter Preview list box below is a preview of your layer list based on the filter options. Unless you've already used the Property Filter tool, there are no filter options, so the Filter Preview list shows all the layers.

3. In the Filter Definition list box, click the blank box just below the Color label. A browse button appears in the box (see Figure 7.24).

FIGURE 7.23

The Layer Properties
Filter dialog box

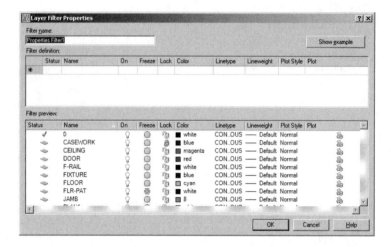

FIGURE 7.24

The browse button
below the Color label
in the Filter Definition
list box

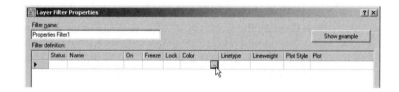

4. Click in the blank box again, and then enter **red**↵. The Filter Preview changes to show only layers that are red. In the current drawing, only one layer has been assigned the color red.

5. Click twice in the blank box below the one you just edited. Again you see a button appear.

6. This time, enter **green**↵. Now the layers that are green appear in the Filter Preview list.

TIP You can also select a color from the Select Color dialog box by clicking the button that appears in the box.

7. In the Filter Definition list, click in the Name column in the third row down. Notice that a cursor appears followed by an asterisk.

8. Enter the letter for the layer names you want to sort and then press ↵. Now you see two new layers added to the Filter Preview whose name begins with the letter you entered.

9. In the Filter Name input box at the upper-left corner of the dialog box, change the name Properties Filter 1 to something more meaningful for this list, and then click OK. Now you see the new filter name in the list box on the left side of the Layer Properties Manager dialog box (see Figure 7.25).

You might also notice that the layer list shows only the layers whose properties conform to those you selected in the Layer Properties Filter dialog box.

FIGURE 7.25
The new filter name appears in the left side of the Layer Properties Manager dialog box.

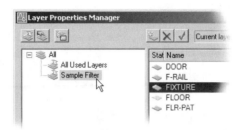

Once you create a new filter, it will be highlighted in the filter list to the left. This tells you that the new filter is the current layer property filter being applied to the layer list to the right. You can change the layer list display by selecting options in the filter list.

1. Click the All option in the filter list at the left side of the dialog box as shown in Figure 7.26.

FIGURE 7.26
Click the All option in the Layer Properties Manager dialog box.

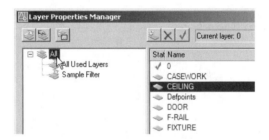

The layer list to the right changes to display all the layers in the drawing. You'll also see a brief description of current layer filter at the bottom of the dialog box.

2. Click the All Used Layer option in the filter list. Now only layers that contain objects are displayed.

3. Click the new list you created. The layer list changes back to the limited set of layers from your filter list.

4. Double-click you new list. The Layer Properties Filter dialog box opens and displays the list of layer properties you set up earlier for that list. You can edit the criteria for your filter by making modifications in this dialog box.

5. Click Cancel to exit the Layer Properties Filter dialog box.

Creating Layer Groups by Selection

Suppose you want to create a layer filter list by graphically selecting objects on the screen. You can use the New Group Filter tool to do just that.

1. In the upper-left corner of the Layer Properties Manager dialog box, click the New Group Filter tool shown in Figure 7.27. You see a new listing appear called Group Filter 1.

FIGURE 7.27

The New Group
Filter tool in the Layer
Properties Manager
dialog box

2. Right-click the Group Filter1 listing, and then choose Select Layers ➢ Add from the shortcut menu. The Layer Properties Manager dialog box temporarily closes to allow you to select objects in your drawing. Notice that your cursor is now a selection cursor.

3. Click a set of objects whose layers you want included in your filter. Press ↵ when you are finished with your selection. The Layer Properties Manager dialog box reappears, and now you see the layers of the objects you selected displayed in the layer list. Also note that Group Filter1 is highlighted in the filter list to the left as shown in Figure 7.28.

FIGURE 7.28

The Group Filter-1 list
after selecting objects

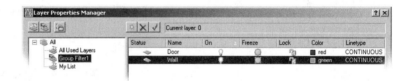

TIP   You may have noticed the Select Layers ➢ Replace option in the shortcut menu in step 2. This option lets you completely replace an existing group filter with a new selection set. It works just like choosing Select Layers ➢ Add.

Earlier, you saw how you can double-click a properties filter to edit a properties filter list. But group filters work in a slightly different way. If you want to add layers to your group filter, you can click and drag them from the layer list to the group filter name. Here's how it's done.

1. In the Layer Properties Manager dialog box, select All from the filter list to the left.

2. Click a layer or set of layers in the layer list to select them. You'll add these layers to the Group Filter1 layer group.

3. Click and drag selected layers to the Group Filter1 listing in the filter list to the left.

4. To check the addition to the Group Filter1 list, click it in the filter list. The selected layers are added to the Group Filter1 list.

To delete a layer from a group filter, follow these steps:

1. With Group Filter1 selected, select the layer name you want to delete from the list, and then right-click it.

2. Select Remove From Group Filter in the shortcut menu. The layer is removed from the Group Filter1 list.

TIP You can also convert a layer properties filter into a group filter. Select the layer properties filter from the filter list, right-click, then choose Convert To Group Filter. The icon for the layer properties filter changes to a group filter icon indicating that it is now a group filter.

Applying Filters to the Properties Toolbar Layer List and Other Options

You'll want to know about some additional options just below the filter list (see Figure 7.29). The Invert Filter option changes the list of layers to show all layers *excluding* those in the selected filter. For example, if your new filter contains red layers, and you select Invert Filter, the layer list displays all layers *except* those whose color is red. The Apply To Layers Toolbar option, when turned on, applies the selected filter to the layer drop-down list found in the Properties toolbar.

FIGURE 7.29
The Invert Filter option and the Apply To Layers Toolbar option.

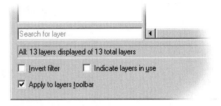

Finally, you'll see a text input box directly below the filter list containing the words *Search for Layer*. You can enter portions of a layer name in this text box to apply additional filters to the layer list currently being displayed. For example, you can enter **G*** in this text input box to display only layers whose name begins with G in the current layer list.

In the next section, I'll give you some tips on how to use layer names with text filters more effectively.

Saving and Recalling Layer Settings

As you start to work with AutoCAD, you'll find that you'll want to set up layers a certain way to edit your drawing. As you progress through your editing session, you'll turn layers on and off. Eventually you want to return to the layer settings you had when you started. You can use the Layer States Manager dialog box to store the way your layers are set up so that you can quickly return to that setup or state when you are done editing.

The ability to save layer states can be crucial when you are editing a file that serves multiple uses, such as a floor plan and reflected ceiling plan. You can, for example, turn layers on and off to set up the drawing for a reflected ceiling plan view and then save the layer settings. Later, when you need to modify the ceiling information, you can recall the layer setting to view the ceiling data. Let's see how the Layer States Manager dialog box works.

Open the Layer Properties Manager dialog box and click the Layer States Manager button to open the Layer States Manager dialog box, as shown in Figure 7.30.

Take a moment to look at the options in this dialog box. This is where you can also specify which layer settings you want saved with this layer state.

Save the current layer state by taking the following steps:

1. Click the New button in the Layer States Manager dialog box to open the New Layer State To Save dialog box shown in Figure 7.31.

FIGURE 7.30

The Layer States
Manager dialog box

FIGURE 7.31

The New Layer State
To Save dialog box

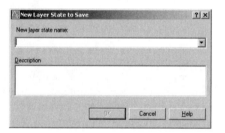

2. Enter a name for the layer state in the New Layer State Name input box. Note that you can also enter a brief description of your layer state. Click OK to return to the Layer States Manager dialog box.

You've just saved a layer state. The following steps demonstrate how you can restore the saved layer state.

3. Click the Layer States Manager button to open the Layer States Manager dialog box.

4. Select the name of the layer state you want to restore from the list, and then click Restore. You return to the Layer Properties Manager dialog box. Notice that the layer settings have changed back to the settings you saved.

The layer states are saved with the file so you can retrieve them at a later date. As you can see from the Layer States Manager dialog box, you have a few other options:

Delete deletes a layer state from the list.

Import imports a set of layer states that have been exported using the Export option of this dialog box.

Export saves a set of layer states as a file. By default, the file is given the name of the current file with the .lay filename extension. You can import the layer state file into other files.

In addition to saving layer states by name, you can quickly revert to a previous layer state by clicking the Layer Previous tool in the left side of the Layers toolbar.

This tool lets you quickly revert to the previous layer settings without affecting other settings in AutoCAD. Note that the Layer Previous mode does not restore renamed or deleted layers, nor does it remove new layers.

Once you become familiar with these layer state tools, you'll find yourself using them frequently in your editing sessions.

TIP The Layerpmode command controls the tracking of layer states. It is normally turned on, but if it is turned off, the Layer Previous tool will not work. To turn it on, enter **Layerpmode↵ On↵**.

Express Tools Layer Options for Managing Layers

The Layer command is one of the most frequently used AutoCAD features, so the Express tools layer options are handy shortcuts for controlling layer settings. If you find yourself having to work with files that other people have created, you might want to review the material in this section.

TIP All the tools discussed in this section have keyboard command equivalents. Check the status bar when selecting these tools from the toolbar or drop-down menu for the keyboard command name.

Saving Layer States through Express Tools

The Express Tools Layer Manager dialog box lets you save layer settings. It performs the same functions as the Layer States Manager button in the Layer Properties Manager dialog box described earlier in this chapter.

Since the Express Tools Layer Manager dialog box has been around longer than the Layer States Manager dialog box, it lets you use layer states from older drawings. This is important as CAD drawings are often brought back from archives after a long period of inactivity. It's not unusual to work on a file that is several AutoCAD versions old.

To use the Express Tools Layer Manager dialog box, Choose Express ➢ Layers ➢ Layer Manager or click the Layer Manager tool in the Express Tools Layers toolbar to open the Layer Manager dialog box, as shown in Figure 7.32.

To save the current layer state, click the Save button to open the Layer State Name dialog box, enter a name for your layer state, and then click OK. When you return to the Layer Manager dialog box, You'll notice that the name you entered for the layer state appears in the list box. You can then close the dialog box.

FIGURE 7.32

The Layer Manager dialog box

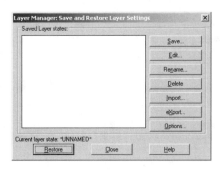

To restore a layer state, click the Layer Manager tool, select the name of the layer state you want to restore from the list, and then click Restore.

The layer states are saved with the file so you can retrieve them later. As you can see from the Layer Manager dialog box, you have a few other options. Here is a listing of those options and what they do:

Edit opens the Layer & Linetype Properties dialog box in which you edit the settings for a layer state. Highlight the layer state from the list, and then click Edit.

Rename renames a layer state in the list.

Delete deletes a layer state from the list.

Import imports a set of layer states that have been exported using the Export option of this dialog box.

Export saves a set of layer states as a file. By default, the file is given the name of the current file with the `.lay` filename extension. You can import the layer state file into other files.

Options displays a list of the states you can save and restore. When you select Options, the Layer Manager Restore Options dialog box opens with a list of checkboxes. You can check the items you want to save as part of the layer state. The list includes all the standard layer properties such as the on/off and freeze/thaw state, lock/unlock, color, linetype, line weight, plot status, and plot style status.

WARNING   The Express Tool Layer Manager dialog box does not share layer states with the Save State and State Manager options in the Layer Properties Manager dialog box. If you start to save layer states in the Express Tool Layer Manager dialog box, you cannot manage layer states using the Layer Properties Manager dialog box and vice versa. You can still use both tools; just don't expect to load layer states across tools.

Exploring Layers with Layer Walk

When you work with a file that has been produced by someone else, you usually have to spend some time getting familiar with the way layers are set up. This can be tedious, but the Express Tools Layer Walk tool can help.

As the name implies, the Express Tools Layer Walk tool lets you "walk through" the layers of a file, visually isolating each layer as you select the layer's name from a list. You can use Layer Walk to select the layers that you want visible, or you can turn layers on and off to explore a drawing without affecting the current layer settings.

To open the LayerWalk dialog box shown in Figure 7.33, choose Express ➤ Layers ➤ Layer Walk or click the Layer Walk tool in the Express Tools Layers toolbar.

FIGURE 7.33
The LayerWalk dialog box

You can click and drag the bottom edge of the dialog box to expand the list so that you can see all the layers in the drawing. You'll see several if not all of the layers in the list highlighted. The highlighted layers are currently turned on and visible. Layers that are not selected in the list are off and not visible. The following list describes how you can use the list to explore the layers in a drawing:

- Ctrl+click any unselected layer in the list to make it temporarily visible without affecting the visibility of the other layers.

- Ctrl+click any selected layer in the list to temporarily turn it off and make it invisible without affecting the visibility of other layers.

- Click a layer name to isolate it. The selected layer will be the only one visible in the drawing.

- Right-click and choose Inverse Selection from the shortcut menu to invert the layer selection. This also inverts the visibility of layers.

- To select layers that do not have objects assigned to them, right-click in the LayerWalk dialog box, and choose Select Unreferenced from the shortcut menu. Since there are no objects on unreferenced layers, all the objects in your drawing disappear.

- You can remove unreferenced layers from the drawing by clicking the Purge button.

- To select all the layers in the list, right-click in the LayerWalk dialog box again, and choose Select All from the shortcut menu. All the layers of your drawing are made visible.

- To unselect all the layers, right-click in the LayerWalk dialog box, and then choose Clear All from the shortcut menu.

You can also lock layers so that they remain visible as you explore the layer in the LayerWalk dialog box. Ctrl+click a set of layers to make them visible, and then right-click and choose Hold Selection from the shortcut menu. Asterisks appear to the left of the selected layer names. Now as you randomly click layer names from the list, the layers with the asterisks remain visible. The Hold Selection option temporarily locks them on so that other selections do not affect their visibility.

Changing the Layer Assignment of Objects

In addition to the Layer Manager and Layer Walk tools, the Express Tools Layers toolbar includes two tools that change the layer assignments of objects. The Match Objects Layer tool is similar to the Match Properties tool, but is streamlined to operate only on layer assignments. Click this tool, select the object or objects you want to change, and then select an object whose layer you want to match.

The Change To Current Layer tool changes an object's layer assignment to the current layer.

Controlling Layer Settings through Objects

The remaining Express Tools in the Layers toolbar let you make layer settings by selecting objects in the drawing. These tools are easy to use: simply click the tool, and then select an object. These tools are so helpful that you might want to consider docking them permanently in your AutoCAD window:

Isolate Object's Layer turns off all the layers except for the layer of the selected object.

Freeze Object's Layer freezes the layer of the selected object.

Turn Object's Layer Off turns off the layer of the selected object.

Lock Object's Layer locks the layer of the selected object. A locked layer is visible but cannot be edited.

Unlock Object's Layer unlocks the layer of the selected object.

Organizing Visual Content through Properties

Part of your work with AutoCAD will involve organizing your drawings visually. You can use color, line weight, and linetypes, such as dashed and center lines, to help keep your drawing orderly and understandable. Color is often used to help identify the layer an object is assigned to or to identify the object's category, such as plumbing or electrical. Color was once the only way to control line weights in AutoCAD, and you might still see drawings that use color to determine line weight. Line weights are also a controllable property, and they can greatly enhance the readability of your drawings. Linetypes have always been used to identify control or datum lines in technical drawings. Center lines, property lines, fences, and other types of noncontinuous lines are essential to any drawing you'll be doing.

You can assign color, line weight, and linetypes through layers. You might notice that layers show color, line weight, and linetypes as part of their attributes. By clicking any one of those attributes in the Layer Properties Manager dialog box, you can change their value. You can also set the color, line weight, and linetype of individual objects.

You've already learned how to set the color of a layer. The following section shows you how to set linetypes and line weights.

Assigning Linetypes to Layers

You will often want to use different linetypes to show hidden lines, center lines, fence lines, or other noncontinuous lines. AutoCAD comes with several linetypes, as shown in Figure 7.34. You then see ISO and complex linetypes, including lines that can illustrate gas and water lines in civil work or batt insulation in a wall cavity. ISO linetypes are designed to be used with specific plotted line widths and linetype scales. For example, if you are using a pen width of 0.5 mm, set the linetype scale of the drawing to 0.5 as well. The complex linetypes at the bottom of the figure are industry-specific.

WARNING Linetypes that contain text, such as the gas sample, use the current text style's height and font to determine the size and appearance of the text displayed in the line. A text height of 0 (zero) displays the text properly in most cases. See Chapter 9 for more on text styles.

AutoCAD stores linetype descriptions in an external file named Acad.lin or Acadiso.lin for metric users. You can edit this file in a word processor to create new linetypes or to modify existing ones, though customizing linetypes is beyond the scope of this book.

LinetypeThe default linetype in a new drawing is the continuous linetype. If you want to use a different linetype, you must load it from the linetype file. Here's how that's done.

1. Open the Layers Properties Manager dialog box, and then select All from the Filter list.

2. Click the word *Continuous* that appears in the layer listing (in the Linetype column) to which you will assign the new linetype. This opens the Select Linetype dialog box, as shown in Figure 7.35. To find the Linetype column, you might need to scroll the list to the right using the scroll bar at the bottom of the list.

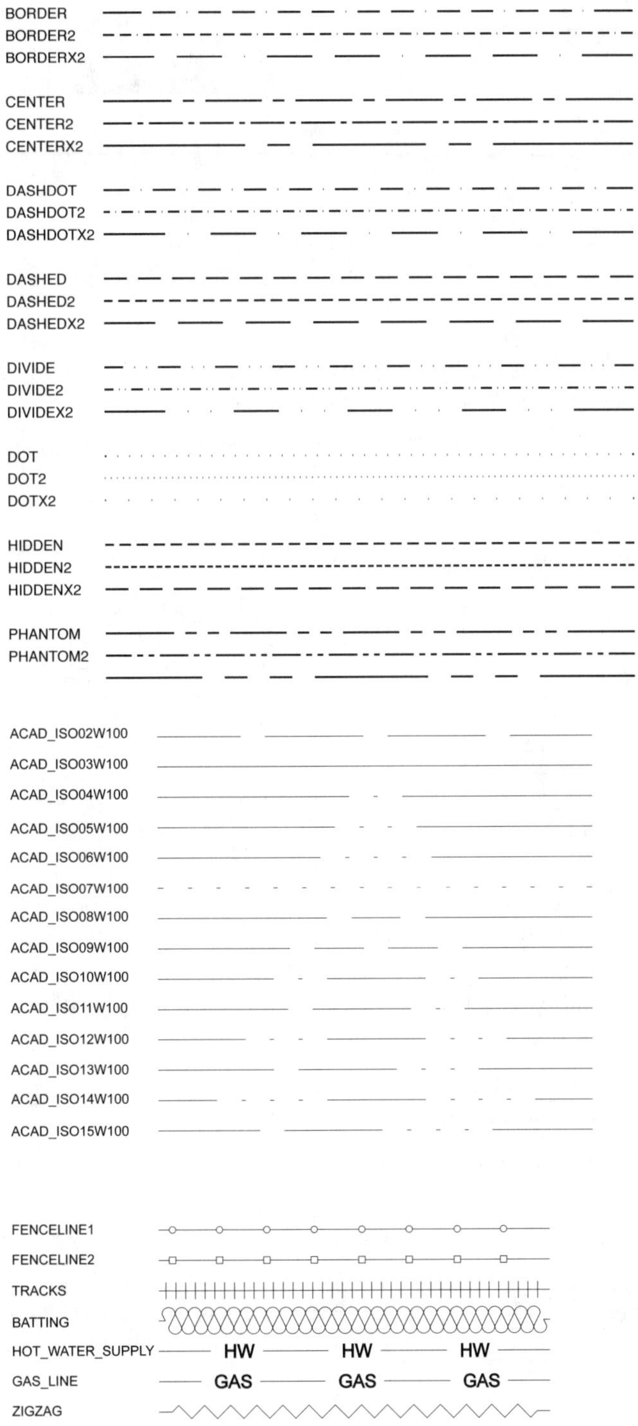

FIGURE 7.34 Standard , ISO, and complex AutoCAD linetypes

FIGURE 7.35

The Select Linetype
dialog box

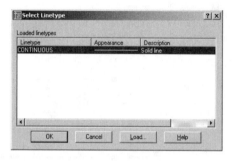

The Select Linetype dialog box displays a list of linetypes to choose from. In a new file, only one linetype is available by default. You must load any additional linetype you want to use. Once a linetype is loaded, it is available for use at any time.

3. Click the Load button at the bottom of the dialog box to open the Load Or Reload Linetypes dialog box shown in Figure 7.36.

FIGURE 7.36

The Load Or Reload Line-
types dialog box

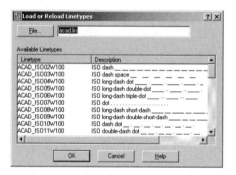

Notice that the list of linetype names is similar to the Layer drop-down list. You can sort the names alphabetically or by description by clicking the Linetype or Description headings at the top of the list.

4. In the Available Linetypes list, scroll down to locate the Dashdot linetype, click it, and then click OK.

5. Notice that the Dashdot linetype is now added to the linetypes available in the Select Linetype dialog box.

6. Click Dashdot to highlight it; then click OK. Now Dashdot appears in the currently selected layer under the Linetype heading.

7. Click OK to exit the Load Or Reload Linetypes dialog box.

Once you've assigned a linetype to a layer, any object assigned to that layer is drawn using that linetype, unless the object is specifically assigned a linetype. Objects can be assigned a linetype on an individual basis through the Properties palette described in Chapter 4.

Controlling Linetype Scale

The appearance of a linetype depends closely on the linetype scale setting in AutoCAD. The linetype scale controls the frequency of the dashes or dots in the linetype. For example, a dashed linetype can appear with 2 dashes per foot in a drawing or 10 dashes per foot, depending on the linetype scale, as shown in Figure 7.37.

FIGURE 7.37
The same linetype using two different linetype scales

You can set the linetype scale in two ways:

◆ To a value that makes noncontinuous linetypes appear properly in the Model tab, which is where you spend most of your time creating and editing drawing

◆ To a value that makes noncontinuous linetypes appear properly when your drawings are displayed and plotted from a layout tab

Linetypes appear properly in one tab but incorrectly in the other, so you have to decide where you want the linetype to appear properly and then set the linetype scale accordingly.

TIP Typically, you can set the linetype scale to the default of 1 and the linetypes appear properly in the layout tabs for plotting. The tricky part is to change the linetype scale setting so that linetypes appear properly in the Model tab.

LINETYPE

By default, the linetype scale is set to 1. This setting often makes noncontinuous linetypes appear as if they were standard continuous lines while in the Model tab. You might want the linetypes to appear as they would when you plot the drawing from the Layout tab. To do this, you need to change the linetype scale to something closer to the scale of the drawing.

Here's an example of how to set the linetype scale for an architectural drawing whose scale is $\frac{1}{4}'' = 1'$.

1. Choose Format ➤ Linetype or select Other from the Linetype drop-down list in the Properties toolbar (see Figure 7.38) to open the Linetype Manager dialog box.

FIGURE 7.38
The Other option from the Linetype drop-down list in the Properties toolbar

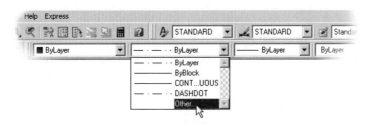

2. Click the Show Details button in the upper-right corner to display some additional options at the bottom of the dialog box, as shown in Figure 7.39.

TIP You might notice that the Linetype tab of the Layer Properties Manager dialog box also contains the Load and Delete buttons that you saw in step 4 of the previous exercise. These offer a way to load or delete a linetype directly, without having to go through a particular layer's linetype setting.

FIGURE 7.39
Additional options in the Linetype Manager dialog box appear at the bottom when you click the Show Details button.

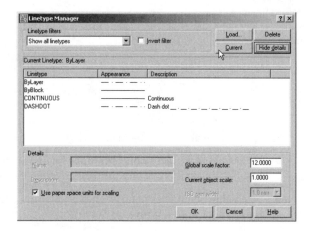

3. Double-click the Global Scale Factor text box, and then type **48**. This is the scale you will need for a ¼″ to a foot scale drawing. Start here. (See the "Understanding Scale Factors" sidebar later in this chapter.)

4. Click OK. If you have drawn any lines using a noncontinuous linetype, these change to reflect the new value.

TIP You can also use the Ltscale system variable to set the linetype scale. Type **Ltscale↵**, and at the LTSCALE New scale factor <1.0000>: prompt, enter **12↵**.

Remember that if you assign a linetype to a layer, everything you draw on that layer is of that linetype. This includes arcs, polylines, circles, and traces.

TABLE 7.1: Scale Conversion Factors

SCALE FACTORS FOR ENGINEERING DRAWING SCALES								
1″ = n	10′	20′	30′	40′	50′	60′	100′	200′
Scale factor	120	240	360	480	600	720	1200	2400
SCALE FACTORS FOR ARCHITECTURAL DRAWING SCALES								
n = 1′-0″	1/16″	1/8″	1/4″	1/2″	3/4″	1″	1½″	3″
Scale factor	192	96	48	24	16	12	8	4

UNDERSTANDING SCALE FACTORS

To properly display linetypes in the Model tab, you need to know which scale factor to use. The scale factor for fractional inch scales is derived by multiplying the denominator of the scale by 12 and then dividing by the numerator. For example, the scale factor for $\frac{1}{4}'' = 1'\text{-}0''$ is $(4 \times 12)/1$, or $48/1$. For $\frac{3}{16}'' = 1'\text{-}0''$ scale, the operation is $(16 \times 12)/3$, or 64. For whole-foot scales, such as $1'' = 10'$, multiply the feet side of the equation by 12. Metric scales require simple decimal conversions. Table 7.1 shows some standard scale conversion factors used in civil and architectural drawings.

You also use scale factors to translate text size in your CAD drawing to the final plotted text size. In AutoCAD, you need to translate the desired final text size to the drawing scale.

When you start adding text to your drawing (see Chapter 9), you have to specify a text height. The scale factor helps you determine the appropriate text height for a particular drawing scale. For example, you might want your text to appear $\frac{1}{8}''$ high in your final plot. But if you draw your text to $\frac{1}{8}''$, it appears as a dot when plotted. The text has to be scaled up to a size that, when scaled back down at plot time, appears $\frac{1}{8}''$ high. So, for a $\frac{1}{4}''$ scale drawing, you multiply the $\frac{1}{8}''$ text height by a scale factor of 48 to get 6″. Your text should be 6″ high in the CAD drawing in order to appear $\frac{1}{8}''$ high in the final plot.

You will use scale factors to specify text height and dimension settings, so understanding them now will pay off later. Plotting to a particular scale will also be easier with an understanding of scale factors.

TIP If you change the linetype of a layer or object but the object remains a continuous line, check the `Ltscale` system variable. It should be set to your drawing scale factor. If this doesn't work, set the `Viewres` system variable to a higher value. (You can set Viewres using the Arc And Circle Smoothness option in the Display tab of the Options dialog box.) The behavior of linetype scales depends on whether you are in Model Space or in a drawing layout. See Chapter 12 for more on Model Space and layouts.

Setting Line Weights

The Lineweight option in the Layer Properties Manager dialog box lets you control the thickness of your lines by adjusting the Lineweight setting. Lineweight settings are designed specifically for printer and plotter output, and you may not see true line weights in the Model tab. They do appear correctly, however, in the layout tabs when you set up AutoCAD to display line weights. Figure 7.40 shows a sample view of a drawing from the layout tab.

FIGURE 7.40

Sample image of different line weights used in AutoCAD

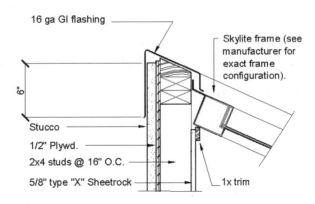

TURNING ON LINE WEIGHT VISIBILITY

By default, AutoCAD does not display line weights in either the Model tab or in the layout tabs. You can turn them on using the Lineweight Settings dialog box shown in Figure 7.41. To open the Lineweight Settings dialog box, choose Format ➤ Lineweight or enter **Lweight⏎** at the Command prompt.

FIGURE 7.41
The Lineweight Settings
dialog box

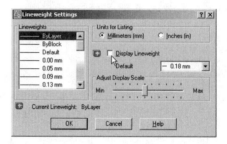

To turn on the display of line weights, click the Display Lineweight option. You can also control the degree to which AutoCAD displays line weights using the Adjust Display Scale slider.

SETTING LINE WEIGHTS THROUGH THE LAYER PROPERTIES MANAGER DIALOG BOX

Just as you can control color and linetypes through layers, you can also control line weights through layers. The Lineweight option in the Layer Properties Manager dialog box controls the line weight for each layer. When you click the Line Weight column for a layer, the Lineweight dialog box opens (see Figure 7.42), showing you the line weight options.

FIGURE 7.42
The Lineweight
dialog box

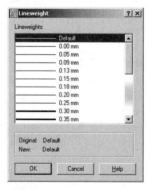

You can select a line weight from the list to assign it to the selected layer or layers. Objects assigned to that layer plot with the assigned line weight.

SETTING LINE WEIGHTS DIRECTLY TO OBJECTS

You can also assign a line weight directly to an object in your drawing. The simplest way to do this is to click the object while no command is active and then select a line weight from the Line Weight Control drop-down list in the Properties toolbar (see Figure 7.43).

FIGURE 7.43

The Lineweight Control drop-down list in the Properties toolbar

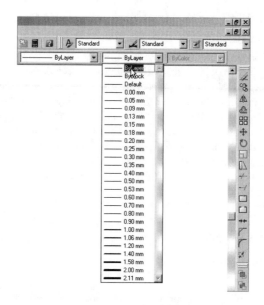

Another place to set line weights for objects is through the Properties palette. Select the objects whose line weight you want to change, and then click the Properties tool in the Standard toolbar. You can then click in the Lineweight option of the Properties palette and select a line weight from the drop-down list (see Figure 7.44).

Yet another way to set line weights is through the plot style tables. If you encounter a drawing in which you seem unable to control the plotted line weights, chances are the line weight settings are set up in the plot style tables for the drawing. See Chapter 12 for more on the plot style tables.

FIGURE 7.44

Lineweight settings in the Properties palette

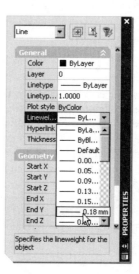

Setting Colors, Linetypes, Linetype Scales, and Line Weights for Individual Objects

If you prefer, you can set up AutoCAD to assign specific colors, linetypes, linetype scales, and line weights to objects, instead of having objects inherit these settings from the layer to which they are assigned. Normally, objects are given default, nongeometric properties called ByLayer, which means each object takes on the color, linetype, linetype scale, and line weight of its assigned layer. (You've probably noticed the word *ByLayer* in the Object Properties toolbar and in various dialog boxes.)

Click the Properties tool on the Standard toolbar to change any properties of existing objects. (See Chapter 4 for more on the Properties tool and palette.) This tool opens the Properties palette that lets you set the properties of individual objects. For new objects, use the Color, Linetype, or Line Weight drop-down list on the Properties toolbar to set the current default values for these properties (see Figure 7.45).

FIGURE 7.45

The Color, Linetype, and Line Weight options on the Properties toolbar

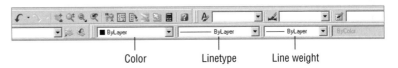

Color   Linetype   Line weight

The Color drop-down list also contains the Select Color option (see Figure 7.46). Click it to open the Select Color dialog box.

FIGURE 7.46

The Select Color option in the Color drop-down list

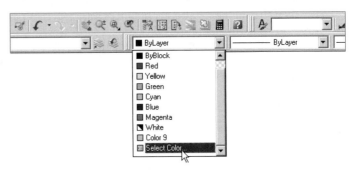

This dialog box lets you select from a broad range of colors. Select a color from the Select Color dialog box, then everything you draw will be in the selected color, regardless of the current layer color.

For linetypes, you can use the Linetype drop-down list in the Properties toolbar to select a default linetype for all new objects. The list shows only linetypes that have already been loaded into the drawing, so you must first load a linetype before you can select it. You can do so by selecting the Other option from the drop-down list shown in Figure 7.47.

FIGURE 7.47

The Other option in the Linetype drop-down list

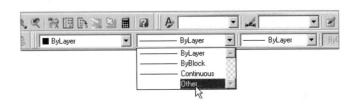

The Line Weight drop-down list displays a list of line weights to choose from.

If you want to set the linetype scale for each individual object, instead of relying on the global line-type scale (the `Ltscale` system variable), you can use the Properties palette to modify the linetype scale of individual objects. (See Figure 7.48.)

FIGURE 7.48

The Linetype scale option in the Properties palette

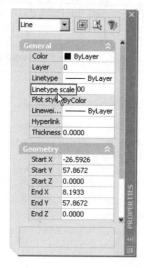

To set the linetype scale to be applied to new objects, set the Linetype Scale value in the Properties palette while no objects are selected. In place of using the Properties palette, you can set the `Celtscale` system variable to the linetype scale you want for new objects.

In the previous section, you saw how to change the global linetype scale setting. This affects all noncontinuous linetypes within the current drawing. You can also change the linetype scale of indi-vidual objects by clicking the Properties button on the Object Properties toolbar. Or you can set the default linetype scale for all new objects, with the Current Object Scale option in the Linetype Man-ager dialog box.

When individual objects are assigned a linetype scale, they are still affected by the global linetype scale set by the `Ltscale` system variable. For example, say you assign a linetype scale of 2 to a dashed line. This assigned scale of 2 is then multiplied by the global linetype scale of 12, for a final linetype scale of 24.

TIP You can also set the default Linetype Scale setting for individual objects using the `Celtscale` system variable. Once it is set, only newly created objects are affected. You must use the Properties tool to change the linetype scale of individual existing objects.

If the objects you draw appear in a different linetype from that of the layer they are on, check the default linetype using the Linetype Control drop-down list on the Object Properties toolbar. You can also choose Format ➤ Linetype. Then, in the Linetype Manager dialog box, highlight ByLayer in the Linetype list, and click the Current button. In addition, check the linetype scale of the object itself, using the Properties palette. A different linetype scale can make a line appear to have an assigned linetype that may not be what you expect.

UNDERSTANDING THE BYBLOCK SETTING

As you explore the Layer Properties Manager dialog box and the various object properties settings, you'll see a setting called ByBlock. ByBlock makes everything you draw white (or black depending on the background color), until you turn your drawing into a block and then insert the block on a layer with an assigned color. The objects then take on the color of that layer. This behavior is similar to that of objects drawn on Layer 0. This option is available if you want objects to have a layer assignment other than zero, but you want the objects to acquire the color or linetype of the block they are combined with. The ByBlock linetype works similarly to the ByBlock color.

Just Enough Summary

AutoCAD's layer system is quite complex and can be daunting to the first-time user. But you don't have to learn everything about layers at one sitting. First, just understand the basics, what layers are used for and that all objects have a layer assignment. Then learn how layers are created and how objects are assigned to layers. Next you'll want to know about the ways layers can be turned on and off. After that, you can explore the other layer options as needed.

In conjunction with layers, you'll want an understanding of how object properties work and how they interact with layers. This is an area you should have at least some familiarity with even as a beginner. Understanding properties will help you understand many of the other ways that AutoCAD can help you organize drawings.

Chapter 8

Blocks, Groups, Xrefs, and DesignCenter

One of AutoCAD's best qualities is its ability to let you get the most mileage from your drawings. AutoCAD includes several features that help you organize your work so that a single drawing can serve multiple purposes. You can also create sets of objects that can be easily reproduced and modified. To get the most out of AutoCAD, you'll want to be as familiar as possible with these organizational features.

One of the most frequently used features is the block, which is a collection of objects that behaves like a single object. Blocks can be duplicated easily, like images from a rubber stamp. And if you need to make a change to several duplicate blocks, you can change one block, and all the copies of that block update to reflect the change.

The difference between blocks and groups is that individual objects within a group are much easier to edit. Copies of groups do not inherit changes from edits made to a group. You can think of the group as a tool to help you keep similar objects together.

Finally, you can import entire drawings if you want to use parts of a drawing as a background. For example, for a large project, one drawing might show the entire floor plan, and several others might show only enlarged portions of that plan. This way, you can get "double duty" from one drawing by using it in several other drawings. Drawings that are imported this way are called external references, or xrefs for short.

Here's a summary of what you'll find in this chapter:

◆ Using Blocks to Organize Objects

◆ Organizing Objects Using Groups

◆ Getting Multiple Uses from Drawings Using External References

◆ Keeping Track of Drawing Components with DesignCenter

◆ Keeping Tools on Hand with Tool Palettes

Using Blocks to Organize Objects

Blocks are one of the oldest methods for grouping objects in AutoCAD. Used properly, they can be a real time-saver. They have the unique ability to be edited globally. For example, you can create a drawing of a chair and then turn it into a block so that the chair behaves as one object. You can then make hundreds of copies of that chair by copying its block form. If you need to modify the chair later, you can modify one copy, and all the other chairs update automatically.

Creating a Block

You can easily create blocks from existing objects by following these steps:

1. In the Draw toolbar, click the Make Block tool, type **B⏎**, or choose Draw ➤ Block ➤ Make to open the Block Definition dialog box (see Figure 8.1).

2. In the Name text box, enter a name for your block. You need to give the block a name to make it easily identifiable from lists or other dialog boxes.

3. In the Base Point section, click the Pick Point button. This option lets you select a base or an insertion point for the block using your cursor. (The insertion point of a block is like its primary grip point. It is the first point you use to locate the block when it is first inserted into a drawing.) After you select this option, the Block Definition dialog box temporarily closes.

TIP The Block Definition dialog box gives you the option of specifying the X, Y, and Z coordinates for the base point, instead of selecting a point.

4. Pick a point that will be useful when you insert the symbol. For example, if it is a symbol for a datum point, pick its center. If it's a symbol for a door, pick the door's hinge location.

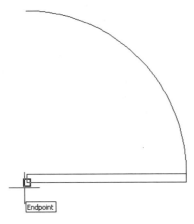

After you select a point, the Block Definition dialog box reopens. Notice that the X, Y, and Z values in the Base Point section now display the coordinates of the point you picked. For two-dimensional drawings, the Z coordinate should remain at 0.

Next, you need to select the actual objects that you want as part of the block.

5. In the Objects section, click the Select Objects button. Once again, the dialog box momentarily closes. You now see the familiar object selection prompt in the Command window, and the cursor becomes an object selection cursor. Select the objects that you want as part of your block.

6. When you've finished your selection, press ⏎ to return to the dialog box.

7. From the Drag-And-Drop Units drop-down list, select Inches. Metric users should select the appropriate metric measurement from the list.

FIGURE 8.1

The Block Definition
dialog box

8. Click the Description list box and enter a brief description of your block.

9. Make sure that the Convert To Block button in the Objects section is checked and that the Create Icon From Block Geometry button is selected in the Preview Icon section. Click OK. The objects you selected in step 5 are now a block with the name you entered in step 2.

TIP You can press ↵ or right-click and choose Repeat Make Block from the shortcut menu to start the Make Block tool again.

When you turn an object into a block, it is stored within the drawing file, ready to be recalled at any time. The block remains part of the drawing file even when you end the editing session. When you open the file again, the block is available for your use. In addition, you can access blocks from other drawings using the AutoCAD DesignCenter and the tool palettes. You'll learn more about the DesignCenter and the tool palettes later in this chapter.

Understanding the Block Definition Dialog Box

The Block Definition dialog box includes several options that can simplify the use of blocks. If you're interested in these options, take a moment to review the Block Definition dialog box as you read these descriptions.

You've already seen how the Name text box lets you enter a name for your block. AutoCAD does not let you complete the block creation until you enter a name.

You've also seen how to select a base point for your block. The base point is like the handle of the block. It is the reference point you use when you insert the block back into the drawing. It is also the primary grip point for the block. In the example given previously, you used the Pick Point option to indicate a base point, but you can also enter X, Y, and Z coordinates just below the Pick Point option. In most cases, however, you will want to use the Pick Point option to indicate a base point that is on or near the set of objects you are converting to a block.

The Objects section lets you select the objects that make up the block. You use the Select Objects button to visually select the objects you want to include in the block you are creating. The Quick Select button to the right of the Select Objects button lets you filter out objects based on their properties.

Other options in the Objects section let you specify what to do with the objects you are selecting for your block. Table 8.1 provides a listing of the options and what they mean.

TABLE 8.1:   Other Block Definition Dialog Box Options

OPTION	PURPOSE
Retain	Keeps the objects you select for your block as they are, unchanged.
Convert To Block	Converts the objects you select into the block you are defining. It then acts like a single object once you've completed the Block command.
Delete	Deletes the objects you selected for your block. This is what AutoCAD did in earlier versions. You might also notice that a warning message appears at the bottom of the Objects section. This warning tells you if you've selected objects for the block. Once you've selected objects, this warning changes to tell you how many objects you've selected.
Preview Icon	Lets you control whether a preview image is stored with the block. This option was added in AutoCAD 2000 and lets you easily locate and identify blocks in a drawing. You can, for example, peek into another drawing file without actually opening the file and browse through the blocks in that file.
Insert Units	Lets you determine how the object is to be scaled when it is inserted into the drawing. By default, this value is the same as the current drawing's Insert value.
Description	Lets you include a brief description or keyword for the block. This option is helpful when you need to find a specific block in a set of drawings.

Inserting a Block

If you delete all the blocks in a drawing, you can still restore a copy of a block at any time, as many times as you want. This is because blocks are stored within the drawing's database and are not removed unless you specifically remove them using the Purge command.

To insert a block into the drawing area, do the following:

1. In the Draw toolbar, click the Insert Block tool or type **I**⏎ to open the Insert dialog box (see Figure 8.2).

2. Click the Name drop-down list to display a list of the available blocks in the current drawing (see Figure 8.3).

3. Click the name of the block you want to insert.

FIGURE 8.2

The Insert dialog box

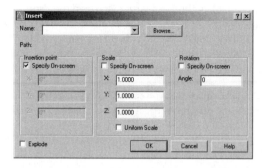

FIGURE 8.3

The Name drop-down
list shows the available
blocks in a drawing.

4. Click OK to display a preview image attached to the cursor. The base point you selected when you created the block is now on the cursor.

5. Click a point to place the block in the drawing.

Scaling and Rotating Blocks

When you insert a block, it appears at the scale and orientation that was used when the block was originally created. In some instances, you might want the block inserted at a rotated angle or at a different size from the original. The Insert dialog box provides two sets of options that let you scale or rotate your block at the time you insert it. If you turn on the Specify On-Screen option in the Rotation section of the dialog box, you are prompted for a rotation angle once you've selected an insertion point. You can specify a rotation angle either by entering an angle value from 0 to 360 or by visually selecting a rotation angle using the cursor. The block rotates with the cursor about the insertion point until you select a rotation angle. You may find that you want the Rotation's Specify On-Screen option turned on most of the time to allow you to adjust the rotation angle of the block while you are placing it in the drawing.

The other options in the Insert dialog box that you did not use are in the Scale section. These options let you scale the block to a different size. You can scale the block uniformly, or you can distort the block by individually changing its X, Y, or Z scale factor. With the Specify On-Screen option unchecked, you can enter specific values in the X, Y, and Z text boxes to stretch the block in any direction. If you turn on the Specify On-Screen option, you'll be able to visually adjust the X, Y, and Z scale factors in real time. Although these options are not used often, they can be useful in special situations if a block needs to be stretched one way or another to fit in a drawing.

You aren't limited to scaling or rotating a block when it is being inserted into a drawing. You can always use the Scale or Rotate tool or modify an inserted block's properties to stretch it in one direction or another.

If you select the block and then open the Properties palette, you'll see the properties for the block, including the X, Y, and Z scale values (see Figure 8.4).

Take a moment to study the Properties palette. Toward the bottom, under the Geometry heading, you'll see a set of labels that show Position and Scale. These labels may appear as Pos… and Sca… if the width of the palette has been adjusted to be too narrow to show the entire label.

TIP Remember that you can click and drag the left or right edge of the palette to change its width or click and drag the vertical separator inside the palette to adjust the width of the columns.

You can change Scale values so that the block is wider or taller than the original block. For example, you can enter 1.5 in the Scale X text box (to the right of the Scale X label) to increase its width by a factor of 1.5.

Once a block has been inserted, you can rotate or uniformly scale it using the Rotate or Scale command.

Importing an Existing Drawing as a Block

Earlier in this chapter, you saw how to create a block from a set of objects in a drawing. You can also treat external drawing files as blocks. For example, you might have drawings of a chair, a table, and other fixtures, each in their own separate file. You can insert those files as if they were blocks in the current drawing. This requires a slightly different way of using the Insert command.

1. In the Draw toolbar, click the Insert Block tool or type **I**↵ to open the Insert dialog box.

2. Click the Browse button to the right of the Name drop-down list to open the Select Drawing File dialog box, which is a standard AutoCAD file dialog box (see Figure 8.5).

3. Locate and select the drawing you want to insert.

FIGURE 8.4
The block properties

FIGURE 8.5

The Select Drawing File
dialog box

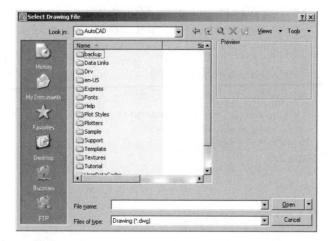

4. Back in the Insert dialog box, click OK to display a preview image of the file attached to the cursor.

5. Click a point to place the block in the drawing.

TIP You can also use Windows Explorer to drag and drop AutoCAD .dwg files into the AutoCAD window.

When you insert a file in this way, the file becomes a block in the current drawing, and like a block, if you erase all instances of the inserted file from the drawing, it remains in the file ready for you to insert again at a later time if needed. Also be aware that if such a block is deleted from a drawing, its original source file remains untouched.

TIP When you insert a drawing file as a block, AutoCAD uses the drawing's origin, 0,0, as the insertion base point. You can modify the base point of any drawing. To do so, enter **base**↵ at the Command prompt, and then select the point you want as the drawing's base point.

EDITING A BLOCK

If you need to make changes to a block, you can use the Block Definition Editor described in Chapter 5. Remember that by updating one block, all instances of the block that appear in a drawing are also updated. This can help you make quick work of repetitive items in a drawing.

If you need to change only one instance of a block, use the Explode command to reduce a block to its constituent parts. If you are working on a project involving multiple AutoCAD users, make sure exploding a block is OK with your coworkers.

Saving Blocks as AutoCAD Drawing Files

As mentioned earlier, whenever you insert a drawing file using the Insert Block tool, the inserted drawing automatically becomes a block in the current drawing. When you redefine a block, however, you do not affect the drawing file you imported. AutoCAD changes only the block within the current file.

You do have the option to save changes to a block back to the original file from which it came. The following steps describe the process.

1. Issue the Wblock command by typing **Wblock↵**, or type **w↵** to open the Write Block dialog box, as shown in Figure 8.6.

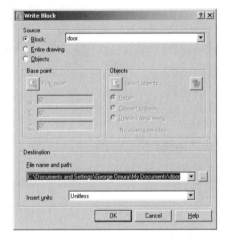

2. In the Source section, click the Block button.

3. Select the name of the block you want to export from the drop-down list. If the block was originally a file you imported, you'll see the original filename in the File Name And Path input box.

4. Click OK.

5. If you are replacing an existing file, you'll see a warning message telling you that the file already exists. Click Yes to confirm that you want to overwrite the old drawing with the new definition.

The Write Block dialog box offers a way to save parts of your current drawing as a file. In the previous exercise, you used the Block option in the Source section to select an existing block as the source object to be exported. You can also export a set of objects by clicking the Objects button. If you choose this option, the Base Point and Objects sections become available. These options work the same way as their counterparts in the Block Definition dialog box that you saw earlier.

Selecting the third option in the Source section, Entire Drawing, lets you export the whole drawing to its own file. This may seem to duplicate the File ➤ Save As option in the menu bar, but saving the entire drawing from the Write Block dialog box actually performs some additional operations, such as stripping out unused blocks or other unused components. This has the effect of reducing file size. You'll learn more about this feature later in this chapter.

Organizing Objects Using Groups

You might want to group objects so that they are connected yet can still be edited individually. For example, consider a space planner who has to place workstations in a floor plan. Though each workstation is basically the same, some slight variations in each station could make the use of blocks unwieldy. Using a block, you would need to create a block for one workstation and then for each variation, explode the block, edit it, and then create a new block. A better way is to draw a prototype workstation and then turn it into a group. You can copy the group into position and then edit it for each individual situation, without losing its identity as a group.

AutoCAD LT offers a different method for grouping objects. If you are using LT, skip this exercise and continue with the following section "Working with the LT Group Manager."

To create a group, you use the Object Grouping dialog box as described here.

1. Type **G⏎** or **Group⏎** to open the Object Grouping dialog box, as shown in Figure 8.7.

FIGURE 8.7

The Object Grouping
dialog box

2. Enter the name for your group in the Group Name text box.

3. Click New in the Create Group section, about midway in the dialog box. The Object Grouping dialog box temporarily closes to allow you to select objects for your new group.

4. At the `Select objects:` prompt, select the objects you want in your group, and then press ⏎.

5. Click OK. You have just created a group.

Now, whenever you want to select the group, you can click any part of it. At the same time, you can still modify individual parts of the group—the desk, the partition, and so on—without losing the grouping of objects.

Toggling Groups On and Off

If you've created a group and now need to edit the individual objects in the group, you can temporarily turn off the group by pressing Shift+Ctrl+A. You will see a message in the Command line indicating whether the groups are on or off. Once they are off, you can edit the individual objects within the group. Press Shift+Ctrl+A again to turn groups back on.

Working with the Object Grouping Dialog Box

Each group has a unique name, and you can also attach a brief description of the group in the Object Grouping dialog box. When you copy a group, AutoCAD assigns an arbitrary name to the newly created group. Copies of groups are considered unnamed, but you can still list them in the Object Grouping dialog box by clicking the Unnamed check box. You can click the Rename button in the Object Grouping dialog box to name unnamed groups appropriately.

Objects within a group are not bound solely to that group. One object can be a member of several groups, and you can have nested groups.

NOTE Here are the options available in the Object Grouping dialog box, which you saw in Figure 8.7. AutoCAD LT users have a different set of options. See the "Working with the LT Group Manager" section that follows this section.

Use the Group Identification section to identify your groups, using unique elements that let you remember what each group is for. Table 8.2 describes the Group Identification options. Table 8.3 shows the Create Group options.

TABLE 8.2:   The Group Identification Options

OPTION	PURPOSE
Group Name	Lets you create a new group by naming it first.
Description	Lets you include a brief description of the group.
Find Name	Finds the name of a group by temporarily closing the Object Grouping dialog box so you can click a group.
Highlight	Highlights a group that has been selected from the group list. This helps you locate a group in a crowded drawing.
Include Unnamed	Determines whether unnamed groups are included in the Group Name list. Check this box to display the names of copies of groups for processing by this dialog box.

TABLE 8.3:   The Create Group Options

OPTION	PURPOSE
New	Creates a new group. The Object Grouping dialog box closes temporarily so that you can select objects for grouping. To use this button, you must have either entered a group name or checked the Unnamed check box.
Selectable	Lets you control whether the group you create is selectable. See the description of the Selectable button in Table 8.4.
Unnamed	Lets you create a new group without naming it.

The Change Group options are available only when a group name is highlighted in the Group Name list at the top of the dialog box. Table 8.4 describes those options.

TABLE 8.4:   The Change Group Options

OPTION	PURPOSE
Remove	Lets you remove objects from a group.
Add	Lets you add objects to a group. While using this option, grouping is temporarily turned off to allow you to select objects from other groups.
Rename	Lets you rename a group.
Re-Order	Lets you change the order of objects in a group.
Description	Lets you modify the description of a group.
Explode	Separates a group into its individual components.
Selectable	Turns individual groupings on and off. When a group is selectable, it is selectable only as a group. When a group is not selectable, the individual objects in a group can be selected, but not the group.

TIP   If a group is selected, you can remove individual items from the group with a Shift+click. In this way, you can isolate objects within a group for editing or removal without having to temporarily turn off groups.

Working with the LT Group Manager

If you are using AutoCAD LT, you use the Group Manager to manage groups. Choose Tools ➤ Group Manager to open the Group Manager dialog box. Table 8.5 describes the tools that are available in the Group Manager. A shortcut to grouping objects is to choose Tools ➤ Group then select the objects you want to group. You may also ungroup an existing group by choosing Tools ➤ Ungroup.

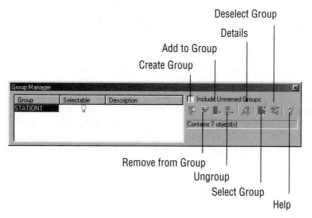

TABLE 8.5:   The AutoCAD 2006 LT Group Manager options

OPTION	USE
Create Group	Converts a set of objects into a group. First select objects then click Create Group.
Ungroup	Ungroups an existing group. Select the group name from the list then click Ungroup.
Add To Group	Adds an object to a group. A group and at least one additional object must be selected before first.
Remove From Group	Removes individual objects from a group. To isolate individual objects in a group, select the group, and then Shift+click to remove individual objects from the selection set. After you isolate the object you want to remove, click Remove From Group.
Details	Lists information about the group. Select the group name from the group list and then click Details.
Select Group	Selects a group by name. Click the group name in the group list and then click Select Group.
Deselect Group	Removes a group from the current selection set. Click the group name in the group list and then click Deselect Group.
Help	Opens the AutoCAD LT Help dialog box and displays information about the Group Manager.

Finding Files on Your Hard Disk

As your library of symbols and files grows, you might begin to have difficulty keeping track of them. Fortunately, AutoCAD includes a utility that lets you quickly locate a file anywhere on your computer. The Find utility searches your hard disk for specific files. You can specify that it search one drive or several or limit the search to one folder. You can limit the search to specific filenames or use wildcard characters to search for files with similar names.

To take a look at the AutoCAD Find dialog box, follow these steps:

1. Choose File ➢ Open to open the Select File dialog box, as shown in Figure 8.8.

2. From the Select File dialog box menu, Choose Tools ➢ Find to open the Find dialog box, as shown In Figure 8.9.

   The Find dialog box has two tabs: Name & Location and Date Modified. The Name & Location tab lets you search for a file based on its location on your computer and the file type. It works in a way that is similar to the Windows Search tool. In the Named text box, enter the name of the file for which you want to search. The default is *.dwg, which in the Type drop-down list causes the Find File utility to search for all AutoCAD drawing files. The Look In drop-down list lets you specify the drive and path to be searched.

3. Click the Date Modified tab. Here you find options that let you search based on the date a file was created (see Figure 8.10).

4. When you're ready, click Cancel to exit the Find dialog box, and then click Cancel to exit the Select File dialog box.

FIGURE 8.8

The Select File dialog box

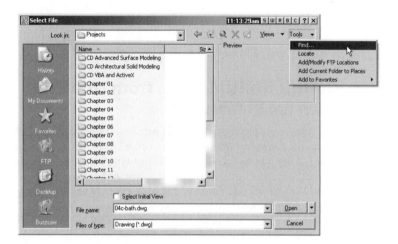

FIGURE 8.9

The Find dialog box

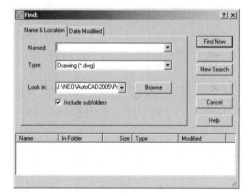

FIGURE 8.10

The Date Modified tab of the Find dialog box

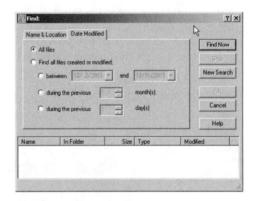

Getting Multiple Uses from Drawings Using External References

You now know that you can insert a drawing file into the current file as a block. You can also insert a drawing file as an *external reference,* or *xref.* The difference between an xref and a block is that an xref does not actually become part of the drawing's database. Instead, an xref is "loaded" along with the current file at startup time. It is as if AutoCAD were opening several drawings at once: the currently active file you specify when you start AutoCAD and any file inserted as an xref.

The unique feature of an xref is that any changes you make to the xref automatically appear in the current file. You don't have to update the xref file manually as you do blocks. AutoCAD also notifies you if the xref file has been altered.

Another advantage of xref files is that since they do not actually become part of a drawing's database, drawing size is kept to a minimum. This results in more efficient use of your hard disk space.

Xrefs are an excellent way to get multiple uses out of one drawing. You can create a floor plan drawing and then use it as an xref in another file to place the plan in a site plan. You can then use the file again for enlarged kitchen and bath plans, and again for a roof plan or overall floor plan. Since you are not duplicating the file, you save on disk and RAM space. And since all these drawings draw from the same source, you can change the original plan, and all its xref instances show the same data. You don't have to update multiple drawings.

When a file is used as an xref, you can do anything to the xref except edit the individual objects in it. You can modify its layer properties, turn layers on and off, scale, rotate, or move the xref, and you can use osnaps to locate geometry. If you need to make changes to the xref, you can either open it directly or use the Refedit command. New and casual users should stick to editing xrefs directly as the Refedit command is a bit tricky to use.

WARNING You cannot xref a file if the file has the same name as a block in the current drawing. If this situation occurs, but you still need to use the file as an xref, you can rename the block of the same name using the Rename command. You can also use Rename to change the name of various objects and named elements.

Attaching a Drawing as an External Reference

You can attach as many files as xrefs as you want in any drawing. The process is fairly simple as shown in the following steps.

ACAD only

WARNING The Open option in the Xref Manager is not available in LT.

1. Choose Insert ➢ Xref Manager, type **XR↵**, or choose Insert ➢ External Reference to open the Xref Manager dialog box (see Figure 8.11).

FIGURE 8.11

The Xref Manager dialog box

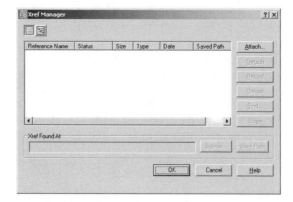

2. Click the Attach button to open the Select Reference File dialog box. This is a typical AutoCAD file dialog box complete with a preview window.

3. Locate and select the drawing file you want to insert, and then click Open to open the External Reference dialog box (see Figure 8.12). Notice that this dialog box looks similar to the Insert dialog box. It offers the same options for insertion point, scale, and rotation.

4. Click OK to proceed with the xref insertion. The drawing is inserted in the default location, which is the origin of the current drawing.

FIGURE 8.12

The External Reference dialog box

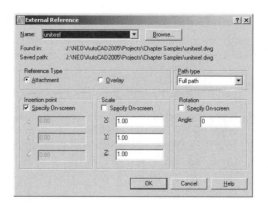

In this example, the simplest default options were used in the External Reference dialog box. These default settings placed the xref in the drawing origin and used the default scale of 1:1 and a default rotation angle of 0. These settings place the xref in the current drawing as it would appear in the original xref file.

If you prefer, you can turn on the Specify On-Screen option for the Insert Point, Scale, and Rotation features, which in turn let you set these values, either through the dialog box using the provided X, Y, Z and Angle text boxes or in the drawing area using your cursor.

TIP If you need to temporarily remove an xref from the current drawing, you can use the Unload option in the Xref Manager dialog box. Select the xref from the list box, and then click Unload. Use the Reload option to restore an xref to full view.

Updating an Xref While You Draw

Since an xref is not actually part of the current drawing, others users can edit the source drawing of the xref even while you are editing the current, referencing drawing. When a file has been modified and saved while you have it open as an xref, the xref icon in the lower-right of the AutoCAD window changes to show an exclamation mark. This alerts you to changes in an xref in the current drawing.

When an xref is present in the current drawing and it has been modified, you can click the xref icon to open the Xref Manager dialog box. The xref that has been changed is indicated by a message in the Status column of the list box, as shown in Figure 8.13.

FIGURE 8.13

The message in the Status column of the Xref Manager dialog box shows that the xref needs to be reloaded.

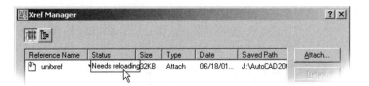

You can then select the xref that needs to be updated and click the Reload button. You can also right-click the xref icon and choose the Reload xref option from the shortcut menu to reload all xrefs in the drawing without opening the Xref Manager dialog box.

Differences between External References and Blocks

Although Blocks and xrefs are quite similar and can be used in similar ways, you will want to keep in mind a few differences:

◆ Any new layers, text styles, or linetypes brought in with cross-referenced files do not become part of the current file. If you want to import any of these items, use the Xbind command.

◆ If you make changes to the layers of a cross-referenced file, those changes are not retained when the file is saved, unless you check the Retain Changes To Xref Layers option in the Open And Save tab of the Options dialog box. This option can be found in the External References (Xrefs) section. This option instructs AutoCAD to remember any layer color or visibility settings from one editing session to the next. In the standard AutoCAD settings, this option is on by default.

TIP   Another way to ensure that layer settings for xrefs are retained is to enter **Visretain**↵ at the Command prompt. At the `New value for VISRETAIN <0>:` prompt, enter **1.**

◆ To segregate layers in xref files from layers in the current drawing, the xref file's layers are prefixed with their file's name. A vertical bar separates the filename prefix and the layer name when you view a list of layers in the Layer drop-down list or the Layer Properties Manager dialog box (as in Unitxref | wall).

◆ You cannot explode xrefs. You can, however, convert an xref into a block and then explode it. To do this, click the Bind button in the External Reference dialog box to open another dialog box that offers two ways of converting an xref into a block.

◆ If an xref is renamed or moved to another location on your hard disk, AutoCAD won't be able to find that file when it opens other files to which the xref is attached. If this happens, you must use the Browse option in the External Reference dialog box to tell AutoCAD where to find the cross-referenced file.

WARNING   Take care when relocating an xref file with the Browse button. The Browse button can assign a file of a different name to an existing xref as a substitution.

Xref files are especially useful in workgroup environments in which several people are working on the same project. For example, one person might be updating several files that are inserted into a variety of other files. Using blocks, everyone in the workgroup must be notified of the changes and must update all the affected blocks in all the drawings that contained them. With cross-referenced files, however, the updating is automatic; so you avoid confusion about which files need their blocks updated.

NESTING EXTERNAL REFERENCES AND USING OVERLAYS

External references can be nested, but this can create problems with circular references. A circular reference is one in which the referencing drawing is actually referenced in an xref. To avoid this problem, use the Overlay option in the External Reference dialog box. If you insert an xref as an overlay, AutoCAD ignores any xrefs that might be attached to the xref you are importing into the current file.

You don't have to limit the use of the Overlay option to circular references. You can use it whenever you want AutoCAD to ignore nested xrefs.

Keeping Track of Drawing Components with DesignCenter

As you start to build a library of drawings, you'll find that you reuse many components. Most of the time, you will probably be producing similar types of drawings with some variation, so you'll reuse drawing components such as layer settings, dimension styles, and layouts. Just keeping track of all the projects you've worked on can be a major task. It's especially frustrating when you remember setting up a past drawing in a way that you know would be useful in a current project, but you can't remember that file's name or location.

The AutoCAD DesignCenter helps you keep track of the documents you use in your projects. You can think of DesignCenter as a kind of super Windows Explorer that is focused on AutoCAD files. DesignCenter lets you keep track of your favorite files and helps you locate files, blocks, and other drawing components. In addition, you can import blocks and other drawing components from one drawing to another by using a simple click and drag. If you are diligent about setting a unit format for each of your drawings, you can use DesignCenter to import symbols and drawings of different unit formats into a drawing, and the symbols maintain their proper size. For example, a 90-cm door symbol from a metric drawing can be imported into a drawing in Imperial units, and the DesignCenter translates the 90-cm door size to a 35.43-inch door.

Getting Familiar with DesignCenter

The DesignCenter interface can be adjusted in a variety of ways so it can vary from installation to installation. Try the following steps to get familiar with DesignCenter.

1. Open AutoCAD to a new file, and then click the DesignCenter tool on the Standard toolbar to open DesignCenter as a floating palette (see Figure 8.14).

FIGURE 8.14
DesignCenter opens as a floating palette.

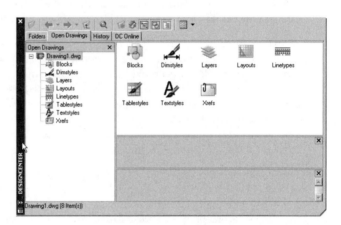

TIP   If your DesignCenter view doesn't look like this, with the DesignCenter window divided into two parts, click the Tree View Toggle tool in the DesignCenter toolbar. The tree view opens on the left side of the DesignCenter window. Click the Home tool to display the contents of the \Sample\ DesignCenter folder.

2. Click the Favorites tool in the DesignCenter toolbar.

DesignCenter displays a listing of the Favorites folder. What you are actually looking at is a view into the C:\Documents and Settings*User Name*\Favorites\Autodesk folder in which *User Name* is your login name. Unless you've already added items to the \Favorites\ Autodesk folder, you see a blank view in the panel on the right. You can add shortcuts to this folder as you work with DesignCenter. You can also see a view showing the tree structure of the files you have open in AutoCAD.

FIGURE 8.15
The components of the
DesignCenter palette

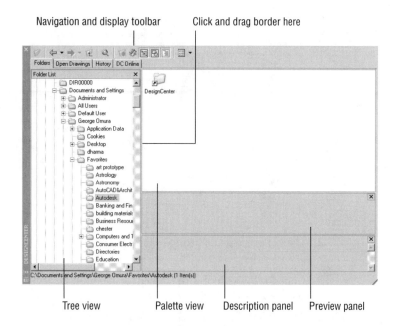

Navigation and display toolbar   Click and drag border here

Tree view   Palette view   Description panel   Preview panel

3. Place your cursor in the lower-right corner of the DesignCenter window so that a double-headed diagonal arrow shows; then click and drag the corner out so that you have an enlarged DesignCenter window that looks similar to Figure 8.15. By the way, the view on the right containing the DesignCenter folder is called the palette view, and the view on the left is called the tree view.

4. Place your cursor on the border between the tree view and the palette view until you see a double-headed cursor. Then click and drag the border to the right to enlarge the tree view until it covers about one-third of the window.

5. Finally, use the scroll bar at the bottom to adjust the tree view so you can easily read its contents.

TIP   Like the tool palettes and the Properties palette, Design Center has an auto-hide feature. To use it, click the double-headed arrow icon near the bottom of the DesignCenter title bar. DesignCenter closes except for the title bar. You can then quickly open DesignCenter by placing the cursor on the title bar.

Once you have it set up like this, you can see the similarities between DesignCenter and Windows Explorer.

NAVIGATING DESIGNCENTER

You can navigate your computer or network using the tree view, just as you would navigate Windows Explorer. There are a few differences, however, as you'll see in the following exercise.

1. In the Design Center toolbar, click the Home tool. The view changes to display the contents of the DesignCenter folder under the \AutoCAD2006\Samples\ folder, as shown in Figure 8.16.

FIGURE 8.16

View of the home location in DesignCenter

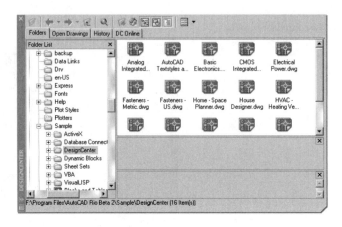

2. Instead of the usual listing of files, you see sample images of each file. These are called *preview icons*.

3. Click the Views tool in the DesignCenter toolbar, and then choose Details from the menu. The palette view changes to show a detailed list of the files in the `DesignCenter` folder.

4. Click the Views tool again, and then choose Large Icon to return to the previous view. The Views tool is similar to the Large Icon, Small Icon, List, and Detail options in Windows Explorer.

If you select a file from the palette view, you'll see a preview of the selected file in the Preview panel of DesignCenter. You can adjust the vertical size of the Preview panel by clicking and dragging its top or bottom border.

You can also open and close the Preview panel by clicking the Preview tool in the Design Center toolbar. The preview can be helpful if you prefer viewing files and drawing components as a list in the main part of the palette view.

Below the Preview panel is the Description panel. This panel displays any text information included with the drawing or drawing element selected in the palette view. To add a description to a drawing, choose File ➤ Properties; to add a description to a block, use the Block Definition dialog box.

You can open and close this panel by clicking the Description tool in the Design Center toolbar. Since the Basic Electronics.dwg file doesn't have a description attached, the Description panel shows the message "No description found."

Both the Preview and the Description panels can offer help in identifying files. Once you find a file, you can click and drag it into a folder in the tree view to organize your files into separate folders.

You can also add files to the `Favorites` folder under the `Windows` folder by right-clicking and then choosing Add To Favorites. The file itself won't be moved to the `Favorites` folder; instead, a shortcut to the file is created in the `Favorites` folder. If you want to organize your `Favorites` folder, open a window to the `Favorites` folder by right-clicking a file in the palette view and choosing Organize Favorites. A window to the `Favorites` folder opens.

VIEWING A *.DWG* FILE'S CONTENTS

You can go beyond just looking at file listings. You can look inside files to view their components. To do this, double-click a file in the palette view. The palette view changes to display a list of the file's contents. From here, you can import any of the drawing components from the DesignCenter palette into an open drawing in AutoCAD. In the tree view, the filename is highlighted.

If the file contains blocks, you'll see Block as an option in the palette view. Double-click the Block listing, and the palette view changes to display a list of blocks in the drawing.

TIP   If the block layers are turned off in the drawing you are viewing, you will not see the block previews.

Opening and Inserting Files with DesignCenter

With DesignCenter, you can locate files more easily because you can view thumbnail preview icons. But often that isn't enough. For example, you might want to locate all files that contain the name of a particular manufacturer in an attribute of a drawing. Once you've found the file, you can load it into AutoCAD by right-clicking the filename in the palette view and then choosing Open In Window.

To insert a file into another drawing as a block, click and drag the file from the DesignCenter palette view into an open drawing window. You are then prompted for insertion point, scale, and rotation angle. If you prefer to use the Insert dialog box, right-click the filename in the palette view, and choose Insert As Block to open the Insert dialog box, which presents the full set of Insert options, as described earlier in this chapter.

Finally, you can attach a drawing as an xref by right-clicking a file in the palette view and choosing Attach As Xref. The External Reference dialog box opens, offering the insertion point, scale, and rotation options similar to the Insert dialog box.

Finding and Extracting the Contents of a Drawing

Aside from the convenience of being able to see thumbnail views of your drawing, DesignCenter may not seem like much of an improvement over Windows Explorer. But DesignCenter goes beyond Windows Explorer in many ways. One of the main features of DesignCenter is that it lets you locate and extract components of a drawing.

For example, you want to find a specific block in a drawing. You remember the name of the block, but you don't remember the drawing you put it in. You can search the contents of drawings using DesignCenter's Search dialog box.

In the DesignCenter toolbar, click the Search tool to open the Search dialog box, which looks similar to the Windows Search dialog box but contains a few extra options. For example, you can use the Look For drop-down list to select the drawing component you are looking for. Choose Blocks if you are looking for a block, or choose Layers or Linetypes to search for those items (see Figure 8.17).

SEARCH OPTIONS

You can use other options in the Search dialog box to narrow your search parameters. You already know that you can specify a particular type of drawing component. You can also specify a location. Table 8.6 lists the search options and their use.

FIGURE 8.17

Options in the Look For drop-down list of the Search dialog box

TABLE 8.6:   The Options in the Search Dialog Box

OPTION	PURPOSE
In	Lets you select the drive you want to search.
Look For Options	Lets you select the type of item to search for. The options are Drawings, Drawings And Blocks, Layers, Layouts, Linetypes, Textstyles, and Xrefs.
Browse	Lets you locate a specific folder to search.
Search Subfolders	Lets you determine whether Search searches subfolders in the drive and folder you specify.
Search Now	Starts the search process.
Stop	Cancels the current search.
New Search	Clears all the settings for the current search so you can start a new search.
Help	Opens the AutoCAD help system to the Search topic.

ADDITIONAL HIDDEN OPTIONS

When you select Drawings from the Look For drop-down list, the Search dialog box displays additional tabs:

The Drawings Tab contains two options:

Search For The Word(s) lets you specify the text to search for in the Drawing Properties fields.

In The Field(s) lets you specify the field of the Drawing Properties dialog box to search through, including filename, title, subject, author, and keyword. You see these fields when you choose File ➢ Drawing Properties.

The Date Modified Tab lets you limit search criteria based on dates.

The Advanced Tab contains three options to further limit your search to specific types of drawing data or to a range of dates:

Containing lets you select from a list of data to search for, including block name, block and drawing description, attribute tag, and attribute value.

Containing Text lets you specify the text to search for in the types of data you select from the Containing option.

Size Is lets you restrict the search to files greater than or less than the size you specify.

AUTOMATICALLY SCALING DRAWINGS AND BLOCKS AT INSERTION

When you first set up a drawing, you can specify the type of units in the Units dialog box using the Drag And Drop Scale drop-down list. DesignCenter uses this information to correctly scale a block or drawing drawn in metric to a drawing that is drawn in the Imperial format and vice versa. The same option is offered in the Block Definition dialog box.

Exchanging Data between Open Files

The DesignCenter usually shows a list of files in tree view, but if multiple files are open in AutoCAD, you can set up DesignCenter to display the drawing components of your open files instead. You can change the tree view to show only the drawing files that are currently open, allowing you to exchange drawing components between open files.

To change the tree view, click the Open Drawings tab. The tree view to the left shows only drawings that are currently open. Click the plus sign (+) next to the filename to explore the drawing components of the file. Once you've located a drawing component, you can click and drag the component from the palette view to the open drawing window. If you prefer to use the Insert dialog box for blocks, right-click the block name in the palette view and choose Insert Block to open the Insert dialog box opens, in which you can set the insertion point, scale, and rotation options.

Just as with drawings, you can see a preview and descriptive text for blocks below the palette view. Earlier in this chapter, I describe the option to save a preview icon with the block when you first create a block. This is where that preview icon can be really helpful. The preview icon gives you a chance to see what the block looks like when you use DesignCenter to browse through your drawing files. If you don't save a preview icon, you'll see the same block icon that was displayed in the previous palette view.

You can also add the text description at the time you create the block. Before saving the block, enter a description in the Description input box of the Block Definition dialog box. If you're updating older drawing files to be used with DesignCenter, you can add text descriptions to blocks using the Make Block tool in the Draw toolbar. Click the Make Block tool, and then, in the Block Definition dialog box, select the name of a block from the Name drop-down list. Enter the description you want for this block in the Description input box, and click OK.

Loading Specific Files into DesignCenter

You've seen how you can locate files using the tree view and palette view. If you already know the name and location of the file you want to work with, you can use a file dialog box to open files in

DesignCenter. Instead of choosing File ≻ Open, click the Load tool in the left end of the DesignCenter toolbar to open the Load dialog box. This is a standard file dialog box that lets you search for files on your computer or network. If you want to open a file in DesignCenter that you've recently opened, you can use the History tab just above the tree view.

Downloading Symbols from DesignCenter Online

Besides allowing you to obtain files and blocks from your computer or network, you can also download symbols directly from Autodesk's DesignCenter Online website. This option offers thousands of ready-to-use symbols for a variety of disciplines.

With a connection to the Internet and DesignCenter open, click the DesignCenter Online tab that appears above the Tree view. The DesignCenter Online symbol categories appear in the tree view, and the palette view shows the same categories in a text view, as shown in Figure 8.18.

Since DesignCenter Online is a website, AutoCAD uses the i-drop feature to bring the symbols into your drawing. With i-drop, you can click and drag symbols from the website into an open drawing. As you can see, the list of symbols is extensive. Many of the symbols are samples from third-party vendors that offer expanded symbols libraries.

FIGURE 8.18

The DesignCenter with the Online tab selected

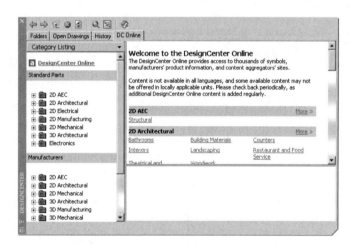

Keeping Tools on Hand with Tool Palettes

One item that has been fairly conspicuous in the AutoCAD window is the Tool palette. The main purpose of the Tool palette is to give you easy access to symbols and patterns that you use frequently. It works by giving you ready access to blocks and other features contained within drawings in your drawing library. In a default AutoCAD setup, the palette offers blocks from drawings in the `Samples` folder of the AutoCAD installation, but you can add your own blocks to the palette just by clicking and dragging them in.

The Tool palettes provide a simple way to keep a set of blocks ready at any time. At first glance, there is no obvious way to add your own tools to the palettes. Adding tools and additional palettes to the Tool palettes is actually fairly simple. The following exercise shows you how it's done.

First, create a new palette for your custom set of objects.

1. Click the Tool Palettes tool in the Standard toolbar to open the Tool palettes.

2. Right-click in a blank spot in the Tool palette, and choose New Tool Palette from the shortcut menu. A new palette opens along with a text box.

3. Enter a name for your new palette. The new palette appears in the Tool palettes with a tab showing the name you just entered.

Now add your custom objects.

1. Open a file containing the block you want to add to the palette.

2. While no command is active, click the block to select it.

3. Click and hold the left mouse button on any part of the block that is not a grip until you see the cursor change to show a small rectangle, as shown in the sample image in Figure 8.19.

4. Drag the block into the Tool palette. The block appears in the Tool palette.

FIGURE 8.19
Selecting and clicking
a block

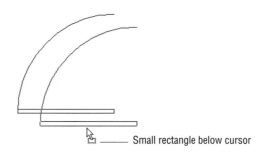

Small rectangle below cursor

You can continue to add other blocks in this way. Once you add a block to your new palette, the block is available at any time while you are editing in AutoCAD. Just click and drag the block from the palette into your drawing.

You do not need the source drawing file open to access the blocks in the palette. AutoCAD remembers which file the block came from and copies the block whenever you click and drag a copy from the palette.

You aren't limited to blocks. You can also place hatch patterns in a palette. If you copy an object into the palette, such as a line or a text object, the command used to create the object is placed in the palette. For example, if you click and drag a text object into the palette, you see the Mtext command in the palette. If you drag a dimension into the palette, you see a dimension symbol that for the particular type of dimension you drag into the palette. For dimensions in particular, you can click the flyout arrow to select a different type of dimension, as shown in Figure 8.20.

In this way, you can create a custom set of tools and symbols in one place in your AutoCAD workspace.

TIP You can used the DesignCenter to add drawing components from multiple files to a Tool palette. Using the DesignCenter, locate the drawing component you want, and then click and drag it into the Tool palette.

FIGURE 8.20

If a dimension is dragged into a palette, the dimension commands appear in the palette.

Deleting Tools and Palettes

If you find you no longer need a block, a pattern, or a command in the palette, right-click it and choose Delete Tool from the shortcut menu. To delete an entire palette, right-click a blank portion of the palette, and then choose Delete Tools from the shortcut menu. Click OK to confirm the deletion.

While deleting a palette, you might decide that you want keep one or two items. You can right-click the tool in a palette and choose Copy to copy the item to another palette. Right-click in another palette and choose Paste to paste the copied item to a different palette.

Customizing a Tool

Other shortcut menu options let you delete entire palettes or rename tools or palettes. You can also edit the properties of symbols in a palette. For example, you can use the shortcut menu options to change the default insertion scale of a block you've stored in a Tool palette.

To do this, right-click a block in the Tool palette, and then choose Properties to open the Tool Properties dialog box, as shown in Figure 8.21. Click the Scale listing, change its value to whatever scale you want for the block, and then click OK.

Once you've made this change, it is inserted at the new scale whenever you drag the block into your drawing from the palette.

Using this method, you can have multiple versions of a block tool at different scales. Make copies of the block tool using the right-click Copy option, and then rename the block tool in the palette. Change the scale of the copy as described in the previous steps using the right-click Properties option.

Once you've set up your block tools at different scales, you can drag and drop the tool appropriate to the scale of your drawing. And as you can see from the Tool Properties dialog box, you can modify other tool properties such as color and layer assignments.

You can use this feature to set up sets of tools for different scale drawings. For example, you can create a palette of architectural reference symbols for $\frac{1}{4}''$ scale drawings, and you can create another palette for $\frac{1}{8}''$ scale drawings.

You can also use the Tool Properties dialog box shown in Figure 8.21 to modify solid fills or hatch patterns you've stored in a Tool palette. For example, you can add several copies of a solid fill to a Tool palette, and then use the Tool Properties dialog box to set a different color for each solid fill.

FIGURE 8.21
The Tool Properties
dialog box

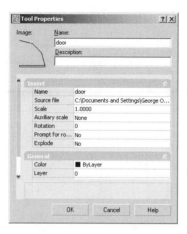

You can perform other types of Tool palettes maintenance operations using the Customize dialog box, which is shown in Figure 8.22. For example, you can change the order of the Tool Palette tabs, or you can group tabs into categories that can be turned on or off. To open the Customize dialog box, right-click Tool Palettes in the Standard toolbar, and choose Customize from the shortcut menu.

To change the order of the tabs, click and drag the tab names up or down in the left panel. If you select a palette in the left panel and right-click, you can rename, delete, import, or export a palette.

WARNING If you use the Export or Import options to move a palette from one computer to another, you must also import or export the drawings that are the source files for the palette tools.

FIGURE 8.22
The Customize
dialog box

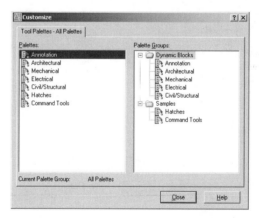

Just Enough Summary

The features covered in this chapter will help you use your drawings more efficiently. With xrefs, you can get multiple uses from a single drawing. Blocks let you easily copy sets of objects and much more. Other features such as the DesignCenter and the Tool palettes help you leverage the work you've done. Once you're comfortable with the basic drawing tools in AutoCAD, make sure you learn about the important features covered in this chapter.

Chapter 9

Creating Text

Even though AutoCAD is primarily a drawing program, you may find that you are actually adding more text than graphics to some of your drawings. In fact, annotation can often consume nearly half the time you spend on an AutoCAD drawing.

Fortunately, AutoCAD provides some familiar tools for creating and editing text. AutoCAD's Mtext command lets you place blocks of text in your drawing as short as a single sentence or as long as several paragraphs. Mtext also contains many familiar text-formatting tools so if you've used a word processor, you should feel at home.

This chapter starts by showing you how to create new text and then goes on to discuss text formatting. You'll also learn how to use text styles and what to do when you only need to ad a short, single-word note. Since you are drawing to a precise scale most of the time, you will have to size your text appropriately for your drawing's scale. If you are creating a new drawing, be sure to check out the section on text scaling.

Finally, since tables are a prominent feature in CAD drawings, you'll learn about AutoCAD's Table command that helps to automate table creation. You'll learn how to can create a table with spreadsheetlike features and how to import spreadsheets as AutoCAD tables.

- ◆ Adding and Formatting Text in AutoCAD

- ◆ Understanding Text and Scale

- ◆ Using Styles to Organize Your Fonts

- ◆ Adding Single Words with the Single-Line Text Object

- ◆ Adding Tables to Your Drawing

Adding and Formatting Text

To add text in AutoCAD, you use the Mtext command, otherwise known as the Multiline Text tool. When you start the command, you must first select a window indicating the area where your text will appear. Once that's done, the Text Formatting toolbar and text panel appear, allowing you to enter the text you want. Here's how this works.

1. Choose Draw ➢ Text ➢ Multiline Text, type **MT**↵, or select the Multiline Text tool from the Draw toolbar.

2. Click the first point indicated in the top image in Figure 9.1 to start the text boundary window. You don't have to be too precise about where you select the points for the boundary because you can adjust the location and size later.

3. Click the second point to indicate the size of the text boundary. The Text Formatting toolbar appears with the text panel superimposed over the area you just selected (see Figure 9.2).

FIGURE 9.1

Indicating the text location with the text boundary

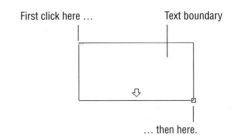

First click here … Text boundary

… then here.

FIGURE 9.2

The Text Formatting toolbar and the text panel

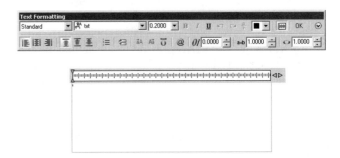

4. Start typing, and the text appears in the text panel. The size and formatting of the text is as it will appear in the drawing. The default font is a native AutoCAD font called Txt. You can also use TrueType fonts and PostScript fonts, but be aware that such fonts can slow down your work in AutoCAD, especially if you have lots of text.

5. Click OK in the Text Formatting toolbar. The text appears in the drawing.

The Text Formatting toolbar and text editor work like any text editor, so if you make a typing error, you can highlight the error and then retype the letter or word. You can also perform other word processing functions such as font and format changes. AutoCAD also automatically wraps text as you type.

AutoCAD offers many of the same tools you expect to see in a word processor. You can format the text for height and font, or you can add bold, italic, or underline with the click of a button.

Adjusting the Text Height and Font

The most common text-editing features you'll want to know about are the text height and font controls. The following example describes how to change an existing multiline text object. The process is similar to text that you are initially adding to a drawing.

1. Double-click an existing Mtext object to display the Text Formatting toolbar and the text in a text panel as shown in the example in Figure 9.3.

2. Select the text you want to reformat in the text panel.

FIGURE 9.3

The Text formatting
toolbar and text panel
with selected text

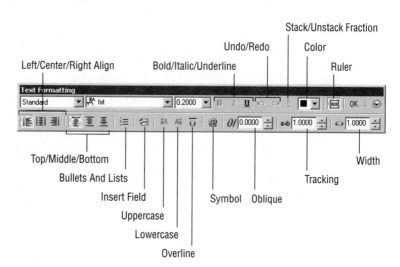

3. In the Text Formatting toolbar, click the Text Height drop-down list and select a text height in drawing units. Or instead of selecting a value, click the current height value and enter a smaller or larger one. The highlighted text changes to a smaller or larger size.

4. Click OK in the Text Formatting toolbar. The text appears in the new height.

To change the font, repeat these steps, but instead of using the Text Height drop-down list, select a font from the Font drop-down list shown in Figure 9.4.

FIGURE 9.4

The Font drop-down list
in the Text Formatting
toolbar

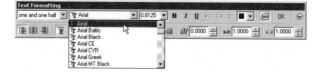

Using Color, Stacked Fractions, Alignment, Lists, and Special Symbols

A variety of additional formatting tools are available in the Text Formatting toolbar. Figure 9.5 shows where these tools are located, and Table 9.1 describes their use. They're fairly straightforward, and if you've used other word-processing programs, you should find them easy to use. Most are common to most word processors, although a few such as Symbol, Oblique, and Width are unique to AutoCAD.

FIGURE 9.5

Additional features of
the Text Formatting
toolbar

TABLE 9.1:   Text Formatting Tools and Their Uses

TOOL	USE
Bold/Italic/Underline	Select text, and then select one of these options to add bold, italic, or underline to the text.
Undo/Redo	Click to undo or redo current edits.
Stack/Unstack Fraction	Select a fraction, and then click this tool to either stack or unstack the fraction text.
Color	Select text, and then choose a color from this drop-down list.
Ruler	Click to turn the ruler at the top of the text panel on or off
Left/Center/Right	Click the appropriate tool to align the text to the left, center, or right side of the text bounding box.
Top/Middle/Bottom	Click the appropriate tool to align the text to the top, middle, or bottom of the text bounding box.
Bullets And Lists	Select a list of text, click this tool, and then select Letter, Number, or Bullet to add letters, numbers, or bullets to the list.
Insert Field	Opens the Fields dialog box allowing you to add a field text. See "Adding Formulas to Cells" later in this chapter for more on fields.
Upper-/lowercase	Select a single letter or set of words, and then select the Uppercase or Lowercase tool to change the selection's case.
Overline	Select text, and then click Overline to add a line across the top of the text.
Symbol	Place the cursor at a location for the symbol, and then click the Symbol tool to find and add a symbol. (See Figure 9.6 for the available symbols.)
Oblique	Select text, and then enter an oblique angle value. The effect is to skew the text characters in a way similar to an italic formatting.
Tracking	Select text, and then enter a tracking value in the Tracking text box. A value greater than 1 increases the spacing between letters, and a value less than 1 decreases the spacing.
Width	Select text, and enter a width value in the Width text box. A value greater than 1 stretches the text, including the letters, horizontally. A value less than 1 compresses the text including the letters.

FIGURE 9.6
Symbols offered by
the Symbol option. (See
Symbol in Table 9.1 for
information on how to
use these symbols.)

Degree	x°	Flow Line	F_L
Plus/Minus	$\pm$	Identity	$\equiv$
Diameter	$\emptyset$	Monument Line	M_L
Almost Equal	$\approx$	Not Equal	$\neq$
Angle	$\angle$	Ohm	Ω
Boundary Line	B_L	Omega	Ω
Center Line	$\mathbb{C}_L$	Property Line	P_L
Delta	Δ	Subscript 2	x_2
Electrical Phase	ϕ	Superscript 2	x^2

Adjusting the Text Boundary

Once you've placed the text in the drawing, you may find that you need to adjust the text boundary or the area that it takes up in the drawing. For example, the text might occupy a space that is too tall and you want to widen the text *boundary window* so it takes up less vertical space. The boundary window is the area within which the text is made to fit. To adjust the bounding box, click the text you want to adjust. The bounding box appears along with grips at each corner. Click a grip, and then drag and click to reposition the grip.

AutoCAD's word-wrap feature automatically adjusts the text formatting to fit the text boundary. This feature is especially useful to AutoCAD users because other drawing objects often affect the placement of text. As your drawing changes, you will need to adjust the location and boundary of your notes and labels.

Setting Indents and Tabs

When you are editing text, you'll notice the ruler at the top of the text panel. Figure 9.7 shows that ruler, including tabs and indent markers.

If you need to set indents, do the following:

1. Double-click the text you want to edit to open the Text Formatting toolbar.

2. Highlight the text whose indent or tab spacing you want to affect.

3. Click and drag the top indent marker to adjust the first line indent. A note appears above the ruler showing the distance of the indent. The text at the first tab remains at its starting location.

FIGURE 9.7

The ruler at the top of the text editor lets you quickly set tabs and indents for text.

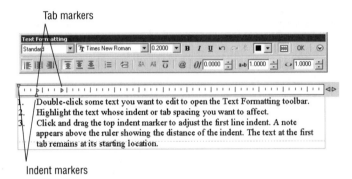

Tab markers

Indent markers

4. Click and drag the bottom indent marker to adjust the indent of the body of the paragraph. The paragraphs moves with the marker. You see a message at the ruler showing the distance of the indent for the body of the text.

5. Click in the ruler to place tab locations. You can click and drag on existing tab locations to adjust them. Remove tabs by clicking and dragging them out of the ruler.

6. Click OK in the Text Formatting toolbar to accept your changes.

You can set paragraphs of a single Mtext object differently, giving you a wide range of indent formatting possibilities. Just select the text you want to set, and then adjust the indent markers.

To set tabs, all you have to do is click in the text panel's Formatting bar (see Figure 9.7). An arrow-shaped marker appears in the text panel ruler, indicating a tab position. You can add as many tab markers as you like. Once placed, the tab markers can be moved with a click-and-drag.

Adjusting Line Spacing

You can set line spacing for existing text, though at first glance at the Text Formatting toolbar, it is not obvious how this is done. Here are the steps to adjust line spacing:

1. Select the text whose line spacing you want to change and right-click to open the shortcut menu.

2. Choose Properties to open the Properties palette.

3. In the scroll bar at the left of the Properties palette, scroll down until you see all the Text group of the palette.

4. Double-click the Line Space Factor value in the Text group (see Figure 9.8).

5. Enter a value that is the multiple of the default line spacing. You can adjust line spacing between the range of 0.5 and 4 times the height of the text.

6. Close the Properties palette. The text line spacing changes to your new specifications.

Another option just below the Line Space Factor option in the Properties palette is Line Space Style. This allows you to choose between an approximate spacing and an exact spacing.

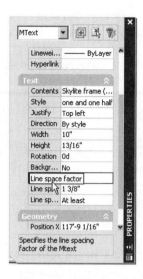

Adding a Background Mask to Text

At times you will need to add text over other graphic elements in your drawing. For example, you might need to place a label over line work or a hatch pattern. In this situation, you will want to add a mask behind your text to make it more readable. You can do this using AutoCAD's Background Mask feature. To use this feature, double-click the text to which you want to add a background, and then when the Text Formatting toolbar appears, right-click the text panel and choose Background Mask from the shortcut menu to open the Background Mask dialog box shown in Figure 9.9.

FIGURE 9.9
The Background Mask
dialog box for text

Turn on the Use Background Mask option, and then click OK. The mask will appear in the color shown in the Color drop-down list. Optionally, you can select a different color from the list or turn on the Use Drawing Background Color option it you want the mask to take on the current background color of the drawing. The Border Offset Factor option lets you control the distance beyond the text that the mask covers.

Making Changes to Multiple Text Objects

One major difference between text in word processors and AutoCAD text is that the AutoCAD text is not all connected as a single block of text. If you want to make changes to the text, you must focus on the specific Mtext object. This can make global changes to text a bit trickier than normal, but you can employ a few tools to make global changes easier.

SCALING MULTIPLE TEXT OBJECTS

You can quickly change the size of text using the Scaletext command. Choose Modify ➤ Object ➤ Text ➤ Scale, or type **Scaletext** at the Command prompt, and then select the text you want to scale. You can select multiple text objects. Press ↵ when you've completed your selection. You see the prompt:

```
[Existing/Left/Center/Middle/Right/TL/TC/TR/ML/MC/MR/BL/BC/BR]<Existing>:
```

Enter the letters corresponding to the location where you want to scale the text. Once you've entered an option, you see the next prompt:

```
Specify new height or [Match object/Scale factor] <Current height>:
```

At this prompt you have three options. You can enter a new height; you can type **M**↵ and then select another text object whose height you want to match; or you can type **S**↵ and then enter a scale factor to scale the text to a specific ratio.

CHANGING JUSTIFICATION OF MULTIPLE TEXT OBJECTS

You've seen how you can change the justification of an individual text object, but you will often find that you need to change the justification of several text objects at one time. AutoCAD offers the Justifytext command for this purpose. To use it, choose Modify ➤ Object ➤ Text ➤ Justify, or type **Justifytext**↵ at the Command prompt. At the `Select object:` prompt, select the text you want to change, and then press ↵ to confirm your selection. You'll see the following prompt:

```
[Left/Align/Fit/Center/Middle/Right/TL/TC/TR/ML/MC/MR/BL/BC/BR] <Left>:
```

Enter the letters corresponding to the type of justification you want to use for the text. Once you've entered an option, the selected text changes to conform to the selected justification option.

Using AutoCAD's Spelling Checker

Although AutoCAD is primarily a drawing program, you will likely be including quite a bit of text in your drawings. If you're like me, you can make frequent spelling mistakes as you rush to get a drawing out. Fortunately, AutoCAD provides a spelling checker. If you've ever used the spelling checker in a typical word processor, such as Microsoft Word, the AutoCAD spelling checker's operation will be familiar to you.

1. Choose Tools ➤ Spelling from the drop-down menu, or type **Sp**↵.

2. At the `Select objects:` prompt, select any text object you want to check. You can select a mixture of multiline and single-line text. When the spelling checker finds a word it does not recognize, the Check Spelling dialog box opens, as shown in Figure 9.10.

TIP You can choose Tools ➤ Quick Select to select all the text in the drawing at once. Quick Select lets you select objects based on their properties or the object type, such as Line or Mtext.

FIGURE 9.10

The Check Spelling
dialog box

In the Check Spelling dialog box, you'll see the word in question, along with the spelling checker's suggested alternate in the Suggestions input box. If the spelling checker finds more than one suggestion, a list of suggested alternate words appears below the input box, just like a typical spelling checker. You can then highlight the desired replacement and click the Change button to change the misspelled word, or you can click Change All to change all occurrences of the word in the selected text. If the suggested word is inappropriate, choose another word from the replacement list (if any), or enter your own spelling in the Suggestions input box. Then choose Change or Change All.

Table 9.2 shows the spelling checker options and their use.

The spelling checker feature includes types of notation that are more likely to be found in technical drawings. It will also check the spelling of text that is included in block definitions.

TABLE 9.2:   The Spelling Checker Options

OPTION	PURPOSE
Ignore	Skips the word.
Ignore All	Skips all occurrences of the word in the selected text.
Change	Changes the word in question to the word you have selected (or entered) from the Suggestions input box.
Change All	Changes all occurrences of the current word when there are multiple instances of the misspelling.
Add	Adds the word in question to the current dictionary.
Lookup	Checks the spelling of the word in question. This option is for the times when you want to find another word that doesn't appear in the Suggestions input box.
Change Dictionaries	Lets you use a different dictionary to check spelling. This option opens the Change Dictionaries dialog box, described in the upcoming section.

Using AutoCAD's Find And Replace Text Feature

Just as the spelling checker plays an important role in CAD drawings, the Find And Replace function found in most word processors is also a welcome tool. AutoCAD's Find And Replace is similar to the same tool in other word processors. A few options, however, work specifically with AutoCAD. Here's how it works.

1. Choose Edit ➤ Find or enter **Find**↵ at the Command prompt to open the Find And Replace dialog box, as shown in Figure 9.11.

FIGURE 9.11

The Find And Replace dialog box

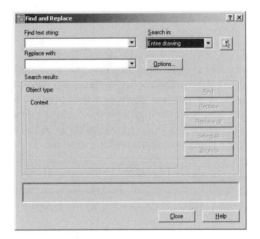

2. Enter the text you want to locate in the Find Text String input box.

3. Enter the replacement text in the Replace With input box.

4. Click Find. When AutoCAD finds the word, it appears in the Context window, along with any other text next to the word.

5. If you have any doubts, click the Zoom To button to display the text in the AutoCAD drawing area.

6. Finally, when you've made certain that this is the text you want to change, click Replace.

If you want to replace all occurrences of a word in the drawing, click Replace All. You can also limit your find-and-replace operation to a specific area of your drawing by clicking the Select Objects button in the upper-right corner of the Find And Replace dialog box (see Figure 9.11).

When you click the Select Objects button, the Find And Replace dialog box closes temporarily to allow you to select a set of objects or a region of your drawing. Find And Replace then limits its search to those objects or the region you select.

You can further control the types of objects that Find And Replace looks for by clicking the Options button to open the Find And Replace Options dialog box, as shown in Figure 9.12.

With this dialog box, you can refine your search by limiting it to blocks, dimension text, standard text, or hyperlink text. You can also specify whether to match case or find whole words only.

FIGURE 9.12

The Find and Replace Options dialog box

Importing Text Files from Other Programs

With multiline text objects, AutoCAD allows you to import ASCII text or Rich Text Format (RTF) files. RTF files can be exported from Microsoft Word and most other word-processing programs and retain their formatting in AutoCAD.

To import text, first select the text from your word processor, and then choose Edit ➢ Copy to copy the text to the Windows Clipboard. In AutoCAD, choose Edit ➢ Paste Special to open the Paste Special dialog box. Click the Paste button, and then select Text from the As list box. Click OK. You'll see the text drag into the drawing area as a bounding box. Click a location to place your text. The inserted text will use the current default text style formatting.

Understanding Text and Scale

AutoCAD allows you to draw at full scale, that is, to represent distances as values equivalent to the actual size of the object. When you later plot the drawing, you tell AutoCAD at what scale you want to plot, and the program reduces the drawing accordingly. This gives you the freedom to enter measurements at full scale and not worry about converting them to various scales every time you enter a distance. Unfortunately, this feature can also create problems when you enter text and dimensions.

You can deal with text in AutoCAD in two ways:

◆ You can add your text in layout space, which has the advantage of letting you specify heights at the actual print size. The drawback is that you cannot edit the text and the graphics in the same workspace. You have to be either in the Layout tab space known as paper space or in the Model tab space also known as floating model space. It can be annoying to have to switch back and forth to edit a drawing full of text.

◆ You can add your text directly in the Model tab. This has the advantage of allowing you to edit text and graphics at the same time without switching between model and paper space. The disadvantage is that you have to scale the text to a size that corresponds to a full-scale drawing.

To help you understand the scale issue when adding text in the Model tab, imagine you are drawing a floor plan at full size on a very large sheet of paper. When you are finished with this drawing, you will need to reduce it to a scale that allows it to fit on an 8.5″ × 11″ sheet of paper. So you have to make your text quite large to keep it legible once it is reduced. This means that if you want text to appear ⅛″ high when the drawing is plotted, you must convert it to a considerably larger size when you draw it. To do this, you multiply the desired height of the final plotted text by a scale conversion factor.

If your drawing is at $\frac{1}{8}"=1'-0"$ scale, you multiply the desired text height, $\frac{1}{8}"$, by the scale conversion factor of 96 to get a height of 12″. This is the height you must make your text to get $\frac{1}{8}"$-high text in the final plot. Table 9.3 shows you some other examples of text height to scale.

TABLE 9.3: $\frac{1}{8}"$-High Text Converted to Size for Various Drawing Scales

DRAWING SCALE	SCALE FACTOR	AUTOCAD DRAWING HEIGHT FOR $\frac{1}{8}"$-HIGH TEXT
$\frac{1}{16}" = 1'-0"$	192	24.0″
$\frac{1}{8}" = 1'-0"$	96	12.0″
$\frac{1}{4}" = 1'-0"$	48	6.0″
$\frac{1}{2}" = 1'-0"$	24	3.0″
$\frac{3}{4}" = 1'-0"$	16	2.0″
$1" = 1'-0"$	12	1.5″
$1\frac{1}{2}" = 1'-0"$	8	1.0″
$3" = 1'-0"$	4	0.5″

Using Styles to Organize Your Fonts

As you start to use AutoCAD, you'll notice a lot of styles—styles for dimensions, styles for plotting, and styles for text. If your drawing is fairly simple, you might not need to worry about text styles. But if you are working with a large drawing project, you'll want to set up a few text styles. If you are working with others on a large project, you'll almost certainly encounter text styles, so it will help to know about them.

You can think of text styles as a way to store your most common text formatting. Styles store text height and font information, so you don't have to reset these options every time you enter text. You might have a style for notes and another for larger drawing labels, and yet another for title block information. And styles also include some settings not available in the Multiline Text Editor.

Creating and Setting a Style

Even if you don't set up a style on your own, the moment you add text to a drawing, you are using a text style. In AutoCAD, the Standard text style is the default. It uses the AutoCAD Txt font and numerous other settings that you will learn about in this section. These other settings include width factor, oblique angle, and default height.

If you've used the instructions in the previous sections of this chapter to create text, you know that you can modify the formatting of a string of text as you enter the text. But for the most part, once you've set up a few styles, you won't need to adjust settings such as fonts and text height each time you enter text. You can select from a list of styles you've previously created and just start typing.

This next exercise shows you how to create a style:

1. Choose Format ➢ Text Style or type **St**⏎ to open the Text Style dialog box (see Figure 9.13).

FIGURE 9.13

The Text Style dialog box

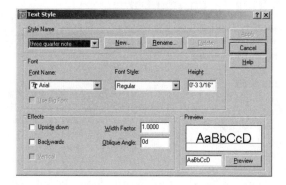

2. Click the New button in the Style Name group to open the New Text Style dialog box.

3. Enter a name for your new style; then click OK.

4. To select a font for your style, click the Font Name drop-down list in the Font group.

5. In the Height input box, enter the text height you want for your style or leave it as 0 if you want more flexibility in determining the text height when you create text.

6. Click Apply, and then click Close.

Once you create a style in this way, your new style becomes the default style whenever you use the Mtext command. You can set the current text style by opening the Text Style dialog box, selecting the desired default style from the Style Name drop-down list, and clicking Apply.

TIP You can use the Rename option in the Text Style dialog box to rename a style.

Using a Text Style

Once you've created a text style, you can easily select it while creating new text. Start the Multiline Text tool in the usual way, and then select the style from the Style drop-down list of the Text Formatting toolbar (see Figure 9.14). When you start to enter text, the style you select is used to format the text.

A newly created style becomes the default style, and you didn't have to explicitly select your new style in order to use it.

You can also change an existing piece of text to a different style by double-clicking an Mtext object and selecting a different style name in the Style drop-down list.

FIGURE 9.14

The Style drop-down list in the Text Formatting toolbar

WARNING The Style option does not affect the style of text if the text has other custom format changes, such as a font and size change from its default settings.

Setting the Current Default Style

Suppose you want all the new text you create to be of a different style than the current default style. You can quickly select a style from the Styles toolbar (see Figure 9.15), which is just to the right of the Standard toolbar.

FIGURE 9.15

The Text Style Control drop-down list in the Styles toolbar toward the top of the AutoCAD window

Once you've done this, the selected style will be the default until you select a different style. AutoCAD records the current default style with the drawing data when you choose File ➤ Save. The next time you work on the file, you the default style is the same.

Now you know how to create a new style. Other settings are available in the Text Style dialog box. Here is a listing of those settings and their purposes. Some of them, such as the Width Factor, can be quite useful. Others, such as the Backwards and Vertical options, are rarely used.

Section	Options	Purpose
Style Name	New	Lets you create a new text style.
	Rename	Lets you rename an existing style. This option is not available for the Standard style.
	Delete	Deletes a style. This option is not available for the Standard style.
Font	Font Name	Lets you select a font from a list of available fonts. The list is derived from the font resources available to Windows, plus the standard AutoCAD fonts.
	Font Style	Offers variations of a font, such as italic or bold, when they are available.
	Height	Lets you enter a font size.
Effects	Upside Down	Prints the text upside down.
	Backwards	Prints the text backward.

Section	Options	Purpose
Effects	Width Factor	Adjusts the width and spacing of the characters in the text. A value of 1 keeps the text at its normal width. Values greater than 1 expand the text, and values less than 1 compress the text.
	Oblique Angle	Skews the text at an angle. When this option is set to a value greater than 0, the text appears italicized. A value of less than 0 (–12, for example) causes the text to "lean" to the left.

Adding Single Words with the Single-Line Text Object

You may find that you are entering a lot of single words or simple labels that don't require all the bells and whistles of the Multiline Text Editor. AutoCAD offers the *single-line text object* that is simpler to use and can speed text entry if you are adding only small pieces of text.

1. Enter **Dt↵** or choose Draw ➢ Text ➢ Single Line Text to issue the Dtext command.

2. At the `Specify start point of text or [Justify/Style]:` prompt, select the starting point for the text. Notice that the prompt offers the Justify and Style options.

3. At the `Specify height:` prompt, enter a height value or indicate a height by clicking two points in the drawing area. You can also just press ↵ to accept the default height.

4. At the `Specify rotation angle of text <0>:` prompt, enter a rotation angle or press ↵ to accept the default, 0°. You can specify any angle other than horizontal (for example, if you want your text aligned with a rotated object). You'll see a text I-beam cursor at the point you selected in step 3.

5. At the `Enter text:` prompt, enter the text you want. As you type, the word appears in the drawing as well as in the Command window.

6. Press ↵ to move the cursor down to start a new line, or click a location in the drawing area to move to an entirely different location to continue your text.

7. Press ↵ without entering text to exit the Dtext command.

You can add single lines of text in different parts of your drawing fairly quickly. Dtext uses the current default text style setting.

If you make a typing error while using Dtext, you can select the text in the drawing with your cursor and make the appropriate changes just as you would in a word processor. You can also paste text from the Clipboard into the cursor location using the Ctrl+V keyboard shortcut or by right-clicking in the Command window to access the shortcut menu.

Even if you don't create a Dtext object, you may encounter them as you edit drawings created from other sources. Fortunately they are easy to edit.

When you double-click a Dtext object, the text highlights and a box appears around the text. You can then either start typing to replace the entire text or click a location to add or delete text, just as you would in any text editor.

If you need to change other properties of single-line text, you can use the Properties palette. Select the Dtext object, and then right-click and choose Properties from the shortcut menu. You can then edit the text-related properties such as style, height, rotation angle, and width factor. (See Chapter 4 for more on the Properties dialog box.)

Adding Tables to Your Drawing

One of the most common text items in a drawing is the table or schedule. Tables are lists of parts that include specifications and part numbers as shown in Figure 9.16. Tables provide vital information about a design that cannot be conveyed through drawings alone.

FIGURE 9.16

A sample schedule created with the Tables tool

No.	Room	Finish				Ceiling Ht.	Area	Remarks
		Floor	Base	Walls	Ceiling			
110	Lobby	B	1	A	1	10'-0"	200sf	
111	Office	A	1	B	2	8'-0"	96sf	
112	Office	A	1	B	2	8'-0"	96sf	
113	Office	A	1	B	2	8'-0"	96sf	
114	Meeting	C	1	B	2	8'-0"	150sf	
115	Breakout	C	1	B	2	8'-0"	150sf	
116	Womens	D	2	C	3	8'-0"	50sf	
117	Mens	D	2	C	3	8'-0"	50sf	

Room Finish Schedule

Frequently, tables are generated in a spreadsheet since the tabular format of spreadsheets fit with the table format. The AutoCAD Table feature gives you an easy way to include tables with your drawing, either by creating them directly in AutoCAD or by importing them from spreadsheet files.

Creating a Table

Before you create your table, you need to know the number of rows and columns you'll want. Don't worry if you are not certain of the exact number; you can always add or subtract them at any time. For practice, you can create a table that contains 4 rows and 5 columns.

Start by creating the basic table layout.

1. Click Table from the Draw toolbar or choose Draw ➢ Table to open the Insert Table dialog box (see Figure 9.17).

2. In the Column & Row Settings group, enter **4** for the columns and **5** for the rows.

3. Click OK. The dialog box closes, and you see the outline of a table follow your cursor.

4. Position the table in the center of your drawing area and click to place the table. The table appears with a cursor in the top cell. You also see the Text Formatting dialog box above the table.

5. Enter a title for your table, and then press ↵. Notice that the cursor moves to the next cell.

6. Click OK to exit the Text Formatting dialog box.

Once you're finished, you will have a table with an additional row—the title row at the top.

FIGURE 9.17
The Insert Table
dialog box

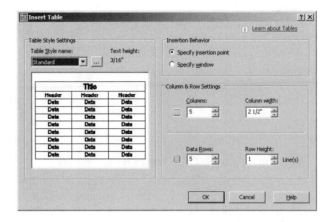

Adding Cell Text

Once you have the table in place, you can easily add text to the individual cells. Just double-click inside a cell to open the Text Formatting toolbar (see Figure 9.18). A text cursor appears inside the cell allowing you to type the text you want. The Text Formatting toolbar lets you format the text.

FIGURE 9.18
A table cell ready for
editing with the Text
Formatting toolbar
above the table

Double-click inside a cell to add text.

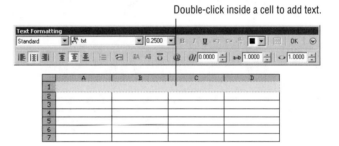

Combining Cells

In formatting your table, you might want to merge adjacent cells to create new headings or for other purposes. Here are the steps to merging cells.

1. Click in the first cell you want to merge.

2. Shift+click in the cell at the other end of the group of cells you want to merge (see Figure 9.19). The group of cells are selected.

3. Right-click in the selected cells, and then choose Merge Cells ➤ All. The selected cells merge into a single cell.

You have the option to restrict the merging of cells to rows (choose Merge Cells ➤ By Row) or to columns (choose Merge Cells ➤ By Column) in the shortcut menu in step 3.

FIGURE 9.19
Selecting a group of cells
in a table

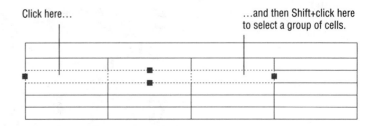

Click here...

...and then Shift+click here
to select a group of cells.

Adjusting Table Cell Text Orientation

You can adjust the orientation of the text in cells to accommodate different table styles. For example, to use space more efficiently, a table frequently has column headings that are oriented vertically. The following shows you how to change the text orientation from horizontal to vertical. Before you start, it will help to have text already placed in the cells you are editing so you can adjust the cell size as you work.

1. Click in the cell to select it.

2. Shift+click in another cell to select a group cells.

3. Click the grip at the bottom of the selected group and move it down. The entire row becomes taller as shown in the sample in Figure 9.20. This provides room for the text when you rotate it.

FIGURE 9.20
A group of cells selected
and made taller

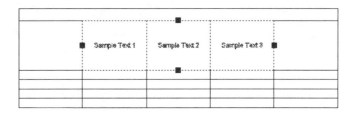

4. Right-click in the selected cells, and then choose Properties from the shortcut menu to open the Properties palette.

5. Click the Text Rotation option in the Content group.

6. Click the drop-down list just to the left of the Text Rotation option and select 90 (see Figure 9.21). The text rotates into a vertical orientation.

   With the text in this orientation, the columns are too wide, so you will want to change the cell width for the selected cells.

7. With the Properties palette still open, click the Cell Width option near the top of the palette, and then enter an appropriate value for the cell width. You might need to experiment with this value until you get something that looks appropriate. The cells change to their new width.

FIGURE 9.21
The Text Rotation option in the Properties palette

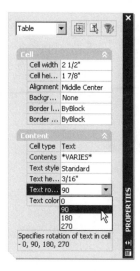

You can also adjust the width of multiple cells by adjusting the grip location as shown in Figure 9.22. For example, instead of changing the cell width value in step 7, you can move the left or right grip of the selected group of cells.

FIGURE 9.22
Adjusting the width of a group of cells

Click and drag either side grip to adjust the width of the group of cells.

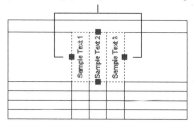

Adjusting Table Cell Text Justification

Besides text orientation, you can also change the justification of text within the cells. Here is how it's done.

1. Select a cell or click in a cell and Shift+click in another cell to select a group.

2. Right-click in the selected cells, and choose Cell Alignment ➤ Middle Left. The text in the cells become centered in their cells.

You can also control the margin between the text and the cell border for the entire table using the Cell Margin options in the Properties palette. Select the entire table, right-click, and choose Properties. In the Properties palette, click the Vertical Cell Margin option or the Horizontal Cell Margin option in the Table group (see Figure 9.23).

FIGURE 9.23
The Vertical Cell Margin
option in the Properties
palette

Adding or Deleting Rows and Columns of Cells

Now suppose you want to delete a row of cells in a table. Here's what to do.

1. Click a cell in the row you want to delete.

2. Right-click, and then choose Delete Row.

To add a row, do the following:

1. Select a cell adjacent to the location where you want a new row

2. Right-click, and choose Insert Rows ➤ Above or Insert Rows ➤ Below, depending on where you want the new row.

You might notice a Delete Columns and Insert Columns option in the shortcut menu that let you add or delete columns. These options function in a similar way to the Delete Rows and Insert Rows options.

Adding Formulas to Cells

One of the greatest benefits of using spreadsheets is that you can apply formulas to the values in a cell. AutoCAD's table feature lets you include formulas in cells so you don't have to rely on an external spreadsheet program when generating tables.

To include formulas, you'll need to employ a special AutoCAD text object called a *field*. A field can be linked with objects in a drawing so that the field displays that object's properties. For example, you can create a field that is associated with a block name. If the block name changes, the field automatically changes as well.

There are several types of fields, each with its own purpose. As a beginner or casual user, you won't have to concern yourself with most of the field types, but if you want to create and use tables, you will want to know how to use the *formula* field, which lets you add formulas to a table cell. The following example introduces you to fields and their use in tables by showing how you can create a cell formula that displays the sum of two other cells. The example uses the table shown in Figure 9.24:

1. Double-click in a cell to select the location for your formula, as shown in Figure 9.24.

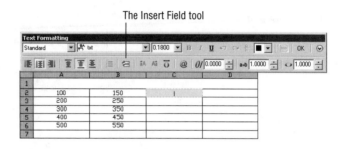

2. Right-click the selected cell, and then choose Insert Field. You can also click the Insert Field tool in the Text Formatting dialog box. (See Figure 9.24 for the location of the Insert Field tool.) The Field dialog box opens (see Figure 9.25).

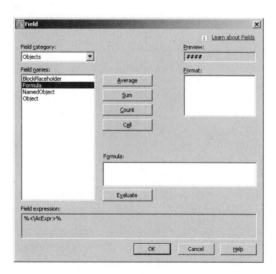

3. Make sure that Objects is selected in the Field category drop down list and that Formula is selected in the Field Names list to the left, and then click the Cell button. The dialog box temporarily closes to allow you to select a cell.

4. Click a cell whose value you want to include in the formula, as shown in Figure 9.26. The Field dialog box reappears, and the cell's address appears in the Formula box near the bottom of the dialog box. In typical spreadsheet form, the cell address is an alphanumeric value with the column given as a letter and the row given as a number. A cell address of A2 is a cell in the column A in row number 2, for example (see Figure 9.27).

FIGURE 9.26
Selecting the cells to
include in the formula

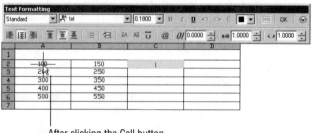

After clicking the Cell button,
select a cell to include in the formula.

FIGURE 9.27
The Formula box with
cell addresses

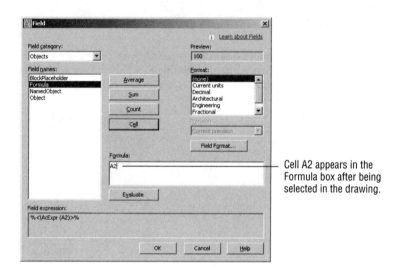

Cell A2 appears in the
Formula box after being
selected in the drawing.

5. Type + (plus sign) as shown in Figure 9.28 to add the value of the selected cell to the value of another cell.

6. Click the Cell button again, and then click another cell whose value you want to add to the first cell. The address of the cell you select appears in the Formula box behind the plus sign you added in the previous step.

7. Click OK. The sum of the two cells appears in the cell you selected in step 1 (see Figure 9.29).

8. Try changing the value in the cell you selected as part of the formula in step 4. The formula cell changes to reflect the new value.

You'll notice that the cell with the formula shows a gray background. This background indicates that the cell contains a field. This background does not print and is there to help differentiate fields from other types of text.

FIGURE 9.28

Adding the plus sign in the Formula box

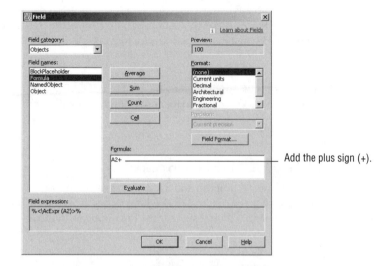

Add the plus sign (+).

FIGURE 9.29

The Cell with the completed formula shows the sum of the selected cells.

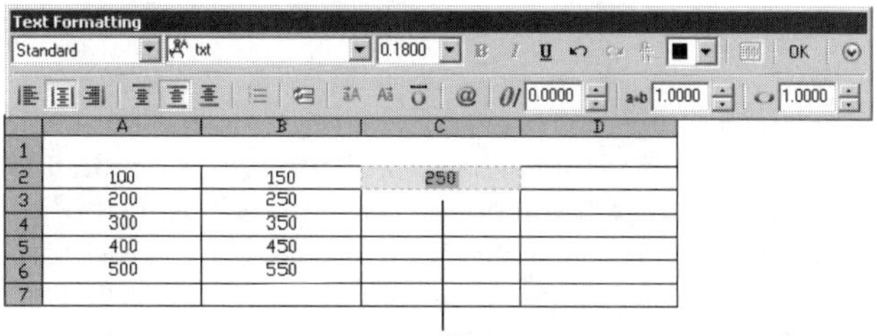

The formula cell showing the addition of cells A2 and B2.
The formula appears as A2+B2 in the Formula box of the Field dialog box.

USING OTHER MATH OPERATIONS

In the previous example, you saw how you can use the plus sign to add the value of two cells. You can string several cells addresses together to add multiple cells as in

    A2+A3+A4...

You can also subtract, multiply, or divide by using the – (subtract or minus), * (multiply or asterisk), or / (divide or hash) signs. To perform multiple operations on several cells, you can group operations with parentheses. For example, if you want to add two cells together and then multiply their sum by another cell, you can use the following format:

    (A2+A3)*A4

You might have noticed the Average, Sum, and Count buttons that appear in the Field dialog box. Average gives the average value of a set of cells, Sum gives the sum, and Count returns the number of cells you select. Clicking one of these buttons temporarily closes the Field dialog box, allowing you to select several cells using a selection window. Once you've selected a set of cells, you'll see a formula appear in the Formula box that automatically applies the operation to the selected cells. For example, clicking the Average button produces a formula similar to the following:

```
Average(A1:B5)
```

A range of cells is indicated using a colon as in A1:B5. You can use this format when entering formulas manually. You can also include a single cell with a range by using a comma as in

```
Average(A1:B5,C6)
```

ADDING FORMULAS DIRECTLY TO CELLS

If you're in a hurry, you can add a formula directly to a cell without using the Field dialog box. To do this, double-click the cell, and then when the Text Formatting toolbar appears, enter the formula with the addition of an = (equal sign) at the beginning as in the following:

```
=A2+A3
```

The cell automatically converts to a formula field with the appropriate value. The only drawback to this method is that you have to decipher the cell address on your own. If you double-click in a cell, the cell row and column labels appear to help you find the appropriate address.

EDITING FORMULAS

Finally, if you want to change a formula, you can double-click the formula cell to open the Text Formatting toolbar. If you prefer to edit the cell using the Field dialog box, select the cell, right-click, and choose Edit Field to open the Field dialog box, with the selected formula in the Formula box. You can then click the Cell button to include individual cells or click the Average, Sum, or Count buttons to include a range, but make sure you delete the Average, Sum, or Count operator from the formula if you do this.

Exporting Tables

In some situations, you'll want to export your AutoCAD table to a spreadsheet program or a database. You can do this through a somewhat hidden option in a shortcut menu. Take the following steps.

1. Select the entire table by clicking in a spot above and to the right of the table. With the crossing selection window, completely enclose the table and click.

2. Right-click anywhere in the table, and then choose Export from the shortcut menu to open the Export Data dialog box. This is a typical file dialog box.

3. Specify a name and location for your exported table data and click Save.

Notice that the file is saved with a .csv filename extension. This is a comma-delimited file and can be read by most spreadsheet programs, including Microsoft Excel. To open the exported file in Excel, choose File ≻ Open to open the Open dialog box, and then select Text File (*.prn, *.txt, *.csv). You can then locate the exported table and open it.

Importing Tables

It's not unusual for a table to be generated in an Excel spreadsheet by someone other than the person drawing plans in AutoCAD. You can easily import Excel spreadsheets into AutoCAD and convert them to AutoCAD tables.

1. In Excel, select the cells you want to export, and then choose Edit ➤ Copy.

2. In AutoCAD, choose Edit ➤ Paste Special to open the Paste Special dialog box (see Figure 9.30).

FIGURE 9.30

The Paste Special dialog box

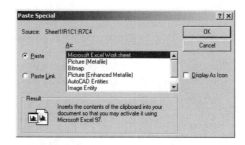

3. Select AutoCAD Entities from the list box, and then click OK. The imported spreadsheet appears at the cursor.

4. Click to place the spreadsheet in the drawing.

Once the spreadsheet is placed, you can use any of the table-editing methods described here to adjust its appearance.

Editing Table Line Weights

The text in a table is not the only part that you want to control. The line work within the table is also important. You can emphasize parts of a table by making the line weight bolder for certain groups of cells, for example.

TIP Before you can see the effects of the line-weight settings for cell borders, you need to turn on the display of line weights. Choose Format ➤ Lineweight, turn on the Display Lineweight setting, and then click OK.

You can control the line weight of cell borders by doing the following:

1. Select a single cell by clicking in it, or select a group of cells by clicking one cell to select it and then Shift+clicking another cell.

2. Right-click and choose Cell Borders to open the Cell Border Properties dialog box (see Figure 9.31). You can use this dialog box to fine-tune the appearance of the line work of the table.

3. Click the Lineweight drop-down list and select a line weight.

FIGURE 9.31

The Cell Border
Properties dialog box

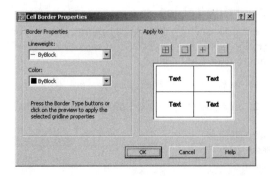

4. Click the Outside Borders button in the Apply To group to tell AutoCAD to change the outer-most borders of the cell or group of cells to the selected line weight (see Figure 9.32).

FIGURE 9.32

The Outside Borders
option in the Cell Border
Properties dialog box

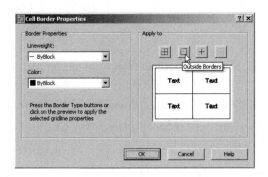

5. Click OK to apply the changes to the cell borders (see Figure 9.33).

FIGURE 9.33

A set of cells with their
border adjusted to a
heavier line weight

The border surrounding the selected cells acquires the line weight.

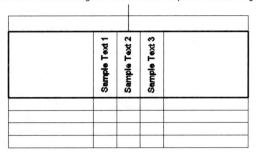

The Cell Borders Properties dialog box also lets you set the line colors by choosing a color from the Color drop-down list before selecting an Apply To option.

In the example, you use the Outside Borders option. Table 9.4 describes all the border options.

TABLE 9.4:   The Apply to Options in the Cell Border Properties Dialog Box

OPTION	PURPOSE
All Borders	Applies the changes to the borders of all the selected cells
Outside Borders	Applies the changes to only the outside borders of a group of cells
Inside Borders	Applies the changes to only the inside borders of a group of cells
No Borders	Lets you select which border you want to affect by clicking the graphic in the Apply To group

If you only want to select the vertical or horizontal inside borders, first click the No Borders button, and then click the desired border in the graphic of the Cell Borders Properties dialog box. As you click lines in the sample image, they lighten or darken to indicate their selection.

Changing Cell Background Colors

In addition to the table borders, you can change the background color for the cells of the table through the Background Fill option in the Properties palette. Select a group of cells in the table that you want to affect (but don't select the entire table), right-click, and choose Properties to open the Properties palette. Click the Background Fill option in the Cell group.

Adding Graphics to Table Cells

One of the more interesting features of the Table tool is its ability to include blocks in a cell. This can be useful if you want to include graphic elements in your table. Adding a block to a cell is a simple process.

1. Click in a cell to select it.

2. Right-click and choose Insert Block to open the Insert A Block In A Table Cell dialog box (see Figure 9.34).

FIGURE 9.34
The Insert A Block In A
Table Cell dialog box

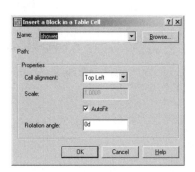

3. Select a block name from the Name drop-down list. You can also click the button to the right of the list to open a file dialog box that allows you to select a drawing file for import to the cell.

4. Once you've selected a block and specified the settings in the Properties group of the dialog box, click OK. The block appears in the cell you've selected.

The Properties group in the dialog box allows you to specify the alignment and size of the inserted block. By default, the Autofit option is turned on. This option adjusts the size of the block to make it fit in the current cell size.

Creating Table Styles

Most users will have a set of table formats they use frequently. Door and window schedules in architectural plans will be fairly similar from project to project, for example.

For this reason, AutoCAD offers custom table styles. You can create a table style that matches some of the formatting you normally use for your projects. Then when you need a table, you can use your custom style and save yourself some table-formatting work.

Table styles allow you to set up the properties of the title, column heads, and data in advance so you don't have to set up those features each time you create a table. When you are ready, you can select your custom table style and specify the number of columns and rows.

To create a table style, take the following steps:

1. Choose Format ➤ Table Style or enter **TS**⏎ to open the Table Style dialog box. You see the Standard table style in the list box shown in Figure 9.35.

FIGURE 9.35

The Table Style dialog box

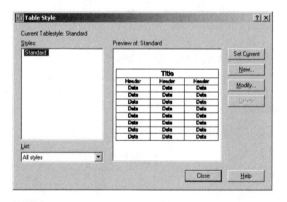

2. Click New to open the Create New Table Style dialog box, as shown in Figure 9.36. This is where you give your new table style a name.

3. Enter a name for your table style and click Continue to open the New Table Style dialog box (see Figure 9.37).

FIGURE 9.36

The Create New Table Style dialog box

FIGURE 9.37
The New Table Style
dialog box

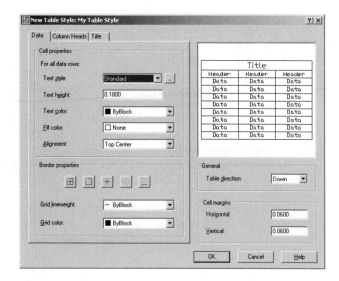

4. Click the Column Heads tab and the Title tab at the top of the dialog box. Notice that options for these tabs are nearly identical to those for the Data tab.

5. You'll learn more about the options in this dialog box next. For now, click OK to close the dialog box.

6. Click Close to exit the dialog box.

In step 5, you'll see that your new table style now appears in the Style list of the Table Style dialog box. If you want to edit an existing table style, select the style from the list and click the Modify button to open the Modify Table Style dialog box, in which you can edit the existing style. The Modify Table Style dialog box is identical to the New Table Style dialog box shown in Figure 9.37.

Once you've created a style, you can select it from the Table Style Settings group of the Insert Table dialog box (see Figure 9.38).

You can also get to the New Table Style dialog box by clicking the browse button just to the right of the Table Style Name drop-down list in the Insert Table dialog box.

FIGURE 9.38
The Table Style Settings
group in the Insert Table
dialog box

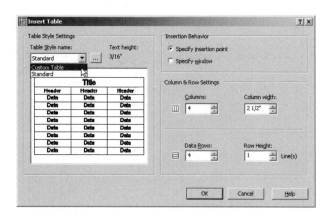

Let's take a closer look at the New Table Style dialog box in Figure 9.37. You saw in step 4 of the previous exercise that the three tabs at the top of the dialog box all contain the same set of options. This allows you to specify the text-formatting options for each of these three table elements: Data, Column Heads, and Title. You can also turn off the column head row or the title row. As you make changes, the graphic to the right shows you how your changes affect your table style.

The Cell Properties group lets you format the text of the table. You can choose the text style, height, color, and alignment. You can select a text style from the Text Style drop-down list, or you can click the button to the right of the drop-down list to open the Text Style dialog box. By offering this option, you can create a new text style if one doesn't exist to suite your needs. The Fill Color option lets you specify a background color for text cells.

The Border Properties group lets you control the color and line weight of the table line work. The options in this group work just like the options in the Cell Border Properties dialog box you saw in an earlier exercise.

The Table Direction option lets you specify whether the table reads from top to bottom or from the bottom up. Finally, the Cell Margins options let you specify the minimum distance between the text and the border of the cell. The Cell Margins options are useful when you find that the text is too close to one of the border lines.

Just Enough Summary

Creating text and editing are tasks that nearly everyone has to tackle at some point. If your job is to just update the text in a drawing, all you have to do is double-click the text and make your changes in the text panel that appears. Format changes are a little more involved, but if you are familiar with most text editors, you will find that AutoCAD's text-editing features follow methods used in most other word processors. Creating text requires some familiarity with methods for scaling your text properly to make it the correct size. Also, placing the text in the Model tab or a Layout tab affects how you deal with text scaling.

Another type of annotation you'll want to know about is dimensioning. In the next chapter, you'll learn about the tools for creating dimensions in AutoCAD and how you can change dimensions as your drawings change.

Chapter 10

Using Dimensions

Dimensions are a key part of technical drawing and drafting. You could almost say that dimensions are the reason we produce CAD drawings in the first place, since they convey critical information about our designs. Before the days of AutoCAD, we used dimensions to communicate specific proportions of a design. But now we can use dimensions to help keep track of critical measurements in a drawing. We can use temporary dimensions to help in this effort.

Adding dimensions to your drawing is fairly easy. The first half of this chapter discusses the types of dimensions available and how to apply them to your drawing. One of the trickier aspects of dimensioning in AutoCAD is understanding scale factors. Just as with text, you have to apply a scale factor to your dimensions before they appear properly in the Model tab of your drawing.

Finally, since there are many standards and styles of dimensioning, AutoCAD provides many options that let you set up dimensions just the way you want. But with so many settings, you might feel just a bit lost when you want to fine-tune the appearance of your dimensions.

- ◆ Understanding the Parts of an AutoCAD Dimension
- ◆ Dimensioning in the Model or Layout Tab
- ◆ Drawing Linear Dimensions
- ◆ Dimensioning Nonorthogonal Objects
- ◆ Adding a Note with an Arrow
- ◆ Using Ordinate Dimensions
- ◆ Adding Tolerance Notation
- ◆ Editing Dimensions
- ◆ Setting Up the Dimension's Appearance

Understanding the Parts of an AutoCAD Dimension

If you were drawing dimensions by hand, you would not need to know the names of the dimension's components. Now that you are using CAD and reading this book, it will help to know these names so you can better understand the discussions that follow in this chapter.

Figure 10.1 shows a typical dimension along with the names of its parts. Not all these parts appear in all styles of dimensions. For example, the dimension line extension is only used in architectural drawings. Also, architectural drawings do not use arrows when dimensioning straight lengths. Instead, a "tick" mark is used, which looks like a diagonal line.

FIGURE 10.1

The components of a dimension for two common styles

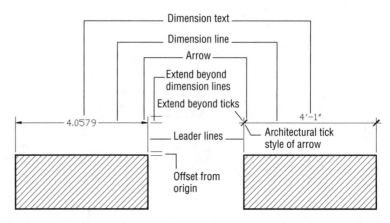

As you read this chapter, you might want to refer to this figure when you need clarification about the names of the dimension components. Toward the end of this chapter, you will find a section called "Setting Up the Dimension's Appearance," which describes how to change the appearance of your dimensions to suit your style of drawing. You'll learn more about the dimension components in that section.

Dimensioning in the Model or Layout Tab

The first big question new users ask regarding dimensioning is which tab to use for dimensioning. Just as with text, you can add dimensions in either the Model tab or a Layout tab. This is an important choice because it affects the way you set up your dimensions. I've mentioned the following points in the section on text and scale, but they bear repeating here with some minor changes:

♦ You can add your dimensions in a Layout tab, which has the advantage of letting you specify sizes of text, arrows, and other dimension features at the actual print size. The drawback is that you cannot see or edit the dimensions while you work on your drawing in a Model tab. You either have to be in the Layout tab space known as paper space or in the Model tab space also known as floating model space. However, dimensions do have a feature called Associative Dimensioning that allows them to automatically adjust to changes in the objects they are dimensioning no mater which tab is used to add dimensions.

♦ You can add your dimensions directly in the Model tab. This has the advantage of allowing you to see and edit text and graphics at the same time without switching between model and paper space. The disadvantage is that you have to apply a scale factor to your dimensions so that their features appear at a correct size when you plot your drawing. (See "The Scale for Dimension Features Group" in Table 10.4 for the scale factor setting.)

Even if you choose to do all your dimensioning in a Layout tab, you will want to know how to work with dimensions that have been drawn in the Model tab. Countless older AutoCAD drawings are dimensioned in Model tab. If you work with AutoCAD professionally, one of those drawings will eventually cross your computer screen.

WHY ARE MY DIMENSIONS SO SMALL?

As you begin to use dimensions in AutoCAD and you are working in a Model tab, you may find that the arrows and text are way too small for your drawing. This usually happens when new users try to dimension a drawing in the Model tab.

If this happens, you'll need to change the way AutoCAD scales dimension components. Just as with text, dimension components such as arrow and text need to be scaled up to appear correctly in the Model tab (see in Chapter 9).Once you know the scale factor for your drawing, do the following.

1. Choose Dimension ➤ Style or click the Dimension Style tool in the Dimension toolbar at the top of the AutoCAD window to open the Dimension Style Manager dialog box.

2. The current dimension style is highlighted in the list to the left. Click the Modify button to the right of the dialog box to open the Modify Dimension Style dialog box.

3. Click the Fit tab at the top of the dialog box.

4. In the Scale For Dimension Features group, enter the scale factor for your drawing in the Use Overall Scale Of text box.

5. Click OK, and then click Close in the Dimension Style Manager dialog box.

Dimension scale is usually not an issue if you are dimensioning in a Layout tab. See "Creating a Dimension Style" later in this chapter for more on the Dimension Style Manager dialog box.

Drawing Linear Dimensions

The most common type of dimension you'll be using is the *linear dimension,* an orthogonal dimension measuring the width and length of an object. AutoCAD provides three dimensioning tools for this purpose: Linear, Continue, and Baseline. These tools are readily accessible from the Dimension drop-down menu.

USING THE DIMENSION TOOLBAR

If you want ready access to dimensioning tools, open the Dimension toolbar and place it in your work area. This toolbar contains nearly all the commands necessary to draw and edit your dimensions. To open the Dimension toolbar, right-click any toolbar, and choose Dimension from the shortcut menu. You can use the tool tips on the toolbar to find the appropriate tool.

Placing Horizontal and Vertical Dimensions

Linear dimensions are those that are aligned either vertically or horizontally. They constitute the bulk of dimensions in most projects. The following steps describe how to apply linear dimensions.

WARNING   Using osnaps is crucial in producing accurate results in all dimensioning tasks.

1. Choose Dimension ➤ Linear from the drop-down menu or enter **Dli**↵ at the Command prompt.

2. At the `Specify first extension line origin or <select object>:` prompt, Shift+right-click and use an osnap to select the exact location on an object, such as an endpoint or an intersection of two lines on the drawing you are dimensioning (see Figure 10.2).

FIGURE 10.2
Using a linear dimension

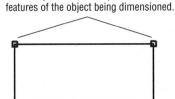
Use osnaps to select endpoints or other features of the object being dimensioned.

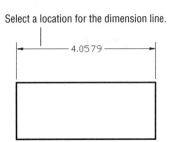
Select a location for the dimension line.

4.0579

TIP The prompt in step 2 gives you the option of pressing ↵ to select an object. If you do this, you are prompted to select the object you want to dimension, rather than the actual distance to be dimensioned.

3. At the `Specify second extension line origin:` prompt, use an osnap to select the other end of the object you are dimensioning, as shown in Figure 10.2.

4. In the next prompt, `Specify dimension line location or [Mtext/Text/Angle/Horizontal/Vertical/Rotated]:`, you'll see a temporary dimension at the cursor location. Position the temporary dimension where you want the dimension to appear, and then click the mouse.

If you prefer to be more precise about the dimension line location, in step 4 you can enter a relative distance from the last point selected.

Continuing a Dimension

You will often want to enter a group of dimensions strung together in a line. You can use the Continue option in the dimension menu to do this. This option assumes that you've already placed one linear dimension and are ready to continue with a string of dimensions from the last dimension.

1. Choose Dimension ➢ Continue or enter **Dco**↵.

2. At the `Specify a second extension line origin or [Undo/Select] <Select>:` prompt, select the next location you want to dimension. (see the left image in Figure 10.3). You can continue to add more dimensions until you press ↵.

If you find that you've selected the wrong location for a continued dimension, click the Undo tool or press **U**↵.

The Continue Dimension option continues from the last dimension you added to the drawing. The last drawn extension line is used as the first extension line for the continued dimension. If you need to continue a string of dimensions from a dimension other than the last one you placed in the drawing, press ↵ at the `Specify a second extension line origin or [Undo/Select]:` prompt in step 2 of the previous example. Then click the extension line from which you want to continue. You can then proceed to add dimensions.

FIGURE 10.3

A continued string of dimensions

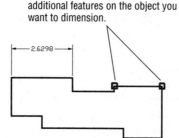

Use the Continue option, and select additional features on the object you want to dimension.

A continued dimension appears after you select each location.

Drawing Dimensions from a Common Base Extension Line

Frequently, you need to dimension from a single datum point, as shown in Figure 10.4. This means that you need several dimensions starting from the same location. To accommodate this, AutoCAD provides the Baseline option.

FIGURE 10.4

A baseline dimension

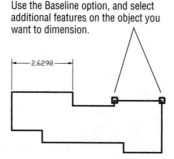
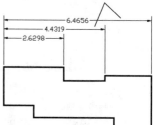

Use the Baseline option, and select additional features on the object you want to dimension.

A baseline dimension appears after you select each location.

As with the Continue option, Baseline assumes that you have already placed at least one other linear dimension in the drawing.

TIP Since you usually select exact locations on your drawing as you dimension, you might want to turn on Running Osnaps to avoid the extra step of selecting Osnaps from the Osnap shortcut menu.

1. Choose Dimension ➢ Baseline or type **Dba**↵ to start a baseline dimension.

2. At the `Specify a second extension line origin or [Undo/Select] <Select>:` prompt, use an osnap to select another feature you want to dimension in your drawing.

3. Press ↵ twice to exit the Baseline Dimension command.

The Baseline Dimension option works in a similar way to the Continue Dimension option, except that Baseline Dimension allows you to use the first extension line of the previous dimension as the base for a second dimension.

TIP The distance between the two horizontal dimension lines is controlled by the Baseline Spacing setting in the Lines And Arrows tab of the Dimension Style dialog box.

Just as with the Continue Dimension option, the Baseline Dimension option continues from the last dimension you added to the drawing by default. If you need to add more baseline dimensions from a dimension other than the last one you placed in the drawing, press ↵ at the `Specify a second extension line origin or [Undo/Select] <Select>:` prompt in step 2 of the previous example. Then click the extension line from which you want to continue. You can then proceed to add dimensions.

Adding a String of Dimensions with a Single Operation

AutoCAD provides a method for creating a string of dimensions using a single operation *while in the Model tab*. The Qdim command lets you select a set of objects instead of having to select points. The following exercise demonstrates how the Qdim command works.

To use Qdim, choose Dimension ➢ Quick Dimension or enter **qdim** ↵. Next, place a crossing selection window around the area you want to dimension. You'll see a string of dimensions at the cursor. Click to place the dimension string in the drawing.

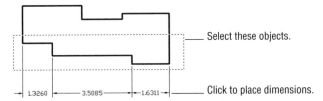

Select these objects.

Click to place dimensions.

USING OSNAP WHILE DIMENSIONING

Dimensions can adjust themselves to changes in the objects they are measuring. To take advantage of this feature, known as *associative dimensioning*, make sure you use osnaps while adding dimensions. The osnaps ensure that you are selecting exact points on objects so that AutoCAD can keep track of what it is you are dimensioning. If you don't know how to use osnaps, see Chapter 2.

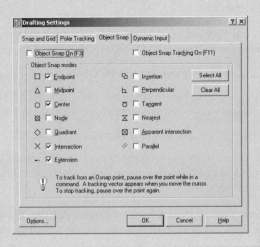

The Qdim command can be a time-saver when you want to dimension a wall quickly. It may not work in all situations, but if the object you're dimensioning is fairly simple, it can be all you need.

TIP This example uses a simple window to select the wall. For more complex shapes, try using a crossing polygon selection window.

Dimensioning Nonorthogonal Objects

Most of your dimensions will be horizontal or vertical, which are handled easily with the linear dimension. But eventually you will need to apply many other types of nonorthogonal dimensions. For example, you might need to dimension a hexagonal shape whose sides are at 30° angles. In this section, you'll find out how to add dimensions to objects that are turned at an angle. You'll also learn about dimensioning arcs and circles.

Adding Nonorthogonal Linear Dimensions

You can add a linear dimension to an object that is not in a horizontal or vertical orientation using the aligned dimension. This type of dimension aligns the dimension line with the two point you select for dimensioning as described in the following steps.

1. Choose Dimension ➤ Aligned or enter **Dal**↵ to start the aligned dimension.

2. At the Specify first extension line origin or <select object>: prompt, use an osnap to select the first edge of the object being dimensioned.

3. At the Specify second extension line origin: prompt, use an osnap again to select the other end of the object being dimensioned.

4. At the Specify dimension line location or [Mtext/Text/Angle]: prompt, you'll see a dimension follow the cursor. Click a point to place the dimension. The dimension appears in the drawing, as shown in Figure 10. 5.

TIP Just as with linear dimensions, you can enter **T**↵ in step 4 to enter alternate text for the dimension.

FIGURE 10.5
The aligned dimension
of a nonorthogonal line

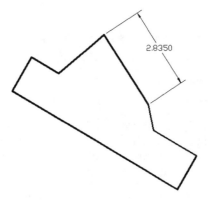

2.8350

You might also need to place a dimension at an angle that is not necessarily aligned with the drawing feature being dimensioned, as shown in Figure 10.6. Here's how to draw this type of dimension.

1. Click the Linear Dimension tool on the Dimension toolbar.

2. At the `Specify first extension line origin or <select> object:` prompt, use an osnap to select an appropriate location on the object being dimensioned.

3. At the `Specify second extension line origin:` prompt, use an osnap again to select the other end of the object being dimensioned.

4. At the `Specify dimension line location or [Mtext/Text/Angle/Horizontal/ Vertical/Rotated]:` prompt, enter **R** ↵ to use the Rotated option.

5. At the `Specify angle of dimension line <0>:` prompt, specify the angle at which the dimension line is to be placed. The angle value you enter is in relation to the X axis of the drawing, so if you enter 0, for example, the dimension line will be horizontal.

6. At the `Specify dimension line location or [Mtext/Text/Angle/Horizontal/ Vertical/Rotated]:` prompt, you'll see the dimension line follow your cursor. Select a point to place the dimension line.

FIGURE 10.6

A nonorthogonal linear dimension that is not aligned with the feature being dimensioned

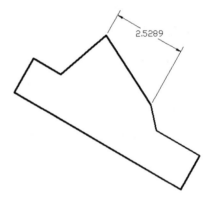

Dimensioning Arcs and Circles

Dimensioning diameters of arcs or circles is fairly simple.

1. Choose Dimension ➤ Diameter or enter **Ddi**↵.

2. At the `Select arc or circle:` prompt, select the circle or arc you want to dimension.

3. At the `Specify dimension line location or [Mtext/Text/Angle]:` prompt, you will see the diameter dimension drag along the circle as you move the cursor. If you move the cursor outside the circle, the dimension changes to display the dimension on the outside. (See the right image in Figure 10.7.)

4. Place the dimension where you want it, and then click the mouse.

FIGURE 10.7
Dimension showing the
diameter of a circle

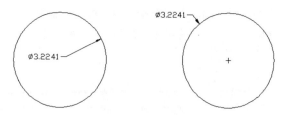

TIP If the dimension text can't fit within the circle, AutoCAD gives you the option to place the dimension text outside the circle as you drag the temporary dimension to a horizontal position.

The Radius Dimension tool on the Dimension toolbar gives you a radius dimension just as the diameter dimension provides a circle's diameter. Figure 10.8 shows a radius dimension on the outside of the circle, but you can place it inside in a manner similar to the diameter dimension. The Center Mark tool on the Dimension toolbar just places a cross mark in the center of the selected arc or circle.

FIGURE 10.8
A radius dimension
shown on the outside
of the circle

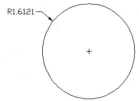

If you are dimensioning a large arc radius, and you can't show the center of the arc within the area of your drawing, you can use a jogged radius dimension (choose Dimension ➤ Jogged) instead of the usual Dimension ➤ Radius option. The Jogged option places a jog in the dimension line to indicate that the center is not shown in the drawing.

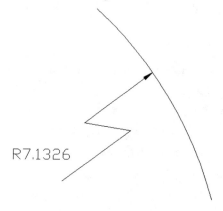

Dimensioning Angles and Arc Lengths

Dimensions aren't always used to show distances. You can use the angular dimension to indicate the angle between features in your drawing. Here's how:

1. Choose Dimension ➢ Angular or enter **Dan**↵ to start the angular dimension.

2. At the `Select arc, circle, line, or <Specify vertex>:` prompt, select the first line whose angle you want to dimension.

3. At the `Select second line:` prompt, select the other line whose angle you want to dimension.

4. At the `Specify dimension arc line location or [Mtext/Text/Angle]:` prompt, the dimension moves to different locations as you move the cursor. This allows you to select the angle to dimension, as shown in Figure 10.9.

FIGURE 10.9

Two examples of an angular dimension

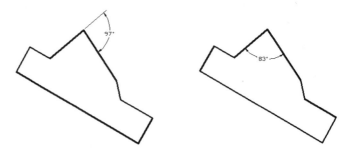

5. When the dimension appears in the location you want, click that point to fix the dimension in place.

In addition to the angle of an arc, you can also dimension the length of an arc. Choose Dimension ➢ Arc Length, and then select the arc whose length you want to dimension. The dimension appears and drags with the cursor. You can then click to place the arc length dimension.

WHY DO MY ANGULAR DIMENSIONS SHOW ONLY WHOLE DEGREES?

By default, AutoCAD's dimensioning feature rounds off angular dimensions to the nearest degree. Follow these steps to show angles less than a whole degree:

1. Select the angular dimension, and then right-click and select Properties to open the Properties palette.

2. Scroll down to locate the Primary Units group.

3. Click the Angle Precision option and select the value you want for the dimension.

You can also change the Angle Precision setting for the current dimension style using the Modify Dimension Styles dialog box, which is the same as the New Dimension Style dialog box. See "Determining the Unit Style Settings for Dimensions" section later in this chapter.

Adding a Note with an Arrow Using the Leader Tool

Next to dimensions, notes are the most common text found in drawings. Choosing Dimension ➤ Leader lets you add a note with an arrow pointing to the object the note describes. Here's how it works:

1. Choose Dimension ➤ Leader or enter **Le↵**.

2. At the `Specify first leader point, or [Settings] <Settings>:` prompt, select a point to indicate the location for the arrow.

3. At the `Specify next point:` prompt, click another point to indicate the other end of the arrow.

4. At the `Specify next point:` prompt, you can continue to select points just as you would draw lines. For this exercise, however, press ↵ to finish drawing leader lines.

5. At the `Specify text width <0">:` prompt, press ↵ or enter a width for your text.

6. At the `Enter first line of annotation text <Mtext>:` prompt, type the label you want to appear for this note.

7. At the `Enter next line of annotation text:` prompt, press ↵ twice to finish the leader. Your note appears with the leader arrow similar to the one in Figure 10.10.

FIGURE 10.10

The leader with a note added

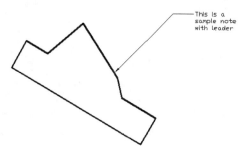

The text in the note will be in the current text style unless you specify another style in the Text tab of the Dimension Styles dialog box. (See the "Setting the Appearance of Dimension Text" section later in this chapter.)

The Leader tool offers a lot of options that are not obviously presented when you are using it. In step 2 of the previous example, after choosing Dimension ➤ Leader, you can enter **S↵** to open the Leader Settings dialog box, which gives you options that let you control the function of the leader.

The options in the Annotation tab of the Leader Settings dialog box let you control the type of annotation that is attached to the leader. AutoCAD uses the Mtext option by default, which places a multiline text object at the end of the leader. If you prefer, you can select an option from this tab to replace the default multiline text. Other options let you include more detailed multiline text options such as text width or framed text.

The options in the Leader Line & Arrow tab give you control over the leader line and arrow. You can select an arrow that is different from the default, or you can constrain the lines to follow a specific angle. You can also select a curved leader instead of straight lines, as shown in Figure 10.11.

FIGURE 10.11
Straight and spline
leader lines

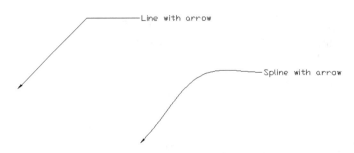

If you don't like the way AutoCAD places the leader next to the text, you can make adjustments through the Attachment tab (see Figure 10.12). Here you can determine where the arrow leader joins the text to which it is attached.

TIP Just as with other dimensions, you can change an existing leader using the Properties palette. For example, you can change the leader line into a spline curve using the Type option in the Properties palette. Select the leader, right-click and select Properties to open the Properties palette. Then in the Miscellaneous group, click the Type option and select Spline With Arrow from the drop-down list.

FIGURE 10.12
The Attachment tab
of the Leader Settings
dialog box

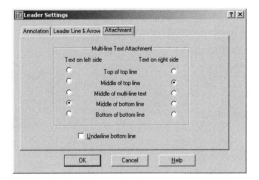

Using Ordinate Dimensions

Ordinate dimensions are used when a dimension in a part is measured from a critical feature. For example, the holes in a machine part may all have to be precisely located in relation to the center of a machine hole in the part, as shown in Figure 10.13. In ordinate dimensions, the dimension labels are shown as X coordinates or Y coordinates from the critical feature.

Before you apply ordinate dimensions, you need to establish the origin of the drawing at the location of the critical feature. You use the UCS to do so.

FIGURE 10.13

An example of ordinate dimensions

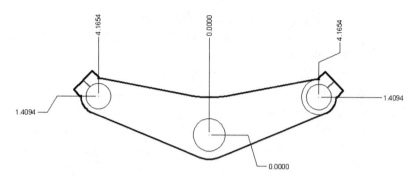

To use AutoCAD's Ordinate Dimension command, follow these steps.

1. Choose Tools ➤ UCS ➤ Origin, or type **UCS↵ OR↵**.

2. At the Specify new origin point <0,0,0>: prompt, click the exact location of the origin of your part.

3. Toggle the Ortho mode on.

4. Choose Dimension ➤ Ordinate or enter **Dor↵** to start the ordinate dimension.

5. At the Specify feature location: prompt, click the item you want to dimension.

TIP The direction of the leader determines whether the dimension will be of the Xdatum or the Ydatum.

6. At the Specify leader endpoint or [Xdatum/Ydatum/Mtext/Text/Angle]: prompt, position the rubber-banding leader that appears at the cursor perpendicular to the coordinate direction you want to dimension. When you have the leader where you want it, click the mouse.

In steps 1 and 2, you used the UCS feature to establish a second origin in the drawing. The Ordinate Dimension tool then uses that origin to determine the ordinate dimensions. You will get a chance to work with the UCS feature in Chapter 17.

You may have noticed options in the Command window for the Ordinate Dimension tool. The Xdatum and Ydatum options force the dimension to be of the X or Y coordinate no matter what direction the leader takes. The Mtext option opens the Multiline Text Editor, allowing you to append or replace the ordinate dimension text. The Text option lets you enter a replacement text directly through the Command window.

TIP As with all other dimensions, you can use grips to adjust the location of ordinate dimensions.

If you turn Ortho mode off, the dimension leader is drawn with a jog to maintain the orthogonal. (Look back at Figure 10.13.)

Adding Tolerance Notation

If you are drawing a part that must be machined within a certain range of dimensions, you can use the Tolerance Dimension option. Tolerance lets you specify a tolerance range for features in your drawing. It produces a note that uses industry standard notation, as shown in Figure 10.14.

FIGURE 10.14

An example of tolerance notation

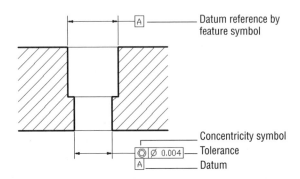

Datum reference by feature symbol

Concentricity symbol
Tolerance
Datum

To use the Tolerance command, type **Tol⏎** at the Command prompt, or choose Dimension ➢ Tolerance from the drop-down menu to open the Geometric Tolerance dialog box (see Figure 10.15).

FIGURE 10.15

The Geometric Tolerance dialog box

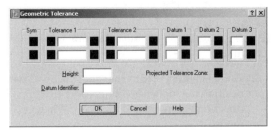

This is where you enter tolerance and datum values for the feature control symbol. You can enter two tolerance values and three datum values. In addition, you can stack values in a two-tiered fashion.

Click a box in the Sym group to open the Symbol dialog box (see Figure 10.16).

FIGURE 10.16

The Symbol dialog box

Figure 10.17 shows what each symbol in the Symbol dialog box represents. The bottom image shows a sample drawing with a feature symbol used on a cylindrical object.

In the Geometric Tolerance dialog box, you can click a box in any of the Datum groups or a box in the right side of the Tolerance groups to open the Material Condition dialog box (see Figure 10.18).

Position (true)	⊕	Flatness	▱
Concentricity	◎	Circularity	○
Symmetry	⊜	Straightness	—
Parallelism	//	Profile	◠
Perpendicularity	⊥	Profile	◠
Angularity	∠	Circular runout	↗
Cylindricity	⌭	Total runout	⌰

Editing Dimensions

As you begin to add more dimensions to your drawings, you will find that AutoCAD occasionally places a dimension text or line in an inappropriate location or that you need to modify the dimension text. In this section, we'll look at how you can modify dimensions to suit those special circumstances.

Although the instructions in this section describe methods for editing specific parts of dimensions, you might be able to adjust dimensions through the Properties palette.

Appending Data to Dimension Text

Most of the time you will accept the dimension value that AutoCAD provides, but you might want to append to that dimension value or even change it entirely. While you are adding dimensions and you see the temporary dimension dragging with your cursor, you can enter **T⏎** to change the dimension text. You can then enter an entirely different text at the Command prompt. You can also use the less than (<) and greater than (>) symbols to add text either before or after the default dimension. For example, if you enter **<> Verify**, the word *Verify* appears after the dimension value. You can click the Properties button on the Object Properties palette to modify the existing dimension text in a similar way.

You can also append text to a dimension that has already been placed in your drawing. Here is an example of how this is done.

1. Choose Modify ➢ Object ➢ Text ➢ Edit or type **ED**↵.

2. Click the dimension whose value you want to edit. The Text Formatting toolbar (see Figure 10.19) appears with the current dimension value highlighted in the text panel.

FIGURE 10.19

A dimension with the
Text Formatting toolbar

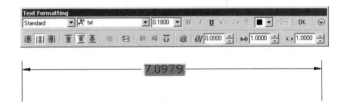

3. Enter the text you want to add.

4. Click OK on the Text Formatting toolbar. The dimension changes to include the text you just added.

In addition to appending to the dimension value, you can do any of the following while editing the dimension text:

◆ Replace the dimension text entirely by deleting the dimension value in the text panel.

◆ Restore a dimension text value that has been modified by entering <>.

◆ Show a blank dimension by replacing the dimension value with a space.

You can also have AutoCAD automatically add a dimension suffix or prefix to all dimensions, instead of just a chosen few, by using the Suffix or Prefix option in the Primary Units tab of the Dimension Style dialog box.

Making Changes to Multiple Dimensions

You can use the Dimension Edit tool to quickly edit existing dimensions and change more than one dimension's text at a time. For example, you can use the Dimension Edit tool to change a string of dimensions to read "Equal" instead of showing the actual dimensioned distance. The following steps show an alternative to using the Properties palette for appending text to a dimension:

1. Type **Ded**↵ at the Command prompt.

2. At the Enter type of dimension Edit [Home/New/Rotate/Oblique]<Home>: prompt, type **N**↵ to use the New option. The Text Formatting toolbar appears with a new dimension value of 0. The 0 is a placeholder indicating where the actual dimension text will appear.

3. Enter the text you want to append to the dimension. If you like, you can delete the 0 dimension to replace the dimension value entirely.

4. Click OK.

5. At the Select objects: prompt, select the dimensions you want to edit. The Select objects: prompt remains, allowing you to select several dimensions.

6. Press ↵ to finish your selection. The dimension changes to include your new text or to replace the existing dimension text.

The Dimension Edit tool is useful in editing dimension text, but you can also use this command to make graphical changes to the text. Here is a listing of the other Dimension Edit tool options:

Home moves the dimension text to its standard default position and angle.

Rotate rotates the dimension text to a new angle.

Oblique skews the dimension extension lines to a new angle. (See the "Skewing Dimension Lines" section later in this chapter.)

Detaching Dimension Text from the Dimension Line

If you try to move the dimension text away from a dimension using the dimension text's grip, you will find that the entire dimension line follows the text. You can separate the dimension from the text by changing one of the settings for the dimension's properties.

1. Click the dimension text to expose its grip.

2. Right-click and choose Properties from the shortcut menu to open the Properties palette.

3. Scroll down the list of properties until you see the Fit options. If you do not see a list of options under Fit, click the downward-pointing arrow to the right to display a new set of options, as shown in Figure 10.20.

4. Scroll down the list farther until you see the Text Movement option.

5. Click the arrow that appears next to the Keep Dim Line With Text listing to open the drop-down list; then select the Move Text, Add Leader option shown in Figure 10.21.

6. Close the Properties palette.

FIGURE 10.20

The Fit options in the Properties palette

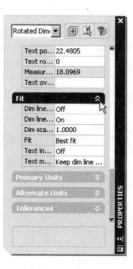

FIGURE 10.21

The Move Text, Add Leader option in the Fit options group

You can now move the text independent of the dimension line. As you do, a leader is drawn from the dimension line to the dimension text.

If you prefer that the leader not appear, you can select Move Text, No Leader in step 7 of the previous example.

Rotating a Dimension Text

You may find that you need to rotate the text of a dimension in conjunction with moving the dimension text.

1. Choose Dimension ➢ Align Text ➢ Angle

2. At the `Select dimension:` prompt, select the dimension whose text you want to rotate.

3. At the `Specify angle for dimension text:` prompt, enter an angle or select two points to indicate an angle visually.

You can also use the Dimension Text Edit tool (Dimtedit command) to align the dimension text to either the left or right side of the dimension line. This is similar to the Alignment option in the Multiline Text Editor that controls text justification.

As you have seen in this section, the Grips feature is especially well suited to editing dimensions. With grips, you can stretch, move, copy, rotate, mirror, and scale dimensions.

WHY DO MY DIMENSIONS APPEAR AS INDIVIDUAL TEXT, LINES, AND ARROWS?

Every now and then, you may encounter a drawing that produces dimensions that are simple text, lines, and arrows. When you edit the parts of the drawing that are dimensioned, the dimensions do not change.

This can be due to a change in an AutoCAD setting called Dimassoc. Dimassoc is set to 2 by default, but if it is set to 0 (zero), AutoCAD draws dimensions as the individual object that constitute the dimension. To restore the default, enter **Dimassoc** at the Command prompt, and then enter **2** ↵.

Skewing Dimension Lines

If you are adding dimensions to an isometric or other axonometric drawing, you will want to skew the dimension lines in relation to the dimension extension lines. You can do this using the Oblique option:

1. Choose Dimension ➤ Oblique, or type **Ded↵ O↵**. You can also select the Dimension Edit tool from the Dimension toolbar, and then type **O↵**.

2. At the Select objects: prompt, select the dimension you want to skew and press ↵ to confirm your selection.

3. At the Enter obliquing angle (Press enter for none): prompt, enter an angle value appropriate to your drawing. The dimension skews so that the extension lines are at the angle you entered (see Figure 10.22).

FIGURE 10.22
A dimension on a 2D isometric drawing using the Oblique option

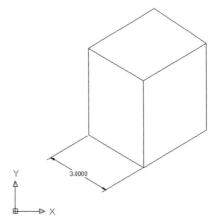

Setting Up the Dimension's Appearance

The default dimensions created by AutoCAD are for mechanical drafting. If you are an architect, you'll want to change the style to follow the standards in that industry. Or perhaps you just want to change the style a little to conform to your particular office's way of doing things.

You can add dimensions using the default settings and then change each dimension so that it appears correctly for your application, but that is extremely time-consuming. Instead, you can use the dimension style feature to set up the appearance of your dimensions beforehand. Once you create a style, you only have to make the style the default and then start dimensioning.

Creating a Dimension Style

Dimension styles are like text styles. They determine the font, size of dimension arrows, and configuration of your dimensions. You might set up a dimension style for special types of arrows or to position the dimension text above the dimension line as in an architectural drawing. You can set up multiple dimension styles for different situations.

1. Choose Format ➢ Dimension ➢ Style or type **D**↵ at the Command prompt to open the Dimension Style Manager dialog box.

2. Select Standard from the Styles list (see Figure 10.23). Metric users should select ISO-25.

FIGURE 10.23

The Dimension Style Manager dialog box with Standard selected

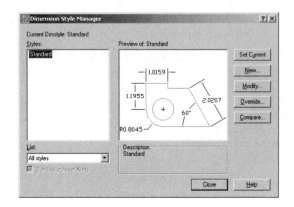

3. Click New to open the Create New Dimension Style dialog box (see Figure 10.24).

FIGURE 10.24

The Create New Dimension Style dialog box

4. With the Copy Of Standard or ISO-25 name highlighted in the New Style Name input box, enter a new name for your style.

5. Click Continue to open the New Dimension Style dialog box, as shown in Figure 10.25.

You are now ready to set up your style's appearance. The New Dimension Style dialog box has several tabs, each of which controls a different aspect of the dimension's appearance.

TIP Since dimensions have so many variables, you may find the number of settings overwhelming. Before you jump in and try to set up a dimension style, skim the introductory paragraph for each tab description given next. You might find that you need to change only a few settings for your style.

SETTING UP THE DIMENSION GRAPHICS

The options in the Lines tab (see Figure 10.25) and the Symbols and Arrows tab (see Figure 10.26) give you control over the appearance of dimension and extension lines, arrowheads, and center marks. Figure 10.27 shows an example of some of the dimension components that are affected by these options. Table 10.1 describes the options in the Lines tab, and Table 10.2 shows the options for the Symbols and Arrows tab. Whenever you change any of these settings, you get immediate feedback on their effect on the dimension's appearance in the graphic that appears in the upper right of the dialog box.

FIGURE 10.25
The New Dimension Style dialog box

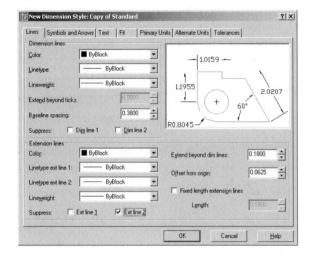

FIGURE 10.26
The Symbols and Arrows tab of the New Dimension Style dialog box

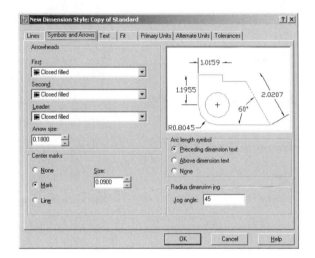

FIGURE 10.27
These dimensions are labeled with the name of the settings that affect their appearance.

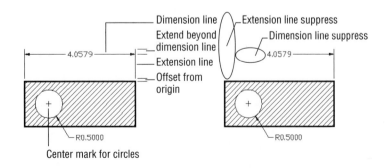

WARNING The value you enter for dimension line component sizes, such as arrow size and offset from origin, should be in the size you want when the drawing is printed. If you are adding dimensions in model space and you need to apply a scale factor, you need to enter a scale factor value in only one place in the Primary Units tab. All other dimension settings are scaled to the value you enter there.

TABLE 10.1: The Lines Tab Settings

THE DIMENSION LINES GROUP	
Color	Sets the color of the dimension line.
Linetype	Sets the linetype for the dimension line.
Lineweight	Sets the line weight for dimension lines.
Extend Beyond Ticks	Sets the distance that the dimension line extends beyond the extension lines.
Baseline Spacing	Specifies the distance between dimensions that use a common baseline.
Suppress	These check boxes let you suppress the dimension line on either side of the dimension text.
THE EXTENSION LINES GROUP	
Color	Sets the color for extension lines.
Linetype Ext Line 1	Sets the linetype for the first extension line.
Linetype Ext Line 2	Sets the linetype for the second extension line.
Lineweight	Sets the line weight for extension lines.
Extend Beyond Dim Lines	Sets the distance that extension lines extend beyond dimension lines.
Offset From Origin	Sets the distance from the extension line to the object being dimensioned.
Fixed Length Extension Lines	Forces the extension lines to be a fixed length set by the Length text box.
Length	Sets the length for extension lines when the Fixed Length Extension Lines option is turned on.
Suppress	Suppresses extension lines indicated by the checked item.

TABLE 10.2:   The Symbols and Arrows Tab Settings

THE ARROWHEADS GROUP	
First	Sets the type of arrowhead to use on dimension lines. By default, the second arrowhead automatically changes to match the arrowhead you specify for this setting.
Second	Sets a different arrowhead from the one set for the first option.
Leader	Sets an arrowhead for leader notes.
Arrow Size	Sets the size for the arrowheads. Enter a value in the final printed size.
THE CENTER MARKS GROUP	
None/Mark/Line	Sets the type of center mark used in radius and diameter dimensions.
Size	Sets the size of the center mark.
THE ARC LENGTH SYMBOL GROUP	
Preceding/Above/None	Sets the location of the arc length symbol for arc length dimensions.
THE RADIUS DIMENSION JOG GROUP	
Jog Angle	Sets the angle for the Radius Dimension Jog symbol.

SETTING UP DIMENSIONS FOR ARCHITECTURAL DRAWINGS

If you need to set up an architectural drawing, follow these steps in the New Dimension Style dialog box:

In the Primary Units tab (see Figure 10.30) follow these steps:

1. In the Linear Dimensions group, open the Unit Format drop-down list and choose Architectural.

2. Select 0´-0 ¼″ from the Precision drop-down list, just below the Unit Format list. The Precision option allows you to set the amount of round off for dimension text. It doesn't actually limit the precision of the drawing.

3. Select Diagonal from the Fraction Format drop-down list and select Diagonal.

4. Turn off the 0 Inches option in the Zero Suppression group.

In the Text tab (see Figure 10.28), follow these steps:

1. In the Text Alignment group, click the Aligned With Dimension Line radio button.

2. In the Text Placement group, open the Vertical drop-down list and select Above.

3. In the Text Placement group, change the Offset From Dim Line value to ¹⁄₁₆. This setting controls the size of the gap between the dimension line and the dimension text.

In the Symbols and Arrows tab (see Figure 10.26), follow these steps:

1. In the Arrowheads group, open the first drop-down list and choose Architectural Tick.

2. In the Arrowheads group, change the Arrow Size setting to 1/8.

3. In the Lines tab (see Figure 10.25), follow these steps:

4. In the Dimension Lines group, highlight the value in the Extend Beyond Ticks input box, and then enter ¹⁄₁₆.

5. In the Extension Lines group, change the Extend Beyond Dim Lines setting to ¹⁄₈.

6. In the Extension Lines group, change the Offset From Origin setting to ¹⁄₈.

In the Fit tab (see Figure 10.29), follow these steps:

1. In the Scale For Dimension Features group, select the Use Overall Scale Of radio button.

2. Double-click the list box just to the right of the Use Overall Scale Of radio button, and then enter the desired scale factor. See Chapter 9 for more on scale factors and text size.

SETTING THE APPEARANCE OF THE DIMENSION TEXT

You can adjust the appearance of the dimension text through the Text tab of the New Dimension Style dialog box. Text style, color, and height are a few of the features that can be adjusted here. You can also specify the default location of the dimension text in relation to the dimension line and extension lines. Figure 10.28 shows the Text tab, and Table 10.3 describes the options in the Text tab.

FIGURE 10.28
The Text tab of the
New Dimension Style
dialog box

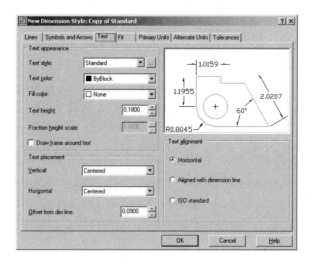

TABLE 10.3:   The Text Tab Settings

THE TEXT APPEARANCE GROUP	
Text Style	Sets the text style for your dimension text. You need to first create a text style using the Text Style dialog box (choose Format ➤ Text Style).
Text Color	Sets the color for your dimension text.
Fill Color	Sets the color for dimension text background.
Text Height	Sets the height for dimension text. This option is only valid for text styles with their height value set to 0 (zero).
Fraction Height Scale	Sets a scale factor for the height of fractional text. This option is only meaningful when Architectural or Fractional is selected in the Primary Units tab.
Draw Frame Around Text	When turned on, draws a rectangle around the dimension text.
THE TEXT PLACEMENT GROUP	
Vertical	Sets the vertical position of the text in relation to the dimension line. Centered places the text in line with the dimension line, and the dimension line is broken to accommodate the text. Above places the text above the dimension line, leaving the dimension line unbroken. Outside places the text away from the dimension line at a location farthest away from the object being dimensioned. JIS places the text in conformance with the Japanese Industrial Standards.
Horizontal	Sets the location of the text in relation to the extension lines. Centered places the text between the two extension lines. 1st Extension Line places the text next to the first extension line and between the two extension lines. 2nd Extension Line places the text next to the second extension line and between the two extension lines. Over 1st Extension Line places the text above the first extension line. Over 2nd Extension Line places the text above the second extension line.
Offset From Dim Line	Sets the distance from the baseline of text to the dimension line when text is placed above the dimension line. Also sets the size of the gap between the dimension text and the endpoint of the dimension line when the text is in line with the dimension line. Can be used to set the margin around the text when the dimension text is in a centered position that breaks the dimension line.
THE TEXT ALIGNMENT GROUP	
Horizontal	Forces the text in a horizontal orientation, regardless of the dimension line orientation.
Aligned With Dimension Line	Aligns the text with the dimension line.
ISO Standard	Aligns the text with the dimension line when it is between the extension lines; otherwise, the text is oriented horizontally.

SPECIFYING TEXT AND ARROW PLACEMENT IN TIGHT SPACES

Quite often, you must place dimensions in such a location that arrows and text will not fit between the extension lines. You can use the options on the Fit tab to specify what AutoCAD should do when the dimension runs out of room. You can also use the Fit tab to specify the overall scale factor for your dimensions, which is especially critical if you add dimensions in the Model tab. Figure 10.29 shows the Fit tab, and Table 10.4 descries the options in the Fit tab.

FIGURE 10.29

The Fit tab of the New Dimension Style dialog box

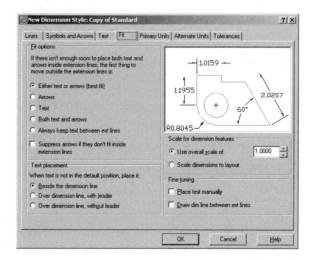

SPECIFYING THE UNIT STYLE SETTINGS FOR DIMENSIONS

The options in the Primary Units tab let you set the format and content of the dimension text, including the unit style for linear and angular dimensions. Figure 10.30 shows the Primary Units tab, and Table 10.5 describes the options in the Primary Units tab.

FIGURE 10.30

The Primary Units Tab of the New Dimension Style dialog box

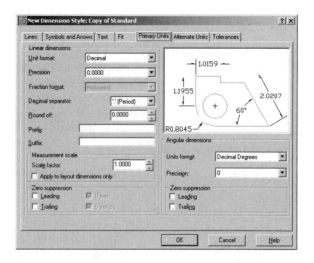

TABLE 10.4:   The Fit Tab Settings

THE FIT OPTIONS GROUP	
Either Text Or Arrows (Best Fit)	Fits either text or arrows between the extension lines depending on which of the two items fit best.
Arrows	Moves arrows outside the extension line first, then text.
Text	Moves text outside the extension line first, then arrows.
Both Text And Arrows	Moves both the text and the arrows outside the extension line.
Always Keep Text Between Ext Lines	Forces the arrows and text to remain between the extension lines.
Suppress Arrows If They Don't Fit Inside Extension Lines	Completely suppresses arrows if they do not fit between the extension lines.
THE TEXT PLACEMENT GROUP	
Beside The Dimension Line	Keeps the text and dimension line together.
Over Dimension Line, With Leader	Allows independent movement of the text and the dimension line. A leader is added if the text is moved from the dimension line.
Over Dimension Line, Without Leader	Allows independent movement of the text and the dimension line.
THE SCALE FOR DIMENSION FEATURES GROUP	
Use Overall Scale Of	This combined radio button and input box sets the overall scale of the dimension components, including text and arrows.
Scale Dimensions To Layout	Scales the dimension components to the scale factor assigned to the paper space viewport in which the drawing appears.
THE FINE TUNING GROUP	
Place Text Manually	Lets you manually place dimension text when the text does not fit between extension lines.
Always Draw Dim Line Between Ext Lines	Forces AutoCAD to draw a dimension line regardless of the width between extension lines.

TABLE 10.5: The Primary Units tab settings

THE LINEAR DIMENSIONS GROUP	
Unit Format	Sets the unit style of the dimension text. The options are Scientific, Decimal, Engineering, Architectural, Fractional, and Windows Desktop.
Precision	Sets the precision of the dimension text. This option rounds off the dimension text to the nearest precision value you set. It does not affect the actual precision of the drawing.
Fraction Format	Specifies how fractions are displayed. The choices are vertically stacked, diagonally stacked, and horizontally stacked. These options apply only to architectural and fractional unit formats.
Decimal Separator	Sets the decimal separator for dimension unit formats that display decimals. You can choose a period, a comma, or a space.
Round Off	Sets the degree of rounding applied to dimension text. For example, you can set this option to 0.25 to round off dimensions to the nearest 0.25, or 1/4, of a unit.
Prefix	Sets a prefix for all linear dimension text. The prefix is added to the beginning of all linear dimension text.
Suffix	Sets a suffix for all linear dimension text. The suffix is added to the end of all linear dimensions text
Measurement Scale: Scale Factor	Multiplies the dimension value by a scale factor. You can set this value to 25.4, for example, to show dimension values in millimeters for drawings created in Imperial units.
Measurement Scale: Apply To Layout Dimensions Only	Applies the measurement scale factor to paper space layouts only.
Zero Supression: Leading, Trailing	Suppresses zeros so they do not appear in the dimension text. For example, with the Leading option selected, 0.50 will be shown as .50 (point five zero). With Trailing selected, it is shown as 0.5.
THE ANGULAR DIMENSIONS GROUP	
Units Format	Sets a format for angular dimensions. The options are Decimal Degrees, Degrees/Minutes/Seconds, Grads, Radians, and Surveyor.
Precision	Sets the precision for the angular dimension text.
Zero Suppression: Leading, Trailing	Suppresses leading or trailing zeros in angular dimensions.

THE ALTERNATE UNITS TAB

The Alternate Units tab lets you apply a second set of dimension text for linear dimensions. You can use this set for alternate dimension styles or units. For example, you can use alternate units to display alternate metric dimension values in addition to the main dimension values in feet and inches. Figure 10.31 shows the Alternate Units tab, and Table 10.6 describes the options in the Alternate Units tab.

To turn on Alternate Units, click the Display Alternate Units check box. AutoCAD then includes an additional dimension text in the format you specify this tab.

FIGURE 10.31

The Alternate Units Tab of the New Dimension Style dialog box

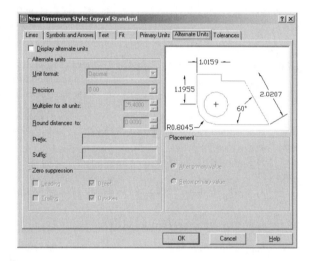

THE TOLERANCES TAB

The options in the Tolerances tab let you add tolerance dimension text and include options for tolerance dimension text formatting. Figure 10.32 shows the Tolerance tab and Table 10.7 gives the description of the options in the Tolerance tab.

FIGURE 10.32

The Tolerance Tab of the New Dimension Style dialog box.

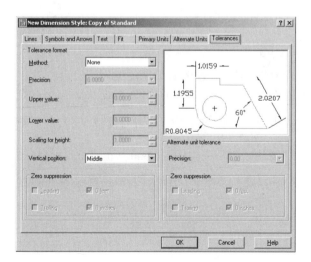

TABLE 10.6:   The Alternate Units Tab Settings

THE ALTERNATE UNITS GROUP	
Unit Format	Sets the unit style of the dimension text. The options are Scientific, Decimal, Engineering, Architectural Stacked, Fractional Stacked, Architectural, Fractional, and Windows Desktop.
Precision	Sets the precision of the dimension text. This option rounds off the dimension text to the nearest precision value you set. It does not affect the actual precision of the drawing.
Multiplier For Alt Units	Sets a multiplier value for the dimension text. This option multiplies the dimension text value by the multiplier value. For example, if you want alternate dimensions to display distances in centimeters even though the drawing was created in inches, you can enter 2.54 for this option.
Round Distances To	Sets the value rounding applied to alternate dimensions.
Prefix	Adds a prefix for all linear alternate dimension text.
Suffix	Adds a suffix for all linear alternate dimension text.
THE ZERO SUPPRESSION GROUP	
Leading, Trailing, Feet, Inches	Suppresses zeros so they do not appear in the dimension text. For example, with the Leading option selected, 0.50 is shown as .50 (point five zero). With Trailing selected, it is shown as 0.5.
THE PLACEMENT GROUP	
After Primary Value	Sets the alternate dimension text to appear behind and aligned with the primary dimension text.
Below Primary Value	Sets the alternate dimension text to appear below the primary dimension text and above the dimension line.

Setting the Current Dimension Style

Before you can begin to use your new dimension style, you must make it the current default.

1. In the Styles list in the Dimension Style Manager dialog box, click the name of style you want to be current.

2. Click the Set Current button in the far-right side of the dialog box.

3. Click Close to exit the Dimension Style Manager dialog box.

You're now ready to use your new dimension style. You can also select a dimension style from the Styles toolbar drop-down list (see Figure 10.33).

TABLE 10.7:   The Tolerance Tab Settings

THE TOLERANCE FORMAT GROUP	
Method	Sets the format for the tolerance dimension text. The options are None, Symmetrical, Deviation, Limits, and Basic. None turns off the tolerance dimension text. Symmetrical adds a plus/minus tolerance dimension. This is a single dimension preceded by a plus/minus sign. Deviation adds a stacked tolerance dimension showing separate upper and lower tolerance values. The Limits option replaces the primary dimension with a stacked dimension showing maximum and minimum dimension values. The Basic option draws a box around the primary dimension value. If an alternate dimension is used, the box encloses both primary and alternate dimension text.
Precision	Sets the precision of the tolerance dimension text. This option rounds off the dimension text to the nearest precision value you set. It does not affect the actual precision of the drawing.
Upper Value	Sets the upper tolerance value for the Symmetrical, Deviation, and Limits tolerance methods.
Lower Value	Lets you set the lower tolerance value for the Deviation and Limits tolerance methods (Dimtm).
Scaling For Height	Sets the size for the tolerance dimension text as a proportion of the primary dimension text height.
Vertical Position	Sets the vertical position of the tolerance text. The options are Top, Middle, and Bottom. The Top option aligns the top tolerance value of a stacked pair of values with the primary dimension text. Middle aligns the gap between stacked tolerance values with the primary dimension text. Bottom aligns the bottom value of two stacked tolerance values with the primary dimension text.
Zero Suppression: Leading, Trailing, Feet, Inches	Suppresses zeros so they do not appear in the tolerance dimension text. For example, with the Leading option selected, 0.50 is shown as .50 (point five zero). With Trailing selected, it is shown as 0.5.
THE ALTERNATE UNIT TOLERANCE GROUP	
Precision	Sets the precision of the alternate tolerance dimension text. This option rounds off the dimension text to the nearest precision value you set. It does not affect the actual precision of the drawing.
Zero Suppression: Leading, Trailing, Feet, Inches	Suppresses zeros in alternate unit tolerance dimensions so they do not appear in the dimension text.

FIGURE 10.33
The Dimension Style drop-down list in the Styles toolbar

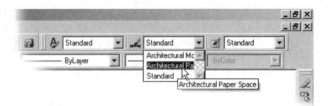

Editing a Dimension Style

Once you've created a dimension style, you can always go back and change it. To do so, you use the Modify option in the Dimension Style Manager dialog box.

1. Choose Format ➤ Dimension ➤ Style or type **D**↵ to open the Dimension Style Manager dialog box. You can also click the Dimension Style tool in the Styles toolbar at the top of the AutoCAD Window (see Figure 10.34).

FIGURE 10.34
The Dimension Style tool in the Styles toolbar

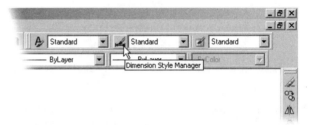

2. Select the name of the dimension style you want to edit in the list box at the left of the dialog box.

3. Click Modify to open the Modify Dimension Style dialog box.

Use the steps in the previous section as a guide to adjust your dimension styles.

Just Enough Summary

As you work with dimensions, you may find that you will make adjustments to the dimension style little by little, until you set up a style just the way you want. Once you've reached that point, you probably won't change your dimension styles often. You can then save your dimension style to a file using the Express Tools, or you can add them to your most frequently used template file so the style is available at all times.

Chapter 11

Gathering Information

AutoCAD drawings can potentially contain a great deal of information. You can you store text based information both as labels in the drawing and as hidden written information, and you can also query graphic elements to find distance and area measurements.

This chapter provides information about how you can store and retrieve information about the drawing. In this chapter, you'll find out how to gather information from your drawing when you're measuring an area or looking for a lost file. You will also find information on how to add textual data to help you when you are doing file searches with DesignCenter. Other topics covered in this chapter include:

- ◆ Measuring Areas
- ◆ Finding the Coordinate of a Point
- ◆ Measuring Distances
- ◆ Measuring Angles
- ◆ Getting the General Status of the Drawing
- ◆ Finding the Time Spent on a Drawing
- ◆ Adding Nondrawing Data to Store with Your Drawing
- ◆ Finding Text in a drawing
- ◆ Locating and Selecting Named Components
- ◆ Finding Missing Support Files

Measuring Areas

One of the first measurement tasks you're likely to need is the area in a drawing. It might be the area of a site plan or the floor space of a commercial building. Before AutoCAD came along, finding the area in a drawing was a tedious and error-ridden job. Now that you are using AutoCAD, you can quickly find areas of all shapes and sizes, and you'll be certain that you have an accurate area calculation.

You can measure an area in several ways. It is easiest to measure an area that is completely bounded by objects. The boundary can be made up of individual objects, or it can be a single closed polyline or spline. You can also find an area by selecting a set of points that define the corners of a boundary. This method is useful for areas that have straight sides such as a typical property line in a city grid.

Measuring the Area of a Polygonal Shape

If you are trying to find the area of a polygonal shape, you can use the Area command. The following steps describe the process.

1. Choose Tools ➤ Inquiry ➤ Area, or type **Area⏎** at the Command prompt.

2. Following the boundary edge, select the corners of your polygon. Use osnaps to make accurate point selections (see Figure 11.1).

FIGURE 11.1

Select points sequentially on a polygonal shape, as shown by the numbers, to find its area.

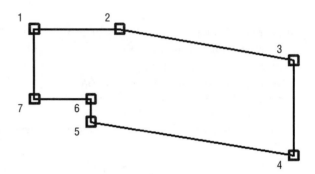

3. When you have come full circle, press ⏎. You see a message in the Command window showing the area and perimeter you just selected.

The shape can be as simple as a box or as complex as the one shown in Figure 11.1. You will get an accurate reading as long as all the sides of the polygon are straight.

Measuring the Area of Complex or Curved Shapes

If the area you want to measure has curves in its boundary or if it is just too complex to use the previous method, the best thing to do is to place a hatch pattern within the boundary. You can then use the Properties palette to find the area. The advantage to this method is that you will always have a way to quickly get an area measurement. At any time, you can look at the properties of the hatch pattern that fills the boundary.

USING THE HATCH COMMAND TO CREATE A POLYLINE OUTLINE

While the main purpose of the Hatch command is to place a hatch pattern in your drawing, hatch patterns can also report the area they occupy. Before you begin, however, you must be sure that the area you are trying to define has a continuous border.

TIP If you're measuring a room with an open doorway, draw a temporary line across the doorway before using the Hatch command. Or, if your drawing contains a door header layer, turn it on to display the door header. Also turn off the layer of any door symbols that might interfere with the creation of a hatch pattern of the entire room.

1. Click the Hatch tool in the Draw toolbar or choose Draw ➤ Hatch to open the Hatch and Gradient dialog box, as shown in Figure 11.2.

FIGURE 11.2

The Hatch and Gradient
dialog box

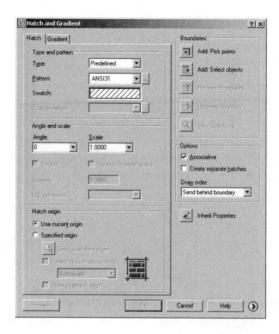

2. Click the Pick Points button. The Hatch and Gradient dialog box closes.

3. At the `Select internal point:` prompt, click in the interior of the area you want to measure. You'll see the area outlined with a dashed line.

4. Press ↵ then at the Hatch and Gradient dialog box, click OK. Hatch draws a hatch pattern on the current layer. You can always change the layer assignment of the hatch pattern later.

5. Select the newly created hatch pattern, right-click, and choose Properties.

6. In the Properties palette, scroll down to the Geometry group to find the area listing, as shown in Figure 11.3.

You can use any hatch pattern you like as they will all report the same area. Once you've obtained the area measurement of the hatch pattern, you can delete it. If you want to keep the hatch pattern for future reference, you can put it on a separate layer and turn that layer off.

TIP If you put the hatch pattern you are using for area calculations on a different layer for future reference, make sure you turn off plotting for that layer. This will prevent you from accidentally including those hatch patterns in your plotted output. See Chapter 7 for more on layer settings.

If there is a gap anywhere in the area you are trying to measure, you may get an error message that the area you are trying to select is not closed. You can use a setting called Gap Tolerance to tell AutoCAD to ignore gaps of a certain size. You can also have the Hatch command place a polyline outline of the hatch area by turning on the Retain Boundaries option in the Hatch and Gradient dialog box. By including a polyline outline, you can delete the hatch pattern and still obtain the area of the polyline outline from the Properties palette just as you would for a hatch pattern (see steps 5 and 6 of the previous example). See Chapter 3 for more information on the Gap Tolerance and Retain Boundaries options.

FIGURE 11.3
The Area listing in the
Geometry group of the
Properties palette

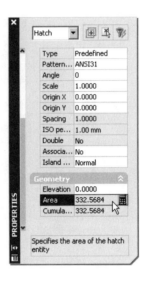

MEASURING AREAS THAT CONTAIN ISLANDS

You might need to measure an area that contains other shapes such as circles or polygons, as shown in Figure 11.4. The hatch command offers the ability to ignore these "islands" within a boundary. If your measurement must exclude these other shapes, make sure that the island detection feature in the Hatch and Gradient dialog box is turned on and set to either Normal or Outer. Island detection is turned on by default.

FIGURE 11.4
An area containing other
shapes, or "islands," that
you do not want in your
area measurement

Islands to be subtracted from the overall area measurement

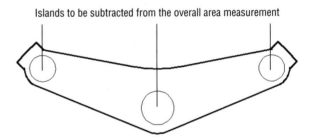

FINDING CUMULATIVE AREA VALUES

If you need to find the cumulative area of several spaces, you can place individual hatch patterns in those spaces, select all the hatch patterns, then open the Properties palette. You will see a Cumulative Area listing in the Geometry group which reports the total area of all of the selected hatch patterns (see the bottom of Figure 11.3).

Another tool you can employ is the QuickCalc calculator. You may have noticed a small calculator icon to the far right of the Area listing of the Properties palette. If you click that icon, the QuickCalc calculator will appear with the area value already displayed.

You can use the Memory function of the calculator to store and add area values, perform conversions, or do any other operation you require. The QuickCalc calculator can also be opened by clicking the calculator icon in the standard toolbar.

Finding the Coordinate of a Point

If you need to find the coordinates of a point in reference to a datum point, you must first set up a UCS with its origin at the datum point. You can then use the ID command to find the coordinate.

1. Choose Tools ➢ New UCS ➢ Origin or enter **UCS** ↵ **Origin** ↵ at the Command prompt.

2. At the Specify new origin point <0,0,0>: prompt, use an osnap to select the datum point.

3. Choose Tools ➢ Inquire ➢ ID Point.

4. At the Specify point: prompt, use an osnap to select the exact point in your drawing. The coordinates are displayed in the Command window.

If a reference datum point is not important, you can skip steps 1 and 2 and start at step 3.

If the coordinate system you are measuring from is at an angle in relation to AutoCAD's default or world coordinate system, you can rotate the UCS about the Z axis before using the ID command.

1. Choose Tools ➢ New UCS ➢ Z.

2. At the Specify rotation angle about Z axis <90>: prompt, enter an angle or select two points to indicate an angle graphically. The UCS rotates to the new angle.

3. Go to step 3 of the previous example to obtain the coordinates of the point you want.

If you'd like to learn more about the UCS, see Chapter 6.

Measuring Distances

Measuring distances is simple.

1. Choose Tools ➤ Inquiry ➤ Distance or enter **Distance** ↵ at the Command prompt.

2. At the `Specify first point:` prompt, use an osnap and select the start point of the distance you want to measure.

3. At the `Specify second point:` prompt, use an osnap to select the end point of the distance. The distance is displayed in the Command window in the following format:

```
Distance = x.xxxx,  Angle in XY Plane = xx,  Angle from XY Plane = x
Delta X = x.xxxx,  Delta Y = x.xxxx,   Delta Z = x.xxxx
```

You are shown both the direct distance and the X, Y, and Z coordinates of the distance. You are also shown the angle within the XY plane and, if the distance is in 3D, the angle from the XY plane.

Measuring Angles

You can use the Distance command described in the previous section to find the angle represented by two points. But what if you want to find the angle between two lines, as in Figure 11.5?

FIGURE 11.5
Using angular dimension to find the angle between two lines

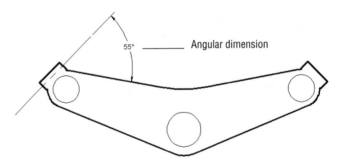

55° ———— Angular dimension

AutoCAD doesn't have a specific command that does this, but you can use the Dimension command to add a dimension that shows you the angle between two lines. Here's how to create an angular dimension.

1. Choose Dimension ➤ Angular or enter **Dimang** ↵ at the Command prompt.

2. At the `Select arc, circle, line, or <specify vertex>:` prompt, select the first line.

3. At the `Select second line:` prompt, select the second line.

4. At the `Specify dimension arc line location or [Mtext/Text/Angle]:` prompt, you will see the angular dimension at the cursor. Move it to the location that best shows the angle you want to measure, and then click the mouse.

TIP   If your drawing contains a lot of textual information you are using for information only, you can create a layer that does not print and then place that information on the nonprinting layer. See Chapter 6 for more information.

By default, AutoCAD's dimensioning feature rounds off angular dimensions to the nearest degree. You can adjust the precision value for dimension styles to show angular values that are less than a whole degree. See the Angular Dimension Group in Table 10.5 of Chapter 10.

Getting the General Status of the Drawing

You can quickly get the status of many drawings settings using the Status command. This command displays the current settings for limits, snaps, and grids, the display area, and other features. This information can help you understand a drawing or help troubleshoot a problem. Here's how it works.

1. Choose Tools ➢ Inquiry ➢ Status or enter **Status** ↵ at the Command prompt.

2. The text screen displays a listing of the current status of the drawing, as shown in Figure 11.6.

FIGURE 11.6

The AutoCAD text screen showing the drawing status

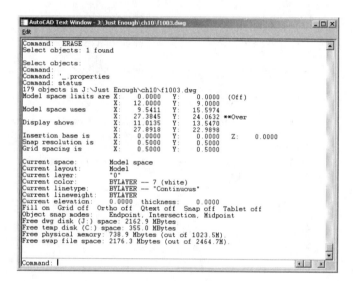

Table 11.1 lists the options shown by the Status command and their meaning.

TABLE 11.1:   The Status Items and Their Meaning

ITEM	MEANING
(Number) Objects In D:\Folder\Subfolder	The number of AutoCAD objects in the drawing.
Model Space Limits Are	The coordinates of the Model tab limits. (See Chapter 3 for more details on limits.)
Model Space Uses	The area the drawing occupies; equivalent to Zoom extents.
**Over:	If present, this item means that part of the drawing is outside the area defined by the drawing limits.

TABLE 11.1:   The Status Items and Their Meaning (CONTINUED)

ITEM	MEANING
Display Shows	The area shown by the current view.
Insertion Base Is, Snap Resolution Is, and Grid Spacing Is	The current default values for these settings.
Current Space	Model (model space) or Layout (paper space) tab
Current Layout	The current tab.
Current Layer	The current layer.
Current Color	The current color.
Current Linetype	The current linetype.
Current Lineweight	The current Lineweight setting.
Current Elevation/ Thickness	The current default Z coordinate, and the current thickness of objects. These are both 3D-related settings.
Fill, Grid, Ortho, Qtext, Snap, and Tablet	The status of these settings.
Object Snap Modes	The current default Osnap setting.
Free Dwg Disk (Drive:) Space	The amount of space available to store drawing-specific temporary files.
Free Temp Disk (Drive:) Space	The amount of space left on your hard drive for AutoCAD's resource temporary files.
Free Physical Memory	The amount of free RAM available.
Free Swap File Space	The amount of Windows swap file space available.

Finding the Time Spent on a Drawing

You might want to find out how much time was actually spent on a drawing for billing purposes or just to keep track of how long a drawing takes. Using the Time command is a quick way to get this information.

1. Choose Tools ➤ Inquiry ➤ Time or enter **Time** ↵ at the Command prompt.

2. The text windows displays the time information, as shown in Figure 11.7.

FIGURE 11.7

The time information in the AutoCAD text window

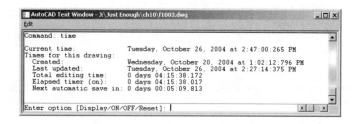

3. At the Enter option [Display/ON/OFF/Reset]: prompt, press ↵ to exit the Time command.

As you can see from Figure 11.7, the information is self-explanatory. You can also turn the timer off by entering **Off** at the prompt in step 3, or you can reset the timer to clear the current values by entering **R** ↵.

Adding Nondrawing Data to Store with Your Drawing

The Preferences dialog box lets you store nondrawing data with your drawing file. This can be textual information such as the project name, people involved in creating the drawing, or comments regarding the drawing. You can even add a keyword in the event that you will need to search for this file using the AutoCAD DesignCenter or the Windows Search tool.

To get to the Preferences dialog box, do the following:

1. Choose File ➢ Drawing Properties to open the Drawing Properties dialog box. The General tab contains formation such as the file size and when the drawing was created (see Figure 11.8).

2. The Summary tab contains the Title, Author, Subject, Keywords, and Comments text boxes in which you can enter data (see Figure 11.9).

3. The Statistics tab (see Figure 11.10) offers editing dates and times. The Custom tab lets you enter further textual data to be stored with the drawing.

FIGURE 11.8

The General tab of the Drawing Properties dialog box

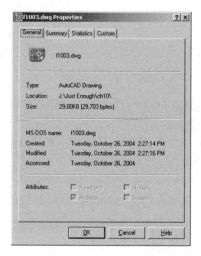

FIGURE 11.9

The Summary tab of the Drawing Properties dialog box

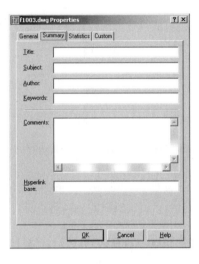

FIGURE 11.10

The Statistics tab of the Drawing Properties dialog box

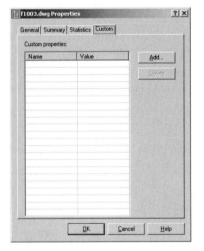

Finding Text in a Drawing

You often have to find a string of text to either replace it or to simply locate a part of a drawing indicated by the text. AutoCAD offers the Find command to help you locate specific text in a drawing, including attribute values and dimension text. Here's how it works.

1. Choose Edit ➢ Find to open the Find And Replace dialog box, as shown in Figure 11.11.

2. In the Find Text String text box, enter the text you want to search for.

3. Make sure Entire Drawing is selected in the Search In drop-down list.

FIGURE 11.11

The Find And Replace
dialog box

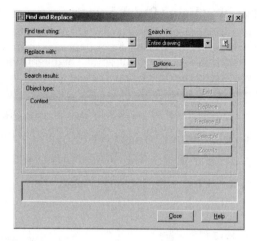

4. Click Find. If the text exists in the drawing, it appears in the Search Results list box.

5. If the text in the list box is not what you are looking for, click Find again.

6. When the appropriate text appears, click the Zoom To button to zoom into the text in the list box.

You can use the Find command to search for attribute text, table text, dimension text, and hyperlinks. If you click the Options button in the Find And Replace dialog box, the Find And Replace Options dialog box appears, allowing you to fine-tune the search criteria (see Figure 11.12).

This is where you can specify whether the search is case sensitive or whether to search for whole words.

FIGURE 11.12

The Find And Replace
Options dialog box

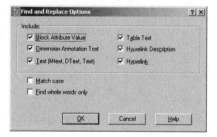

Locating and Selecting Named Components

As your drawings become more complex, you'll have a harder time finding specific items you need to edit. For example, you might need to replace the text style of some notes that have been set improperly. You have a couple of tools that can help you find items in your drawing based on their name or the name of a property they possess. You can use the Quick Select feature, which is actually intended to select objects based on their properties. You can also use the DesignCenter, which can show you graphic representations of named components in your drawing.

Searching Using Quick Select

You can locate objects based on the type of object or a property using the Quick Select tool. If the object has a name, such as a block, for example, you can also locate it with this tool. Although Quick Select is intended as a selection tool, since it highlights the objects in your drawing, you can see where the selected objects are in the drawing and then use the zoom feature to zoom in on their location.

The following example shows how you can find a block in a drawing:

1. Choose Tools ≻ Quick Select to open the Quick Select dialog box.

2. Select Entire Drawing from the Apply To drop-down list.

3. Select Block Reference in the Object Type drop-down list.

4. In the Properties list, select Name.

5. In the Operator list, select Equals, as shown in Figure 11.13.

FIGURE 11.13

The Quick Select dialog box with Equals selected in the Operator list

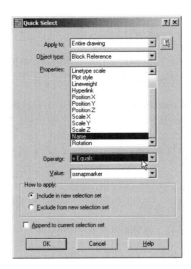

6. Locate the name of the block you want in the Value drop-down list.

7. Click OK. You will see the selected objects highlighted in the drawing.

One feature you'll want to be aware of is the Operator list. By default, it shows Equals, but you can also base your selection on properties that are not equal to the settings you select. If the selection criteria involve a numeric value, you can also use greater-than or less-than operators.

You can also use the Design Center to locate named items such as blocks, linetypes, text styles, and dimension styles.

Viewing a List of Named Components

If you don't necessarily need to find a named element in a drawing, but just want to see a listing of them, you can use the DesignCenter. The DesignCenter shows you not only the named components in open drawings, but also named components in other drawing files. You can even search folders containing drawing files to locate a particular named component. You can find a detailed discussion of the DesignCenter in Chapter 7.

Finding Missing Support Files

Sometimes a drawing appears incomplete or incorrect due to missing support files. If font files are missing, AutoCAD attempts to substitute another font, but your text will not appear as it was intended. Or if a custom linetype was used for parts of the drawing, they will not appear correctly. Whole parts of a drawing will be missing if AutoCAD can't find Xrefs.

If you open an AutoCAD drawing and find that you are missing support files such as these, it may be that you only need to direct AutoCAD to the proper location for these files.

Locating Xrefs

If you open a drawing and most of it appears to be missing, chances are an Xref has been misplaced. You will know that an Xref is missing because you will see a text string that starts with the word *Xref* and is followed by a search path, as shown in Figure 11.14.

FIGURE 11.14

Text shown in place of a missing Xref

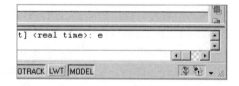

Xref C:\Documents and Settings\George Omura\My Documents\New Folder\Office Plan.dwg

Another clue that you are missing an Xref is an exclamation point in the lower-right corner of the AutoCAD window (see Figure 11.15).

FIGURE 11.15

The lower-right corner of the AutoCAD window shows an exclamation point with a paper clip icon.

If this happens to you, do the following:

1. Choose Insert ➢ Xref Manager, click the exclamation point in the lower-right corner of the AutoCAD window, or enter **Xref** ↵ at the command prompt to open the Xref Manager dialog box, as shown in Figure 11.16.

2. You'll see the name of the missing Xref in the list box. Make note of the filename, and then use the Windows Search utility (choose Start ➢ Search ➢ Files Or Folders) to find the missing file.

FIGURE 11.16

The Xref Manager dialog box

3. Back in AutoCAD, select the filename in the Xref Manager dialog box, and then click Browse to open the Select New Path dialog box.

4. Browse to the location of the missing file and select it.

5. Back in the Xref Manager dialog box, you should see that the exclamation point has changed to a reload symbol, as shown in Figure 11.17.

FIGURE 11.17

The Xref Manager dialog box showing the Reload symbol in the Status column

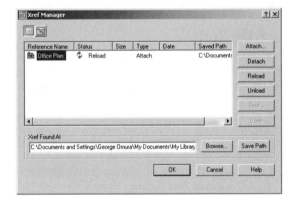

6. Click OK. The missing portion of the drawing appears.

7. If you want AutoCAD to remember this new location for the Xref, click the Save Path button in the lower-right corner of the Xref Manager dialog box.

Another option is to first look at the name of the search path shown in the drawing or in the Xref Manager dialog box, as shown in Figure 11.18.

This tells you where AutoCAD expects to find the file. Use the Windows Search utility to find the missing Xref, and then place it in the path indicated by the Xref Manager search path. You can also place the file in the same folder as the current drawing.

FIGURE 11.18

Hover over the Saved Path column to display the search path for the Xref.

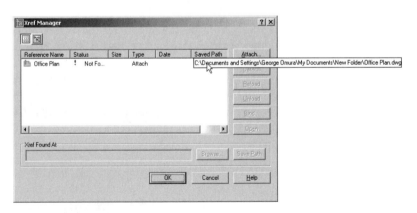

Locating Fonts, Linetypes, and Hatch Patterns

AutoCAD relies on external files for fonts, linetypes, and hatch patterns. Occasionally you encounter a drawing that cannot find one or all these external files, in which case the drawing produces the wrong display for these items. This often happens when you receive files from another source, such as a consultant or a client.

If the support files are in the same folder as the drawing that uses them, you shouldn't have a problem, but you may find that, for whatever reason, you have to maintain the folder structure from the original source location. In this case, the support files may not be where AutoCAD expects to find them.

Using the Options dialog box, you can tell AutoCAD to look in a specific location for these support files.

1. Choose Tools ➢ Options or type **Options** ↵ in the Command line to open the Options dialog box.

2. Make sure the Files tab is selected, as shown in Figure 11.19.

FIGURE 11.19

The Files tab in the Options dialog box

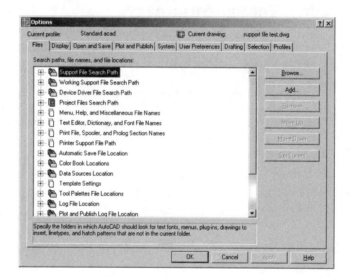

3. Click the plus sign to the left of the Support File Search Path option. The option expands to show a list of the current search paths.

4. Click the Add button, and then click the Browse button to open the Browse For Folder dialog box (see Figure 11.20).

5. Find the location of your support files, and then click OK. The new location appears in the Support File Search Path list box.

6. Click OK to exit the Options dialog box.

FIGURE 11.20
The Browse For Folder
dialog box

Just Enough Summary

In this short chapter, you've seen some of the most important features in AutoCAD. Finding measurements is perhaps the simplest yet most useful AutoCAD tool. Other information, such as the time spent editing or getting the overall settings in one view, can save time and guesswork if you're managing a project.

Other features discussed in this chapter can help you troubleshoot a problem. Locating missing files is a fairly common task, especially if you are sharing files with another office, and the Status command is often the first step in diagnosing other file-related problems.

Chapter 12

Laying Out and Printing Your Drawing

Printing in AutoCAD is a bit more complicated than in other applications and for a good reason. You will often be required to print a drawing multiple times over the course of a project, and you will want your drawings to be consistent from one print to the next. And since AutoCAD is a graphics program, you spend a greater amount of time laying out your drawings on a sheet in order to visually organize your work.

This chapter covers two aspects of printing: preparing your drawing's final appearance in a Layout tab and printing your drawing. The Layout tabs let you organize your drawing in a precise way and include standard drawing borders and titles and give you flexibility in the scale and orientation of your drawing on the printed sheet. Finally, you can get an accurate view of how your drawing will look before you commit it to paper.

AutoCAD's printing feature offers more than just orientation and sheet sizes. You can store your printer settings so you can easily and accurately reproduce prints. Since AutoCAD offers some advanced 3D capabilities, you can combine 3D views with 2D drawings. You can even include information about the file so you can easily identify the source for the printed drawing.

If you're new to AutoCAD, and you need to get started with printing, you'll want to read the first section of this chapter carefully. It provides an overview of the layout and printing features in a tutorial format. The sections that follow give you more detailed information about Layout tabs and how to use them. After the sections on layouts, you'll find more detailed information on how to print your drawing and the settings associated with printing. Here's an overview of the topics covered in this chapter:

- ◆ Setting Up a Drawing for Printing
- ◆ Printing Your Drawing
- ◆ Storing Your Printer Settings
- ◆ Controlling Color, Lines, and Fills though Plot Styles
- ◆ Assigning Named Plot Styles Directly to Layers and Objects
- ◆ Converting a Drawing from Color Plot Styles to Named Plot Styles

Setting Up a Drawing for Printing

In most programs, you choose File ➢ Print and send your drawing to the printer. Although you can do this in AutoCAD, the best way to control your print results is to set up how your drawing will look in the Layout tab.

In this section, we'll take a look at how you can set up the scale and location of your drawing on the printed page exactly as you want it. To help you get familiar with the process, the first part is a tutorial showing you the parts of the Layout tab and how they behave. You'll then learn how to set the scale and location of your drawing on the printer medium before you actually send the drawing to the printer.

Exploring the Layout Tab

When you're ready to print your drawing, you'll need to do a little setup first. The Layout tabs help you set up your drawing precisely the way you want it to appear before you print. The following steps introduce the Layout tab.

1. Open a new drawing and add a few objects such as rectangles and circles. We'll use these to show how the Layout tab works.

2. Click the Layout tab. You see your objects appear within a rectangle, which itself is inside a white rectangular area, as shown in Figure 12.1.

FIGURE 12.1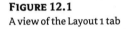
A view of the Layout 1 tab

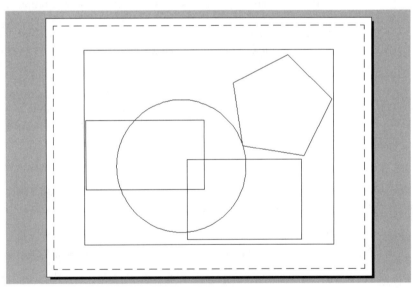

The white area represents the paper onto which your drawing will be plotted. It appears over a gray area, and you see a drop shadow behind the white space. The dashed line indicates the non-printable border of your printer. Finally, the solid rectangle that frames your drawing is a *viewport*, which is like a window into your Model tab drawing. This viewport behaves like any other AutoCAD object in that it has properties that you can edit through the Properties palette. You can set the viewport's layer, linetype, and color assignment, and you can change its width and height using grips.

EXPLORING THE VIEWPORT

The viewport has a few properties that are quite unusual. First, it displays the drawing you created in the Model tab. It also has properties that control the exact scale of the view it displays. You can also pan and zoom the view so you're not fixed to any one view within the viewport.

1. Try selecting part of your drawing by clicking inside the viewport. Nothing is selected. This is because you are currently in the layout space, otherwise known as *paper space*. Later you'll see how you can reach into the viewport to edit your view while still in the Layout tab.

2. Click the viewport border, right-click, and choose Properties from the shortcut menu. You can see from the Properties palette that the viewport is just like any other AutoCAD object with layer, linetype, and color assignments. You can even hide the viewport outline by turning off its layer.

3. Close the Properties palette, and then with the viewport still selected, press Delete or click the Erase tool in the Modify toolbar. The view of your drawing disappears.

This shows you that the viewport is like a window into the drawing you created in the Model tab. Once the viewport is erased, the drawing view goes with it.

1. Type **U↵** or click the Undo button in the Standard toolbar to restore the viewport.

2. Click the Paper button in the status bar, as shown in Figure 12.2.

FIGURE 12.2

The Paper button in the status bar

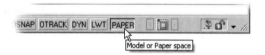

The button label changes to Model, and you'll notice that the viewport border becomes thicker. By clicking the Paper button, you changed to *floating model space*. Floating model space allows you to edit the drawing within the viewport as if you were in the Model tab.

Take a closer look at the viewport, and you'll see that the UCS icon appears within the viewport. The viewport looks as if it is a miniature version of the Model tab. In fact, that's exactly how floating model space behaves. You can think of floating model space as a shortcut to the contents of the Model tab.

3. Click any of the objects you drew at the beginning of this exercise. You can now select objects within the viewport.

4. Try zooming and panning your view. Changes in your view only take place within the boundary of the viewport.

5. Choose View ➢ Zoom ➢ All or type **Z↵ A↵** to display the entire drawing in the viewport once again.

6. Click the Model button in the status bar to return to paper space. The viewport border returns to its original thickness, and the UCS icon disappears from within the viewport.

This exercise shows you the unique characteristics of the Layout tab. The objects within the viewport are inaccessible until you enter floating model space by clicking the Paper button in the status bar.

The Layout tabs can contain as many viewports as you like, and each viewport can hold a different view of your drawing. You can size and arrange each viewport in any way you like, giving you the freedom to lay out your drawing as your needs dictate.

TIP Nothing prevents you from drawing in the Layout tab around and on top of a viewport. In fact, some users find it convenient to draw dimensions and notes in the Layout tab to help keep drawing notation consistent when multiple viewports are present. Another common practice is to add title blocks and borders in the Layout tab to frame your drawing. Items you draw in the paper space of the Layout tab will not appear in the Model tab.

SELECTING A PAPER SIZE AND ORIENTATION

In a totally new AutoCAD setup and with a new drawing, AutoCAD assumes that you want to print your drawing in an 8 ½″ × 11″ sheet of paper, so that is the size of the default paper area shown in the Layout tab. If you have a printer capable of printing larger formats, you can set up the layout to show larger sizes and different drawing orientations. The following introduces the Page Setup Manager and the Page Setup dialog boxes.

1. Choose File ➢ Plot or right-click the Layout tab at the bottom of the AutoCAD window and choose Plot to open the Plot dialog box, as shown in Figure 12.3.

FIGURE 12.3
The Plot dialog box

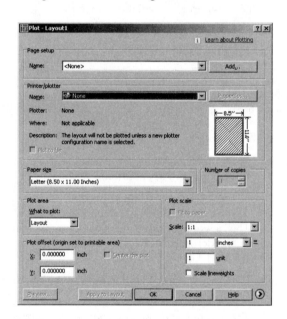

2. Click the Name drop-down list in the Printer/Plotter group, and select the printer you want to use.

3. Click the More Options button in the lower-right corner of the dialog box. It's the round button with the right pointing arrow (see Figure 12.4).

FIGURE 12.4
The More Options button

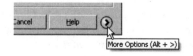

4. In the Drawing Orientation group, select the Landscape or Portrait radio button that appears in the lower-right corner of the dialog box.

5. To ensure that your drawing prints in black and white instead of color or shades of gray, select monochrome.ctb from the Plot Style Table drop-down list, as shown in Figure 12.5.

FIGURE 12.5

The Plot Style Table drop-down list showing the monochrome.ctb option

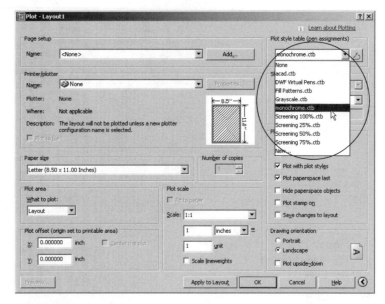

After making your changes, you can save the settings for use in other Layout tabs. This saves you from having to set up each layout that you create and use.

1. At the top of the Plot dialog box, click the Add button in the Page Setup group, as shown in Figure 12.6.

2. In the Add Page Setup dialog box, you can enter a name for your setup, or just accept the default name offered by AutoCAD (see Figure 12.7). Click OK to return to the Plot dialog box.

3. Click the Apply To Layout button at the bottom of the dialog box to save the settings you just made.

4. Click Cancel to exit the dialog box without printing your drawing.

When you return to the Layout tab, you may notice some subtle differences in the dashed line that shows the nonprintable area of your printer. Since every printer is different, this area depends on your specific printer selection.

The next time you open the Plot dialog box, you will see the same settings you entered in the previous example. You can then click OK to go ahead with your print.

This section has given you a brief tour of the layout features in AutoCAD. The rest of the chapter describes the methods you'll need to know to fine-tune your printer output, starting with the issue of scale.

FIGURE 12.6
The Add button in the
Page Setup group

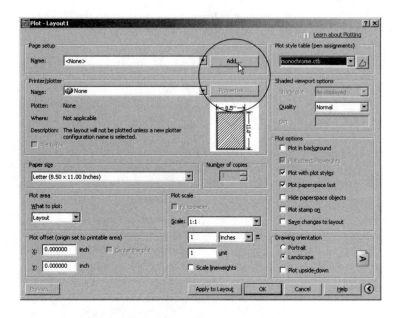

FIGURE 12.7
The Add Page Setup
dialog box

Using the Layout Tab to Scale Down Your Drawing

In the Model tab, you draw everything at full scale. When you are ready to print, you need a way to scale down your drawing to fit on a piece of paper. The Layout tab is like the staging ground where you can adjust your Model tab drawing to fit a sheet of paper. You can choose from a set of standard scales for your Model tab drawing so that it fits onto the paper size you have selected for your output. If you don't know the scale to use, you can try various ones to find one that allows your drawing to fit your paper. The following steps describe the process.

To set the scale of a viewport in a Layout tab, take the following steps.

1. In a Layout tab, click the viewport border to select it, right-click, and choose Properties from the shortcut menu to open the Properties palette for the viewport.

2. Scroll down the Properties palette to locate the Standard Scale option under the Misc category. Click this option, and you'll see a list box to the right, as shown in Figure 12.8.

FIGURE 12.8

A list of scales in the
Properties palette

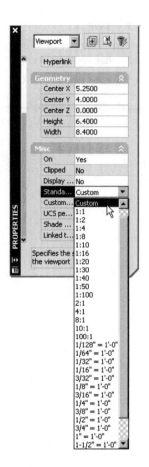

3. Open the list box and select a scale that you want to use. The view in the viewport changes to reflect the new scale.

4. Close the Properties palette.

In step 3, you saw that you can select a scale for a viewport from the Properties palette. If you look just below the Standard Scale option, you'll see the Custom Scale option. You can enter a scale factor in the Custom Scale text box for scales that are not listed in the Standard Scale option.

Creating Additional Viewports

Quite often, you will want several views of your Model tab drawing visible in the Layout tab. For example, you might have a wall section at one scale and enlarged details at another and want both to appear in the Layout tab.

ADDING A SINGLE VIEWPORT

You can add as many viewports as you need through the Viewports dialog box, but if you only need to add one, here's what you can do.

1. Choose View ➢ Viewports ➢ New Viewports to open the Viewports dialog box.

2. Make sure the New Viewports tab is selected, and then select the Single option in the Standard Viewport list, as shown in Figure 12.9.

FIGURE 12.9

The Single option selected in the New Viewports tab

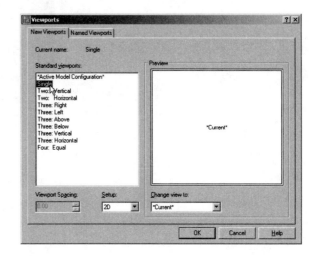

3. Click OK.

4. At the Specify first corner or [Fit] <Fit>: prompt, click a point in the layout for the first corner of the new viewport.

5. At the Specify opposite corner: prompt, you'll see the corner of the new viewport follow the cursor. Click a point to place the other corner of the viewport.

Don't worry if your viewport isn't exactly the size you want it. You can adjust the size of the viewport by selecting its border and then clicking a corner grip to move the corner.

If you want the viewport to cover the entire layout, you can type **F** ↵ in step 4 to use the Fit option. This immediately places the viewport in the layout that extends all the way to the edge of the printable area of the layout.

ADDING MULTIPLE VIEWPORTS AT ONCE

The Viewports dialog box contains several options that let you add multiple viewports at one time. In step 2 of the previous example, you are asked to select the Single option. If you select another option, such as the Three: Above option, for example, you will see a preview of the viewport layout in the preview panel to the right (see Figure 12.10). This shows you the arrangement of the selected option as it will appear when you finally place the viewport.

Once you select an option and click OK, you can place the viewport as described in steps 4 and 5 of the previous example. You can also enter **F** ↵ in step 4 if you want the viewports to fill the layout.

FIGURE 12.10
The Three: Above
option in the Viewports
dialog box

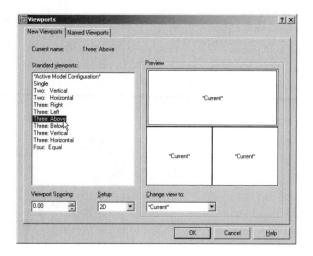

OTHER MULTIPLE VIEWPORT OPTIONS

Some other options also let you control the views that appear in each of the viewports. By default, the current model space view is placed in all the viewports as indicated in the preview area. You can click a preview viewport and then select a view from the Change View To drop-down list shown in Figure 12.11.

FIGURE 12.11
The Change View To
drop-down list at the
bottom of the Viewports
dialog box

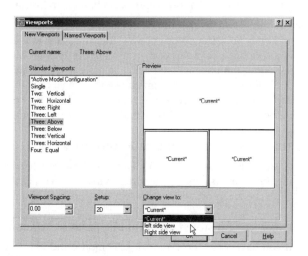

You must first save a view in the Model tab before this option shows anything other than Current.

Another option is the Setup drop-down list (see Figure 12.12). This option lets you select between 2D and 3D views. If you select 3D, the preview panel displays a top, bottom, side, or isometric view option.

You can then use the Change View To drop-down list to select the type of view you want for each viewport.

FIGURE 12.12
The Setup option at the bottom of the Viewports dialog box

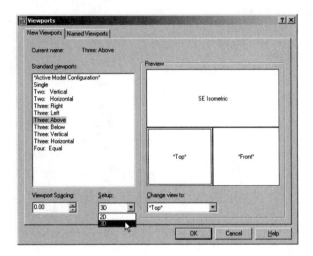

Controlling How Viewports Display and Print

Several other settings let you control the way viewports display and print your drawing. You can turn the display of your drawing off entirely, lock the view to prevent accidental pans and zooms, and set up a 3D view to plot a hidden line or rendered view.

LOCKING THE VIEWPORT VIEW FROM PANS AND ZOOMS

You might end up spending a fair amount of time setting up your viewport view for the proper scale and view area. But you can easily alter the scale accidentally, just by going to floating model space and zooming in to a part of the view. For this reason, AutoCAD offers a way to lock the viewport view so zooms and pans will not alter the scale or view contents.

To lock the viewport from pans and zooms, click the viewport border to select it, right-click, and choose Display Locked ➢ Yes. Once this is done, you can use the pan and zoom tools to move about in the viewport, but you won't affect the actual viewport view.

TURNING THE VIEWPORT DISPLAY ON OR OFF

Another lesser-used viewport feature is the ability to turn the view on or off. If you encounter a drawing with empty layout viewports, chances are you can turn on the display by doing the following: Click the viewport border to select it, right-click, and choose Display Viewport Objects ➢ Yes.

PRINTING A 3D MODEL WITH HIDDEN LINES OR SHADED

If you have a viewport view of a 3D model and you want that model to print as a hidden line view or as a shaded view, you can do the following: Click the viewport border to select it, right-click, and choose Shaded Plots ➢ Hidden or Shaded Plots ➢ Rendered. Your view of the model won't change but when you plot the layout, the 3D model appears as a hidden line or rendered view.

Setting Layers for Individual Viewports

You can control the layer settings for each individual viewport in a Layout tab. This can be helpful when you want to show the same view of a drawing in different ways. For example, you can draw a single floor plan in the Model tab with different types of information on different layers. Then in a Layout tab, you can create multiple viewports showing the same view but with different layer settings in each viewport to show the different elements. If your drawing is a floor plan, you might want a layout that shows one viewport with the furniture layer turned on and another viewport with an electrical layout layer turned on and the furniture turned off, as shown in Figure 12.13.

You're already familiar with the sun icon farthest to the left. This is the Freeze / Thaw icon that controls the freezing and thawing of layers globally. Several columns to the right of that icon is a sun icon with a transparent rectangle. This icon controls the freezing and thawing of layers in individual viewports. The next exercise shows you firsthand how it works.

FIGURE 12.13

A layout with two viewports, each showing the same view with different layer settings

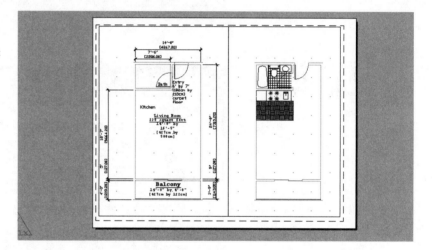

1. Click the Paper button on the status bar to go to floating model space.

2. Click in the viewport whose layers you want to control.

3. Open the Layer Properties Manager dialog box.

4. Locate the layer you want to turn on or off; then click its name to isolate this layer in the list (see Figure 12.14).

5. Look for the Current VP Freeze column for the selected layer. You might need to widen the Layer Properties Manager dialog box or use the scroll bar at the bottom of the dialog box to do this. The Current VP Freeze column is the second column from the right side of the dialog box. The icon looks like a transparent rectangle over a sun. The sun tells you the layer is on for the current viewport (see Figure 12.15).

FIGURE 12.14

A single layer selected in the Layer Properties Manager dialog box

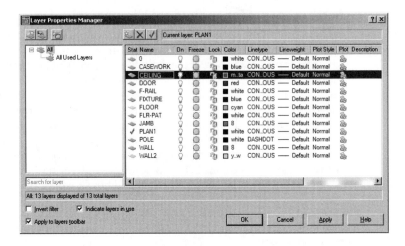

FIGURE 12.15

The Current VP Freeze option in a layer listing

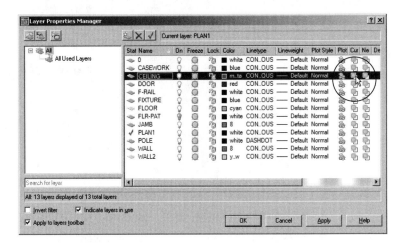

6. Click the Current VP Freeze icon to turn the layer off for the current viewport. The sun changes to a snowflake.

7. Click OK when you are finished. The selected viewport changes to reflect the layer changes you made.

You can also use the Layer Control drop-down menu in the toolbar to freeze layers in individual viewports. Proceed with the steps in the previous example, but instead of opening the Layer Properties Manager dialog box in step 3, open the Layer Control drop-down list shown in Figure 12.16.

Select the layer you want to affect from the drop-down list, and then click the sun icon with the small rectangle to turn the layer off.

If you find that a layer does not display in a viewport and you want it turned on, you might need to turn it on or thaw it globally by using the On/Off or Freeze/Thaw column of the Layer Properties Manager dialog box.

FIGURE 12.16
The Layer Control
drop-down list

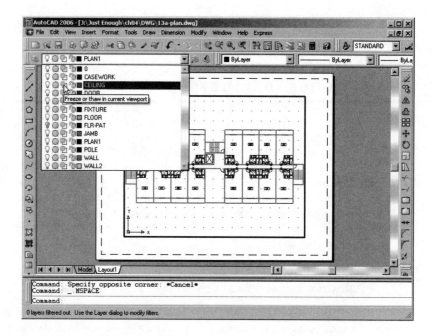

Adding Layouts

In a new drawing, AutoCAD provides two Layout tabs labeled Layout 1 and Layout 2. You're not limited to two layouts. For small projects with only a handful of drawings in the printed set, you can set up a layout for each sheet in the set.

If you need more Layout tabs, you can easily duplicate an existing layout by doing the following:

1. Right-click the Layout tab you want to duplicate.

2. Choose Move or Copy from the shortcut menu to open the Move Or Copy dialog box.

3. Select the name of the layout you want to copy and turn on the Create A Copy option at the bottom of the dialog box (see Figure 12.17).

4. Click OK. A new Layout tab appears. The new tab contains the name of the original tab from which the copy was made plus a number in parentheses indicating that it is a copy of the original.

FIGURE 12.17
The Move Or Copy dialog
box with the Create A
Copy option turned on

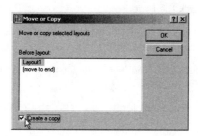

To rename the new tab, or any tab for that matter, right-click the tab and choose Rename from the shortcut menu to open the Rename Layout dialog box. Enter a new name and click OK.

The new tab will have the same printer settings as the original tab.

Printing Your Drawing

Once your layout is set up, you are ready to print your drawing. If you read the first part of this chapter, you saw how you can right-click the Layout tab and choose the Plot option to open the Plot dialog box. From there, you can print your drawing after making a few adjustments. In that first example, you selected a printer, paper size, and paper orientation. These are the most common settings, but eventually, you'll have to use some of the other settings in the Plot dialog box.

In this section, you'll find descriptions for each group of options in the Plot dialog box. Some options are fairly common, such as those in the Drawing Orientation group, but others may be totally new to you, such as those in the Plot Area group. You might want to skim this section so you have an idea of what all the options are for and then later, when you have some special needs, you can refer to the topic you need.

HOW DO I GET MY COLORS TO PRINT IN BLACK AND WHITE?

By default, AutoCAD prints your drawings just as they appear in the AutoCAD window, including the colors you assign to layers or objects. The AutoCAD colors are helpful when you are editing because they can help you visually organize your drawing, but most of the time, you want to print your drawings in black and white. You can use plot styles to automatically convert colors to black or shades of gray. You'll find more on plot styles in the section "Using AutoCAD's Predefined Plot Styles" later in this chapter.

Selecting and Storing Printer Settings

The Printer/Plotter group lets you select a printer and make setting changes to the printer you select. At first glance, these settings look like those of any other Windows program, but there is an important difference. You can save changes you make to a printer's properties and later recall them. Here's how it works.

1. Choose File ➤ Plot or right-click the Layout tab at the bottom of the AutoCAD window and choose Plot to open the Plot dialog box.

2. From the Name drop-down list in the Printer/Plotter group, select a printer.

3. Click the Properties button to open the Plotter Configuration Editor dialog box.

4. Make a change to any of the properties in this dialog box (see the next section "Printer Configuration Options").

5. Click OK. You'll see the Changes To A Printer Configuration File dialog box, as shown in Figure 12.18.

6. Enter a name for this printer configuration that will remind you of the settings, and then click OK.

The next time you use the Name drop-down list to locate a printer, you will see the name of the printer configuration file you just created. You can then select that configuration file to use those printer settings. This saves you from having to remember settings you used to print a drawing.

A single printer can have multiple configuration files. You can create a configuration for custom paper sizes or any other settings you find useful in the Plotter Configuration Editor dialog box.

Configuration files end with the .PC3 filename extension. They are normally stored in the Plotters folder under the C:\Documents and Settings*User Name*\Application Data\Autodesk\ AutoCAD 2006\R16.1\enu\ folder. *User Name* is your login name. You can get to this folder quickly by choosing File ➢ Plotter Manager.

Printer Configuration Options

The printer configuration options vary somewhat from printer to printer, but here are some general guidelines for using the Plotter Configuration Editor dialog box. These options include items such as the port your printer is connected to, the quality of bitmap image printing, custom paper sizes, and printer calibration, which lets you adjust your plotter for any size discrepancies in output.

The Plotter Configuration Editor dialog box has three tabs: General, Ports, and Device And Document Settings. The General tab displays a list of Windows drivers that this configuration uses, if any, and there is a space for your own comments. The Ports tab lets you specify where your plotter data is sent. You can also select the AutoSpool feature, which allows you to direct your plot to an intermediate location for distribution to the appropriate output device. The Device And Document Settings tab is the main part of this dialog box. The main list box contains options in a hierarchical list, similar to a listing in Windows Explorer (see Figure 12.19).

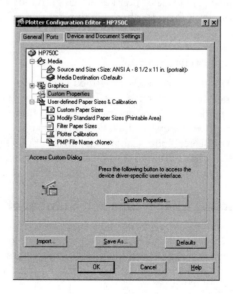

The list has four main categories: Media, Graphics, Custom Properties, and User-Defined Paper Sizes & Calibration. Not all the options under these categories are available for all plotters. When you select an item from this list, the area just below the list displays the options associated with that item.

MEDIA

Many printers offer options for choosing the source and size of printer media and for the media type. If the Source And Size option is available, the media option lets you select them. Duplex Printing, when available, allows for double-sided printing in printers that support this feature. Media Destination, when available, lets you select a destination for output such as collating or stapling in printers that support such features.

GRAPHICS

These options give you control over color depth, dots per inch, and the rendering of shaded areas. You can adjust your output for better color or faster speed. One popular setting is Merge Control, which controls how overlapping lines are drawn.

CUSTOM PROPERTIES

These options are actually the same as those you find when you edit your printer properties through the Windows Start menu. (Choose Start ➢ Settings ➢ Printers And Faxes, right-click the printer whose properties you want to edit. and choose Properties.) The main difference here is that settings you make through this option are saved in a plot configuration file.

USER-DEFINED PAPER SIZES

Several settings relate to paper sizes that fall under the heading of User-defined Paper Sizes. For some printers, the Custom Paper Sizes option offers the ability to create a nonstandard paper size. Another similar option is Modify Standard Paper Size. As the name implies, this option lets you change the standard paper sizes. Filter Paper Sizes is handy for printers that offer a large number of paper sizes. You can limit the sizes shown in the Plot dialog box by selecting the sizes you want to appear from a list.

PLOTTER CALIBRATION

Another option in the User-Defined Paper Sizes heading is Plotter Calibration. This feature is significant because it lets you adjust the aspect ratio of your image on the printed page. If you find that your printer stretches your drawing in one direction, it may need to be calibrated. The Plotter Calibration option offers a way to adjust your printer so it produces a properly proportioned print.

If you select Plotter Calibration, the Calibrate Plotter button appears in the lower half of the dialog box. Click this button to start the Calibrate Plotter wizard. You can follow the instructions in the wizard to fine-tune the width and height ratio of your printer output.

Selecting a Paper Size and Number of Copies

These options are fairly obvious. You can select a paper size from the Paper Size drop-down list and set the number of copies in the Number Of Copies text box. One feature of the Paper Size option is not obvious. You can control the paper sizes that are displayed by editing the properties for the current printer. See the preceding "Printer Configuration Options" section.

Determining What View Will Print

You can be selective about the part of your drawing that prints. The Plot Area group offers the What To Plot drop-down list. This list contains several options that determine the view that is sent to the printer. Typically, you print from a layout, so you use the Layout option. But at other times, you might want to print from the Model tab and select a specific view. The other options offer different ways to select the area to print. Table 12.1 shows those options and describes their typical use.

TABLE 12.1:   The What To Plot Options

OPTION	USE
Limits	Available in the Model tab only. It uses the limits of the drawing to determine what to print. This is the same view you see in model space when you choose View ➤ Zoom ➤ All.
Layout	Uses the current layout as the print area.
Extents	Uses the extents of the drawing as the area to print. This is the same view that you see on the screen if you choose View ➤ Zoom ➤ Extents.
Display	Uses the current display as the area to print.
Window	Asks you to select a window to indicate the area you want to plot. The dialog box temporarily closes to allow you to select points.

The Scale option in the Plot Scale group affects how these options appear in the final printed sheet. Typically, if you are using the Layout option, you can use the default scale of 1:1 in the Plot Scale group. You will have to calculate the proper scale for the Limits, Extents, Display, and Window options, or if the scale is not important, you can use the Fit To Paper option.

Adjusting the Location of Your Printed Image

You can adjust the position of your drawing on the printed sheet by changing the options in the Plot Offset group. X and Y options let you adjust the location of the printed image by increasing the X and Y coordinate value. The default zero X and zero Y location is the lower-left corner of the printable area. (Remember that the printable area is represented by a dashed line in the Layout tab view.)

If you prefer, you can set up AutoCAD to use the corner of the paper as the origin instead of the printable area. The Plot And Publish tab of the Options dialog box (choose Tools ➤ Options) offers the Specify Plot Offset Relative To button group. This group offers two radio buttons: Printable Area and Edge Of Paper. You can select the option that makes the most sense for you.

Setting the Print Scale

If you are printing from a Layout tab, you can usually keep this setting at 1:1. You have the option to alter that scale using the options in the Plot Scale group. For example, if you want to print a drawing at half its intended size, you can specify a scale of 1:2 in the Scale drop-down list. Or if you are printing a 3D view from the Model tab, you can use the Fit To Paper option.

For the most part, you need to set the plot scale only if you are plotting from model space and are using one of the options in Table 12.1 other than Layout. It that is what you are doing, be sure that the scale you select allows your drawing to fit on the paper size you select in the Paper Size group. You can use the Preview button in the lower-left corner of the Plot dialog box to check.

SELECTING A SCALE

To use the scale options, open the Scale drop-down list and select a scale. The proportions of the scale then appear in the inch= and unit text boxes. For metric users, the text boxes are labeled mm= and unit. If you want to use a scale that is not listed in the Scale drop-down list, select Custom, and then enter the appropriate values in the inch= or mm= and unit text boxes.

ADJUSTING LINE WEIGHTS TO YOUR SCALE

AutoCAD lets you set line weights in your drawing. When your drawing is plotted through a Layout tab, AutoCAD faithfully prints the line weights you've selected. But often, you want to print a half-size view or your layout, and you want the line weights reduced to half their specified size. To ensure your line weights are scaled to your half-size prints, make sure the Scale Lineweights setting is turned on. AutoCAD then applies the selected scale to line weights.

Options for Printing 3D Views

When you are working with 3D models in AutoCAD, you can view them as wireframe, hidden line, or shaded views. A wireframe view shows all the lines in the model as if you could see through it. Hidden views give you a more realistic view by hiding the parts you normally wouldn't see. The Shaded view adds a bit more realism by giving the surfaces of the model a solid, colored appearance.

You can apply these view options to your printed output through the Shaded Viewport Options group in the Plot dialog box. This group offers three main options.

◆ The Shade Plot drop-down list

◆ The Quality drop-down list

◆ The DPI (dots per inch) text box

TIP If you don't see the Shaded Viewport Options group, click the More Options button in the lower-right corner of the Plot dialog box.

The Shade Plot options in the Plot dialog box are not available if you are plotting from a Layout tab. Instead, you can control this value by doing the following:

With the Plot dialog box closed, select the view containing the 3D view. Right-click, and then choose Shaded Plots from the shortcut menu. Finally, from the cascading menu select the option that you want to apply to the viewport. The choices are As Displayed, Wireframe, Hidden, and Rendered. (LT users will not have the Rendered option.) As Displayed plots the 3D view as it appears in the viewport. Hidden plots your 3D view with hidden lines removed. Rendered renders your 3D view before plotting.

Plot Options

The Plot Options group contains some general settings that you can use to control your printer output.

Plot In Background　If you are printing a fairly large file that will take some time, you can use this option to print in the background. You can then get back to work while AutoCAD prints.

Plot Object Lineweights　If you set line weights by object or layer, this option prints line weights as you specified them.

Plot With Plot Styles　Plot styles give you control over the way colors, line weights, area fills, and the corners of lines are printed. You can use this setting to specify whether to use plot style settings. See the section "Controlling Color, Lines, and Fills though Plot Styles" later in this chapter.

Plot Paperspace Last　When you are printing from a Layout tab, this option determines whether objects in paper space are drawn before or after objects in model space.

Hide Paperspace Objects　AutoCAD offers controls over 3D hidden line views in viewports through the shortcut menu or the Properties palette for a selected viewport. In the event that a 3D model has been drawn in the Layout tab in paper space, this option prints paper space objects using hidden lines.

Plot Stamp On　You can add a plot stamp to your printer output using this option. The plot stamp prints information about the current drawing that can be helpful to anyone viewing the printed copy. When you activate Plot Stamp On, the Plot Stamp Settings button appears.

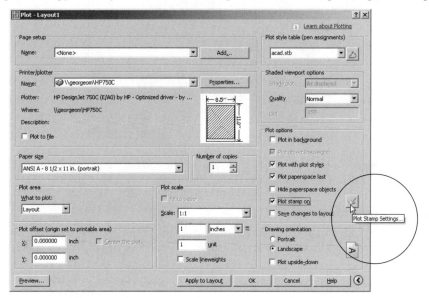

You can click this button to gain access to the Plot Stamp dialog box.

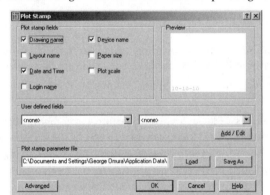

This dialog box lets you determine the information included in the plot stamp. The Advanced tab opens the Advanced Options dialog box, which lets you specify the location and orientation of the plot stamp. It also lets you adjust font and text size.

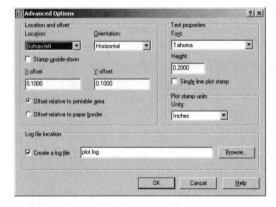

Save Changes To Layout   When this option is turned on, the changes you make to the Plot dialog box settings are saved with the current layout.

Drawing Orientation

As with most programs, you can control the orientation of the document you are printing. Here you have the typical Landscape and Portrait options plus the Plot Upside-Down option.

Storing Your Printer Settings

You'll most likely have to print an AutoCAD drawing many times over the course of a project. Not only that, but each time you print a drawing, you will want to use the exact same settings. To help you keep consistency in your printing, AutoCAD offers the Page Setup Manager dialog box.

If you did the exercise at the beginning of this chapter, you encountered the Page Setup option in the Plot dialog box. There, you made some plotter settings and then saved the settings as a page setup called Setup1. You don't have to save your printer settings in a setup, but doing so can be a real time-saver.

The Page Setup group at the top of the Plot dialog box lets you select from a drop-down list of setups you've created. You can also create and manage setups through the Page Setup Manager dialog box. You can get to the Page Setup Manager and edit or create new setups by doing the following:

1. In AutoCAD, choose File ➢ Page Setup Manager, or right-click a Layout tab and choose Page Setup Manager to open the Page Setup Manager dialog box, as shown in Figure 12.20.

FIGURE 12.20
The Page Setup Manager dialog box

2. Click the New button to open the New Page Setup dialog box, as shown in Figure 12.21.

FIGURE 12.21
The New Page Setup dialog box

3. To create a new page setup, enter a name in the New Page Setup Name input box, and then select a prototype setup from the Start With list box. AutoCAD offers the name of Setup 1 as a default for a new setup, but it will be helpful to give your setup a name to help you remember the purpose of the setup.

4. Click OK when you are finished. The Page Setup dialog box opens again. This is nearly identical to the Plot dialog box with a few options made unavailable.

5. Make your custom settings, and then click OK. You return to the Page Setup Manager dialog box. You'll see your new page setup in the Current Page Setup list box.

6. You can select a page setup from the list box and then click the Set Current button to make it the current page setup for the layout. You can also select a page setup from the Page Setup group of the Plot dialog box (see Figure 12.22).

FIGURE 12.22

Select a page setup from the Page Setup group of the Plot dialog box.

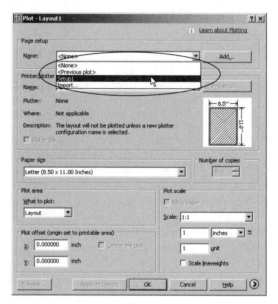

Page Setups are stored with the drawing, but if you want to import a setup from another drawing, you can do so by clicking the Import option in the Page Setup Manager dialog box. A standard file dialog box opens in which you can select a drawing file that contains the page setup you want to import. Here the trick is to remember the drawing in which you stored the desired setup.

The current page setup applies to the current Layout tab, but once you create a new page setup, it is displayed as an option in the Page Setup Manager dialog box for all other Layout tabs.

Controlling Color, Lines, and Fills through Plot Styles

When you print your drawing, AutoCAD attempts to reproduce your drawing's appearance in the Layout or Model tab. However, you might want to change the way certain parts of the drawing appear in the printed output. For example, you might want all line work in black instead of the AutoCAD colors, or you might want filled areas in shades of gray instead of solid fills. To accomplish these effects without actually converting all your objects to the color black, you need to employ plot styles.

You can think of plot styles as a way to translate the colors and fills in an AutoCAD drawing into different colors or patterns. You can control whether the color red on your AutoCAD screen is printed in black or gray or even green, or you can control whether an area filled in solid black is screened to a 30 percent shade. The plot styles also let you specify whether the lines forming the corners of a rectangle are rounded or square, as shown in Figure 12.23.

FIGURE 12.23
Plot styles can translate colors and fills into shades of gray and half-tone screens.

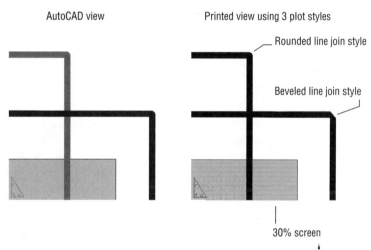

AutoCAD view

Printed view using 3 plot styles

Rounded line join style

Beveled line join style

30% screen

You can use two types of plot styles: *color* and *named*. Color plot styles let you control printer output based on the color you assigned to the objects in your drawing. For example, you can tell AutoCAD to print the color red as black using a 50 percent screen or as a line width of 0.5 mm. This is a method similar to the one used by early versions of AutoCAD, and it persists today, mainly because many old drawings are still in use.

Named plot styles operate in a different way. They let you give a name to a set of printer parameters that include line weight, color, percent screen, or the corner condition of line work. You can then apply that named set of parameters, called a plot style, to objects or layers. If you are coming from another CAD program, you may be more familiar with this method of assigning printer parameters to objects in a drawing.

Using AutoCAD's Predefined Plot Styles

AutoCAD comes with a set of plot styles you can use right away. There are actually two sets; one for color plot styles and another for named plot styles. You can select the plot styles from the Plot Style Table drop-down list of the Plot or Page Setup dialog box (see Figure 12.24).

FIGURE 12.24

Selecting a plot style
from the Plot Style Table
drop-down list of the
Page Setup dialog box

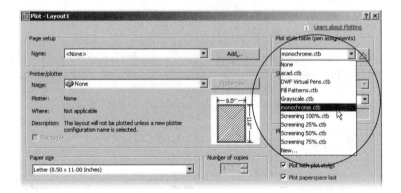

Table 12.2 lists and describes the predefined color plot styles available in AutoCAD. Table 12.3 lists the predefined named plot style tables.

You may find that you can do most of your work with these standard plot style tables. At other times, you will be required to use office standard plot style tables for your projects.

TABLE 12.2: The Standard Color Plot Style Tables

PLOT STYLE	PURPOSE
Acad.ctb	Converts the first 8 AutoCAD colors to black when printing
DWF Virtual Pens.ctb	Converts AutoCAD colors to virtual pens of the same color in DWF files
Fill Patterns.ctb	Converts the first 9 AutoCAD colors into fill patterns
Grayscale.ctb	Converts all AutoCAD colors into grayscale equivalents on printers that support this feature
Monochrome.ctb	Converts all AutoCAD colors into black
Screening xxx%.ctb	Converts all AutoCAD colors into a screened value indicated by the plot style name (*xxx* is the screen percentage)
New	Starts the Add Color Dependent Plot Style Table Wizard to allow you to create a new plot style

TABLE 12.3:   The Standard Named Plot Style Tables

PLOT STYLE	PURPOSE
Acad.stb	Plots AutoCAD colors as they are displayed in the drawing area.
Autodesk-Color.stb	Includes screened "colors" from solid (100%) to 10 percent. Uses object color for printed color.
Autodesk-MONO.stb	Same as the Autodesk-Color.stb but converts colors to black.
Monochrome.stb	Converts all AutoCAD colors to black.
New	Starts the Add Name Dependent Plot Style Table Wizard to allow you to create a new plot style.

Choosing between Color and Named Plot Style Tables

If you need to create your own plot style tables, decide which type of plot style table you want to use. Named plot styles are more flexible than color plot styles, but if you already have a library of AutoCAD drawings set up for a specific set of plotter settings, the color plot styles are a better choice. Color plot styles are the most similar to users of the older method of assigning AutoCAD colors to plotter pens.

The type of plot style table assigned to a drawing depends on the template you use to start a new drawing. The acad.dwt template file uses color plot style tables, and the acad - Named Plot Styles.dwt template file uses named plot styles.

You can also set up AutoCAD to use color or named plot style tables for the default drawing that appears when you start AutoCAD. The Options dialog box offers controls over the default plot style used for the drawing*x*.dwg default drawing(*x* is the drawing number). Here's how to make those settings.

1. Choose Tools ➤ Options to open the Options dialog box, and then click the Plot And Publish tab.

2. Click the Plot Style Table Settings button to open the Plot Style Table Settings dialog box.

3. In the Default Plot Style Behavior For New Drawings button group, click the Use Color Dependent Plot Styles radio button.

4. Click OK, and then click OK again to return to the drawing.

Once you've set up AutoCAD for color plot style tables, any new drawings you create are allowed to use only color plot style tables. You can change this setting at any time for new files, but once a file is saved, the type of plot style that is current when the file is created is the only type of plot style available to that file. If you find that you need to change a color a plot style to a named plot style drawing, see the section entitled "Converting a Drawing from Color Plot Styles to Named Plot Styles" later in this chapter.

Creating a Plot Style Table

If you are using color plot style tables, you can create a plot style table file (with the `.ctb` filename extension) for different styles of drawings. You might create one for presentation drawings in which certain colors and screened solid fills are assigned to colors in your drawing. Or you might have specific screen settings you use frequently when printing monochrome prints. The following steps describe how you can create your own color plot style table.

1. Open a drawing; then click the Layout 1 tab.

2. Right-click, choose Page Setup Manager to open the Page Setup Manager dialog box, and then click Modify.

3. In the Plot Style Table button group, open the drop-down list and select New. If the current drawing uses color plot style tables, you will see the Add Color-Dependent Plot Style Table Wizard. If it uses a named plot style, you'll see the Add Name-Dependent Plot Style Table Wizard, as shown in Figure 12.25.

FIGURE 12.25

The Add Name-Dependent Plot Style Table Wizard first screen

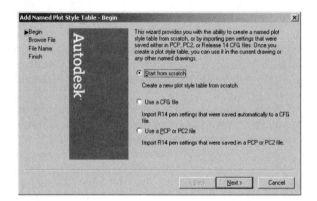

4. Click the Start From Scratch radio button, and then click Next.

5. The next screen of the wizard asks for a filename. You can also specify whether this new plot style table will be the default for all drawings or whether you want to apply this plot style table just to the current drawing. Enter a name for the filename and click Next.

6. The next screen of the wizard lets you edit your plot style and assign the plot style to your current, new, or old drawings. You'll learn about editing plot styles a bit later.

7. Click Finish to return to the Page Setup dialog box. Once you have created a color plot style, you can go ahead and make setting changes.

Editing and Using Plot Style Tables

Once you've created a plot style, you'll want to set it up the way you want. In the Page Setup dialog box, open the Plot Style drop-down list and select the new plot style you want to edit (see Figure 12.24). Click the Edit button to open the Plot Style Table Editor dialog box. The Edit button is the one just to the right of the Plot Style Table drop-down list. Click the Form View tab, which is shown at the top of Figure 12.26.

FIGURE 12.26

The Plot Style Table Editor dialog box, open at the Form View tab

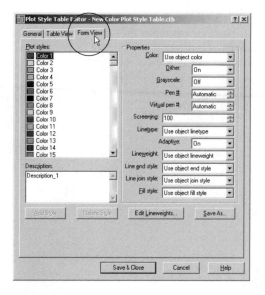

TIP Plot style table files are located in `C:\Documents and Settings\Username\Application Data\Autodesk\AutoCAD 2005\R16.1\enu\Plot Styles`. You can also edit them by locating the plot style file you want to edit and double-clicking it.

The Plot Style Table Editor dialog box has three tabs that give you control over how each color in AutoCAD is plotted. The Form View tab lets you select a color from a list box and then set the properties of that color using the options on the right side of the tab.

Understanding the Options in the Plot Style Table Editor

Once you get to the Plot Style Table Editor dialog box, you will see quite a few options. These options are the same for both the named and color plot style tables. The main difference is that the color plot style table lists all 256 of the AutoCAD colors as plot styles. Named plot style tables list only a single plot style. You can add other plot styles and name them.

THE GENERAL TAB

The General tab contains information regarding the plot style you are currently editing. You can enter a description of the style in the Description box. This can be useful if you plan to include the plot style with a drawing you are sending to someone else for plotting.

The File Information group gives you the basic information on the file location and name, as well as the number of color styles included in the plot style table.

The Apply Global Scale Factor To Non-ISO Linetypes check box lets you determine whether ISO linetype scale factors are applied to all linetypes. When this item is checked, the Scale Factor input box becomes active, allowing you to enter a scale factor.

THE TABLE VIEW TAB

The Table View tab offers the same settings as the Form View tab described next, only in a different format (see Figure 12.27). Each plot style is shown as a column with the properties of each plot style listed along the left side of the tab. To change a property, click the property in the column.

FIGURE 12.27
The Table View tab of the Plot Style Table Editor dialog box

To apply the same setting to all plot styles at once, right-click a setting you want to use from a single plot style, and choose Copy from the shortcut menu. Right-click the setting again, and then choose Apply To All Styles from the shortcut menu.

THE FORM VIEW TAB

To modify the properties of a plot style or color, select it from the list at the left and then edit the values in the Properties button group in the right side of the dialog box (see the Form View tab in Figure 12.28 later in this section). For example, to change the screen value of the Color 3 style in a color plot style table, highlight Color 3 in the Plot Styles list, double-click the Screening input box, and enter a new value.

You can select several plot styles at once from the list by selecting the first item and then Shift+clicking the last item in a group. Or you can Ctrl+click individual items.

The following describes the other settings in the Form View tab.

Description   This option allows you to enter a description for each individual color.

Dither [Enable Dithering]   Dithering enables your plotter to simulate colors beyond the basic 256 available in AutoCAD. Although this option is desirable when you want to create a wider range of colors in your plots, it can also create some distortions, including broken, fine lines and false colors. For this reason, dithering is usually turned off. This option is not available in all plotters.

[Convert to] Grayscale   This option converts colors to grayscale.

[Use Assigned] Pen #   This option lets you specify what pen number is assigned to each color in your drawing. This option only applies to pen plotters.

Virtual Pen #   Many inkjet and laser plotters offer "virtual pens" to simulate the processes of the old-style pen plotters. Frequently, such plotters offer as many as 255 virtual pens. Plotters with virtual pens often let you assign AutoCAD colors to a virtual pen number. This is significant if the virtual pens of your plotter can be assigned screening width, end style, and joint styles. You can then use the virtual pen settings instead of using the settings in the Plot Style Table Editor dialog box. This option is most beneficial for users who already have a library of drawings that are set up for plotters with virtual pen settings.

You can set up your inkjet printer for virtual pens under the Vector Graphics listing of the Device And Documents Setting tab of the Plotter Configuration Editor dialog box.

Linetype   If you prefer, you can use this setting to control linetypes in AutoCAD based on the color of the object. By default, this option is set to Use Object Linetype. I recommend that you leave this option at its default.

Adaptive [Adjustment]   This option controls how noncontinuous linetypes begin and end. This option is on by default, which forces linetypes to begin and end in a line segment. With the option turned off, the same linetype is drawn without regard for its ending. In some cases, this may produce a line that appears incomplete.

Line End Style   This option lets you specify the shape of the end of simple lines that have a line weight greater than zero.

Line Join Style   This option lets you determine the shape of the corners of polylines (see Figure 12.28).

FIGURE 12.28
The Line Joint Style options

Fill Style   This option lets you set up a color to be drawn as a pattern when used in a solid filled area. The patterns appear in the drop-down list, as shown in Figure 12.29:

Add Style   Clicking this button lets you add more plot styles or colors.

Delete Style   Clicking this button deletes the selected style.

Save As   Clicking this button lets you save the current plot style table.

FIGURE 12.29

The Fill Style options

Assigning Named Plot Styles Directly to Layers and Objects

With color plot style tables, you have to rely on the AutoCAD colors to control how objects are printed. But with named plot styles, you are not limited to object colors to control the way an object prints. Color plot styles are easier to manage for the beginning user, but if you are an advanced user or if you are used to a CAD program that allows you to control printing properties of each individual object, you'll want to know how to use named plot styles.

Assigning Plot Styles to Objects

Once you've set up AutoCAD to use named plot styles, you can begin to assign plot styles to objects through the Properties palette. Here are the steps to take to assign plot styles to objects.

1. Assign a plot style to your drawing layout. Choose File ➢ Page Setup Manager, and then click the Modify button.

2. In the Page Setup dialog box, select the named plot style table from the Name drop-down list in the Plot Style Table group. Make sure the Display Plot Styles check box is checked, and then click OK.

3. Click Close to close the Page Setup Manager dialog box.

   Once you've selected a named plot style table, you can begin to apply plot styles to individual objects. Next make sure the plot styles will be displayed in the drawing.

4. Choose Format ➢ Lineweight, make sure there is a check in the Display Lineweight check box, and click OK.

5. Set up your view so you see a close-up of the lower-left corner unit.

6. In the status bar at the bottom of the AutoCAD window, click the Paper button to switch to floating model space. This lets you select objects in the drawing while in a Layout tab (see Figure 12.30).

FIGURE 12.30

The Model or Paper Space button in the status bar

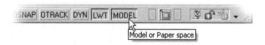

7. Select the objects to which you want to assign a plot style, right-click, and choose Properties from the shortcut menu.

8. In the Properties palette, click the Plot Style option. The option turns into a drop-down list with a downward-pointing arrow to the far right (see Figure 12.31). Click the downward-pointing arrow, and then select Other from the list to open the Select Plot Style dialog box, as shown in Figure 12.32.

9. Select the name of the plot style you want to use, and click OK. Notice that style you selected now appears as the value for the plot style in the Properties palette. Close the Properties palette.

FIGURE 12.31
The Plot Style drop-down list in the Properties palette

FIGURE 12.32
The Select Plot Style dialog box

10. Choose View ➤ Regen All. If you have the line weight visibility turned on, you'll see the results in the Drawing Editor. You can also assign plot styles to individual objects through the Plot Style Control drop-down list, as shown in Figure 12.33.

FIGURE 12.33
The Plot Style Control drop-down list in the Styles toolbar

11. Select the objects, and then select the plot style from the Plot Style Control drop-down list. This allows you to select a plot style in a manner similar to the Layer & Linetype drop-down list. If you are using a color plot style table like the one you created in earlier exercises, the Plot Style Control drop-down list is unavailable.

Assigning Named Plot Style Tables to Layers

If you prefer, you can assign named plot styles to layers. This has a similar effect to using the color plot style tables. The main difference is that with named plot style tables, you assign the plot style tables directly to the layer instead of assigning a plot style to the color of a layer. Here's how to assign a plot style table to a layer.

1. Choose Format ➤ Layers or click the Layer Properties Manager tool (shown in Figure 12.34) to open the Layer Properties Manager dialog box.

FIGURE 12.34
The Layer Properties Manager tool in the Layer toolbar

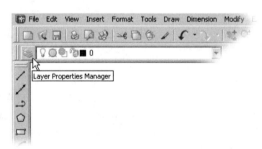

2. Select a layer or set of layers whose plot style you want to change.

3. Click Normal in the Plot Style column of the selected layers (see Figure 12.35). You may have to scroll to the right to see the Plot Style column. The Select Plot Style dialog box opens, as shown in Figure 12.36.

4. Select the plot style you want to assign to the layer or layers from the Plot Styles list, and then click OK. The Layer Properties Manager dialog box opens again.

5. Close the Layer Properties Manager dialog box; then choose View ➤ Regen All. Your view of the plan changes to reflect the new plot style assignment to the layers you modified.

FIGURE 12.35
Click Normal in the
Plot Style column of
the selected layer.

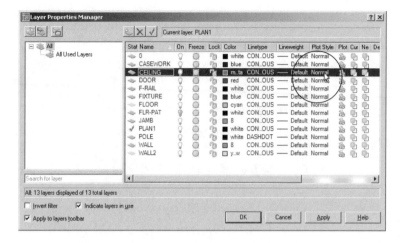

FIGURE 12.36
The Select Plot Style
dialog box

Converting a Drawing from Color Plot Styles to Named Plot Styles

If you work in an office where drawings from other offices frequently cross your desk, you may eventually need to convert a drawing from a color plot style to named or vice versa.

To convert a color plot style drawing to a named plot style drawing, you need to use the Convertctb and Convertpstyles commands. This conversion is a two-part process. In the first part, which is needed only the first time you perform the conversion, you convert a color plot style table file into a named plot style table file. You can then convert the drawing file.

1. Open the AutoCAD drawing you want to convert.

2. At the Command prompt, enter **Convertctb↵** to open the Select File dialog box, in which you can select a color plot style table file; these files have the filename extension `.ctb`.

3. Select the color plot style you want to convert with the drawing, and then click Open to open the Create File dialog box. This dialog box allows you to provide a name for the converted file. For example, if you opened the `Acad.ctb` file in step 1, you might want to give the new file the name `AcadConvert` so you know that it is a converted `.ctb` file. AutoCAD automatically adds the `.stb` filename extension. Click Save. AutoCAD creates a new named plot style table file.

Once a color plot style table is converted, you can go ahead and convert the drawing as described next:

1. Open the file you want to convert and enter **Convertpstyles↵** at the Command prompt. You will see a warning message to make sure you've converted a `.ctb` file to a `.stb` file.

2. Click OK. The Select File dialog box opens.

3. Select the converted `.stb` file you created using the Convertctb command. The current drawing is converted to use a named plot style table.

The process for converting a drawing that uses named plot styles to one that uses color plot styles is a bit simpler. You only need to use the Convertpstyles command. When you do, you will see a warning message telling you that all the named plot styles will be removed from the drawing. Click OK to convert the drawing.

Just Enough Summary

There is a lot to learn when it comes to printing in AutoCAD, but it's worth the effort to become as familiar as you can with the process. By mastering the printing process, you will have better control over the appearance of your drawings. You'll be able to organize your drawings in a clearer fashion, and you'll get more consistent output from print to print.

The documents you produce in AutoCAD will most likely be used to convey detailed information. Someone may rely on your work to construct a building or manufacture a crucial part, so mastering these printing tools is essential.

Index

Note to the reader: Throughout this index **boldfaced** page numbers indicate primary discussions of a topic. *Italicized* page numbers indicate illustrations.

Symbols and Numbers

@ sign
    for break without gap, 142
    and Dynamic Input display, 44, 45
    for relative coordinates, 36–37
↵ (Enter key), 6
2D objects
    adding thickness, **150**
    arcs, **74–76**, *75*
    circles, **73–74**
    curves, **76–81**
        ellipse, *76*, **76–77**
        elliptical arc, *77*, **77–78**
        polylines, **80–81**
        smooth curves, **78–80**
    hatch patterns and solid fills,
        85, **85–99**
        basics of placing, **86–87**
        boundary hatch options, **94–99**
        editing hatch area, **91**
        modifying hatch pattern, **92–94**
        positioning accurately, **89–90**
        predefined patterns, **87–88**, *88*
        solid fills, **88**
    to layout drawing, **101–106**
        construction lines, **103–106**
        dividing objects in specified
            lengths, **102**
        marking equal divisions, **102**
        marking points in drawing,
            101–102
    lines, **72**
    parallel lines, **81–82**
    regular polygons, **100**
    revision clouds, *83*, **83–85**
        based on object shape, **84–85**
        freehand, 84
2P option for circles, 73
3D extrusions, objects for, 164
3D Face, 151
3D modeling, 147. *See also* surface 3D
    modeling
    manipulating objects in 3D space,
        179–181, *180*
    methods, **147–148**
    printing with hidden lines or
        shading, 342
    solid, 147, *147*
    viewing options, **181–189**
        3Dorbit, *184*, **184–189**
        adjusting distance, 186
        Camera command for viewport
            setup, *182*, **182–183**, *183*
        focal length, 189
        panning, 187

    rotating view, 184–186
    saving and restoring views,
        189–191
3D Object dialog box, *163*, 163
3D Orbit toolbar, 16
3D solids, polylines to create, **166**
3D view
    printing, **350**
    saving, **189–191**
    for surface modeling, *149*, **149–150**
3Dorbit command, 184
    Distance option, 186
3P option for circles, 73, *74*

A

absolute coordinates, 36–37
Acad.ctb plot style table, 356
acad.dwt template file, 21
Acadiso.lin external file, 216
Acad.lin external file, 216
Acad.stb .ctb plot style table, 357
ACR (AutoCad Command
    Reference), 32
Add Page Setup dialog box, 337, *338*
Add To Group option, in LT Group
    Manager, 238
Adjust Clipping Planes option, of
    3Dorbit command, 189
Adjust Distance option, of 3Dorbit
    command, 188
alignment
    of dimension text, 309
    of linear dimensions with
        nonorthogonal objects, *291*,
        291–292
    object snaps (osnaps) for, **132–133**
    when rotating object, **139–141**, *140*
All option
    for Select objects: prompt, 124
    for zoom, 26
American Institute of Architects, 194
AND Boolean keyword, 31
Angle option, for Chamfer
    command, 129
angles
    dimensions for, **294**
    measurement units, 46, *47*
    measuring, *322*, **322–323**
    for polar coordinates, 40, *41*
    Polar Tracking snap to, 52
    precision, 294
    for rectangular array, 135
annotation. *See* text
Apparent Intersection option, for
    osnap, 62

Arc tool (Draw toolbar), *19*, 28, *29*, **74–76**,
    75, 155
arcball, **184–186**
architectural drawings
    dimensions for, **307–308**
    scale factors, 220
Architectural length option, 46
arcs, **74–76**, *75*
    converting to polyline, 144
    dimensions for, **292–293**, *293*
    dimensions for lengths, **294**
    elliptical, *77*, **77–78**
    for joining end to end, **125–127**
Area command, 318
area measurement, **317–321**
    of complex or curved shapes,
        318–321
        cumulative values, 320–321
        with islands, 320
    of polygonal shape, **318**
array cell, 136, *136*
Array dialog box, *134*, **134–135**
    to copy rows and columns,
        135–136, *136*
Array tool (Modify toolbar), *19*, 134, 135
arrows, for dimensions, 286, 307
ASCII text, importing, 265
associative dimensioning, 286, 290
Associative option, for hatch patterns,
    91, *92*
attaching drawings as xrefs, **241–242**.
    See also xrefs (external references)
AUG (AutoCAD User Guide), 32
AUGI (AutoCAD User Group
    International), 23
auto-hide, for DesignCenter, 245
AutoCAD, "chatting" with, 7
AutoCAD Command Reference
    (ACR), 32
AutoCAD coordinate system, **35–45**, *36*
    experimenting with, **37–39**
AutoCAD LT, Group Manager, *237*,
    237–238
AutoCAD User Group International
    (AUGI), 23
AutoCAD User Guide (AUG), 32
AutoCAD window, **1–20**, *2*
    Command window, **6**
    drawing area, **5–6**
    layout tabs, **26–28**, *27*. *See also*
        Layout tabs; Model tab
    menu bar, **7–11**
    panning and zooming, **24–26**, *25*
    toolbars, **11–20**. *See also specific*
        toolbars
        flyouts, *12*, *12*

list of, 16–17
locking, **14**
moving, **13–14**
opening and closing, **15**
tool tips, **12**, *13*
UCS icon, 6, *6*, 149
Autodesk-Color.stb plot style table, 357
Autodesk-MONO.stb plot style table, 357
Autoselect, 109–111
AutoSnap feature, 62–63
AutoSpool feature, for printer, 347
average, in tables, 277–278
axes of ellipse, major and minor, 76

B

Back Clipping On option, of 3Dorbit command, 189
background
color for table cells, **281**
of default drawing, 3
mask for text, **261**
Backspace, 23
backwards text, 268
base point
for blocks, 229
for insertion, origin as, 233
for Move command, 132
option for grips, 113–114, *114*
providing, **133**
baseline dimension, *289*, 289
bisecting construction lines, 105
bitmap images, deleting, 125
black and white, printing in, 337, 346
Block Definition dialog box, 228–230, *229*
Block Definition Editor, 142
Block Editor toolbar, 143, *143*
Block Editor window, 142–143, *143*
blocks, **227–234**
adding to tool palette, 251
automatic scaling at insertion, 249
color and linetype for, **199**
converting xrefs to, 243
creating, **228–229**
editing, **142–144**, 233
exploding, 144
Freeze and Thaw effect on, 201
importing drawings as, **232–233**
inherited changes, 227
inserting, **230–231**
saving as drawing files, **234**
scaling and rotating, **231–232**
in table cells, 281
vs. xrefs, 240, **242–243**
Bold tool (Text Formatting toolbar), *257*, 258
Boolean operations, 170
for regions, 106
for searches in Help, 31

borders of table cells, line weight of, 279–281
Bottom Align tool (Text Formatting toolbar), *257*, 258
boundary set for hatch patterns, 96–97
boundary window for text, **259**
Break at Point tool (Modify toolbar), *19*
Break option, for Pedit command, 145
Break tool (Modify toolbar), *19*, 141
breaking objects in two, **141–142**
Browse For Folder dialog box, *332*
Bullets And Lists tool (Text Formatting toolbar), *257*, 258
"bullnose," 125
ByBlock, 226

C

CAD drawings. *See* drawings
CAD Standards toolbar, 16
calibration of printer, 348
calligraphy style clouds, *83*, 85
Camera command, **182–183**, *183*
camera, distance from target, 186
canned 3D surfaces, *163*, 163
Cartesian coordinate system
positive and negative values in, 41, *42*
relative coordinates, **40–41**
cascading menu, 7
cell address, 275
Cell Border Properties dialog box, *280*, 280–281
cells. *See* tables
Celtscale system variable, 225
center
of circle, 73
of ellipse, 77, *77*
Center Align tool (Text Formatting toolbar), *257*, 258
Center Mark tool (Dimension toolbar), 293
Center option
for osnap, 62
for zoom, 25
Chamfer command, *127*, **127–129**, *128*
for 3D solids, 172
Chamfer tool (Modify toolbar), *20*, 127
Check option, for solid editing, 179
Check Spelling dialog box, 262–263, *263*
Circle tool (Draw toolbar), *19*, 24, 73–74
circles, **73–74**
dimensions for, **292–293**, *293*
drawing, 22
circular pattern, placing copies in, **134–135**
circular references, for nested xrefs, 243
Circumscribed polygon, *100*
Clean option, for solid editing, 179
Clipboard (Windows), for importing text, 265, 269

Clockwise, for angle values, 47
Close option, for Pedit command, 145
closing toolbars, **15**
color
for blocks, **199**
for dimension lines, 306
for dimension text and background, 309
dithering to simulate, 360
for gradient fill, **97–99**, *98*
for layers, 194, *195*, 216
object property set ByLayer, 198
for objects, 224–225
plot styles for, **355–361**
printing in black and white, 346
for table cell background, **281**
of table cell borders, 280
Color drop-down list (Text Formatting toolbar), *257*, 258
Color Faces option, for solid editing, 178
color plot styles, 355
converting to named plot styles, **365–366**
vs. named plot styles, 357
Color property, 119
columns in tables, adding or deleting, **274**
columns of objects, Array dialog box to copy, **135–136**, *136*
combining solids in 3D modeling, *170*
combining solids, in solid 3D modeling, 170
comma-delimited file (.csv), 278
command prompt, 4, 6, 29
options list, 10
Command window, 3, 4, **6**
commands
on menus, **9–11**
options list, **28–29**
Communication Center, 4, 5, **33–34**
Welcome dialog box, 33, *33*
Configuration Settings dialog box, 34
Construction Line tool (Draw toolbar), *18*
Construction lines, **103–106**
bisecting, 105
multiple through a point, 104
parallel to existing, 105–106
rays as, 106
construction objects, layer for, 141
context-sensitive help, **32–33**
context sensitive menus, 6
contiguous line segments, 72
Continuous Orbit option, of 3Dorbit command, 188
Convert to Block option, for blocks, 230
Convertctb command, 365–366
Convertpstyles command, 365–366
coordinates, **35–45**, *36*
experimenting with, **37–39**
for moving objects, 113
of point, *321*

polar, 28, 37, *37*
    relative, 39–40
        specifying, 40
readout, *4*
relative Cartesian, **40–41**
Copy command, in 3D space, 179, *180*
Copy Faces option, for solid editing, 178
Copy Object tool (Modify toolbar), *18*
Copy option, for grips, 113
copying objects, **133**
    with Array, **134–136**
corners in solid 3D modeling, filleting, *172*, **172**
count, in tables, 277
Create Group option, in LT Group Manager, 238
Create New Dimension Style dialog box, 304, *304*
Create New Table Style dialog box, 282
Crossing option, for Select objects: prompt, 124
Crossing Polygon option, for Select objects: prompt, 124
crossing window
    for selecting objects, 110–111
    to stretch object vertices, *138*, 138
.csv file extension, 278
.ctb file extension, 366. *See also* color plot styles
Current VP Freeze column, in Layer Properties Manager dialog box, 203
cursors
    in 3D orbit, 184, *185*
    Command window prompts at, **42–45**, *43*
    as crosshair, 3–4
    isoplane, *55*
    modes, 49
    PointSelection mode of, 39
    for selection, *107*
curved shapes, area measurement, **318–321**
curved shapes with meshes in surface 3D modeling, **159–163**
    canned 3D surfaces, 163
    facet count for mesh, 162, *162*
    line to set mesh direction, 160–161, *161*
    mesh definition with 4 edges, *162*, 162
    revolving shape, *161*, **161–162**
    stretching surface between objects, **159–160**, *160*
curves, **76–81**
    ellipse, *76*, **76–77**
    elliptical arc, *77*, **77–78**
    polylines, **80–81**
    smooth curves, **78–80**
Cylindrical format, for specifying distance, 181

D

Decimal Degrees angle option, 47
Decimal length option, 46
decimal separator, 312
Decurve option, for Pedit command, 145
default document, 1, 45
    background, 3
    plot style tables for, 357
default font, 256
default options, 28
default system for angle specification, *41*
default text style, **268–269**
Deg/Min/Sec angle option, 47
Del key, 125
Delete option, for blocks, 230
Deleted Faces option, for solid editing, 178
deleting
    layer state, 212, 214
    layers, 197
        from group filter, 210
    objects, **125**
    rectangle, 10–11
    table rows or columns, **274**
    tools and palettes, 252
    viewport, 27
Description option, for blocks, 230
Description panel, in DesignCenter, *245*, 246
Deselect Group option, in LT Group Manager, 238
Design Center, 47, **243–250**, *244*, *245*
    auto-hide for, 245
    exchanging data between open files, **249**
    for list of named components, 328
    loading specific files, **249–250**
    navigating, **245–246**
    Online tab, 246
    opening and inserting files with, **247**
    thumbnail preview icons in, 247
Design Center Online, downloading symbols from, **250**
DesignCenter tool (Standard toolbar), 244
DesignCenter toolbar
    Favorites tool, 244
    Home tool, 245, *246*
    Tree View Toggle tool, 244
    Views tool, 246
Details option, in LT Group Manager, 238
Developer help, 33
dialog boxes, **8–9**
Dimang command, 322
Dimassoc variable, 302
Dimension menu
    ➢ Align Text ➢ Angle, 302
    ➢ Aligned, 291
    ➢ Angular, 294, 322
    ➢ Arc Length, 294
    ➢ Baseline, 289

    ➢ Continue, 288
    ➢ Diameter, 292
    ➢ Jogged, 293
    ➢ Leader, 295
    ➢ Linear, 287
    ➢ Oblique, 303
    ➢ Ordinate, 297
    ➢ Quick Dimension, 290
    ➢ Style, 287
    ➢ Tolerance, 298
Dimension Style Manager dialog box, 287, *304*, 304
    for setting current style, 314
Dimension Styles dialog box
    Primary Units tab, 300
    Text tab, 295
Dimension toolbar, 16
    Center Mark tool, 293
    Dimension Style tool, 287
    Radius Dimension tool, 293
dimensions
    adding string with single operation, *290*, **290–291**
    common base extension line for, *289*, **289–290**
    components, **285–286**, *286*
    continuing, **288**, *289*
    editing, **299–303**
        appending data, **299–300**
        changes to multiple, **300–301**
        detaching text from dimension line, **301–302**
    linear, **287–291**
        horizontal or vertical, 287–288, *288*
    in Model tab or layout tabs, **286**
    for nonorthogonal objects, **291–294**
        arcs and circles, **292–293**, *293*
    ordinate, **296–297**, *298*
    rotating text, **302**
    size of, 287
    skewing lines, 303, *303*
    styles, **303–314**. *See also* New Dimension Style dialog box
        editing, **316**
        setting current, **314**
    tolerance notation, *298*, **298–299**
        symbols, *299*
    troubleshooting, 302
Dimtedit command, 302
Direct Distance method, for relative coordinates, 42, 45
direction, Drawing Units option, 47
distance
    in 3D space, 179
    from camera target, 186
    measuring, **322**
    specifying exact, **39–45**
Distance option, for Chamfer command, 129
dithering, 360
Divide command, 101, **102**

docked toolbars, 3, 14
downloading symbols, from Design
  Center Online, **250**
Drafting Settings dialog box
  Object Snap tab, *59*, 64
  Polar Tracking tab, *51*, 51–52
  Snap and Grid tab, *54*, **55–58**
    aligning grid to object, 57–58, *58*
    isometric 2D drawing setup, *55*,
      55–56
    rotating grid, snap and cursor,
      56, 56
    X and Y spacing, 55
Drag-And-Drop Scale, 47
dragging toolbars, 3
Draw menu
  ➤ Arc, 75
    ➤ Continue, 75
  ➤ Block ➤ Make, 228
  ➤ Circle
    ➤ 2 Points, 73
    ➤ 3 Points, 73
    ➤ Tan Tan Radius, 74
    ➤ Tan Tan Tan, 73
  ➤ Construction Line, 104
  ➤ Ellipse
    ➤ Arc, 77
    ➤ Axis, 76
  ➤ Hatch, 86
  ➤ Point
    ➤ Divide, 102
    ➤ Measure, 102
    ➤ Multiple Points, 101
    ➤ Single Point, 101
  ➤ Polygon, 100
  ➤ Polyline, 72, 80
  ➤ Ray, 106
  ➤ Rectangle, *10*, 10, 22
  ➤ Revision Cloud, 84
  ➤ Solids
    ➤ Extrude, 165, 174
    ➤ Revolve, 176
    ➤ Sphere, 163
  ➤ Spline, 78, 81
  ➤ Surfaces
    ➤ 3D Face, 151
    ➤ 3D Surfaces, 163
    ➤ Edge Surface, 162
    ➤ Revolved Surface, 161
    ➤ Ruled Surface, 159
    ➤ Tabulated Surface, 160
  ➤ Table, 270
  ➤ Text
    ➤ Multiline Text, 255
    ➤ Single Line Text, 269
Draw Order toolbar, 16
Draw toolbar, 3, 16, **18–20**
  Arc tool, 28, *29*, **74–76**, *75*, 155
  Circle tool, 24, 73–74
  Ellipse tool, 76, 77
  Hatch tool, 86
  Insert Block tool, 230, 232

Line tool, 37–38, **72**
  Osnap options, 61, *61*
Make Block tool, 228
Multiline Text tool, 255
Polyline tool, 72, 80, 157
Rectangle tool, 22
Revision Cloud tool, 84
Spline tool, 78
Table tool, 270
drawing area, **5–6**
  checking size, 21
  determining boundaries, **47–50**
  dimensions, 22
  Grid feature, **52–53**
    Limits command and, 50
drawing assemblies, setting at
  intervals, 103
Drawing Properties dialog box, 325
  General tab, *325*
  Statistics tab, 325, *326*
  Summary tab, 325, *326*
drawing, starting, **20–22**, 24
Drawing Units dialog box, 21, 45–47, *46*
Drawing1.dwg, 1, 45
drawings
  attaching as xrefs, **241–242**
  automatic scaling at insertion, 249
  finding and extracting contents with
    Design Center, **247–249**
  finding missing support files,
    329–331
  general status information, *323*,
    323–324
  importing as blocks, **232–233**
  from previous AutoCAD
    versions, 213
  setup, **45–52**
    drawing units, **45–46**
  setup for printing, **334–346**. *See also*
    printing
    Layout tabs, *334*, **334–337**
    paper size and orientation,
      336–337
  storing nondrawing data with, **325**
  tracking time spent on, **324–325**, *325*
Dtext command, 269
duplex printing, 348
Dview command, 189
DWF Virtual Pens.ctb plot style
  table, 356
.dwg files
  saving blocks as, **234**
  viewing contents, 247
  Windows Explorer to drag and
    drop, 233
DYN button, *4*, 4, 9, *42*, 42
Dynamic Input, 4, 5, **42–45**
  displaying options, 44
  editing objects with grips and,
    115–118, *116*
  turning off, 9
Dynamic option, for zoom, 25

E

Edge option, for Trim or Extend, 131
Edgesurf command, 162
Edit Block Definition dialog box, 142, *142*
Edit menu
  ➤ Find, 264
  ➤ Paste Special, 265, 279
Edit Vertex option, for Pedit
  command, 145
editing, 107. *See also* Modify toolbar
  blocks, 233
  lines, 72
  locking layers for, **205**
  objects, 107
  objects using grips
    copy, mirror, rotate, scale or
      stretch, 113–114
    and Dynamic Input, **115–118**
    stretching lines, 111–113
  polylines, **144–146**
  preventing accidental changes, **205**
  in solid 3D modeling, **177–179**
ellipse, *76*, **76–77**
Ellipse Arc tool (Draw toolbar), *19*
Ellipse tool (Draw toolbar), *19*
ellipsis (...) in menus, 8
elliptical arc, 76, *77*, **77–78**
Endpoint option, for osnap, 62, 1
  32–133, *133*
endpoints
  automatic snap to, 59
  grips to move, 114
  joining, 125–127
Engineering drawing scales, scale
  factors, 220
Engineering length option, 46
Enter key, 6
Erase tool (Modify toolbar), *18*, 125
erasing. *See* deleting
Escape, 23
Excel
  importing spreadsheets to
    AutoCAD, 279
  opening exported table in, 278
exchanging data between open files, **249**
exclamation point icon, *329*, 329
EXit option, for Pedit command, 146
Exit option, of 3Dorbit command, 187
Explode command, 72, 144
  for multilines, 82
Explode tool (Modify toolbar), *20*, 144
exploding polylines, 80
Export Data dialog box, 278
exporting
  layer state sets, 212, 214
  tables, **278**
Express menu ➤ Layers
  ➤ Layer Manager, 213
  ➤ Layer Walk, 214
Express Tools Layer Manager dialog
  box, **213–214**

Express tools layer options, **213–216**
    changing object assignment, 215
    controlling settings through objects,
        215–216
    exploring with Layer Walk, **214–215**
    saving layer states, **213–214**
Express Tools Layer toolbar
    Change To Current Layer tool, 215
    Freeze Object's Layer, 215
    Isolate Object's Layer, 215
    Layer Manager tool, 213
    Layer Walk tool, 214
    Lock Object's Layer tool, 216
    Match Objects Layer tool, 215
    Turn Object's Layer Off, 215
    Unlock Object's Layer tool, 216
Extend command, for lines, 72
Extend tool (Modify toolbar), *19*
extending objects, 130–131, *131*
Extension option, for osnap, 62
Extents option, for zoom, 26
external files, persistence after
    erasing, 125
External Reference dialog box, *241*,
    241–242, 247
    Overlay option, 243
external references. *See* xrefs (external
    references)
extracting contents of drawing, with
    Design Center, **247–249**
Extrude Faces option, for solid
    editing, 178
extruding in solid 3D modeling
    along path, **174–175**, *175*
    polyline, **163–167**, *165*

F

facet count for mesh, in surface 3D
    modeling, *162*, 162
Favorites folder, 246
Favorites tab, in help, 32
feet (measurement unit), 45
Fence option, for Select objects:
    prompt, 124
Field dialog box, *275*, 275
    Formula box with cell addresses, *276*
fields, for table formulas, 274
File menu
    ➤ Close, 20
    ➤ Drawing Properties, 325
    ➤ New, 20
    ➤ Open, 238
    ➤ Plot, 346
    ➤ Plotter Manager, 347
    ➤ Print, 334
    ➤ Save As, 21
files
    exchanging data between open, **249**
    finding missing support files, **329–331**
    opening and inserting with Design
        Center, **247**

Fill Patterns.ctb plot style table, 356
Fillet command, **125–127**
    for lines, 72
    No Trim option, 126–127, *127*
Fillet tool (Modify toolbar), *20*, 172
filleting corner in solid 3D modeling,
    172, **172**
fills. *See* hatch patterns and solid fills
Find and Replace dialog box, for text,
    264, **264**, 326–327, *327*
Find and Replace Options dialog
    box, *265*
Find dialog box, **238–239**
    Date Modified tab, *240*
    Name & Location tab, *239*
finding
    drawing contents with Design
        Center, **247–249**
    layers, 206
    missing support files, **329–331**
Fit option, for Pedit command, 145
Fit Tolerance option, for spline, 78, *79*, 80
floating model space, 203, 335
floating toolbars, 3, 14
    opening, 15
flyouts, *12*, **12**
focal length in perspective view, 189
fonts
    finding, **331**
    style setting for, 268
Format menu
    ➤ Dimension ➤ Style, 304, 316
    ➤ Layer, 194, 364
    ➤ Linetype, 219, 225
    ➤ Lineweight, 279
    ➤ Point Style, 101
    ➤ Table Style, 282
    ➤ Text Style, 267
    ➤ Units, 45
formula field, 274
formulas in tables, **274–278**
fraction, format of, 312
Fractional length option, 46
freehand revision cloud, **84**
Freeze Object's Layer (Express Tools
    Layer toolbar), 215
Freeze option, for layers, 201
From option, for osnap, 62
Front Clipping On option, of 3Dorbit
    command, 189

G

gap tolerance, for hatch patterns, 97
Geometric Tolerance dialog box, *298*, 298
Geometry section of Properties
    palette, *120*
Gouraud shade, 173, *173*
grab bars, for toolbar, *13*, 13
gradient fill, colors and patterns for,
    97–99
Gradient tool (Draw toolbar), *20*

Grads angle option, 47
graphics
    adding to table cells, **281–282**
    printer control options, 348
grayscale, 361
    printing, 337
Grayscale.ctb plot style table, 356
"Grid too dense to display" message, 53
grids, **52–53**
    changing settings, **54–58**
        aligning grid to object, 57–58, *58*
        isometric 2D drawing setup, *55*,
            55–56
        rotating grid, snap and cursor,
            56, 56
        X and Y spacing, 55
    Limits command and, 50
    snapping to, **53–54**
grips, 49, 111
    editing objects with
        copy, mirror, rotate, scale or
            stretch, 113–114
        and Dynamic Input, **115–118**,
            116
        stretching lines, 111–113
    vs. Move and Copy commands, 132
    of polylines, 144
    shortcut menu, *112*
    turning on, 111
group filter
    adding layers to, 210
    converting layer properties filter
        to, 211
    deleting layers from, 210
groups, 227
    for object organization, **235–239**
    toggling on and off, 235

H

hard disk space, xrefs and, 240
Hatch and Gradient dialog box
    for area measurement, 318–319, *319*
    expanded box, *95*
    Gradient tab, *97*, **97–99**
    Hatch tab, *86*
    Inherit Properties option, 87
    options, **94–99**
    origin settings, 89, *89*
hatch boundary extents, 90, *91*
Hatch Edit dialog box, Hatch tab, *92*,
    92–98
Hatch Pattern Palette, *89*, 93
hatch patterns and solid fills, 85, **85–99**
    for area measurement, 318
    basics of placing, 86–87
    boundary hatch options, **94–99**
        behavior of patterns and fills,
            95–97
    editing hatch area, **91**
    finding files, **331**
    matching with other properties, 99

modifying hatch pattern, **92–94**
plot styles for, **355–361**
positioning accurately, **89–90**
predefined patterns, 87–88, *88*
solid fills, **88**
in tool palette, 251
Hatch tool (Draw toolbar), *20*, 86
help, **30–34**
   Ask Me tab, *31*, 31–32
   Contents tab, *30*
   context-sensitive, **32–33**
   Favorites tab, 32
   Index tab, 32
   Search tab, 31
   Search the Web option, 32
Help menu, 30
Help option, in LT Group Manager, 238
hidden line view, printing, 342, 350
Hide command, 151, 152
highlighting objects for selection, 108
Home option, for Dimension Edit
   tool, 301
horizontal line, restricting line to, 39, 50
hot grip, 111
HSL (hue, saturation, luminance) color
   model, 196
Hyperlink property, 119

I

icons
   in menus, 7
   thumbnail previews in
      DesignCenter, 247
   on toolbars, 12, 18
   UCS, 6, *6*, 149
ID command, 321
Imperial measurement system, 45
imported objects, automatic scaling, 47
importing
   drawing as block, **232–233**
   layer state sets, 212, 214
   page setups, 354
   tables, **279**
   text files, 265
Imprint option, for solid editing, 178
In option, for zoom, 26
inches, 45
indents for text, **259–260**, *260*
Index tab, in help, 32
Info palette, 33
Inquiry toolbar, 16
Inscribed polygon, *100*
Insert A Block In A Table Cell dialog box,
   281, 281–282
Insert Block tool (Draw toolbar), *19*,
   230, 232
Insert dialog box, 230–231, *231*
Insert Field tool (Text Formatting
   toolbar), *257*, *258*, 275
Insert menu
   ➢ External Reference, 241
   ➢ Xref Manager, 241, 329

Insert option
   for osnap, 62
   for Pedit command, 146
Insert Table dialog box, 270, *271*, *283*
Insert toolbar, 16
Insert Units option, for blocks, 230
inserting
   blocks, **230–231**
   files with Design Center, *247*
   graphics in table cells, **281–282**
   table rows or columns, **274**
insertion base point, origin as, 233
Interfere command, *171*, 171
Internet, 33
intersection of solids, *170*, 171
Intersection option, for osnap, 62
islands
   and area measurement, 320
   for hatch patterns, *96*, 96
ISO linetypes, 216, *217*
Isolate Object's Layer (Express Tools
   Layer toolbar), 215
isometric 2D drawing, setup, *55*, 55–56
isometric views, *168*
isoplane cursors, *55*
Italic tool (Text Formatting toolbar),
   257, 258

J

Join option, for Pedit command, 145
Join tool (Modify toolbar), *19*
joining objects, **125–131**
   end to end with intermediate arcs,
      125–127
   extending or trimming lines to other
      objects, 129, **129–131**, *130*, *131*
justification
   for multiple text objects, 262
   of table cell text, **273**, *274*
Justifytext command, 262

K

keyboard command equivalent
   for menu item, 8
   for tool, 12

L

Last option, for Select objects:
   prompt, 124
lathe, *161*, 161–162
Layer & Linetype Properties dialog
   box, 214
Layer Control drop-down list, *345*
Layer Manager dialog box, 213
Layer Properties Manager dialog box,
   193, **196–197**, *197*, 343, 364, *365*
   ByBlock, 226
   Color icon, *195*
   Current Layer tool, 197

Current VP Freeze column, 203, *344*
Delete Layer tool, 197
lightbulb icon, 201, *202*
Lineweight option, 221–223, *222*
lock icon, 205, *205*
Model/Paper space button, *204*
New Layer button, *194*, 194
New Properties Filter tool, 207, *208*
New VP Freeze column in, 203
printer icon, *205*, 205
snowflake icon, 202
sun icon, 202, *203*
Layer property, 119
Layer State Manager, 207
Layer State Name dialog box, 213
Layer States Manager dialog box,
   211, *212*
Layer toolbar, *3*, 16
Layerpmode command, 213
layers
   controlling list, **206–211**
      creating groups by selection,
         209–211
      filtering by properties, **207–209**
   creating and assigning, **193–199**
      assigning to objects, **198–199**
   Express tools layer options, **213–216**
      changing object assignment, 215
      controlling settings through
         objects, **215–216**
      exploring with Layer Walk,
         214–215
      saving layer states, **213–214**
   finding, **206**
   locking for printing and editing, **205**
   organizing visual content through
      properties, **216–225**
      assigning linetypes, **216–218**
      colors, linetypes and line
         weights for objects, **224–225**
      controlling linetype scale,
         219–221
      setting line weights, **221–223**
   plot style assignment to, **364**
   for point objects as visual
      markers, 102
   saving and recalling settings,
      211–213
   selecting all, 206
   setting current, **200**
   visibility, **201–205**
      controlling with Freeze and
         Thaw, 202
      in individual viewports of
         Layout tab, **203–205**
      on/off option, 201–202
   in xref files, 243
Layers toolbar, Layer list, 198–199,
   199, 200
LayerWalk dialog box, *214*, 215
Layout tabs, *4*, *5*, **26–28**, *27*, *334*, **334–337**
   adding, **345–346**
   adding text, 265

dimensions in, **286**
drawing displayed in, 27
linetype scale in, 219
multiple views in, 339–341
for scaling down drawing, **338–339**
Layouts toolbar, 16
leader lines, *286*
Leader Settings dialog box, 295
    Attachment tab, *296*
Left Align tool (Text Formatting toolbar),
    257, 258
lightbulb icon, in Layer Properties
    Manager dialog box, 201, *202*
Limits command, 48–50
line spacing for text, **260**
Line tool (Draw toolbar), *18*, 37–38, **72**
    Close option, 41
    Osnap options, *61*, 61
line weights, **221–223**, *222*
    adjusting to scale for printing, 350
    for dimension lines, 306
    for layers, 216
    for objects, 224–225
    for tables, **279–281**
    visibility, 222
linear dimensions, **287–291**
    horizontal or vertical, 287–288, *288*
    for nonorthogonal objects, *291*,
        291–292
lines, **72**
    converting to polyline, 144
    stretching, 111–113
Linetype Manager dialog box,
    219–220, *220*
Linetype property, 119
linetype scale, for objects, 119, 224–225
linetypes, *217*
    for blocks, **199**
    for dimension lines, 306
    finding files, **331**
    for layers, **216–218**
    loading from linetype file, 216
    for objects, 224–225
    Plot Style Table Editor setting
        for, 361
    plot styles for, **355–361**
    scaling, *219*, **219–221**
Lineweight dialog box, *222*, 222
Lineweight property, 119
Lineweight Settings dialog box, *222*, 222
Load dialog box (Design Center), 250
Load Or Reload Linetypes dialog
    box, *218*
lock icon, in Layer Properties Manager
    dialog box, *205*, 205
Lock Object's Layer tool (Express Tools
    Layer toolbar), 216
locking
    layers for printing and editing, **205**
    toolbars, **14**
    viewport from pan and zoom, 342
Lowercase tool (Text Formatting
    toolbar), *257*, 258

LT Group Manager, *237*, **237–238**
Ltscale system variable, 220, 221, *225*
Ltype gen option, for Pedit
    command, 145

M

macros, moving or copying in, 132
Make Block tool (Draw toolbar), *19*, 228
marquee, 108
Match Properties tool (Standard
    toolbar), 99
Material Condition dialog box, 298, *299*
math operations in tables, **277–278**
Measure command, 101, **102**
measurement systems, selection, 45
menu bar, 3, *3*, **7–11**
    keyboard command equivalent for
        item, 8
    triangular pointer in menus, 8
merging table cells, **271**
meshes for curved shapes, **159–163**
    canned 3D surfaces, 163
    facet count for mesh, 162, *162*
    line to set mesh direction, 1
        60–161, *161*
    mesh definition with 4 edges, *162*,
        162
    revolving shape, *161*, **161–162**
    stretching surface between objects,
        159–160, *160*
Method option, for Chamfer
    command, 129
metric measurement system, 45
Mid Between 2 Points option, for
    osnap, 62
Middle Align tool (Text Formatting
    toolbar), *257*, 258
Midpoint osnap, 60, *61*, 62
midpoints, automatic snap to, 59
Mirror option, for grips, 113
Mirror tool (Modify toolbar), *19*
model space of AutoCAD, 26
Model tab, *4*, 5, 26
    adding text, 265
    dimensions in, **286**
    linetype scale in, 219
Modify Dimension Styles dialog box, 294
Modify II toolbar, 16
Modify menu, *7*, 7
    ➤ 3D Operation ➤ Rotate 3D, 153
    ➤ Break, 141
    ➤ Chamfer, 127
    ➤ Erase, 125
    ➤ Explode, 144
    ➤ Extend, 131
    ➤ Fillet, 172
    ➤ Move, 132
    ➤ Object
        ➤ Polyline, 80, 144, 157
        ➤ Text ➤ Edit, 300
        ➤ Text ➤ Justify, 262
        ➤ Text ➤ Scale, 262

    ➤ Offset, 82
    ➤ Rotate, 139
    ➤ Scale, 137
    ➤ Solid Editing
        ➤ Intersect, 171
        ➤ Subtract, 169
        ➤ Union, 170
    ➤ Stretch, 138
    ➤ Trim, 130
Modify Table Style dialog box, 283
Modify toolbar, 3, 7, 16, **18–20**
    Array tool, 134, 135
    Break tool, 141
    Chamfer tool, 127
    Erase tool, 125
    Explode tool, 144
    Extend tool, 131
    Fillet tool, 172
    Move tool, 132
    Rotate tool, 139
    Scale tool, 137
    and Select objects: prompt, **123–124**
    Stretch tool, 138
    Trim tool, 130
Monochrome.stb plot style table, 357
monochrome.ctb plot style table, 337, 356
More option, of 3Dorbit command, 188
mouse, scroll wheel for zoom, 24–25
Move command, in 3D space, 179, *180*
Move Faces option, for solid editing, 178
Move option, for Pedit command, 146
Move Or Copy dialog box, *345*, 345
Move tool (Modify toolbar), *19*, 132
moving
    objects, **132–133**
    toolbars, **13–14**
Mtext command, 251, 255
    default style, 267
Multiline command, 81
Multiline Text tool (Draw toolbar), 18,
    18, *20*, 255
multilines, 82
Multiple option
    for Chamfer command, 129
    for Fillet command, 127
    for Select objects: prompt, 124
Multiple Point tool (Draw toolbar), *19*

N

named plot styles, 355
    assigning to layers, **364**
    assigning to layers and objects,
        362–364
    vs. color plot styles, 357
    converting color styles to, **365–366**
names
    for blocks, 229
    of layer groups, 207
    of layer state, changing, 214
    of layers, 194
    locating and selecting by, **327–328**

for User Coordinate System, 156, 169
viewing list of components with, 328
"natural language" questions in help, 31
NEAR Boolean keyword, 31
Nearest option, for osnap, 62
negative values, in Cartesian coordinate system, 41, *42*
nested block, editing, 143
nested groups, 236
New Dimension Style dialog box, 304
Alternate Units tab, 313, *313*, 314
for architectural drawings, 307–308
Fit tab, 310, *310*, 311
Lines tab, 304, *305*, 306
Primary Units tab, *310*, 310, 312
Symbols and Arrows tab, 304, *305*, 307
Text tab, *308*, 308–309
Tolerances tab, 313, *313*, 315
New Features workshop, 33
New Group FIlter, for layers, 207, **209–211**, *210*
New Layer State To Save dialog box, 211, *212*
New Page Setup dialog box, *353*, 353–354
New Properties Filter tool, in Layer Properties Manager dialog box, 207, *208*
New Property FIlter, for layers, 207
New Table Style dialog box, 282–284, *283*
New View dialog box, *191*
New VP Freeze column, in Layer Properties Manager dialog box, 203
Next option, for Pedit command, 145
Node option, for osnap, 62
nondrawing data, storing with drawing, **325**
None option, for osnap, 62
nonorthogonal objects, dimensions for, **291–294**
nonprintable border of printer, *334*, 334
nonprinting layer, 141
to store information, 322
normal clouds, *83*
NOT Boolean keyword, 31
notes, Leader tool for adding, *295*, **295–296**
NURBS curves, 78

O

Object Grouping dialog box, *235*, **236–237**
Object option, for zoom, 25
Object Properties toolbar
ByLayer, 224
Properties tool, for hatch pattern editing, 92
Object Selection cursor, *49*, 49
Object Snap toolbar, 17
Object Snap Tracking, 49, **64–67**

object snaps (osnaps), 37, **59–64**
for alignment, **132–133**
for dimensions, 287, 290
location setup, **59**
options list, **62–63**
selecting on the fly, **61–62**
and Snapang for grid alignment with object, *57*
in surface 3D modeling, *152*, **152–153**
turning off, 61
using, *60*, **60**
objects. *See also* 2D objects; blocks; xrefs (external references)
adding to tool palette, 251
aligning grid to, 57–58, *58*
aligning UCS with, 167
assigning layers to, **198–199**
automatic scaling of imported, 47
breaking in two, **141–142**
controlling layer settings through, **215–216**
copying, *133*
with Array, **134–136**
dividing into specified lengths, **102**, *103*
editing, 107
erasing, **125**
groups for organizing, **235–239**
joining, **125–131**
end to end with intermediate arcs, **125–127**
extending or trimming lines to other objects, *129*, **129–131**, *130*, *131*
line weight setting, 222–223, *223*
linetype scale, 225
linetypes for, 218
moving, **132–133**
plot style assignment to, **362–364**
Properties palette for controlling, **118–121**, *119*
revision clouds based on, **84–85**
rotating, **139–141**
scaling, *137*, **137–138**
selecting, **107–111**
practice, 108–109
Select objects: prompt, **123–124**
standard method, 107–108
with windows, 109–111, *110*
stretching, **138**, *138*
stretching surface between, **159–160**, *160*
oblique angle for text, 269
Oblique option, for Dimension Edit tool, 301
Oblique tool (Text Formatting toolbar), *257*, 258
Offset command, 81–82, *82*
for lines, 72
Offset Faces option, for solid editing, 178
offset printing, PANTONE color book for, 196

Offset tool (Modify toolbar), *19*
online resources, 33
open files, exchanging data between, **249**
Open option, for Pedit command, 145
opening files, with Design Center, **247**
opening toolbars, **15**
Options dialog box, 9, *9*, 331
Drafting Settings tab, 62–63
Files tab, *331*
for Color Book location, 196
Selection tab, 111
OR Boolean keyword, 31
Orbit Maintains Z option, of 3Dorbit command, 188
Orbit option, of 3Dorbit command, 188
Orbit uses AutoTarget option, of 3Dorbit command, 188
ordinate dimensions, **296–297**, *298*
orientation
for printing, 336–337, 352
of table cell text, **272–273**
origin
of drawing, 41
of grid, 57–58
of hatch patterns, 89–90, *90*
as insertion base point, 233
for ordinate dimensions, 297
settings for User Coordinate System, 154
Ortho mode, *50*, 50
orthographic views, *168*
Osnap button, 60, *60*, 61
Osnap marker with tool tip, 49, *49*
Osnap mode, 60
Osnap Tracking, **64–67**
turning off, *108*, 108
Osnap Tracking marker, 65, *65–66*
osnaps. *See* object snaps (osnaps)
Out option, for zoom, 26
overlays, 243
Overline tool (Text Formatting toolbar), *257*, 258

P

Page Setup Manager dialog box, *353*, **353–354**
Palette view, in DesignCenter, *245*
palettes. *See* Tool palettes
Pan option, of 3Dorbit command, 187
panning and zooming, **24–26**, *25*
by exact distance and direction, 26
locking viewport from, 342
Pantone colors, **195–196**
paper
printable area, 28
size for printing, 336–337
user-defined, 348
paper space, 335
adding text, 265
parallel lines, **81–82**, *82*
Parallel option, for osnap, 62
parallel projection view, 184

Paste Special dialog box, 265, *279*
patterns. *See also* hatch patterns and
   solid fills
   for gradient fill, **97–99**
.PC3 file extension, 347
Pedit command, 80, *80*, **144–146**, 158
   edit options, 145–146
   Fit option, 81, *81*
Perpendicular option, for osnap, 62
perspective view, 184
   focal length in, 189
   panning, 187
pickbox, 108
Plot dialog box, 336, *336*, 346
   expanded box, *337*, *351*, 351–352
plot stamp, 351
Plot Stamp dialog box, *352*, 352
Plot Style property, 119
Plot Style Table Editor dialog box,
   359–361
   Form View tab, *359*, 360–361
   General tab, 359
   Table View tab, 360, *360*
plot style tables
   creating, 358
   editing and using, **358–359**
   for printing, **355–361**
      assigning to layers, **364**
      assigning to objects, **362–364**
      color vs. named, **357**
      converting from color to
         named, **365–366**
      predefined, *356*, **356–357**
      to set line weights, 223
plotter calibration, 348
Plotter Configuration Editor dialog box,
   347–348
   Device and Document Settings
      tab, *347*
Point Filters option, for osnap, 62
point objects, **101–102**, *102*
   coordinates of, *321*
   multiple construction lines through
      single, 104
Point Selection cursor, 39, 49, *49*
Point Style dialog box, *101*, 101–102
polar coordinates, 28, 37, *37*
   relative, 39–40
   specifying, 40
Polar Tracking, 39, 49, **50–51**
   modifying behavior, **51–52**
Polar Tracking vector, 28, 29
Polygon tool (Draw toolbar), *19*
polygons
   area measurement, **318**
   regular, *100*, **100**
Polyline command, 72
Polyline option, for Fillet command, 127
polyline spline curve, converting to true
   spline curve, 81
Polyline tool (Draw toolbar), *19*, 72, 157
polylines, *72*, 72, 76
   Chamfer command on, *128*

for complex shapes, 148
to create 3D solids, **166**
editing, **144–146**
exploding, 144
extruding solids from, 163–167
Fillet command on, **126**
outline for area measurement, 319
for smooth curves, 78, **80–81**
in solid 3D modeling, revolving,
   175–176, *176*
in surface 3D modeling, **157–159**
   3D curves, *157*, **157**
   polyline paradox, 159
   "solid" appearance, *158*, **158**
position, of hatch patterns, **89–90**
positive values, in Cartesian coordinate
   system, 41, *42*
PostScript fonts, 256
precision
   of dimension text, 312
   Drawing Units option, 47
   of tolerance dimension text, 315
predefined UCS, in solid 3D
   modeling, **167**
Preferences dialog box, 325
prefix, for dimensions, 300, 312
Preset Views option, of 3Dorbit
   command, 188
Preview Icon option, for blocks, 230
preview icons, 246
Preview panel, in DesignCenter, *245*, 246
Previous option
   for Pedit command, 145
   for Select objects: prompt, 124
   for zoom, 25
printable area of paper, 28
printer icon, in Layer Properties
   Manager dialog box, *205*, 205
printing
   3D views, **350**
   drawing position on page, 349
   drawing setup for, **334–346**
      adding layouts, **345–346**
      layers for individual viewports,
         343, **343–344**
      Layout tabs, *334*, **334–337**
      paper size and orientation,
         336–337
      scaling down, **338–339**
      viewport control, **339–342**
   Layout tabs for organizing, 333
   locking layers for, **205**
   offset, PANTONE color book f
      or, 196
   orientation, 352
   Plot Options group, **351–352**
   plot styles for, **355–361**
      assigning to layers, **364**
      assigning to objects, **362–364**
      color vs. named, **357**
      converting from color to
         named, **365–366**
      predefined, *356*, **356–357**

table creation, **358**
   table edit and use, **358–359**
printer configuration options,
   347–348
scaling, **349–350**
selecting and storing printer
   settings, **346–347**
storing printer settings, **353–354**
view selection for, **349**
Project option, for Trim or Extend, 131
Projection option, of 3Dorbit
   command, 188
prompts, **49**
properties, filtering layers by, **207–209**
Properties palette, 3, *198*, 224
   for assigning layers to objects, 198
   Auto-hide button, 120, *120*
   for blocks, *232*, 232
   Browse button, *121*
   to control objects, **118–121**, *119*
   for dimensions, Fit options, *301*, *302*
   for line weights, *223*, 223
   Linetype scale option, *225*
   Misc group, list of scales, *339*
   Pattern category, *94*, 94
   Plot Style drop-down list, *363*
   Table group, Cell Margin options,
      273, *274*
   Text group
      Line Space Factor, 260, *261*
      Text Rotation, 273
Properties tool (Standard toolbar),
   118, 223
Properties toolbar, 3, 16, 224
   Color drop-down list, *224*
   Layer list, applying filters, 211, *345*
   Layer Properties Manager tool,
      193, *194*
   Line Weight drop-down list, 222,
      223, *225*, 225
   Linetype drop-down list, *219*,
      224, 224
Property Settings dialog box, *99*
Purge command, 230

Q

Qdim command, 290
Quadrant option, for osnap, 62
Quick Select dialog box, **328**, *328*
QuickCalc calculator, *321*, 321

R

Radians angle option, 47
radius, 73
Radius Dimension tool (Dimension
   toolbar), 293
Radius option, for Fillet command, 127
Ray command, 101
rays, as Construction lines, 106
Realtime option, for zoom, 25

Rectangle tool (Draw toolbar), *19*, 22
redo, 23, *257*, *258*
Refedit command, 142, 240
Refedit toolbar, 17
Reference option
    for Rotate command, *139*, 139–140
    for Scale command, 137
reference rectangle, 48
Reference toolbar, 17
Regen option, for Pedit command, 146
region object, 106
Region tool (Draw toolbar), *20*
regular polygons, **100**, *100*
relative coordinates
    Cartesian, **40–41**
    Direct Distance method for, 42
    polar, 39–40
Remove From Group option, in LT
    Group Manager, 238
Render toolbar, 17
    Hide, 158
Reset View option, of 3Dorbit
    command, 188
restoring
    layer state, 214
    User Coordinate System (UCS),
        156–157
Retain option, for blocks, 230
retaining boundaries, for hatch
    patterns, 96
Return key, 6
Revcloud command, Object option, 84
reversing actions, 23
Revision Cloud tool (Draw toolbar), *19*
revision clouds, *83*, **83–85**
    based on object shape, **84–85**
    freehand, 84
revolving polyline, in solid 3D modeling,
    175–176, *176*
revolving shape, in surface 3D modeling,
    161, **161–162**
Revsurf command, 161
RGB (red, green, blue) color model, 196
Rich Text Format (RTF) files,
    importing, 265
Right Align tool (Text Formatting
    toolbar), *257*, 258
right-clicking, 6
Rotate Faces option, for solid editing, 178
Rotate option, for Dimension Edit
    tool, 301
Rotate tool (Modify toolbar), *19*, 139
rotating
    blocks, **231–232**
    dimension text, **302**
    grid, snap and cursor, *56*, 56
    objects, **139–141**, *140*
        in surface 3D model, *153*, **153**
    text, 272–273
    views with arcball, **184–186**
Rotation option, for ellipse, 76
rounded corner, 125
    with Fillet command, 126, *126*

rounding, of dimensions, 312
rows and columns, Array dialog box to
    copy, **135–136**, *136*
rows in tables, adding or deleting, **274**
RTF (Rich Text Format) files,
    importing, 265
rubber-banding, 39
rubber-banding line, 26, *38*
ruler, 259–260, *260*
Ruler tool (Text Formatting toolbar),
    257, 258
Rulesurf command, 159
Running Osnap, 60
    turning off, 108, *108*

S

Save Drawing As dialog box, 21
saving
    3D view, **189–191**
    blocks as drawing files, **234**
    layer settings, **211–213**
    User Coordinate System (UCS),
        156–157
scale factors, **221**
    for dimension line components, 306
    multiple tools for different, 252
Scale option
    for grips, 113
    for zoom, 25
Scale tool (Modify toolbar), *19*, 137
Scaletext command, 262
scaling
    automatic for drawings and blocks
        at insertion, 249
    blocks, **231–232**
    conversion factors, 220
    Layout tabs and, **338–339**
    linetypes, *219*, **219–221**
    multiple text objects, 262
    objects, *47*, *137*, **137–138**
    for printing, **349–350**
    and text, **265–266**
Scientific length option, 46
Screening xxx%.ctb plot style table, 356
scroll wheel on mouse, for zoom,
    24–25, 111
Search dialog box in DesignCenter,
    247–249
    Look For drop-down list, *248*
Search the Web option, in help, 32
Select Color dialog box, 194, *195*, 224
    Color Books tab, *196*, 196
    Index Color tab, 195
    True Color tab, *195*, 195
Select Drawing dialog box, 232, *233*
Select File dialog box, 238–239, *239*
Select Group option, in LT Group
    Manager, 238
Select Linetype dialog box, 216, *218*
Select Plot Style dialog box, *363*, *365*
Select Template dialog box, *20*, 20–21

selecting
    all layers, 206
    colors to indicate mode, 5
    grips, *112*, 112
    objects, **107–111**
        practice, 108–109
        Select objects: prompt, **123–124**
        standard method, 107–108
        with windows, 109–111, *110*
    rectangle, 10–11
selection set, 108
selection window, 5
separating solids, in solid 3D modeling,
    170, 170
Shade Modes option, of 3Dorbit
    command, 188
Shade toolbar, 17
shaded view
    printing, 342, 350
    in solid 3D modeling, *173*, 173
Shell option, for solid editing, 179
shortcut menu, 6
    for command options, 7
    for grips, *112*
    to lock toolbars, 14
    of toolbars, 15
single-line text object, to add words,
    269–270
size of object, scaling, *137*, 137
Sketch command, 106
skewed text, 269
smooth curves, **78–80**
Snap mode
    changing settings, **54–58**
        aligning grid to object, 57–58, *58*
        isometric 2D drawing setup, *55*,
            55–56
        rotating grid, snap and cursor,
            56, *56*
        X and Y spacing, 55
    with grids, **53–54**
Snapang command, 56
Snapbase command, 58, 89
snowflake icon, in Layer Properties
    Manager dialog box, 202
solid 3D modeling, *147*, 147, **163–179**
    combining and separating solids,
        170, *170*
    editing options, **177–179**
    extruding along path, **174–175**, *175*
    extruding shape, **163–167**, *165*
    filleting corner, *172*, **172**
    intersection, *170*
    predefined UCS, **167**
    revolving polyline, **175–176**, *176*
    shaded view, **173**, *173*
    subtracting 3D shapes, **169–171**, *170*
solid fills. *See* hatch patterns and solid
    fills
Solids Editing toolbar, 17
Solids toolbar, 17
sorting layers in Layer Properties
    Manager dialog box, 197

Spelling Checker, **262–263**
Spherical format, for specifying
    distance, 181
splash screen, 1
Spline option, for Pedit command, 145
Spline tool (Draw toolbar), *19*, 78
splines, 76
    for smooth curves, 78, *79*
Splinesegs system variable, 158
Stack Fraction tool (Text Formatting
    toolbar), *257*, 258
standard cursor, *49*
Standard text style, 266
Standard toolbar, *3*, 17
    DesignCenter tool, 244
    Match Properties tool, 99
    Pan Realtime tool, 24
    Properties tool, 118, 223
    Redo tool, 23
    Tool Palettes tool, 251
    Undo tool, 23, 39
        for erasing, 125
    Zoom Previous tool, 24
    Zoom Window tool, *12*, 12, 24
standard window, for selecting objects,
    110–111
Start menu ➢ All Programs ➢ Autodesk
    ➢ AutoCAD 2006, 1
Startup dialog box, 2
status bar, *3*, *4*
    command description in, 8, 18
    controlling display, 5
    Grid button, 50
    Paper button, *335*, 335
    Snap button, 53
Status command, 323
.stb file extension, 366. *See also* named
    plot styles
Straighten option, for Pedit
    command, 146
Stretch tool (Modify toolbar), *19*, 138
stretching
    objects, *138*, *138*
    surface between objects,
        159–160, *160*
styles
    for dimensions. *See also* New
        Dimension Style dialog box
        editing, **316**
        setting current, **314**
    for tables, **282–284**
    for text, **266–269**
        creating, **266–267**
Styles toolbar, *3*, 17
    Text Style Control drop-down
        list, *268*
subtracting 3D shapes, **169–171**, *170*
suffix, for dimensions, 300, 312
sum, in tables, 277
sun icon, in Layer Properties Manager
    dialog box, 202, *203*
surface 3D modeling, *148*, **148–163**
    3D view, *149*, **149–150**

adding 3D surface, *151*, **151–152**, *152*
adding thickness, *150*, **150**
canned 3D surfaces, *163*
curved shapes with meshes, **159–163**
    canned 3D surfaces, 163
    facet count for mesh, *162*, 162
    line to set mesh direction,
        160–161, *161*
    mesh definition with 4 edges,
        162, 162
    revolving shape, *161*, **161–162**
    stretching surface between
        objects, **159–160**, *160*
object snaps in, *152*, **152–153**
with polylines, **157–159**
    3D curves, **157**, *157*
    polyline paradox, 159
    "solid" appearance, *158*, *158*
rotating objects, *153*, **153**
User Coordinate System (UCS), *154*,
    154–157
Surfaces toolbar, 17
Surveyor's Units, 46, 47
SW Isometric view, *149*
Swivel Camera option, of 3Dorbit
    command, 188
Symbol dialog box, *298*
Symbol tool (Text Formatting toolbar),
    257, 258
symbols, 259
    downloading from Design Center
        Online, **250**
    setting at intervals, 103

T

T square, 50. *See also* Ortho mode
Table Style dialog box, *282*, 282
tables, *270*, **270–284**
    adding cell text, **271**
    adding graphics to cells, **281–282**
    adding or deleting rows or
        columns, **274**
    cell background colors, **281**
    cell text justification, **273**, *274*
    cell text orientation, **272–273**
    combining cells, **271**
    creating, **270**
    editing line weights, **279–281**
    exporting, **278**
    formulas in, **274–278**
    importing, **279**
    styles for, **282–284**
Tables tool (Draw toolbar), 20
tabs for text, **259–260**, *260*
Tabsurf command, 160
Tangent option
    for osnap, 62
    for Pedit command, 146
Taper Faces option, for solid editing, 178
Temporary Track Point option, for
    osnap, 62, **67–68**

text, **255–265**. *See also* tables
    adding single words, **269–270**
    background mask, **261**
    boundary adjustment, **259**
    changing multiple objects, **261–262**
    default style, **268–269**
    Find and Replace, **264**, **326–327**, *327*
    fonts, 256–257
    height, 256–257
    importing files, **265**
    indents and tabs, **259–260**, *260*
    Leader tool for adding notes, *295*,
        295–296
    line spacing, **260**
    and scale, 221, **265–266**
    Spelling Checker, **262–263**
    styles, **266–269**
        creating, **266–267**
Text Formatting dialog box, 275
Text Formatting toolbar, **255–256**, *256*,
    257, 258
    for dimensions, 300, *300*
    Font drop-down list, 257, *257*
    Style drop-down list, 267, *267*
    Text Height drop-down list, 257
Text Style dialog box, *267*, 267, **268–269**
Text toolbar, 17
Thaw option, for layers, 201
thickness
    adding in surface modeling, *150*, **150**
    for arc, *155*, 155
    of objects, 148
Through option, for Offset command, 82
thumbnail preview icons, in
    DesignCenter, 247
Time command, **324–325**
time consumption, tracking for drawing,
    324–325, *325*
tolerance notation in dimensions, *298*,
    298–299, 313, 315
    symbols, 299
Tool palettes, *3*, *4*, **250–253**
    closing, 9
    creating, 251
    customizing tool, **252–253**
    deleting tools and palettes, 252
    locking, 14
Tool Properties dialog box, 252, *253*
tool tips, **12**, *13*, 18
toolbars, *3*, **11–20**. *See also specific toolbars*
    flyouts, **12**, *12*
    list of, 16–17
    locking, **14**
    moving, **13–14**
    opening and closing, **15**
    shortcut menu, 15
    tool tips, **12**, *13*
Tools menu
    ➢ Drafting Settings, 51
    ➢ Drawing Limits, 48
    ➢ Group, 237
    ➢ Group Manager, 237

➢ Inquiry
   ➢ Area, 318
   ➢ ID Point, 321
   ➢ Status, 323
   ➢ Time, 324
➢ Move UCS, 167
➢ Named UCS, 156
➢ New UCS
   ➢ 3point, 154
   ➢ Origin, 321
➢ Options, 8–9, 62
➢ Orthographic UCS ➢ Front, 167
➢ QuickSelect, 262, 328
➢ Spelling, 262
➢ UCS ➢ Origin, 297
➢ Ungroup, 237
Top Align tool (Text Formatting toolbar), 257, 258
top view of 3D model, 183
tracking point, 64
Tracking tool (Text Formatting toolbar), 257, 258
Tracking vector with coordinate readout, 49, 49
Tree view, in DesignCenter, 245
triangular pointer in menus, 8
Trim command
   for arc, 76
   for Fillet command, 126–127
   for lines, 72
Trim option, for Chamfer command, 129, 129
Trim tool (Modify toolbar), 19, 130
true colors, **195–196**
TrueType fonts, 256
Turn Object's Layer Off (Express Tools Layer toolbar), 215
Txt font, 256

U

UCS dialog box, 156, 156
UCS icon, 6, 6, 149
UCS II toolbar, 17
UCS toolbar, 17
Underline tool (Text Formatting toolbar), 257, 258
undo, **23**, 39
   for erasing, 125
   tool in Text Formatting toolbar, 257, 258
   for Trim or Extend, 131
Undo option, for Pedit command, 145
Ungroup option, in LT Group Manager, 238
units of measurement, 21
   selecting, **45–46**
Unlock Object's Layer tool (Express Tools Layer toolbar), 216

unselecting objects, 108
Unstack Fraction tool (Text Formatting toolbar), 257, 258
Uppercase tool (Text Formatting toolbar), 257, 258
upside down text, 268
User Coordinate System (UCS), 6
   naming, 169
   predefined, **167**
   for surface 3D modeling, 154, **154–157**
      creating, 154–155

V

version of AutoCAD, 1
   information about, 33
vertical line, restricting line to, 39, 50
vertical text orientation, 272
View dialog box, 190
   Named Views tab, 190
   Orthographic & Isometric Views, 190
View menu, 8, 8
➢ 3D Orbit, 184
➢ 3D Views
   ➢ Plan View ➢ Named UCS, 183
   ➢ Plan View ➢ World UCS, 183
   ➢ SWIsometric, 149, 164
➢ Hide, 151, 152, 166
➢ Named Views, 190, 191
➢ Pan
   ➢ Point, 26
   ➢ Realtime, 24
➢ Regen, 152, 166
➢ Shade
   ➢ 2D Wireframe, 173
   ➢ Gouraud Shade, 173, 176
➢ Viewports, ➢ New Viewports, 340
➢ Zoom
   ➢ All, 49, 53, 335
   ➢ All Programs ➢ Autodesk, 48
   ➢ Extents, 48
   ➢ Out, 150
   ➢ Previous, 24
   ➢ Window, 24
   options list, 25–26
View toolbar, 17
viewports, 27
   creating, **339–341**
   display and printing, **342**
   floating model space of, 203
   layer visibility in, **203–205**
   in Layout tab, 334, **335–336**
   scale for, 338
   setting layers for, **343–344**

Viewports dialog box, 340, 340
   adding multiple viewports, 340, 341
Viewports toolbar, 17
Viewres system variable, 221
views
   for 3D modeling, **181–189**
      3Dorbit, 184, **184–189**
      adjusting distance, 186
      Camera command for viewport setup, 182, **182–183**, 183
      focal length, 189
      panning, 187
      rotating view, 184–186
      saving and restoring views, **189–191**
   orientation, 6
   orthographic and isometric, 168
virtual pens, 361
visibility of layers, **201–205**
   controlling with Freeze and Thaw, 202
   in individual viewports of Layout tab, **203–205**
   on/off option, 201–202
Visretain command, 243
Visual Aids option, of 3Dorbit command, 188

W

Wblock command, 234, 234
Web toolbar, 17
width of table cell group, 273, 273
Width option, for Pedit command, 145, 146
Width tool (Text Formatting toolbar), 257, 258
window mullions, polylines to create, 158, 158
Window option, for Select objects: prompt, 124
Window Polygon option, for Select objects: prompt, 124
Windows Clipboard, for importing text, 265, 269
Windows Explorer, to drag and drop .dwg files, 233
windows, for selecting objects, 109–111, 110
wireframe view, 150, 151, 165, 165
   displaying, 173
   printing, 350
word-wrap, 259
words, single-line text object to add, **269–270**
workpoints, 49. See also grips
Workspaces toolbar, 17
World Coordinate System, 6, 154
   switching between UCS and, 156

X

X axis, *180*
X coordinate, entering, 36
X grid spacing, changing, 55
Xbind command, 242
Xline command, 101, **103–106**
Xline tool (Draw toolbar), *18*
Xref Manager dialog box, *241*, 241,
    329, *329*
xrefs (external references), 227, **240–243**
    attaching drawing as, **241–242**
    vs. blocks, **242–243**
    converting to block, 243
    editing, **142–144**
    as external files, 125
    finding, **329–330**
    nesting, 243
    updating, **242**
XY coordinate, 4

Y

Y axis, *180*
Y coordinate, entering, 36
Y grid spacing, changing, 55

Z

Z axis, 150, 179, *180*
Z coordinate, 5, 36, 179
zero suppression, 312
Zoom Extents option, of 3Dorbit
    command, 188
Zoom option, of 3Dorbit command, 188
Zoom toolbar, 17
Zoom Window option, of 3Dorbit
    command, 188
zooming. *See also* panning and zooming
    scroll wheel on mouse for,
        24–25, 111

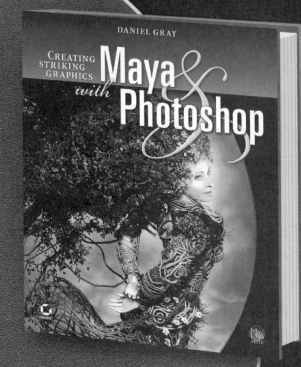

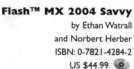

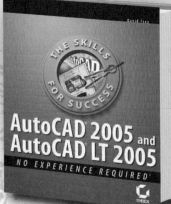

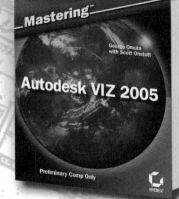